HOW TO DRAW MANGA

volume 5

Developing Shoujo Manga Techniques

HOW TO DRAW MANGA Volume 5: Developing Shoujo Manga Techniques
by The Society for the Study of Manga Techniques

First published in 1997 by Graphic-sha Publishing Co., Ltd.
This English edition was published in 2002 by
Graphic-sha Publishing Co., Ltd.

The members of The Society for the Study of Shoujo Manga Techniques:
Kaoru Kajiwara, Tadashi Kudo, Reiko Kudo, Ryo Kagami

Cover drawing:	Kaoru Kajiwara
Production incorporated by:	Studio Pinewood Inc.
Title logo design:	Hideyuki Amemura
Photographs:	Yasuo Imai
English cover design:	Shinichi Ishioka
English edition layout:	Shinichi Ishioka
English translation:	Língua fránca, Inc. (an3y-skmt@asahi-net.or.jp)
Japanese edition editor:	Motofumi Nakanishi (Graphic-sha Publishing Co., Ltd.)
Foreign language edition project coordinator:	Kumiko Sakamoto (Graphic-sha Publishing Co., Ltd.)

All of the tones used for the illustrations in this book were screen tone and IC tone manufactured by Letraset.
The manga illustrations were all written on TOO manga paper.

Distributor:
Japan Publications Trading Co., Ltd.
1-2-1 Sarugaku-cho, Chiyoda-ku, Tokyo, 101-0064
Telephone: +81(0)3-3292-3751 Fax: +81(0)3-3292-0410
E-mail: jpt@jptco.co.jp
URL: http://www.jptco.co.jp/

First printing: June 2002

ISBN 4-88996-081-3
Printed in China by Everbest printing Co., Ltd.

Table of Contents

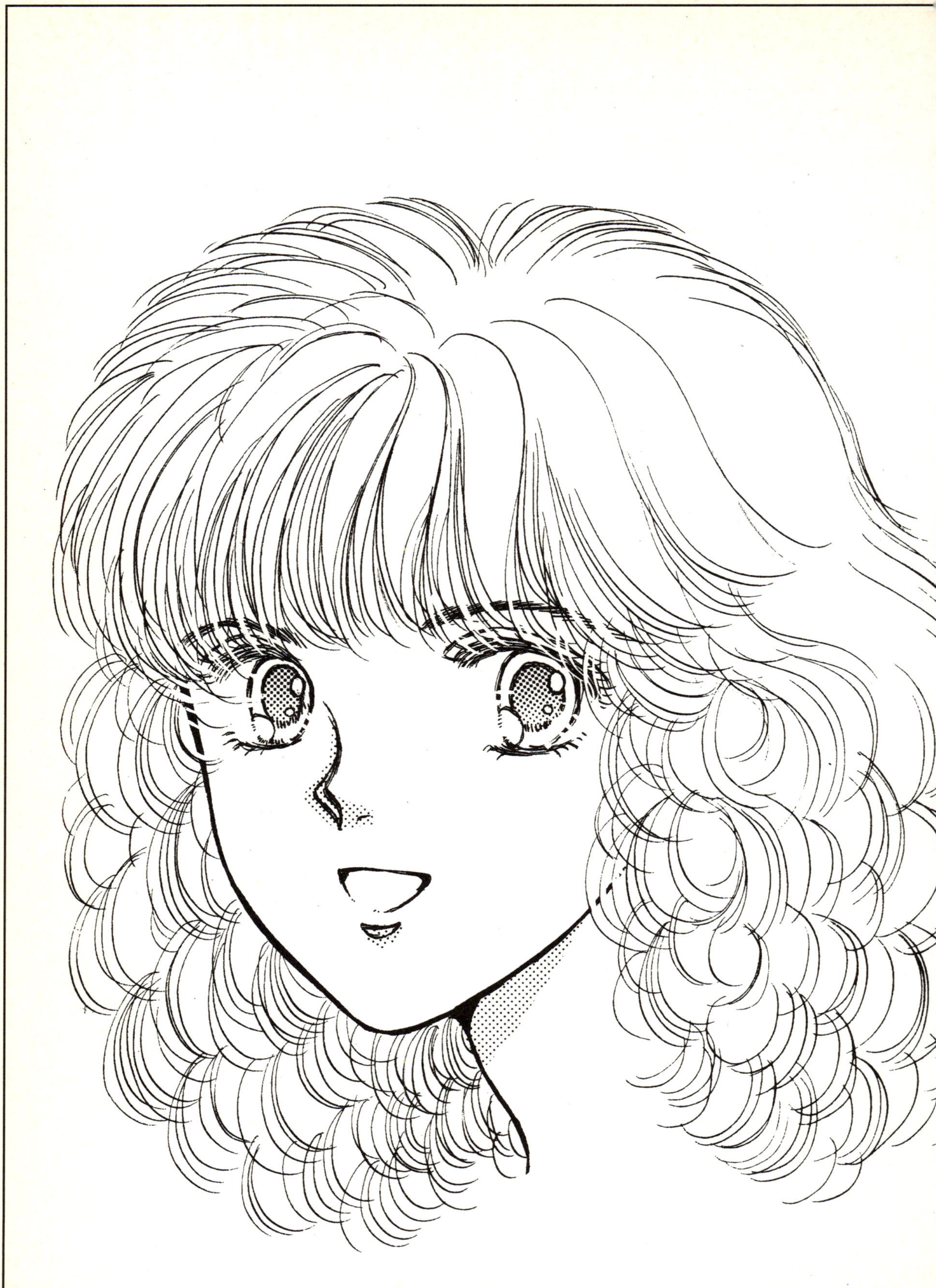

Chapter 1
How to Draw Characters

Basics of How to Draw Faces

Do not think of the face as being flat. Think of it as a rounded sphere as you draw. The eyes, nose, mouth, eyebrows, ears, and other parts all have their proper positions, so be careful.

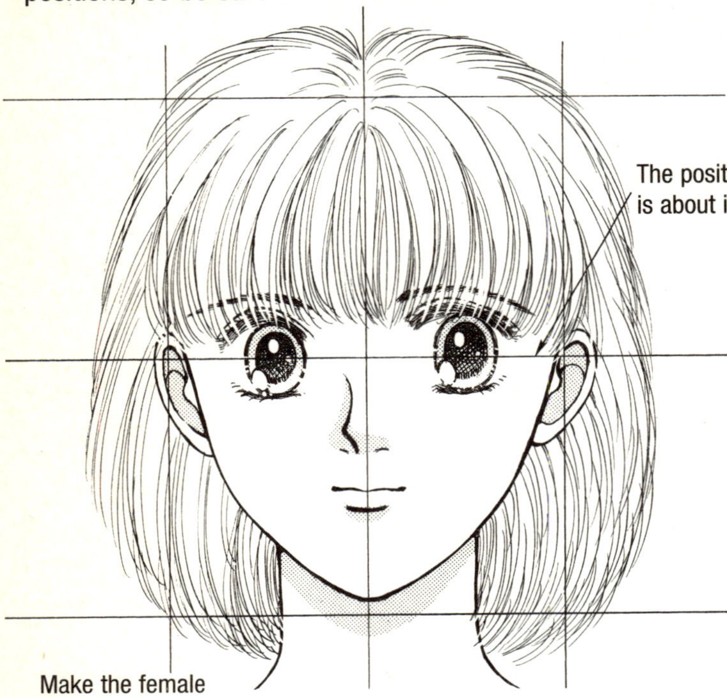

Front Side

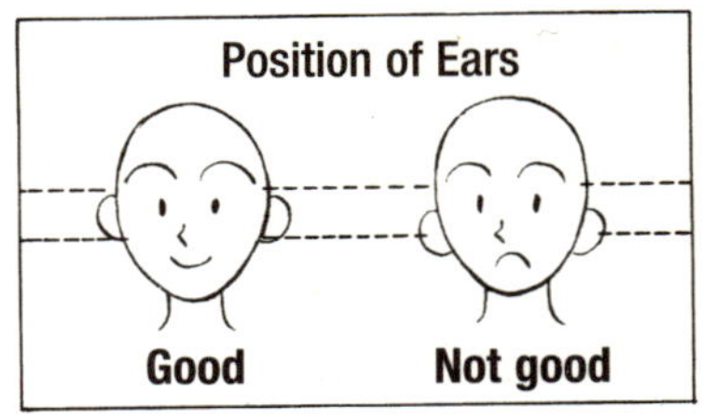

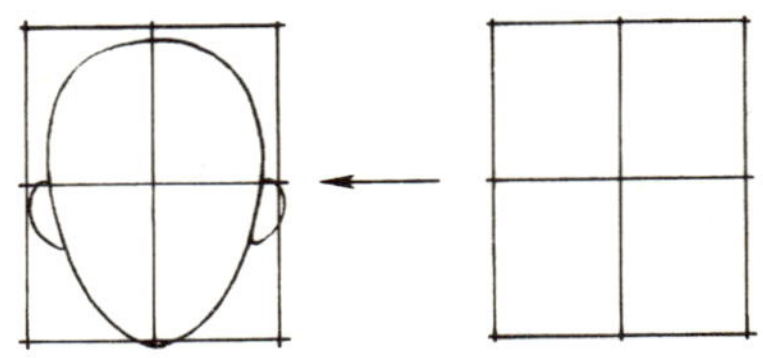

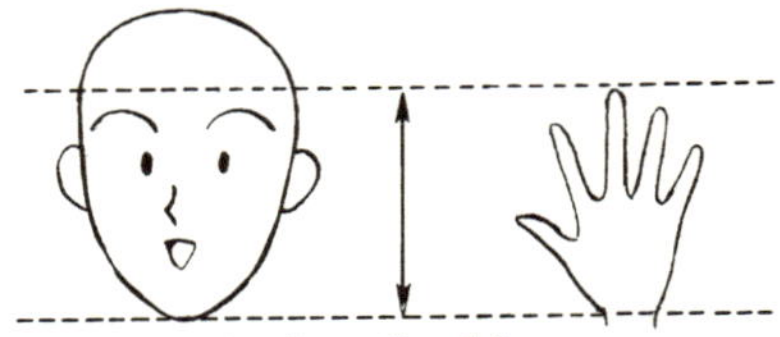

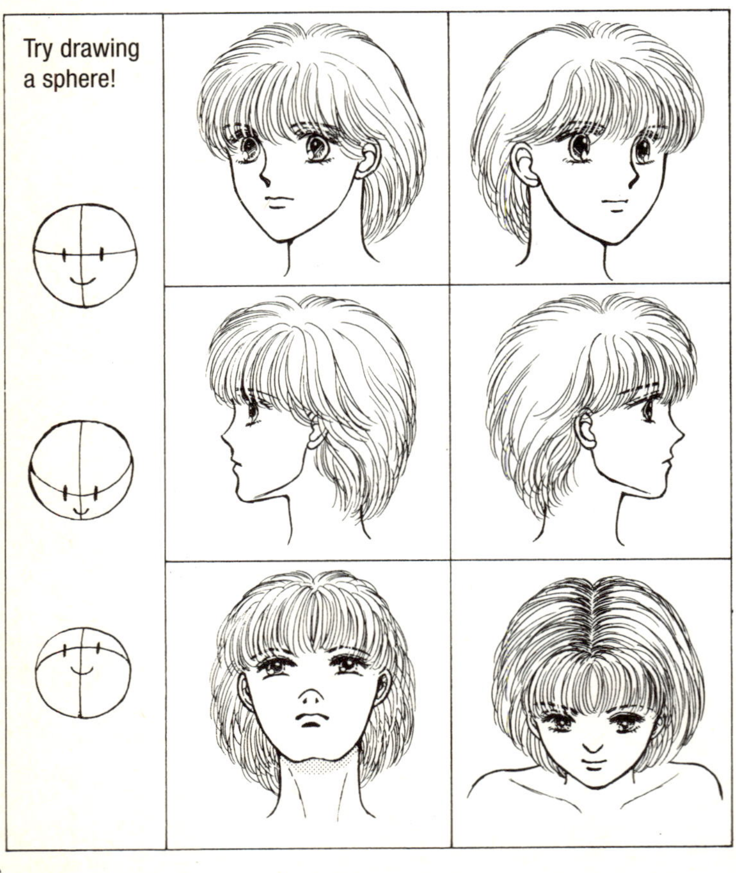

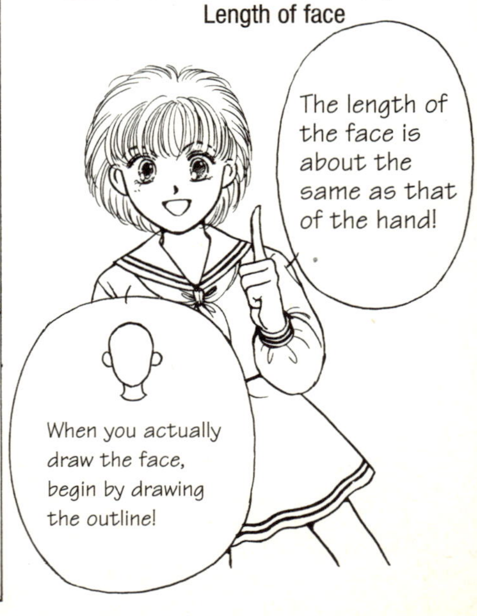

Each Part as Seen from a Variety of Angles

☆Pay attention to the balance between the ears, nose, and neck!

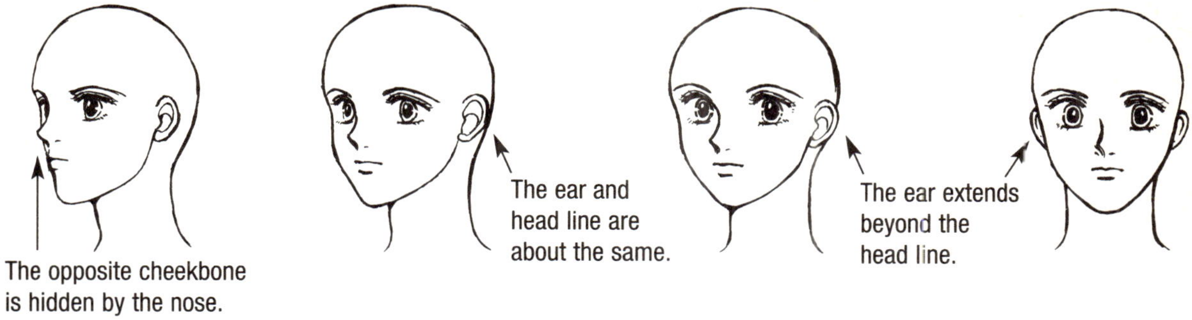

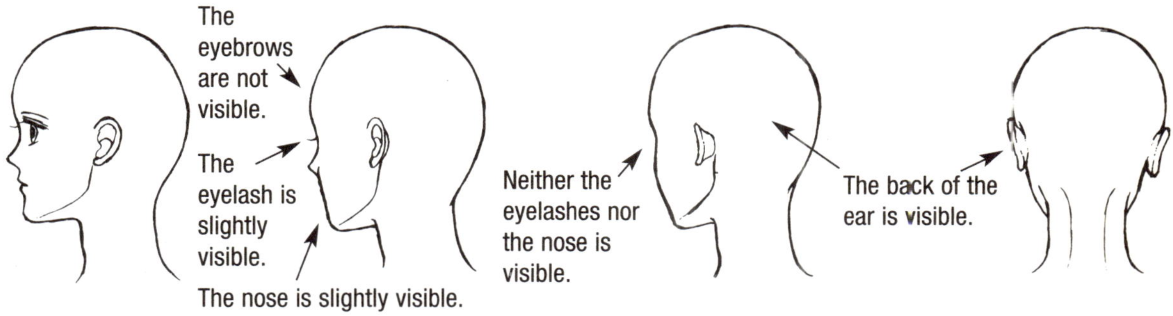

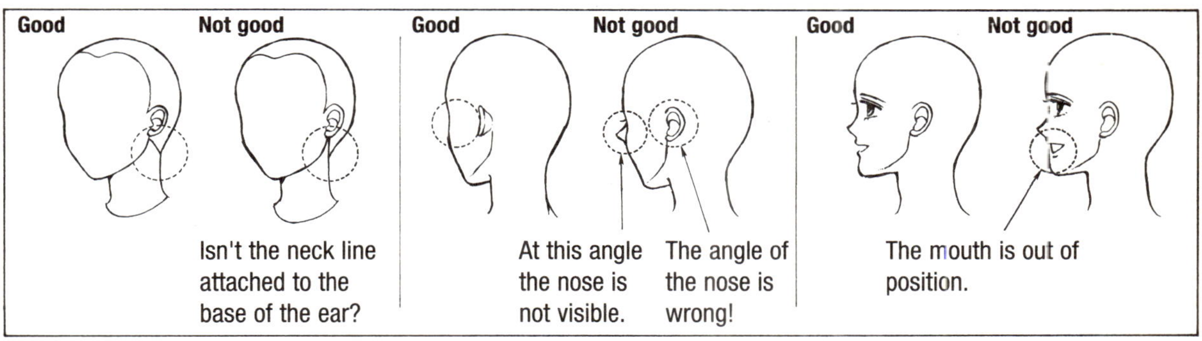

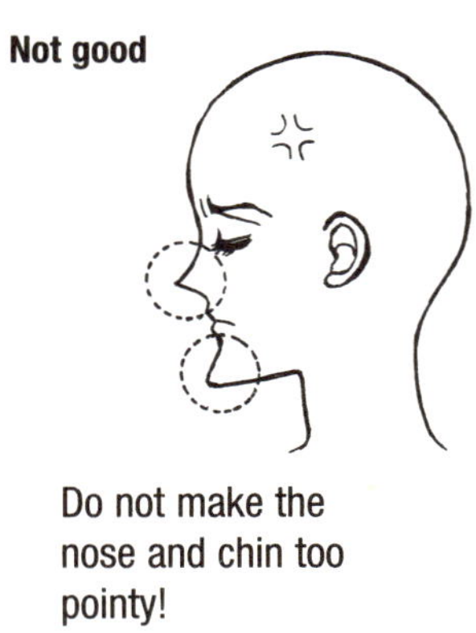

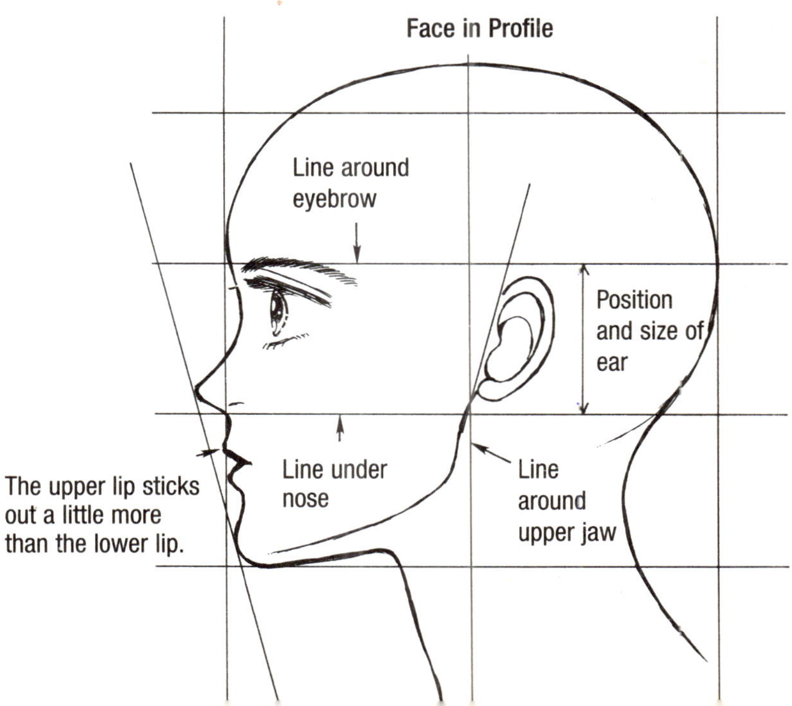

Balance Between Head and Neck

Length of Neck

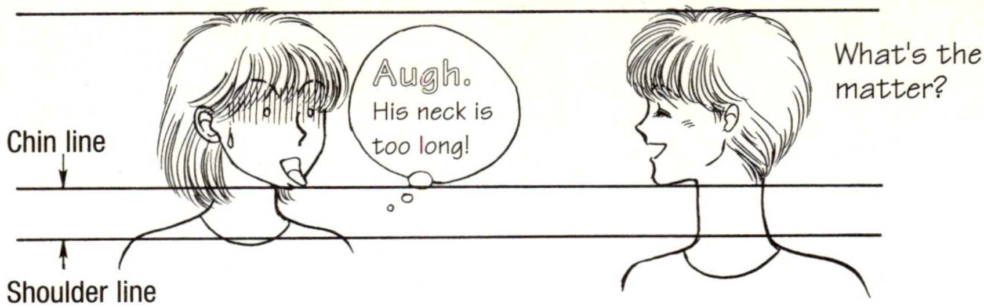

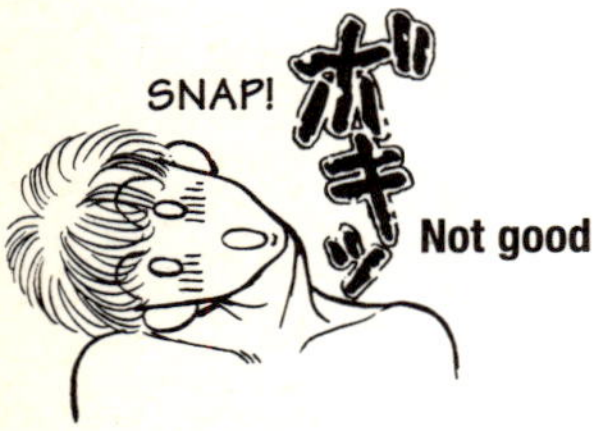

The neck doesn't bend this far!

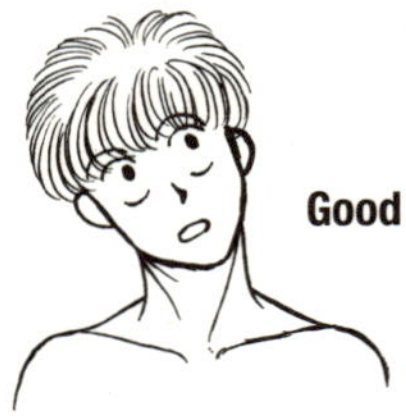

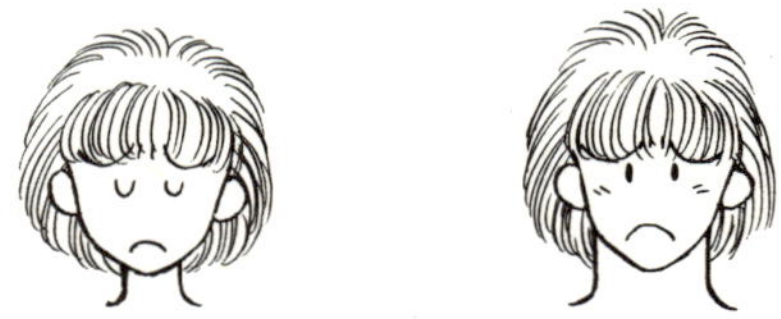

The neck is too thin. The neck is too thick.

Looking Back

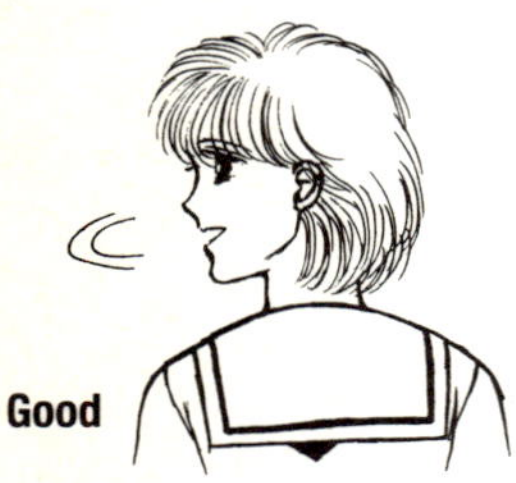

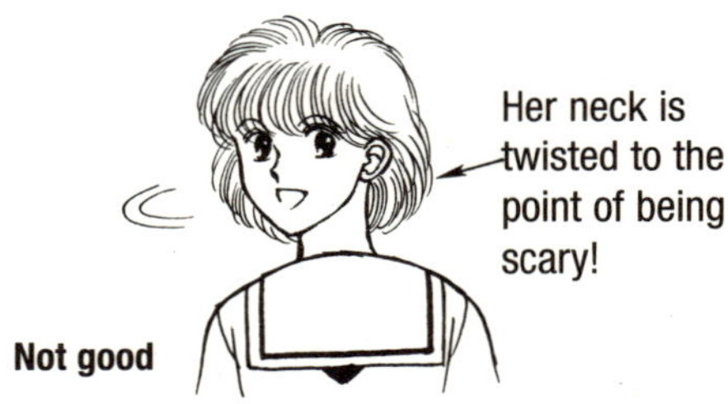

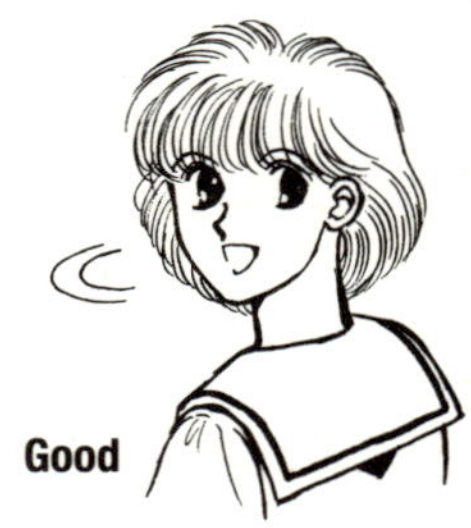

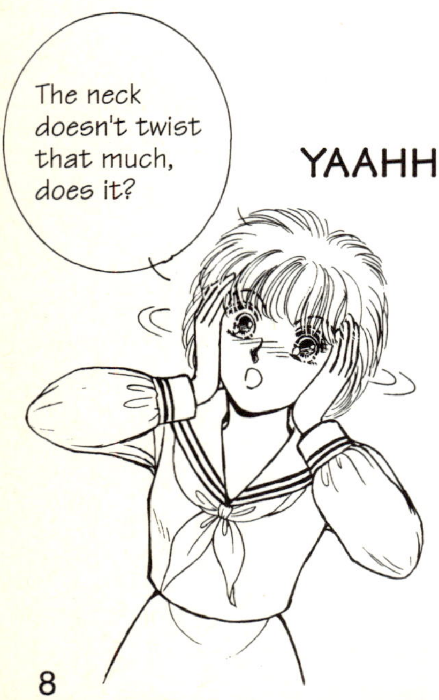

Looking Up

The neck bone protrudes slightly.

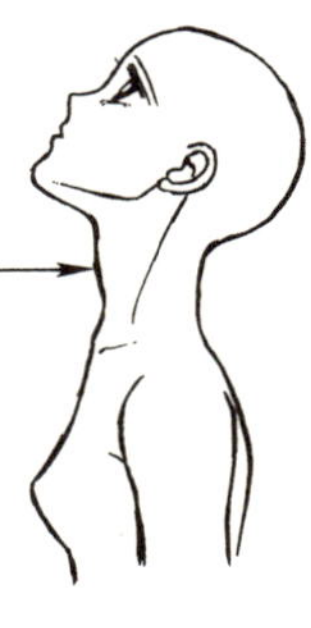

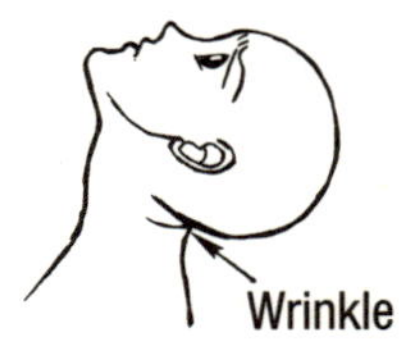

This is about the limit (requires bending backwards).

Looking Down

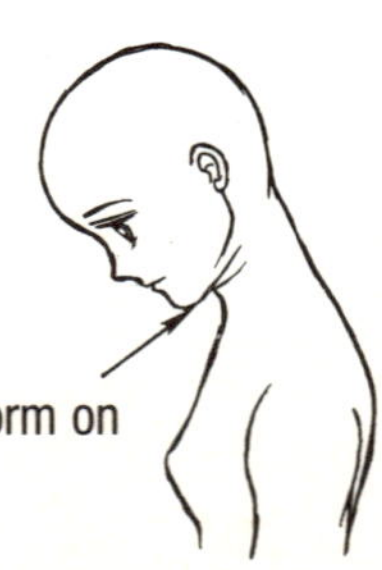

Wrinkles form on the neck.

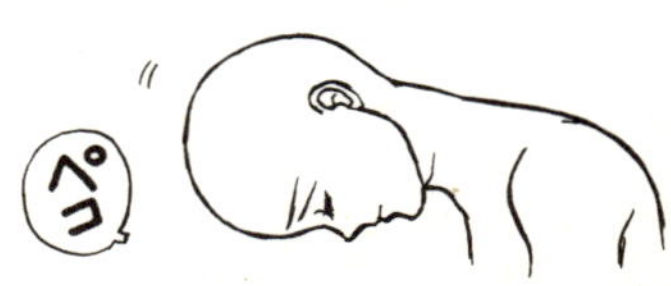

This angle is impossible to attain without bending the back.

Let's try drawing faces from a variety of angles.

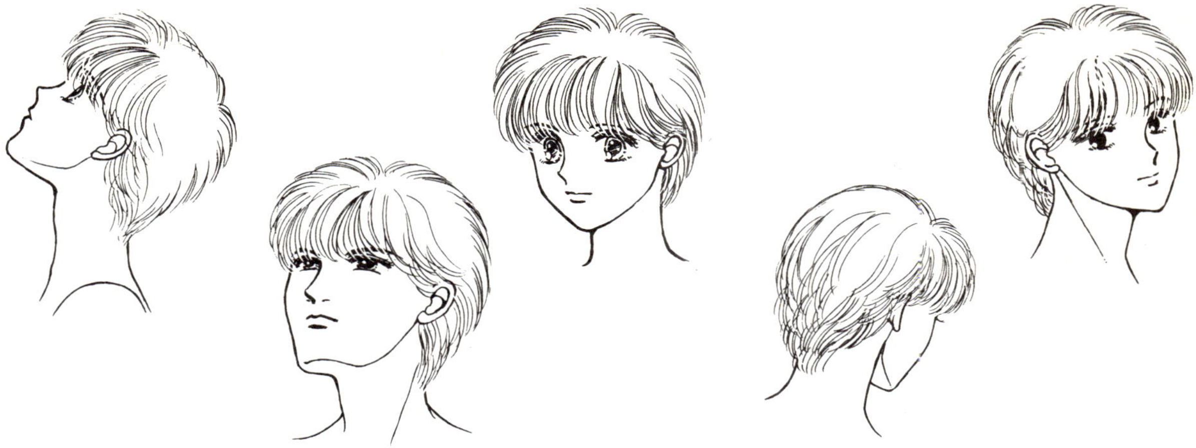

The size of the eyes and the position of the nose are wrong on the face marked with X.

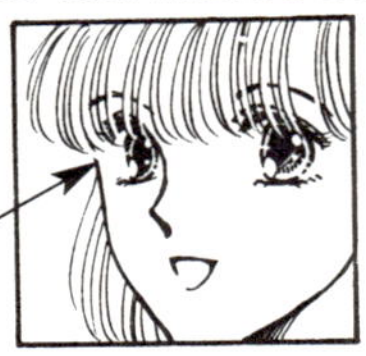

The far eye is smaller.

× **Not good** **Good**

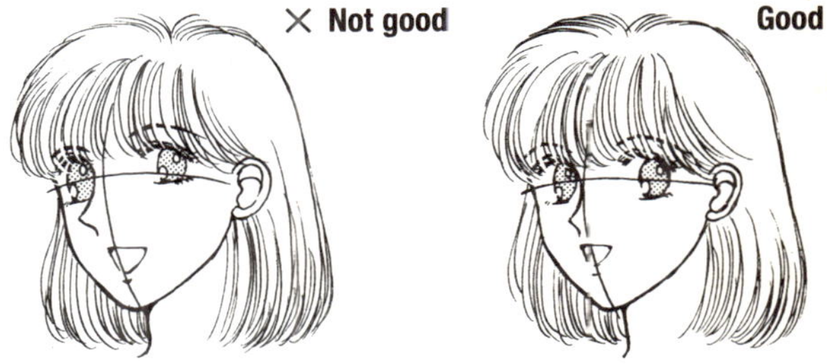

Some ways to check to see if a drawing is distorted are to look at it in a mirror, look at it upside down, and asking a friend or other third party to look at it.

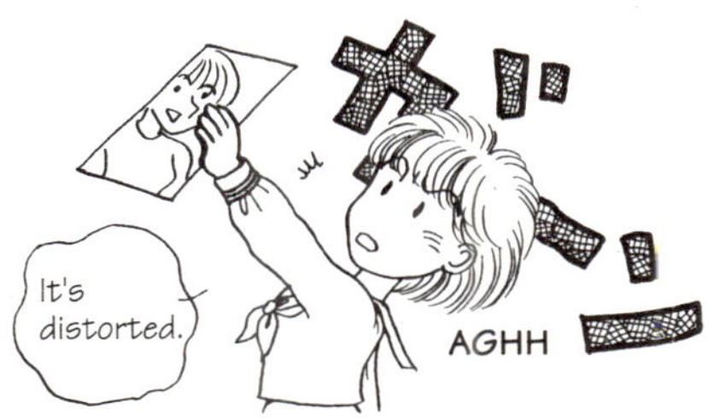

Differentiating Faces

- Make the eyes of children big.
- Think about the difference in bone structure between fat and thin people.
- The amount of hair decreases with age.

In the case of elderly characters, do not just add wrinkles to a young face!

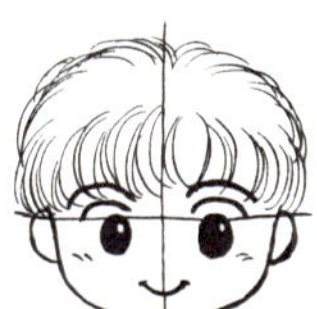

Child

Draw the face a little lower than the center line.

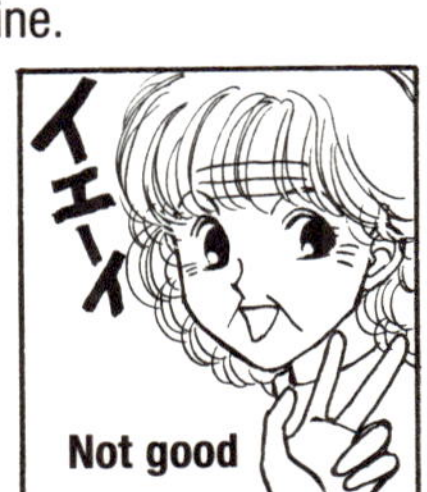

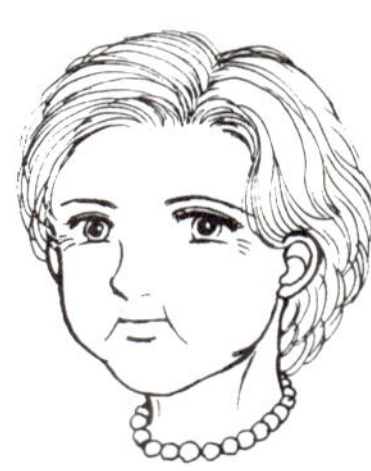

Middle-aged woman

The tails of the eyes and cheeks are low.

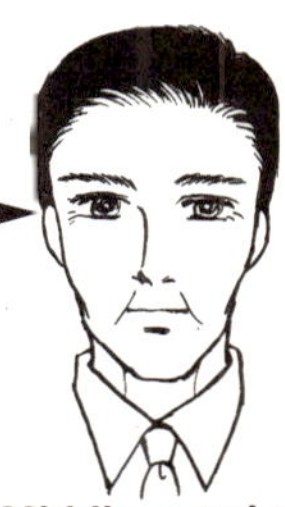

Middle-aged man

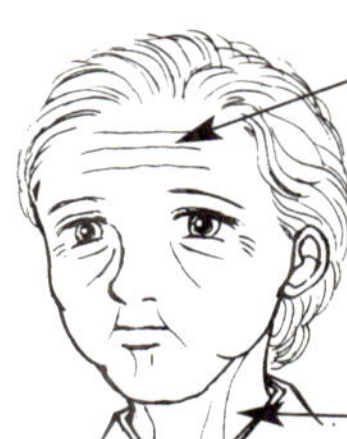

There are more wrinkles.

The shoulder line is also lower.

Neck muscle

Elderly woman

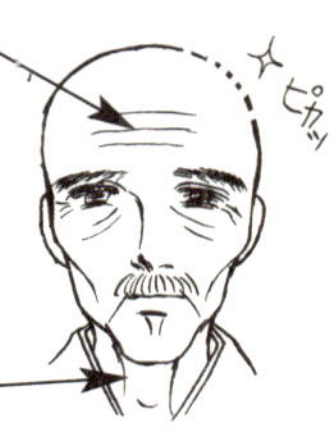

Elderly man

Let's try giving characters expressions!

Facial expressions differ depending on height of the eyebrows, the size of the eyes, and how the mouth is opened. Having a hand near the face will make the face more expressive.

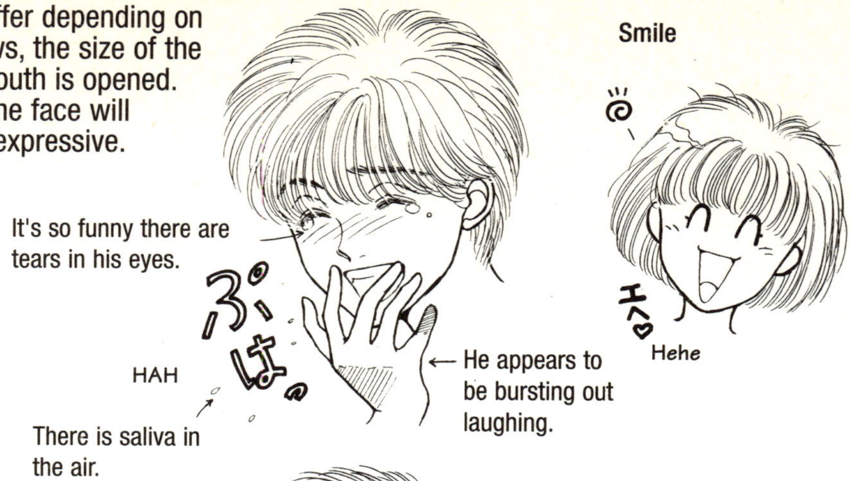

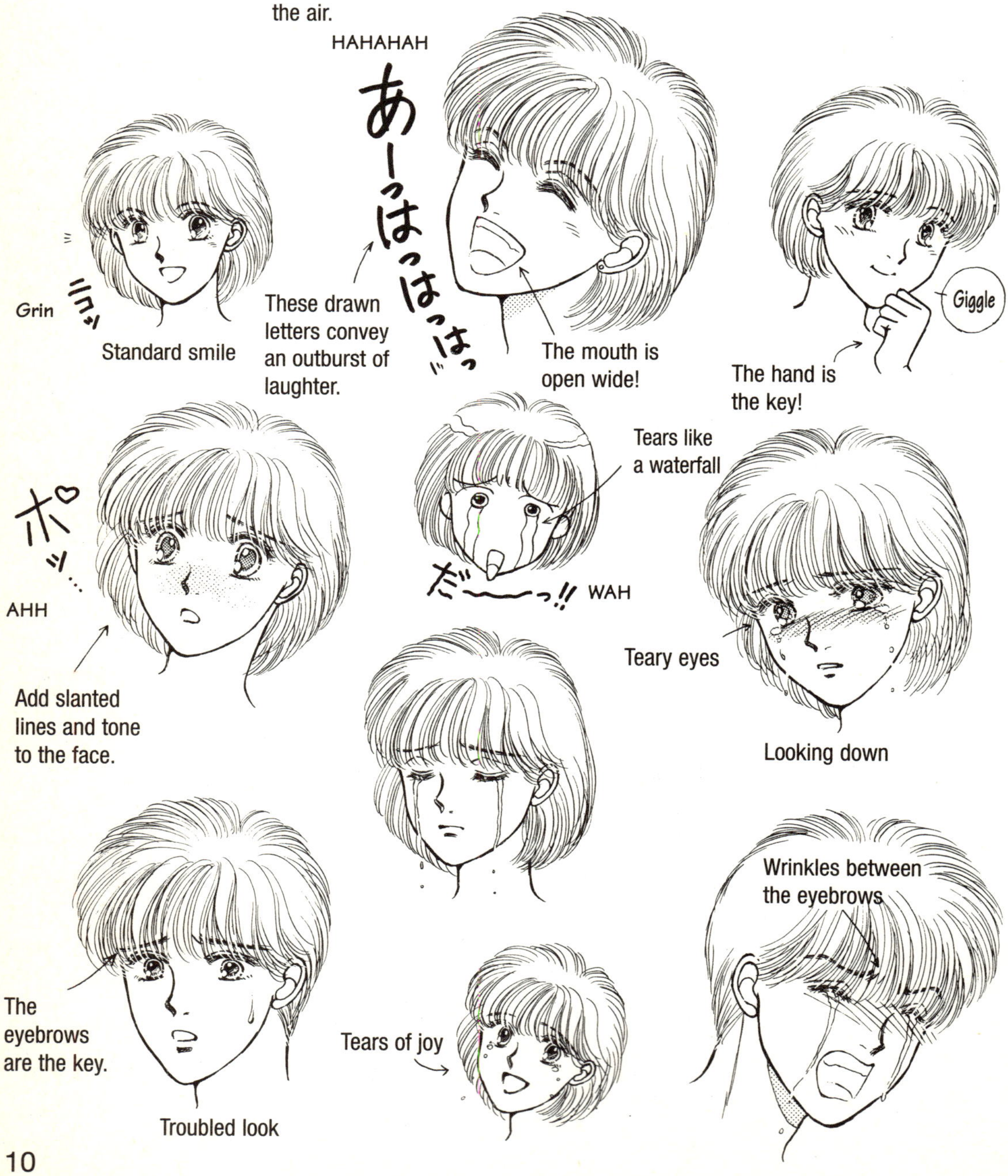

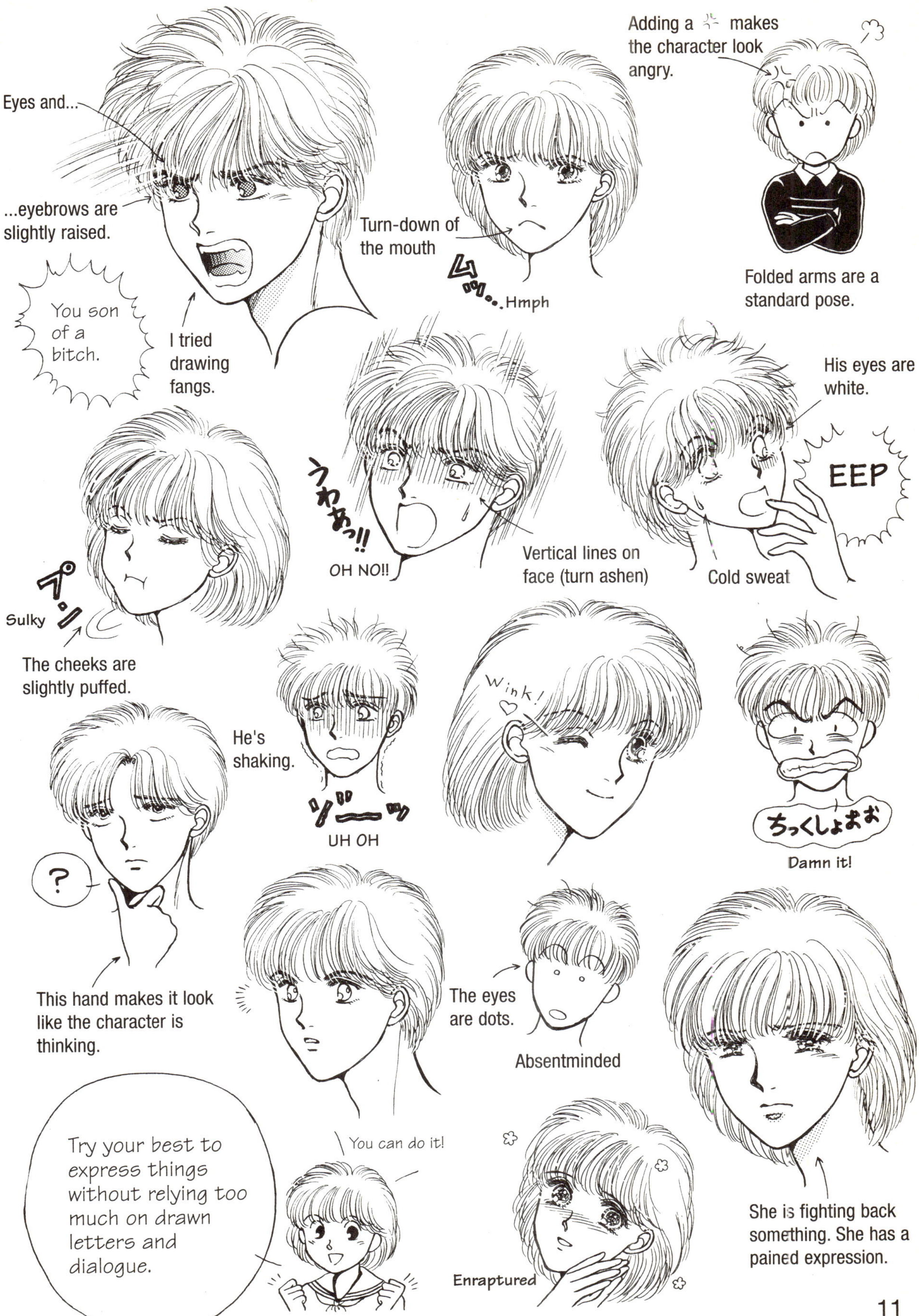
Eyes and...
...eyebrows are slightly raised.
You son of a bitch.
I tried drawing fangs.
Turn-down of the mouth
Hmph
Adding a makes the character look angry.
Folded arms are a standard pose.
うわあっ!!
OH NO!!
Vertical lines on face (turn ashen)
His eyes are white.
EEP
Cold sweat
Sulky
The cheeks are slightly puffed.
He's shaking.
UH OH
Wink!
ちっくしょぉお
Damn it!
?
This hand makes it look like the character is thinking.
The eyes are dots.
Absentminded
Try your best to express things without relying too much on drawn letters and dialogue.
You can do it!
Enraptured
She is fighting back something. She has a pained expression.

How to Draw Hair (Hairstyles)

Straight Hair

Adding a few stray hairs will make the hair look natural.

This female parts her hair in the middle.

Draw the hair one size larger than the sketch of the head.

Adding volume to the hair will make it look like a wig.

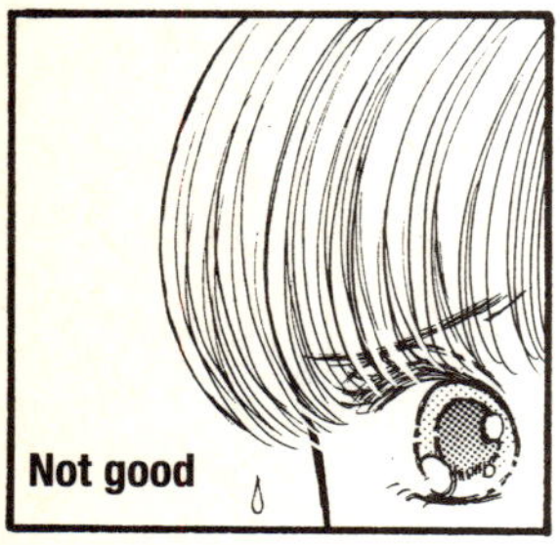

Looks like it was hardened with hair spray.

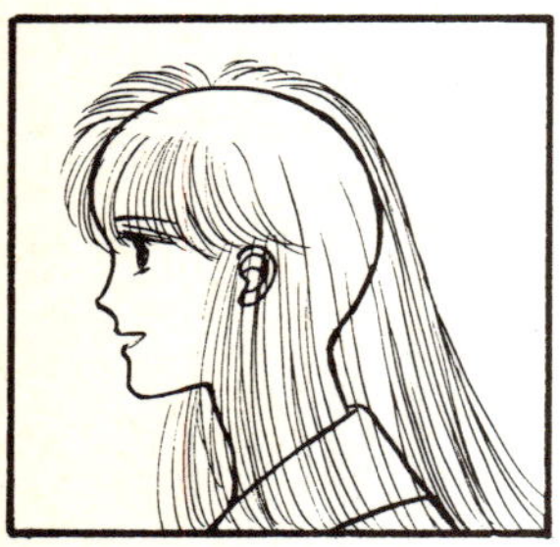

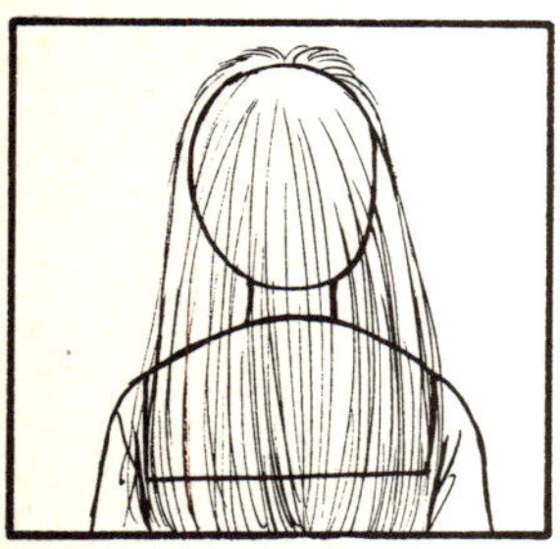

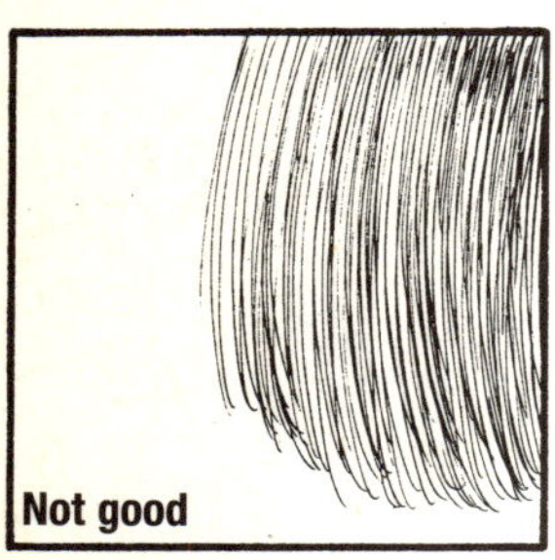

The hair looks spooky because there are too many strands. The lines are monotonous and hard.

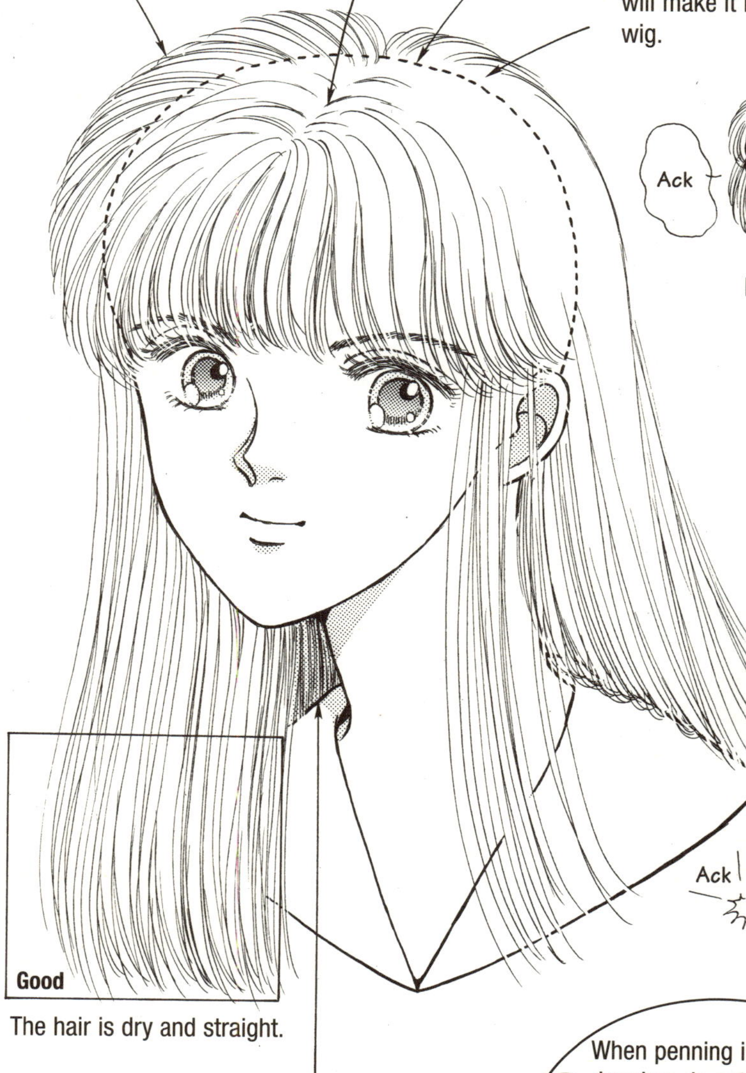

The hair is dry and straight.

The inner side is shaded. Use tone in this instance.

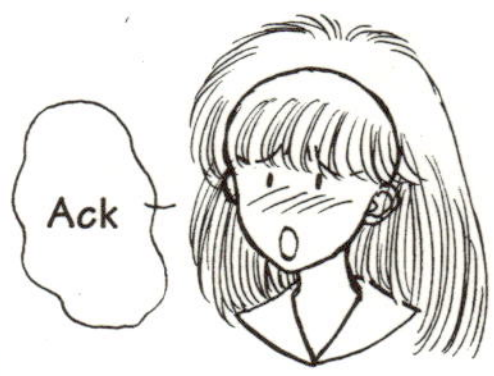

Large head

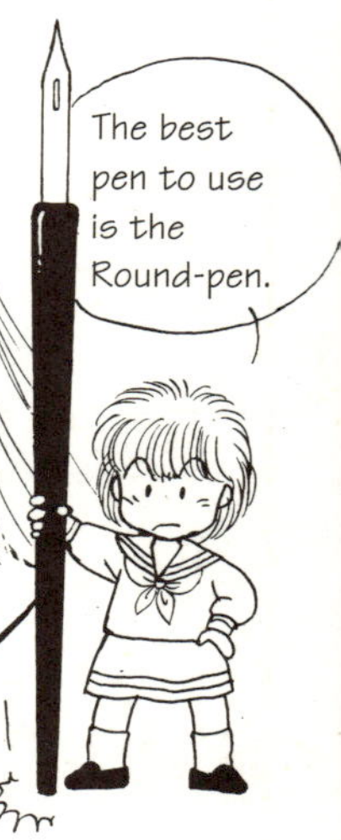

Key Point When penning in the drawing, do not get hung up on the lines of the rough sketch. Relax and draw in light, sustained bursts without stopping the pen midway through lines.

Solid Hair

Solid hair is black hair with India ink in it. There are various types depending on how it is rendered.

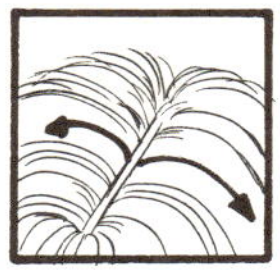

Hairline

Be aware of the hairline and whirl of hair.

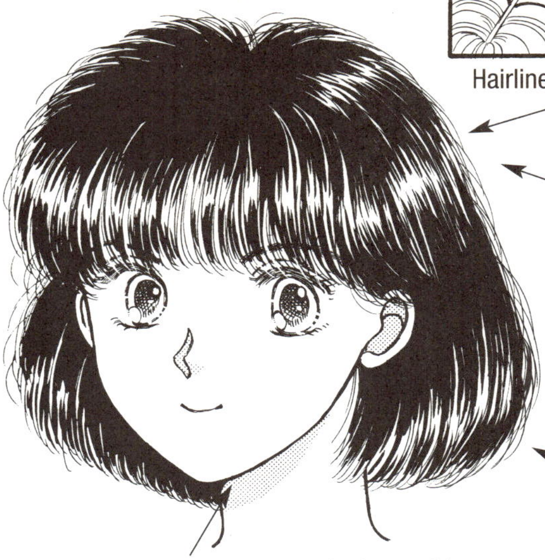

Part where light hits the hair.

Add sheen so that it appears to be wrapping around the other side.

Add thin lines.

Do not add sheen to the inner side because it is shaded.

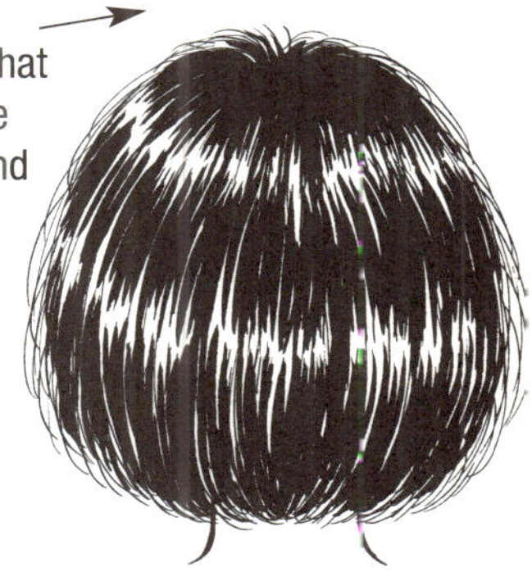

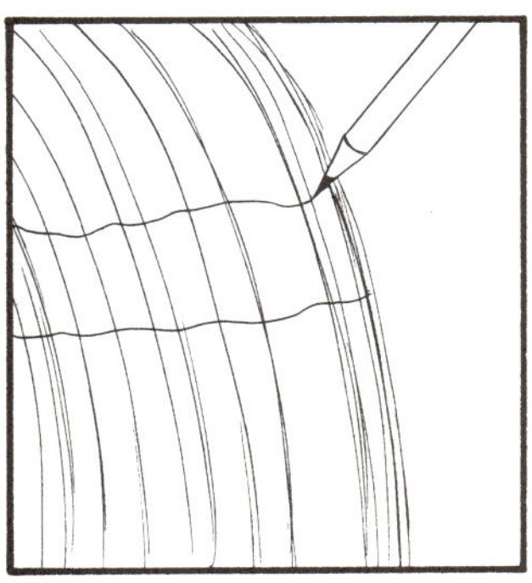

1 Use a pencil to draw guidelines for adding sheen.

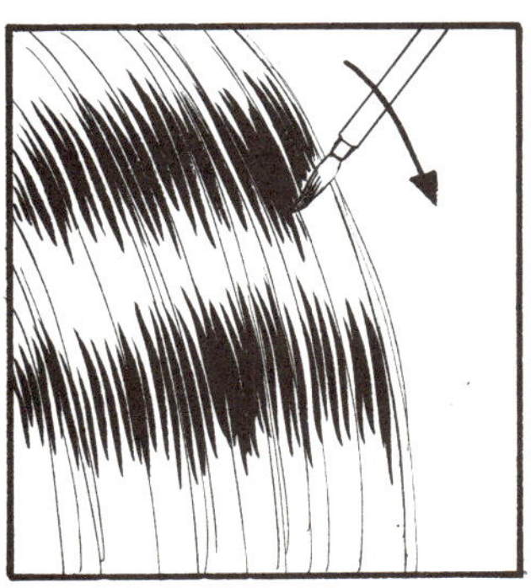

2 Use a pen or brush to draw lines while noting the flow of the hair (make the ends of the lines narrow).

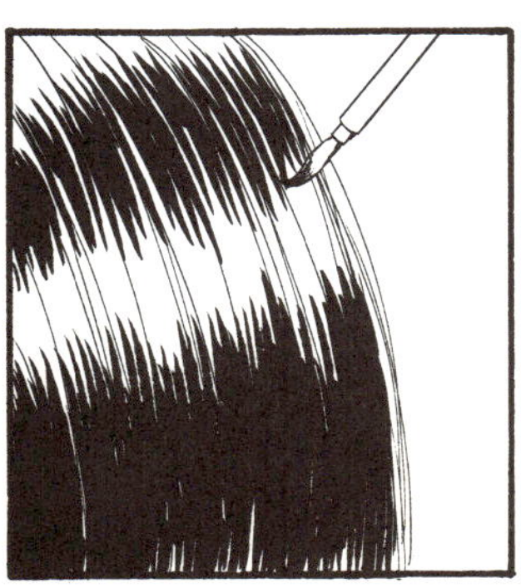

3 Paint black making use of the lines drawn in Step 2. A thin brush is best.

⁂ Use a stiff brush where the ends will not split.

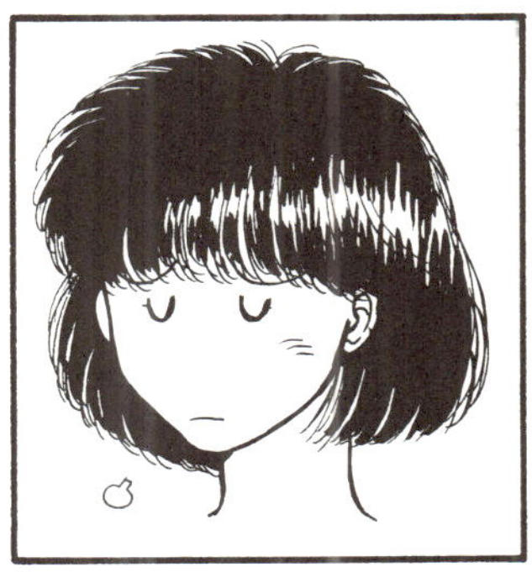

Not good

If you ignore the shape of the head when you add the sheen, the head will look flat.

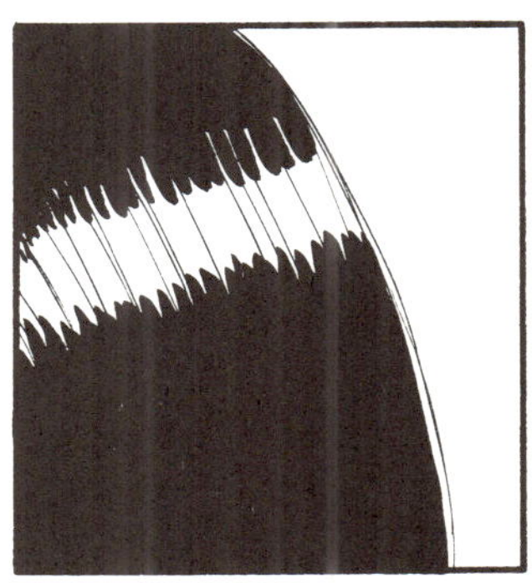

Not good

There should not be a clear border between the sheen and the solid block.

Other Types of Solid Hair

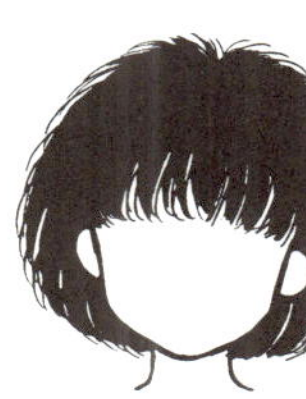

No sheen

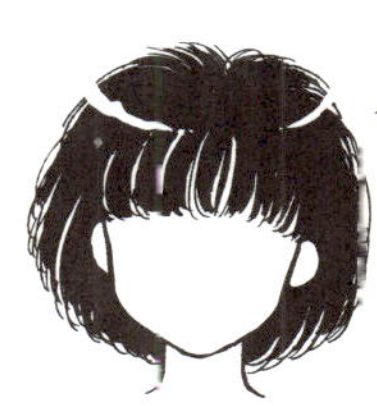

Animation style

Add white or leave some white in the shape of the sheen.

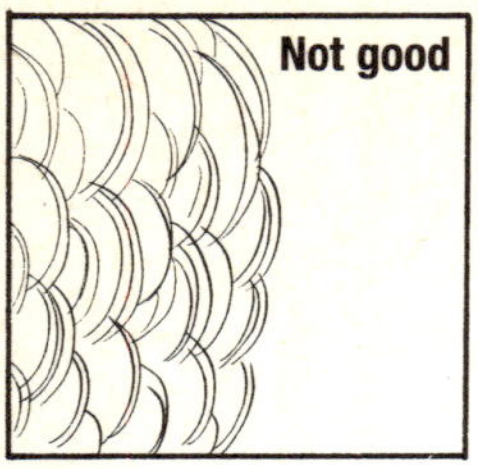

The hair looks hardened with hair spray and heavy.

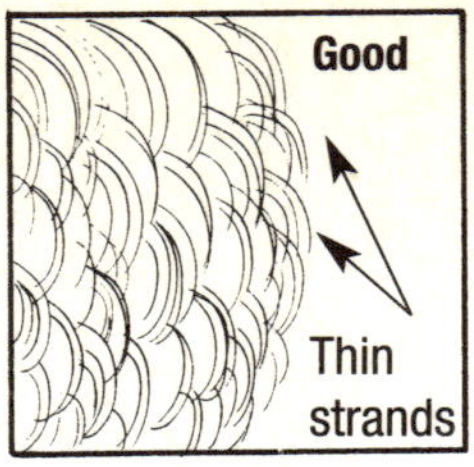

Adding several strands of thin hair to the outside will make it look natural.

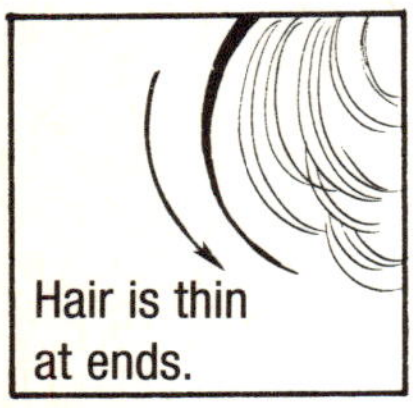

Hold the pen lightly and draw with a flick the closer you get to the end of the hair. The lines will be unsteady and hard if you draw slowly.

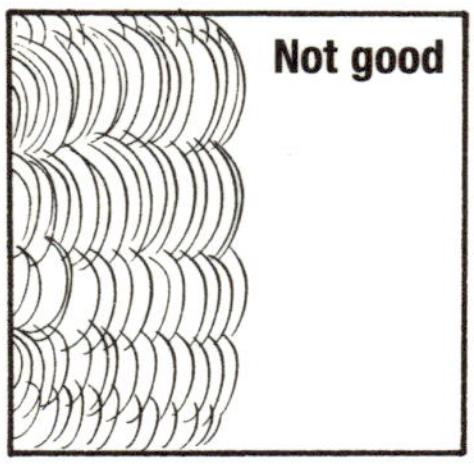

It will look outdated and hard if the lines are uniform and the thickness of the lines is constant.

Permed Hair

Hold the pen lightly and draw in a relaxed and nimble fashion in order to get the fluffy look of a perm.

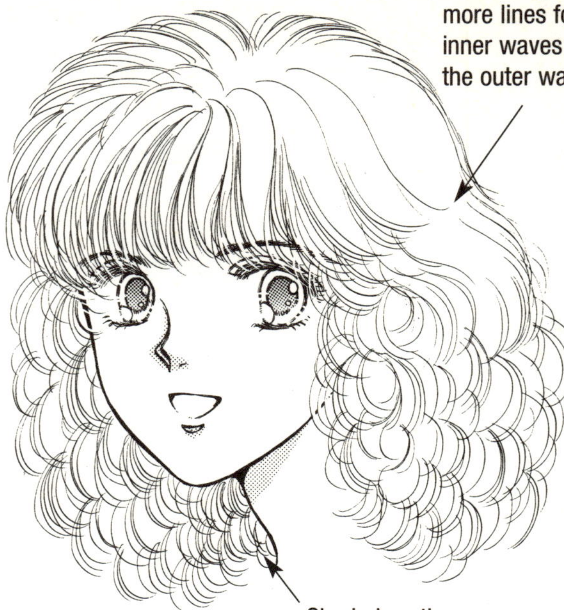

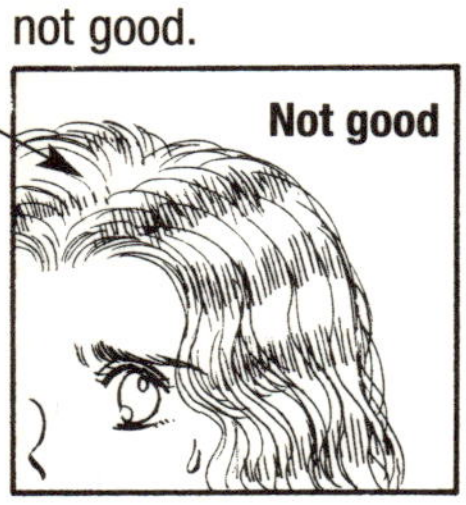

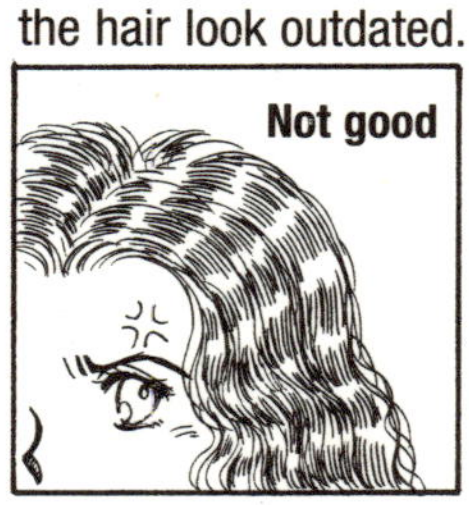

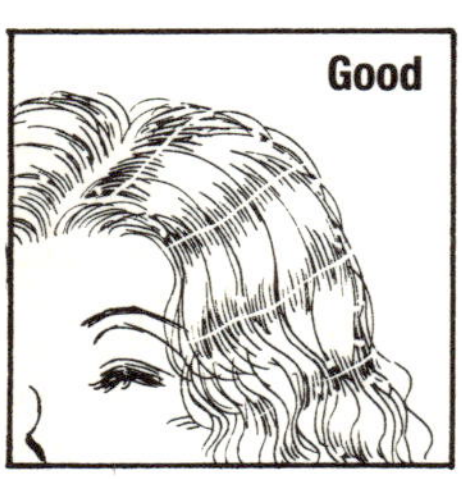

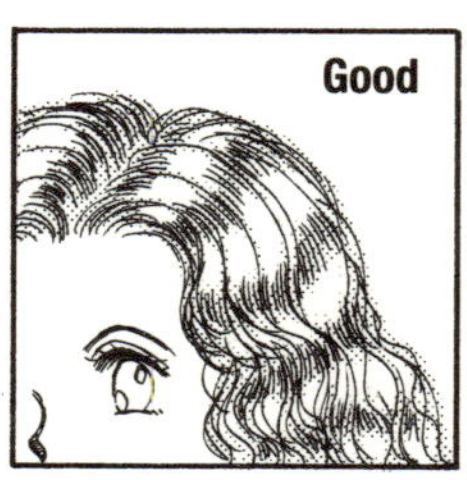

It is also good to add tone to some parts.

Fair Hair

Add sheen while being aware of the flow of the hair, the shape of the head, and how the light hits the hair.

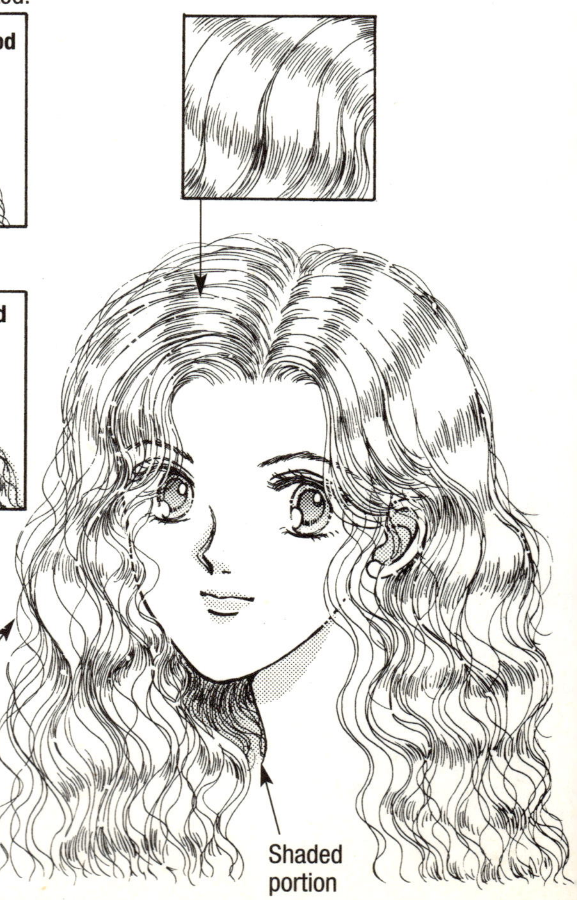

Short Hair

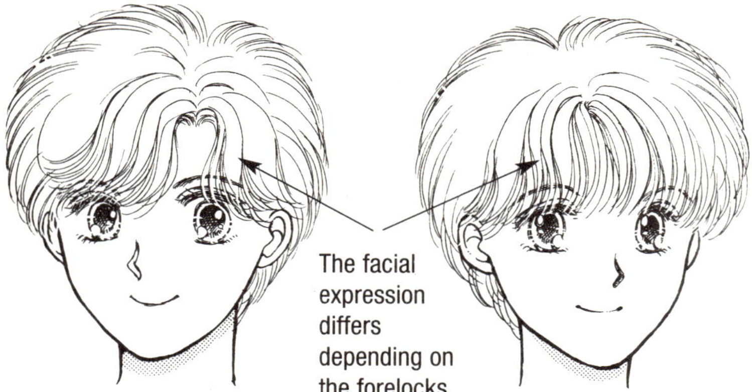

The key to short hair is the cut!

The facial expression differs depending on the forelocks.

In the case of sheer, think about how the light hits the hair.

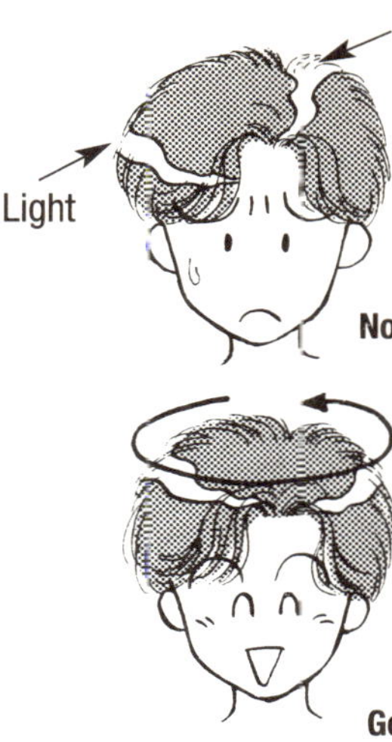

Sheen like an angel's halo.

Pay attention to the part in the hair.

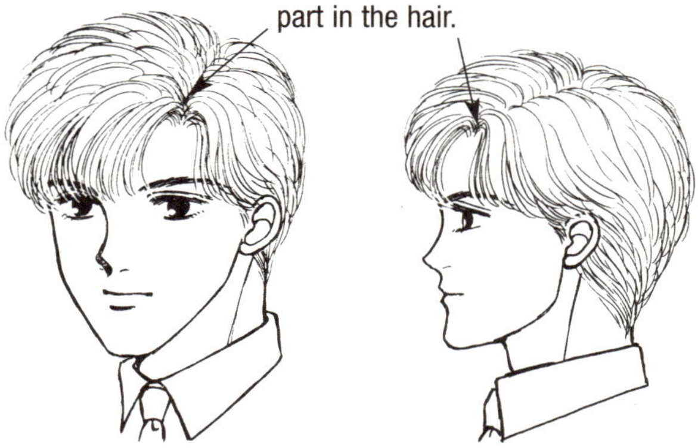

Pay attention to the flow of the hair.

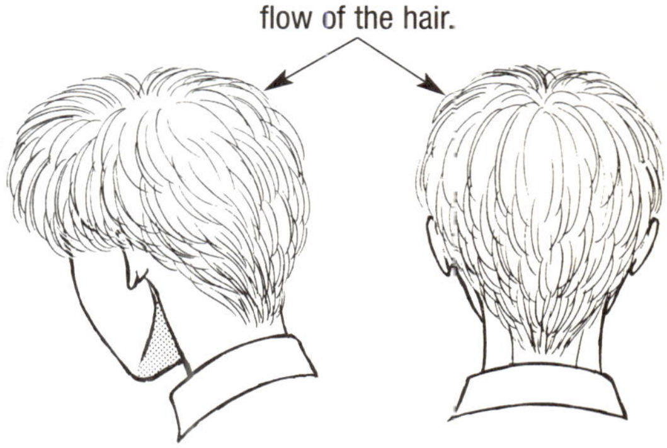

Hair with Tone

There are a variety of types depending on the type of tone and how the tone is scraped.

Create sheen by scraping the tone.

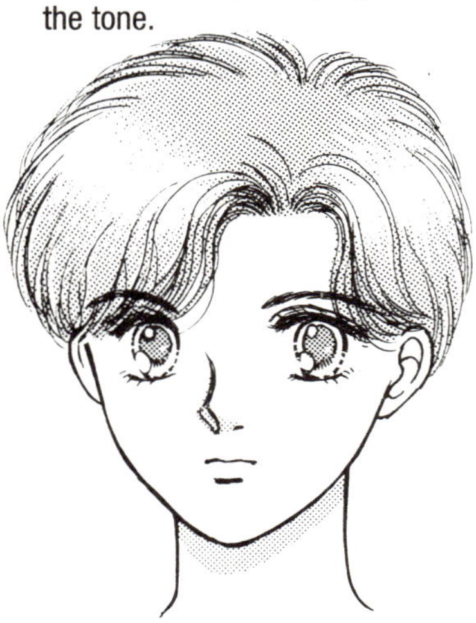

Use tone here and there (the hair will look fair).

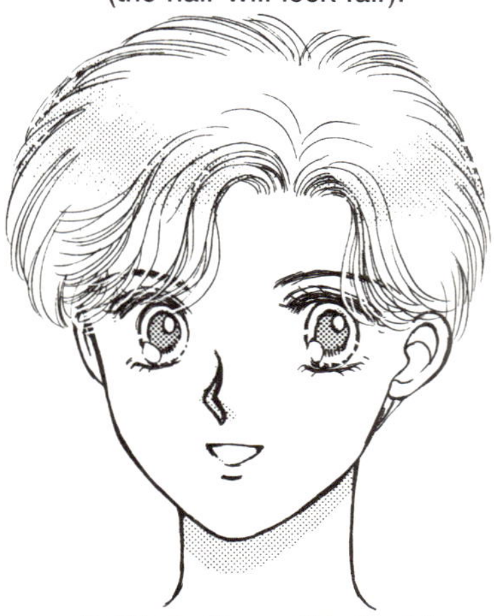

In this instance, it is best to avoid dark tones.

Solid black and tone

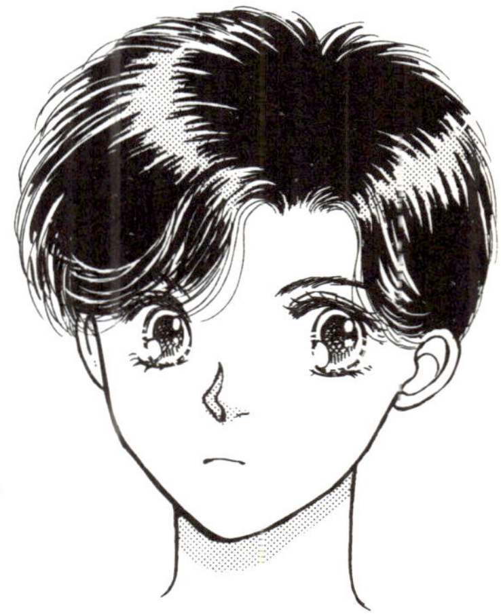

Paint the hair black, add tone after the ink has dried completely, and scrape. Pay attention to the balance between the black and tone.

Other Hairstyles

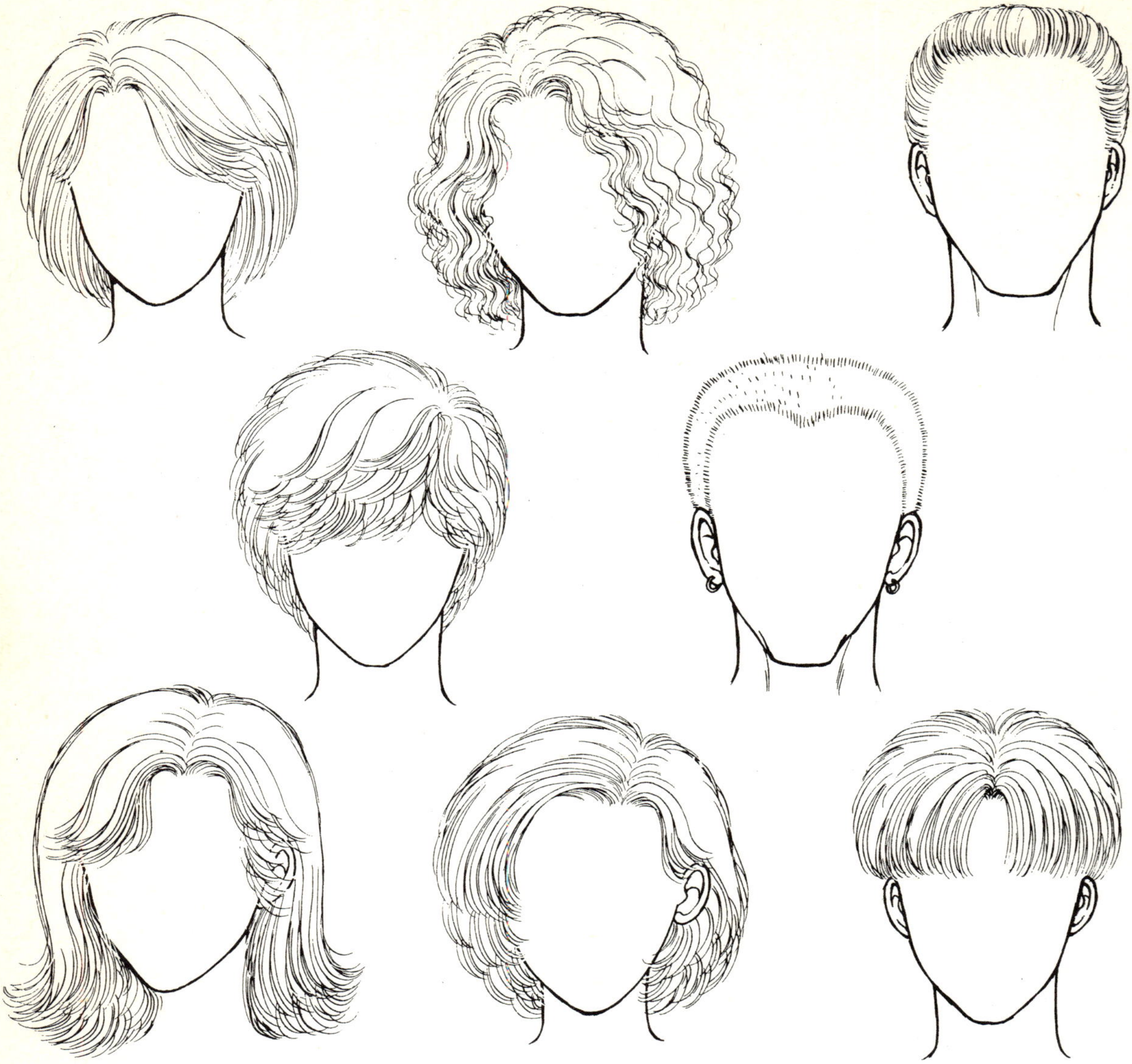

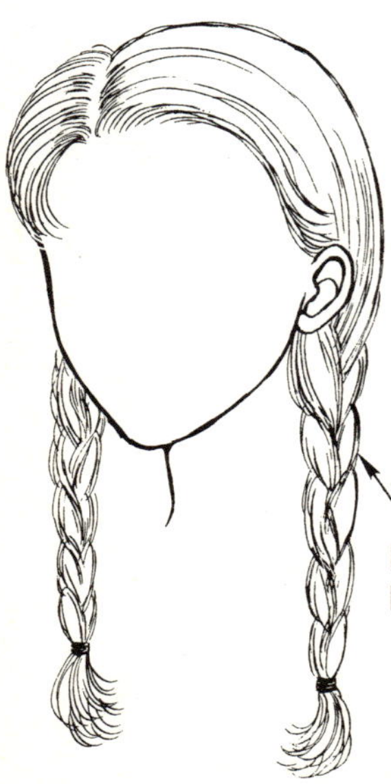

Make sure the hair looks braided.

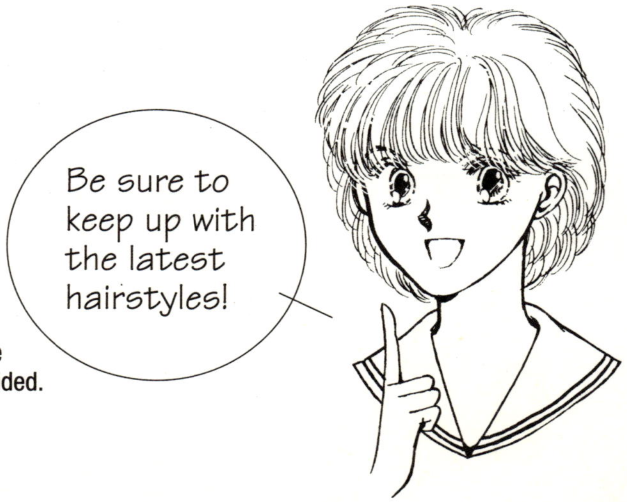

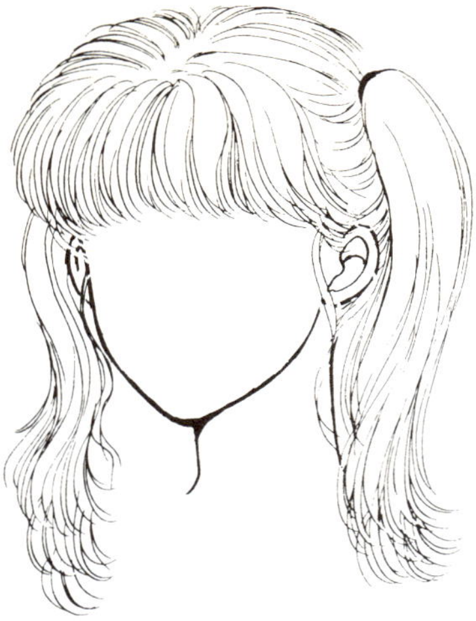

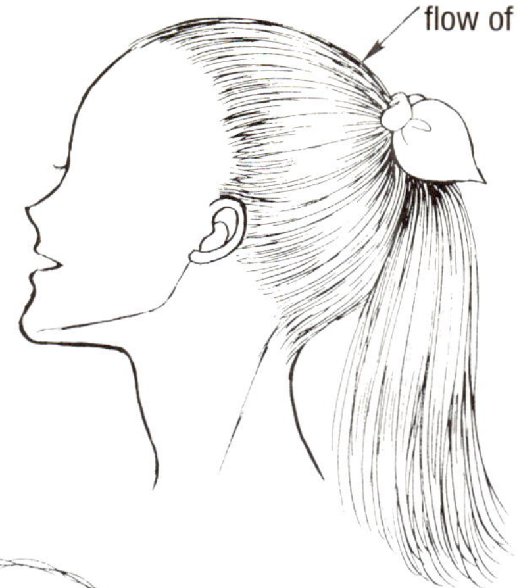

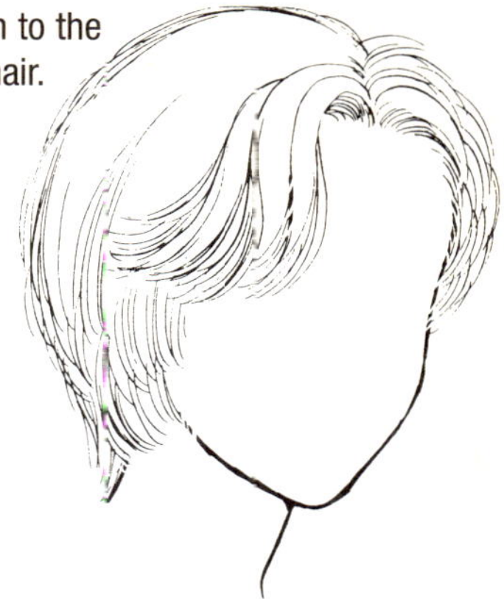

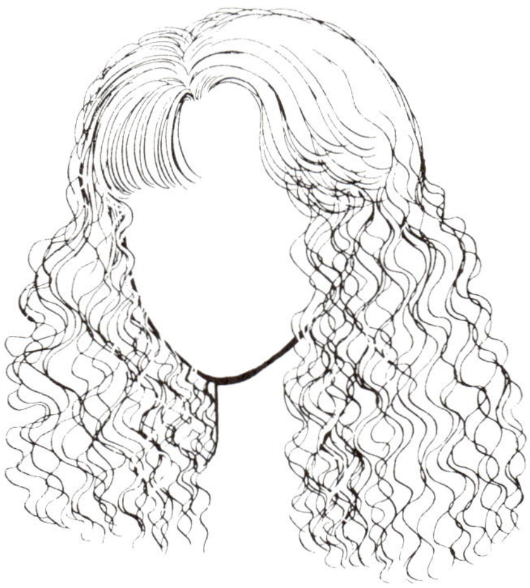

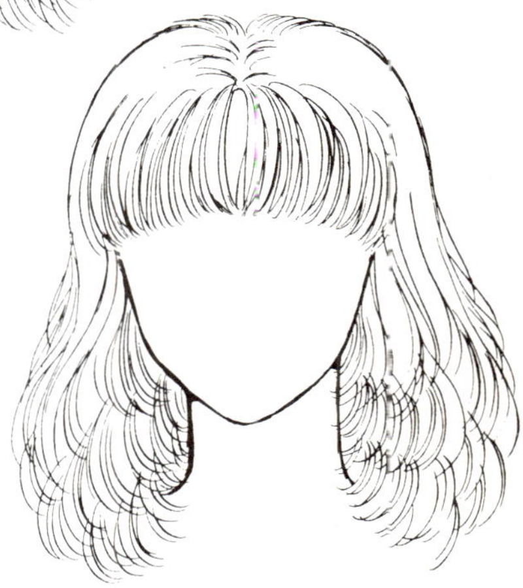

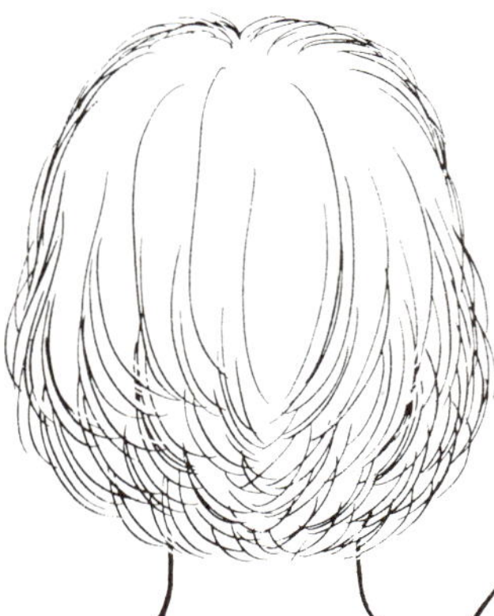

Back

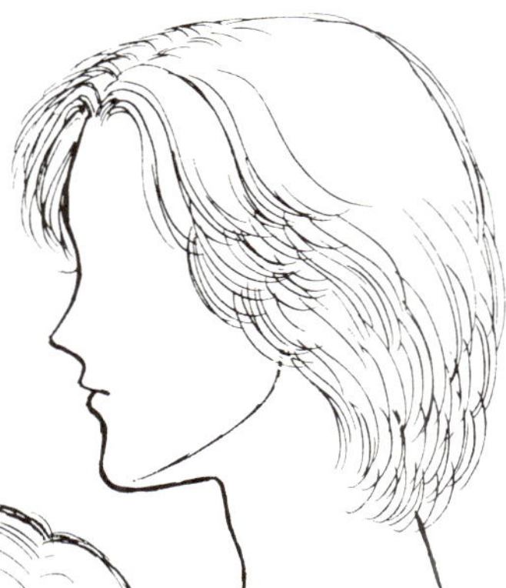

Side

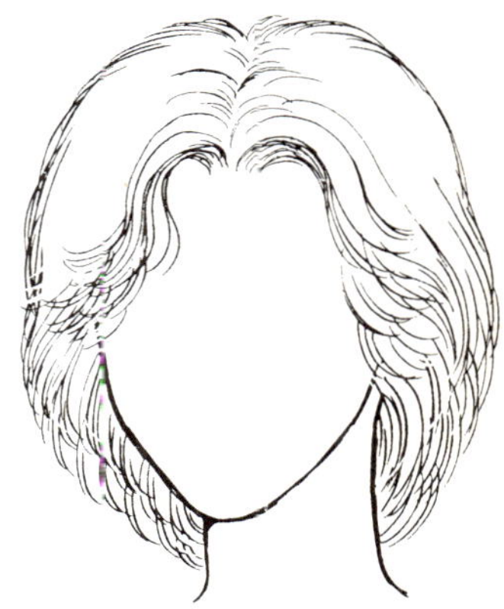

Front

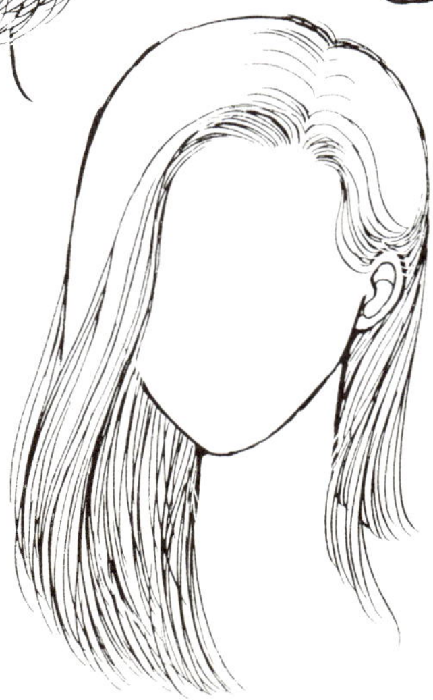

Body as a Whole

The position of the head and heels is determined after deciding the height. If the character is to have a head-to-body ratio of 1:7, then divide the body into seven parts based on the size of the head.

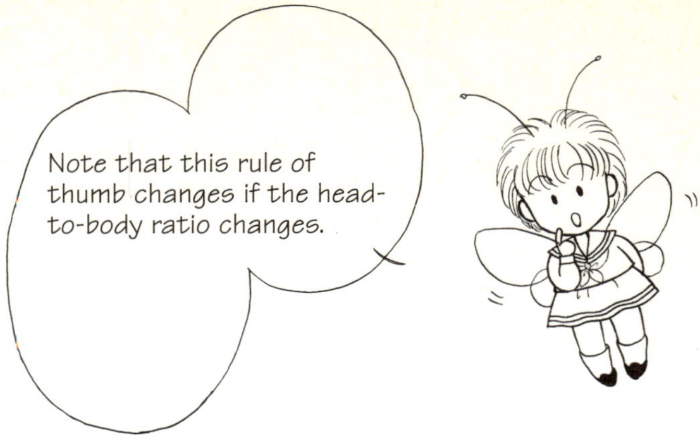

It is best for females to have a head-to-body ratio of 1:7 or 1:8 (the character below is 1:7).

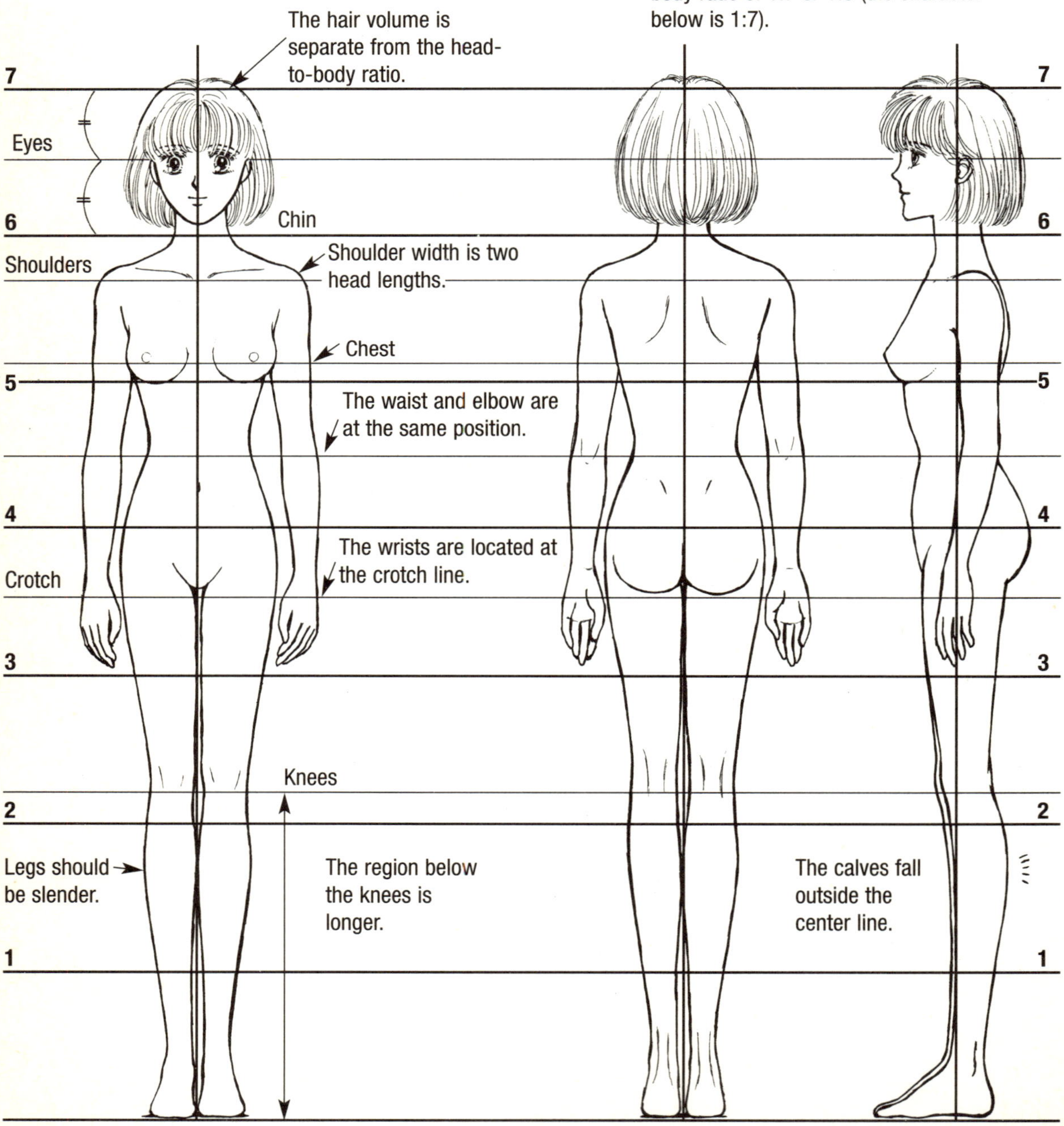

Males have broader shoulders than females and bigger bones. Don't forget to add muscle!

It is best for males to have a head-to-body ratio of 1:8 or 1:9. A ratio of 1:10 is stretching it (the character below is 1:8).

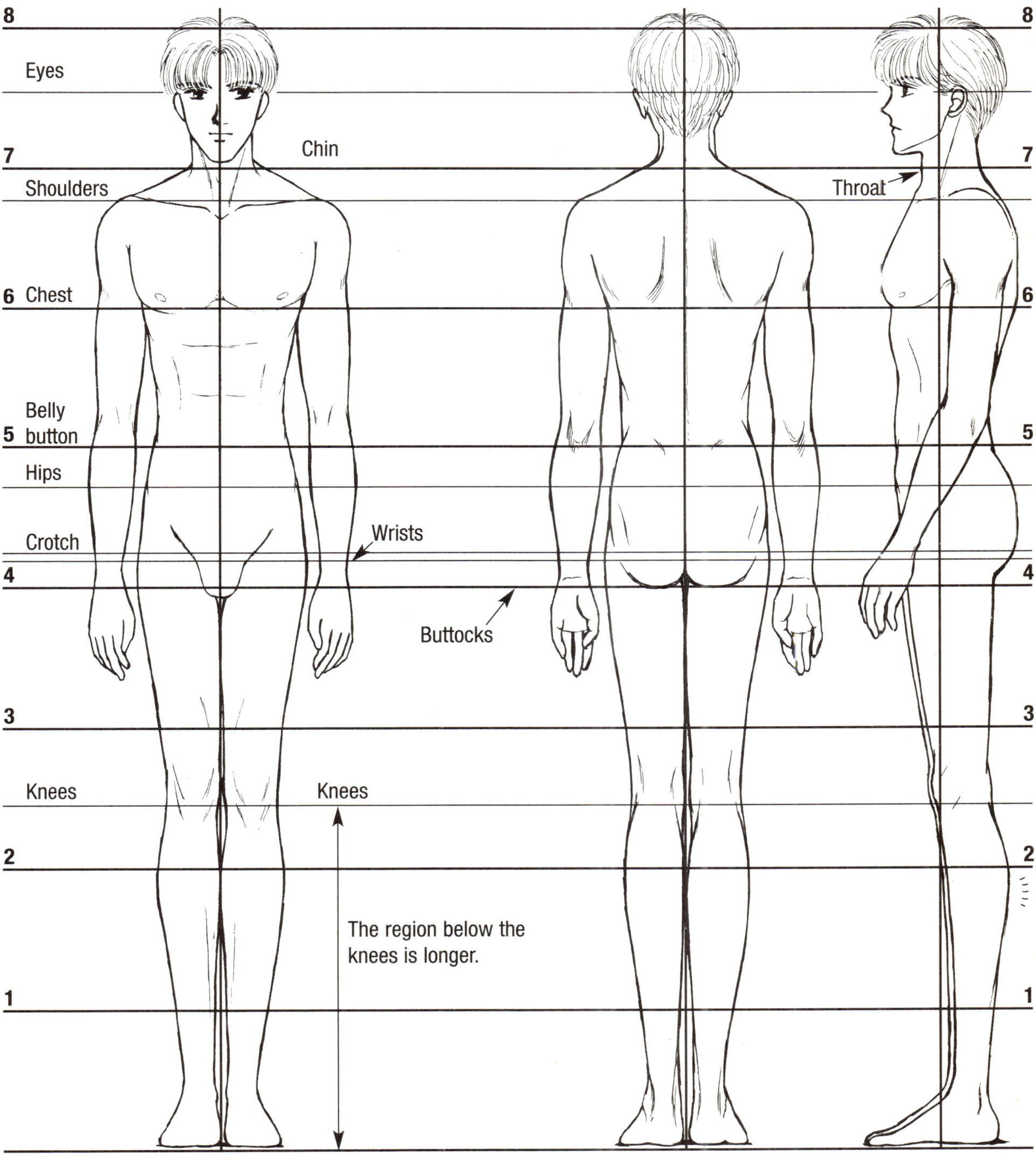

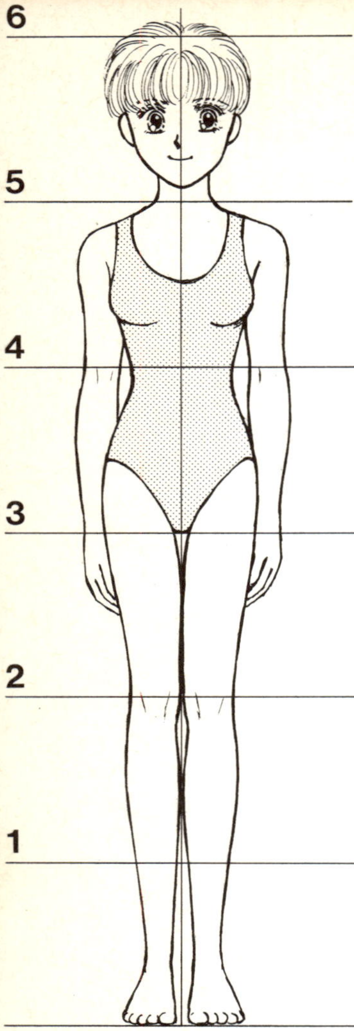

It can be difficult to draw short people and children if they have a head-to-body ratio of 1:7 or 1:8.

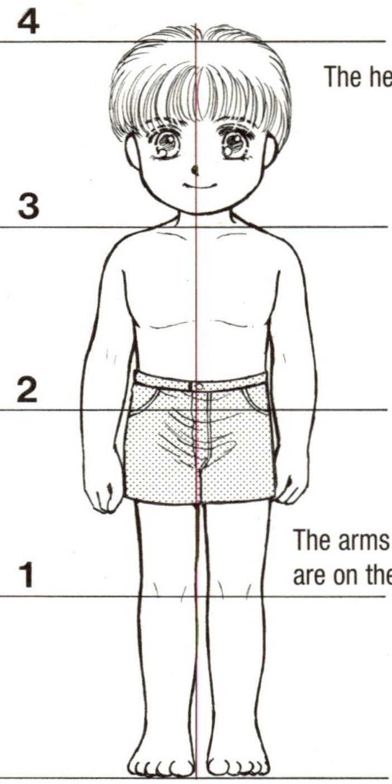

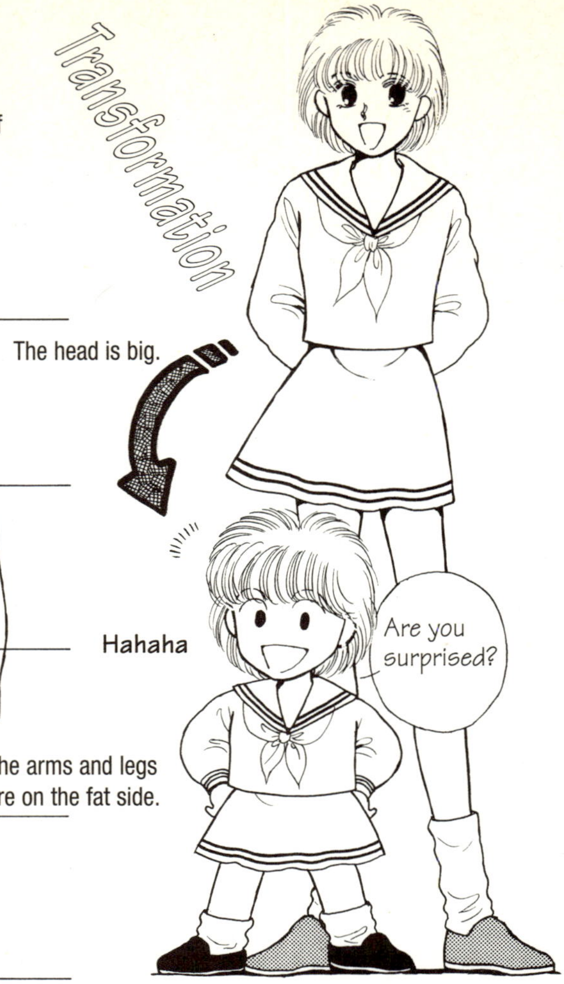

Higher grades of elementary school (head-to-body ratio of about 1:5.5 to 1:7)

Lower grades of elementary school (head-to-body ratio of about 1:4 or 1:5)

Comical (head-to-body ratio of 1:3) Toddlers should also be a ratio of 1:3.

The length of the arms when extended is the same as the length of the body.

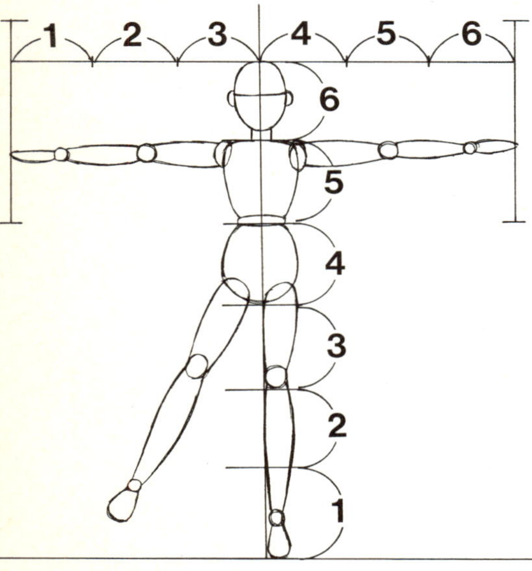

Center of Gravity

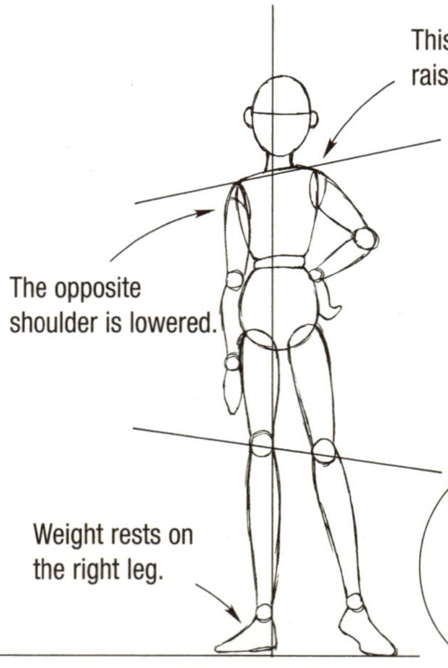

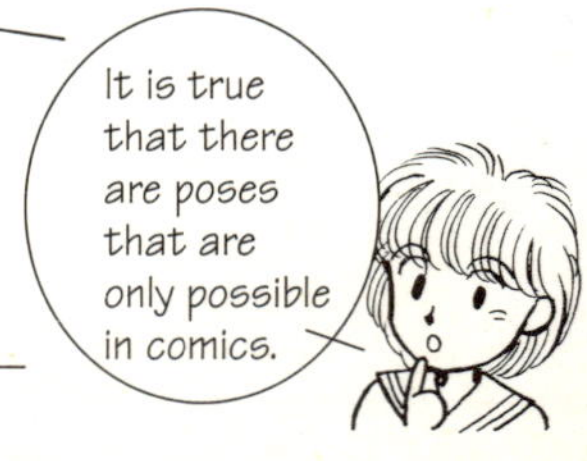

Low and high angles

Low and high angles are used when you want a scene with tremendous impact, want to express a psychological effect, or draw a building and a character.

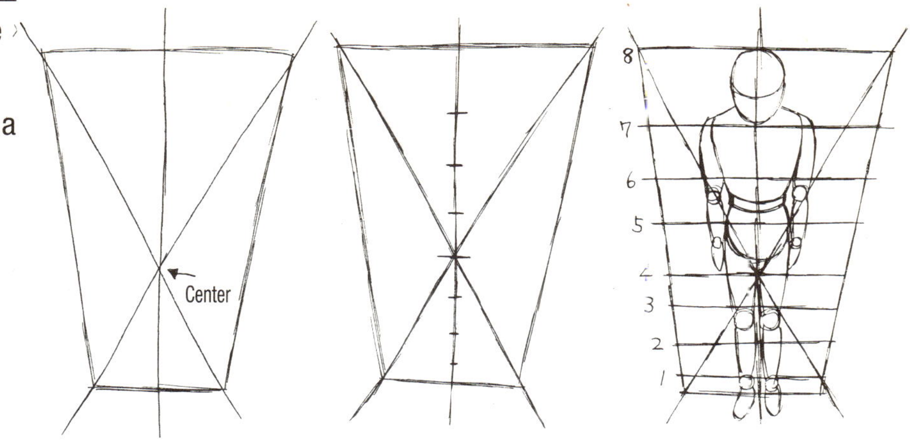

1 Draw a rough sketch. **2** Divide by the number of heads based on the center. **3** Add the character.

Low Angle (Looking Up From Below)

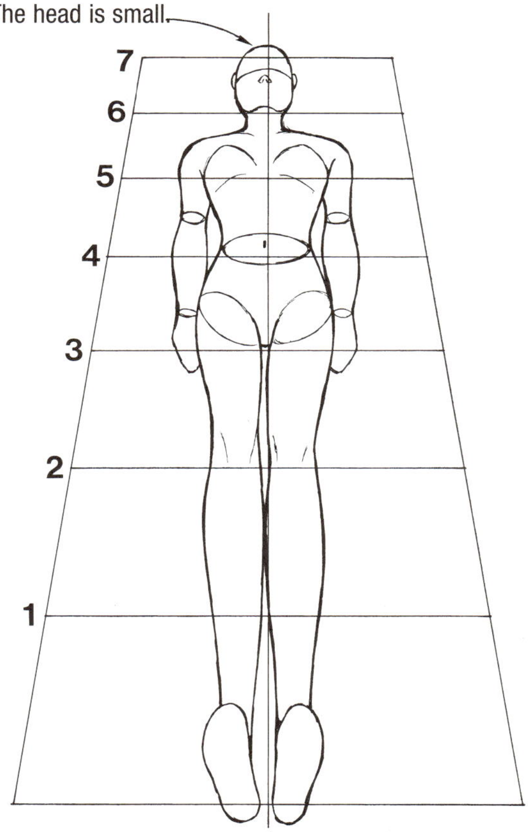

High Angle (Looking Down From Above)

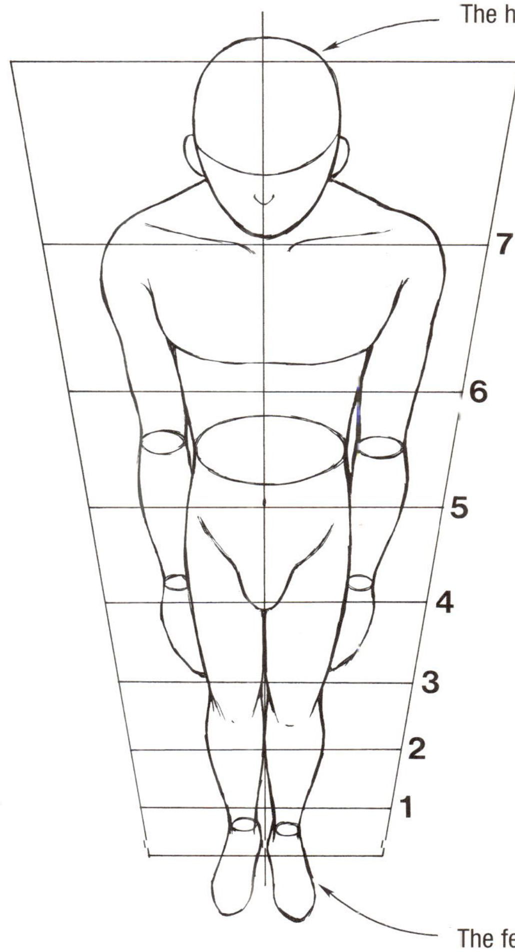

Try drawing from a variety of angles!

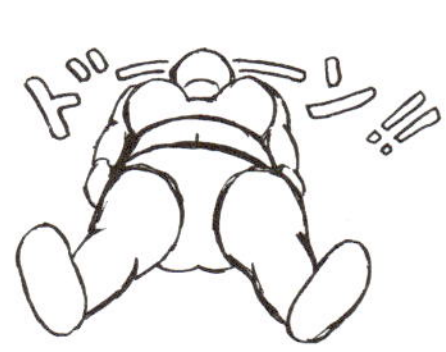

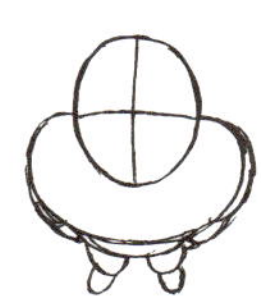

Let's give characters movement!

Basic Walking Motion

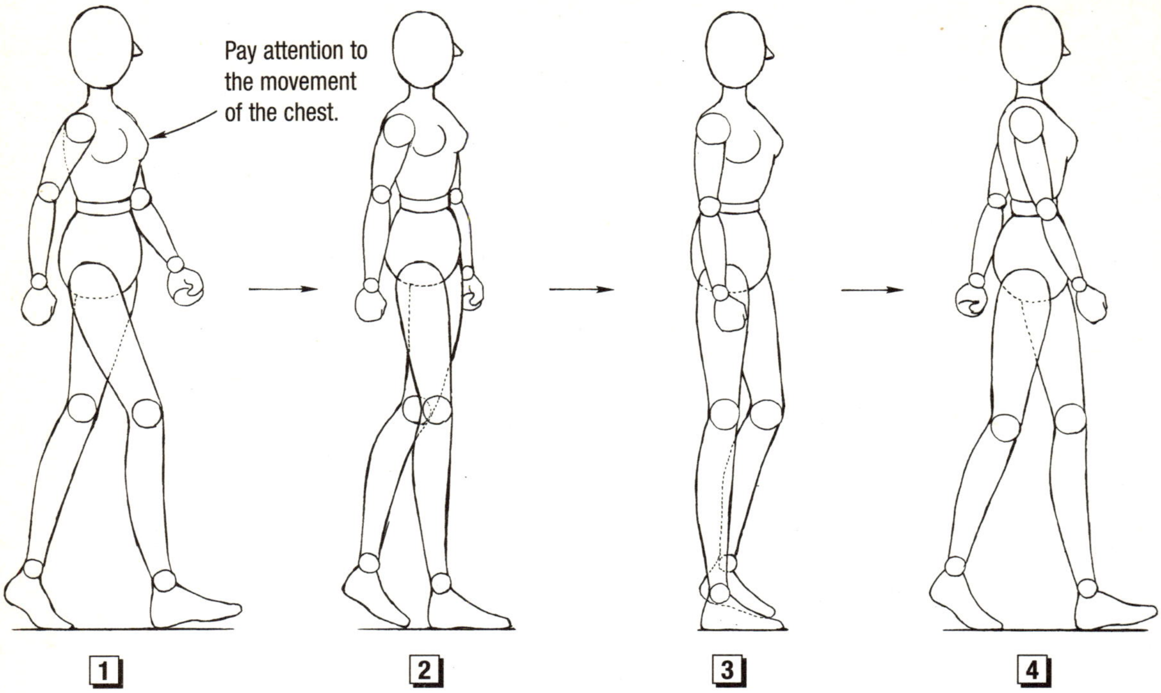

Basic Running Motion

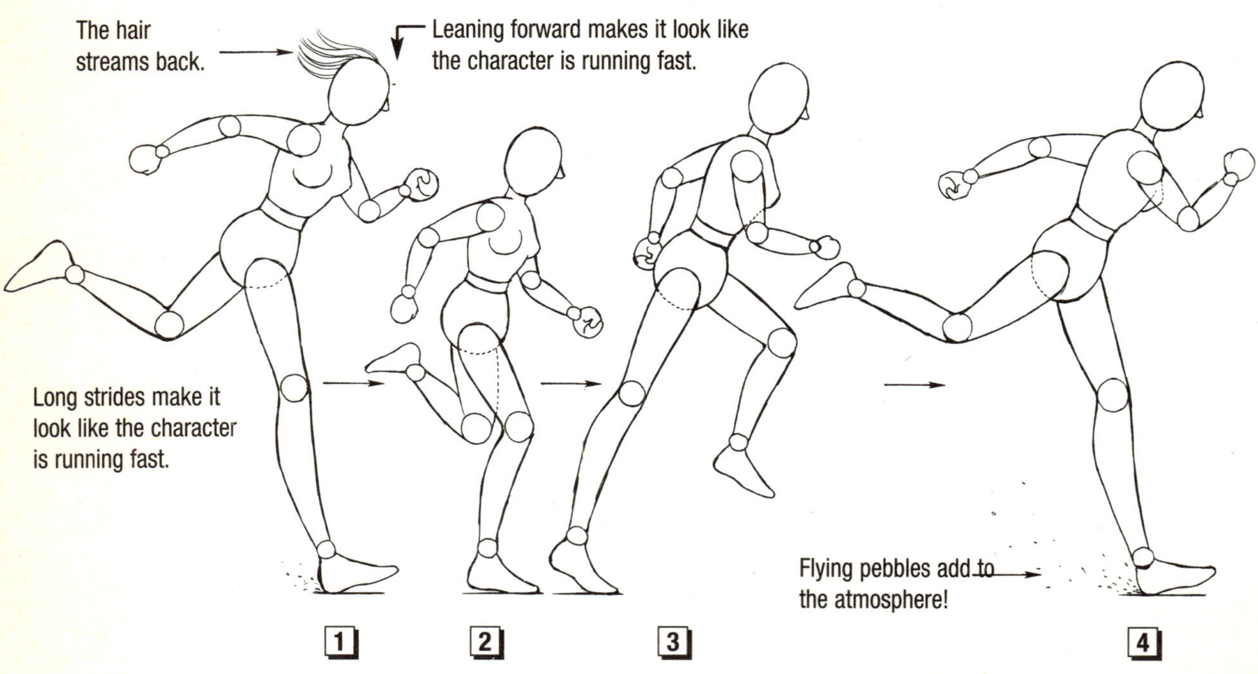

Walking

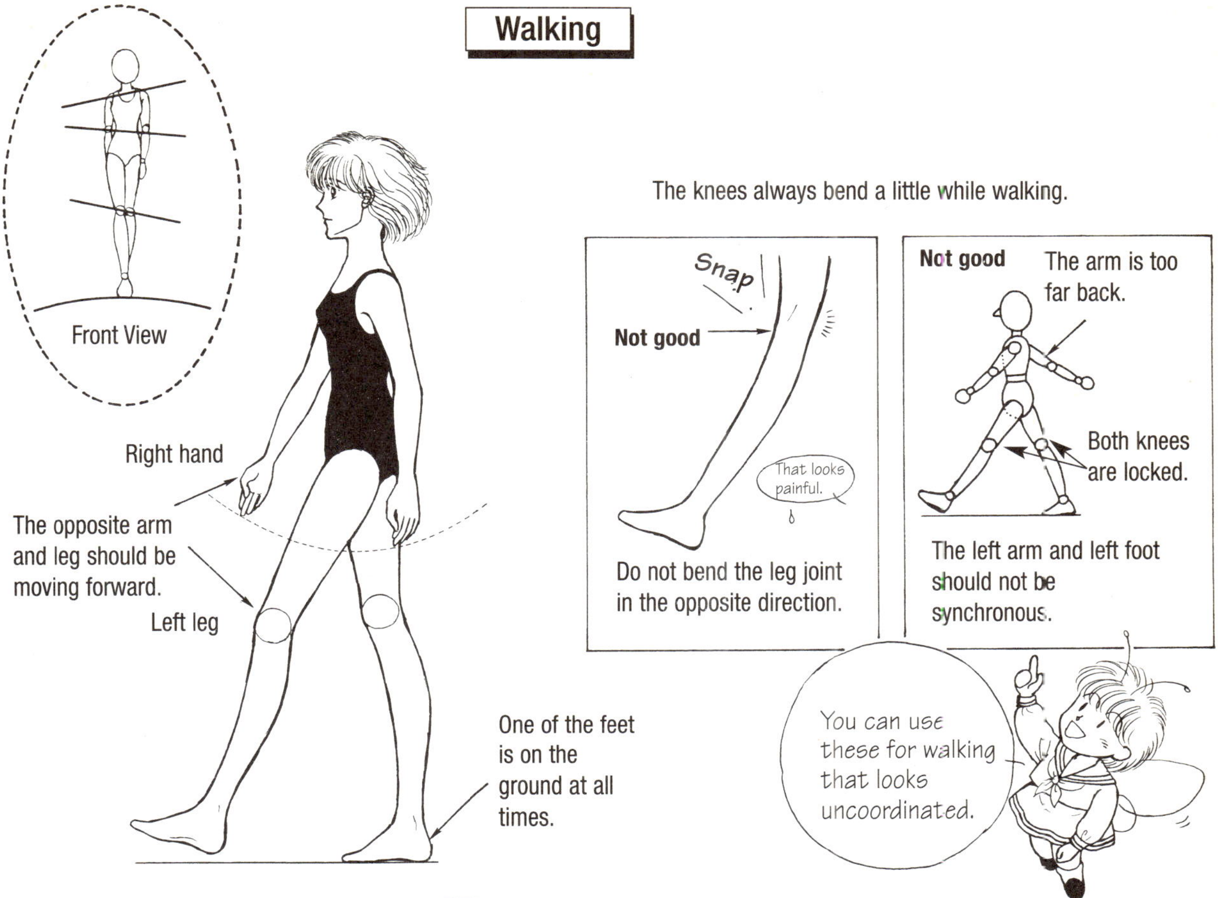

Running

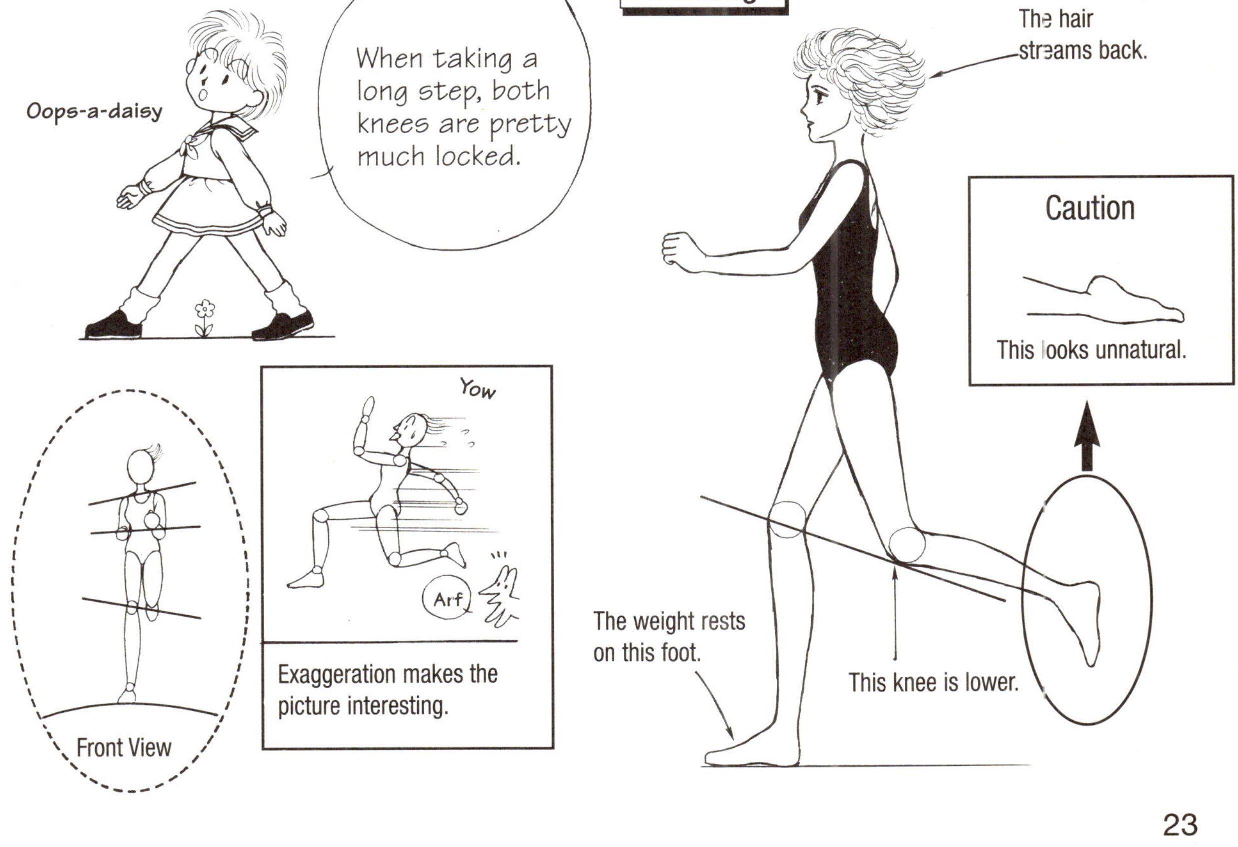

A Variety of Actions

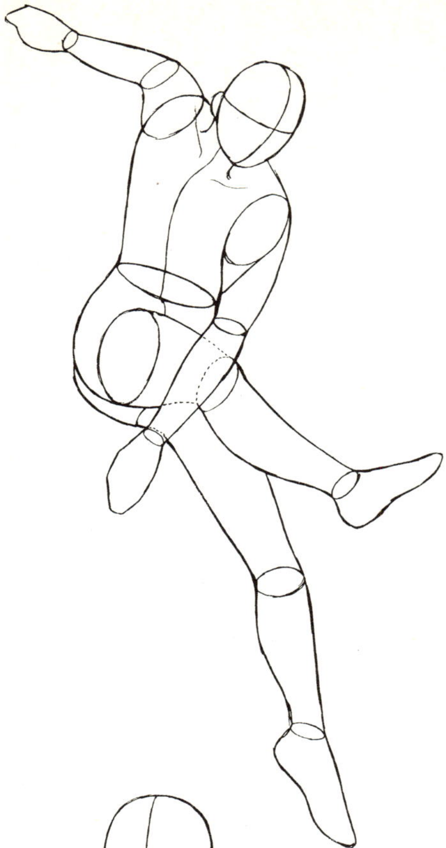

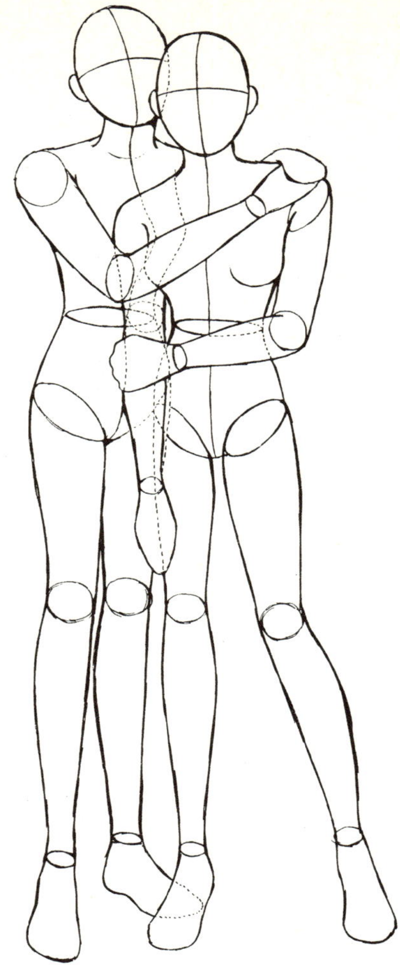

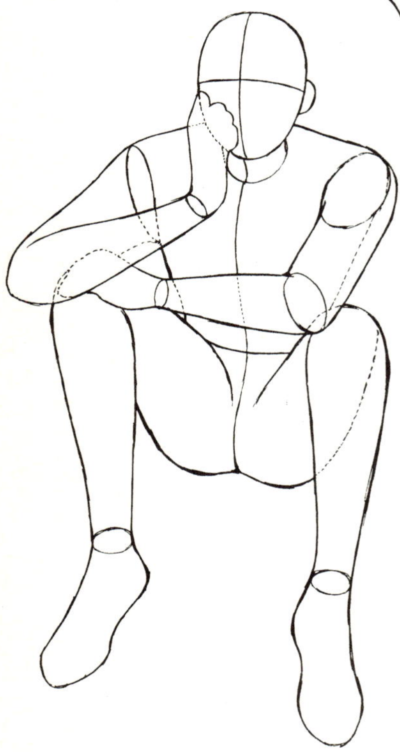

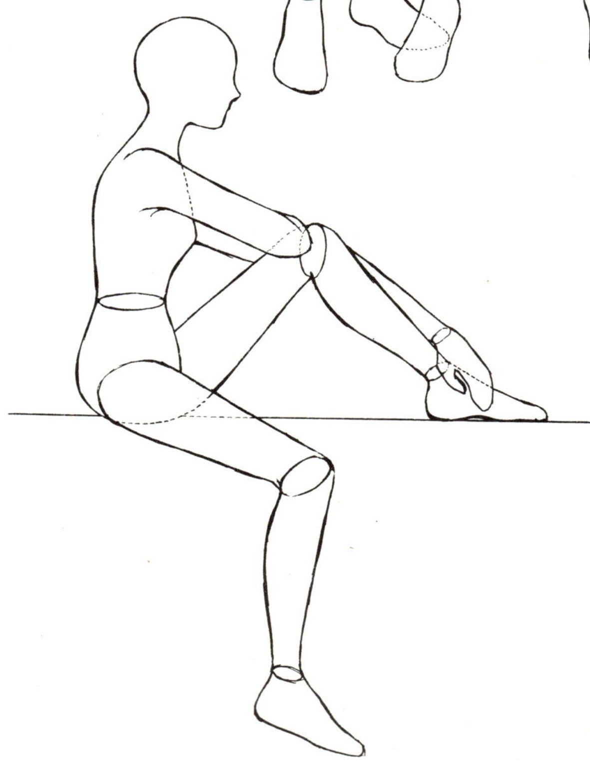

Hands and Feet

Try drawing hands from a variety of angles, paying attention to finger length, width, and joints.

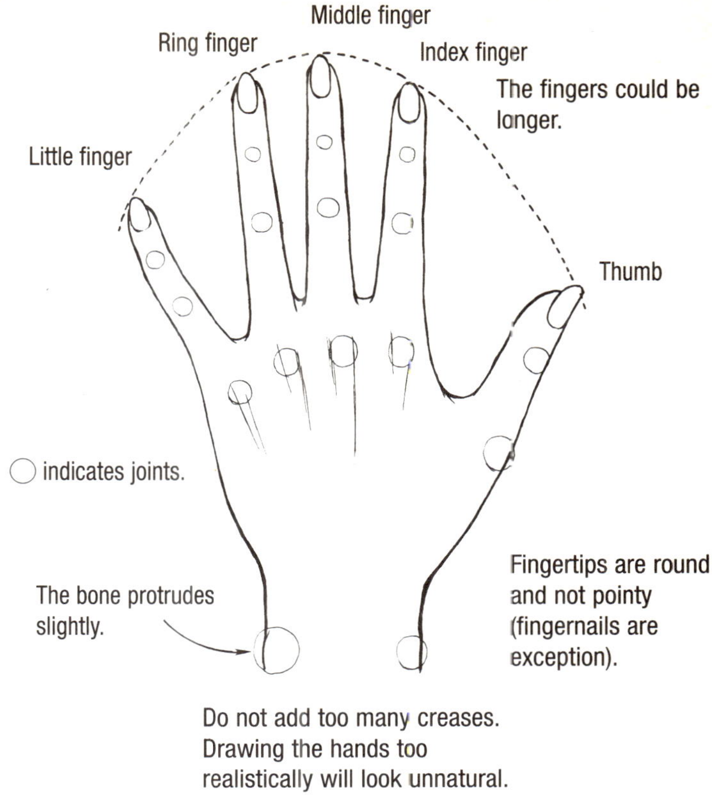

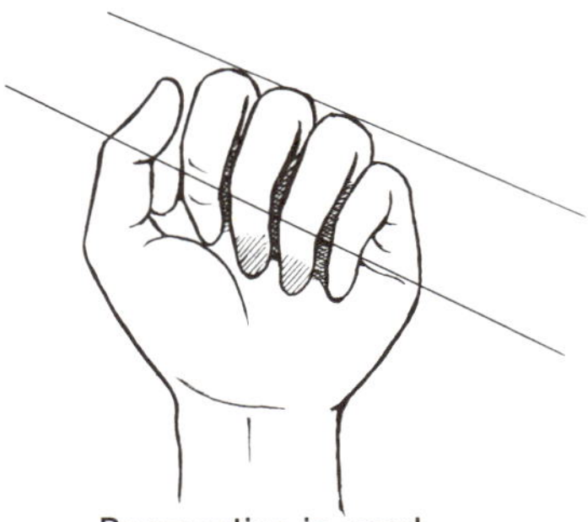

Perspective is used for hands as well.

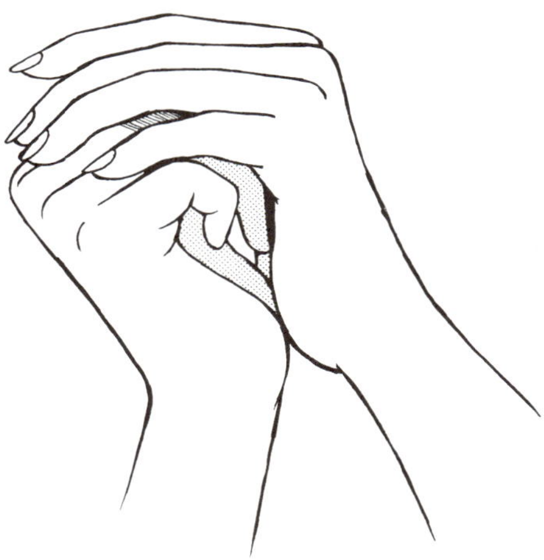

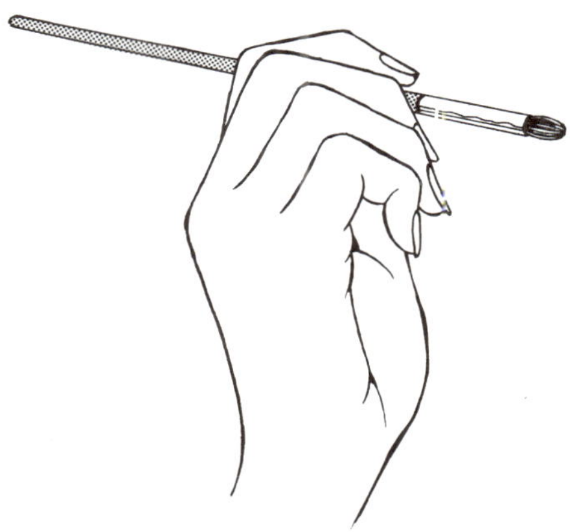

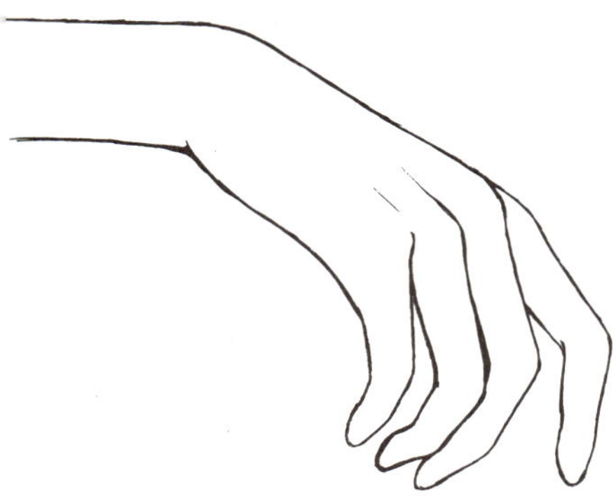

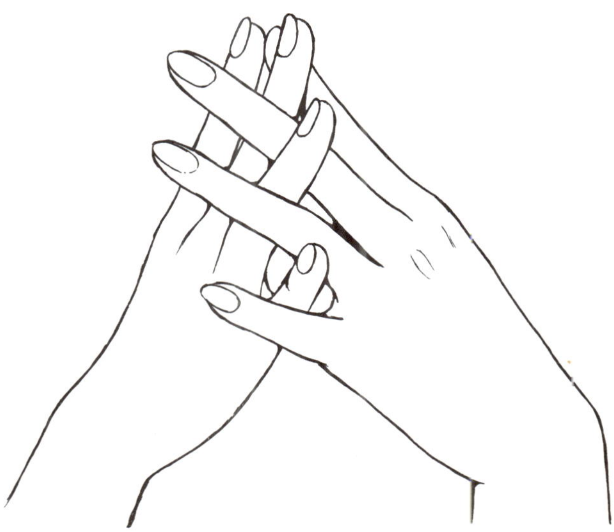

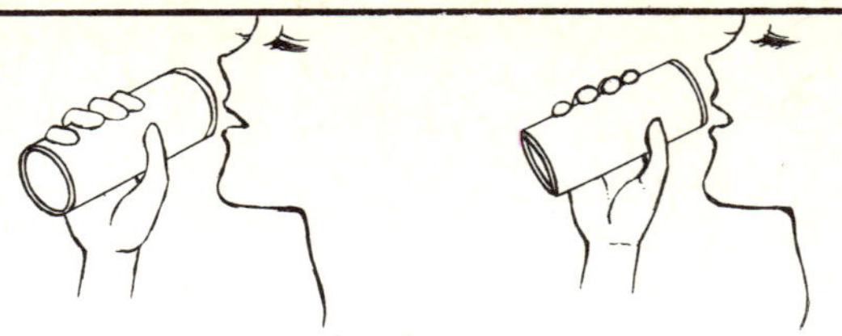

When holding a can or other object, you can strike the right balance by also drawing the parts of the hand and can that are not visible.

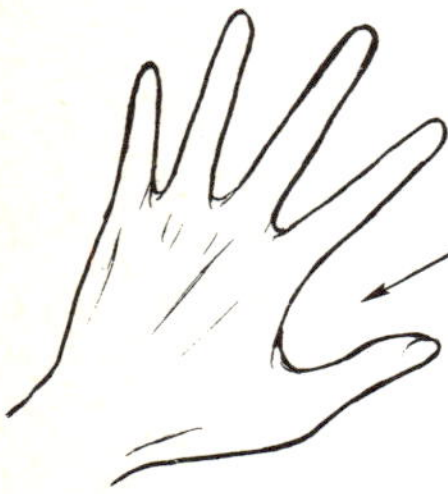

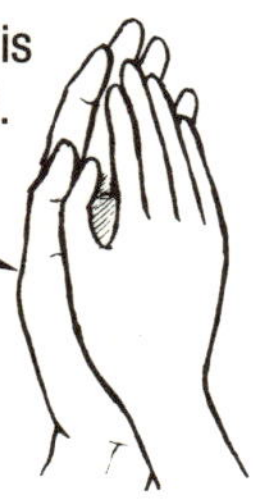

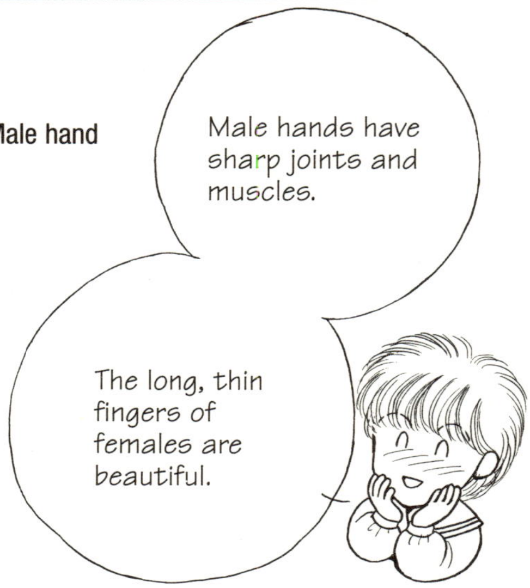

Common Mistake

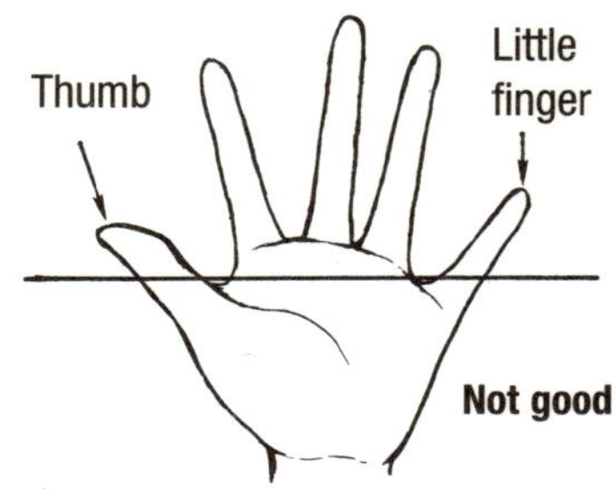

It is a mistake to have the base of the thumb and the base of the little finger at the same level.

Try drawing feet in a variety of poses as well.

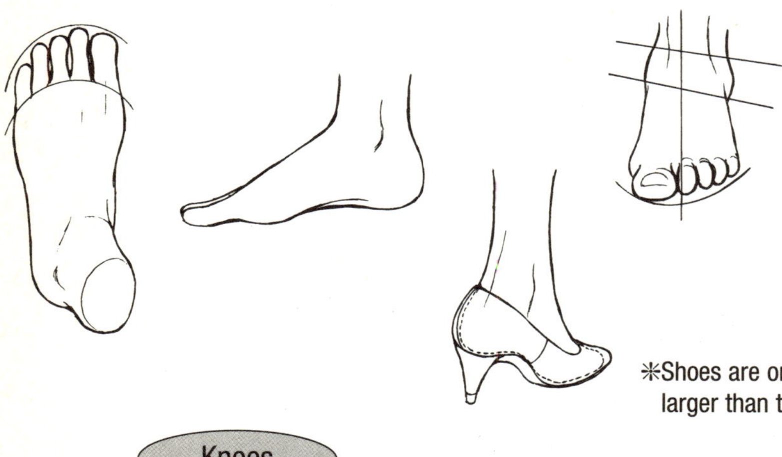

※Shoes are one size larger than the feet.

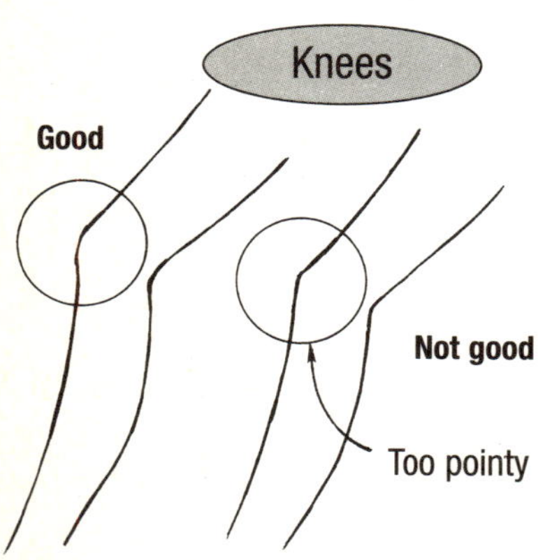

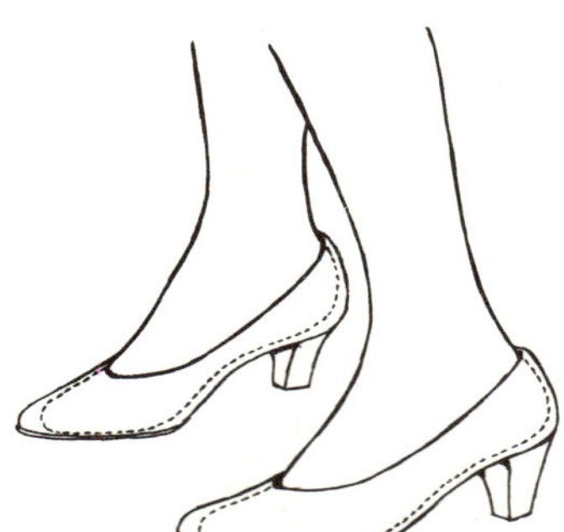

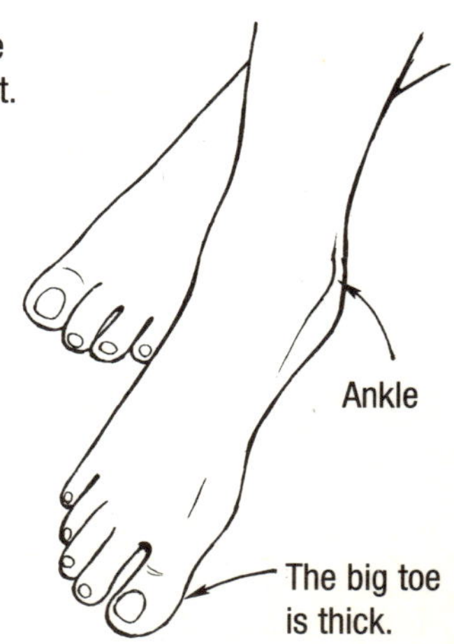

Compilation of common mistakes

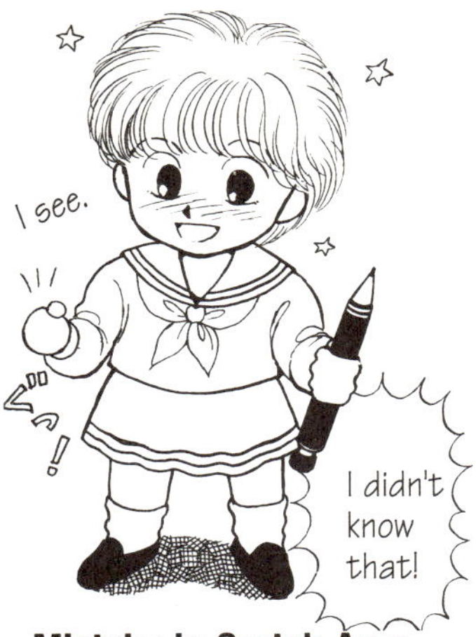

From the Neck to the Shoulders and Arms

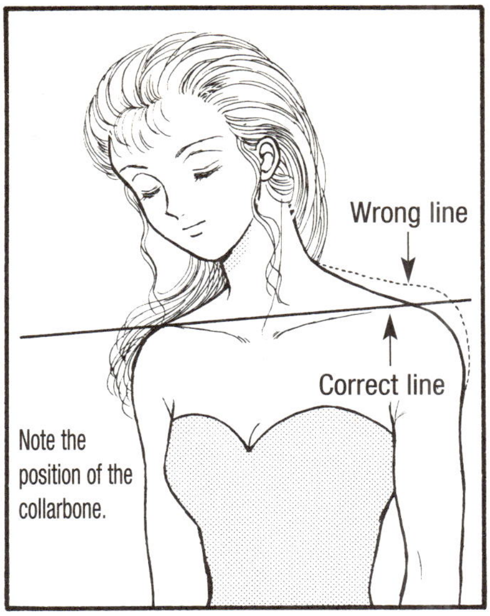

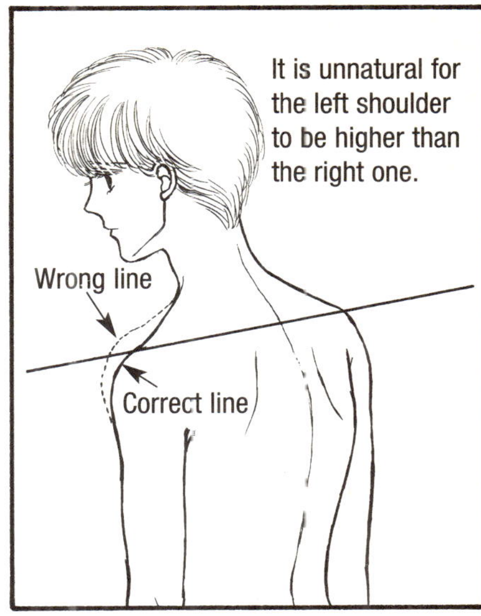

Mistake in Crotch Area

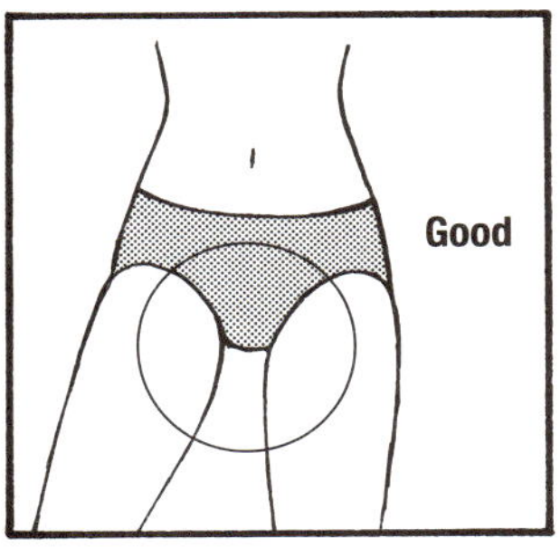

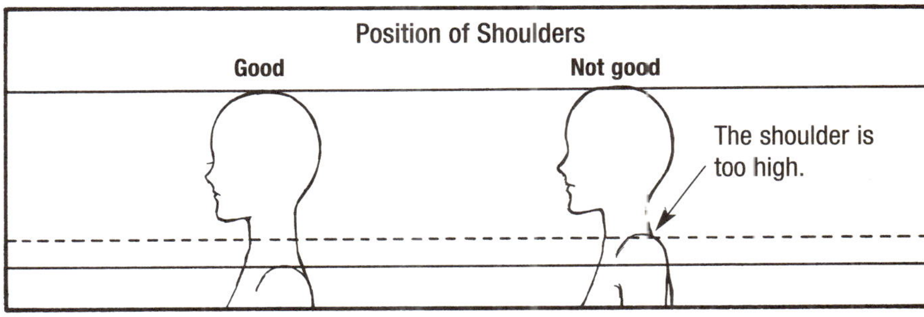

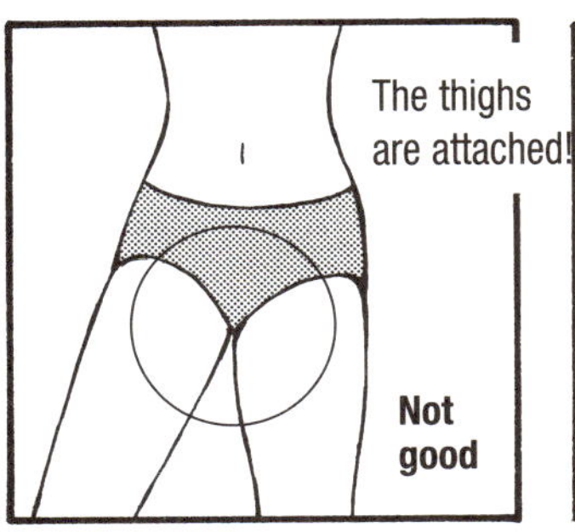

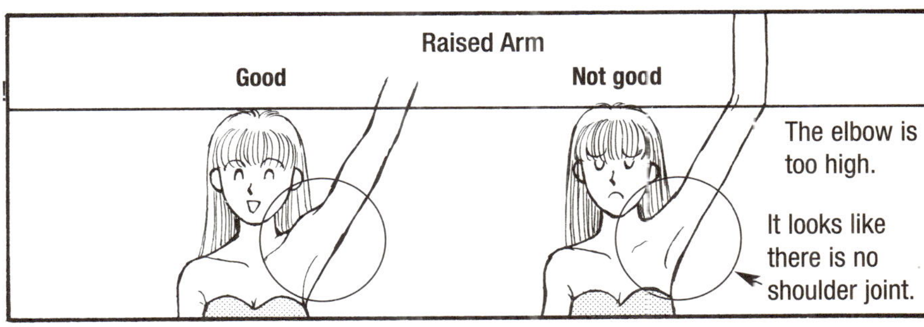

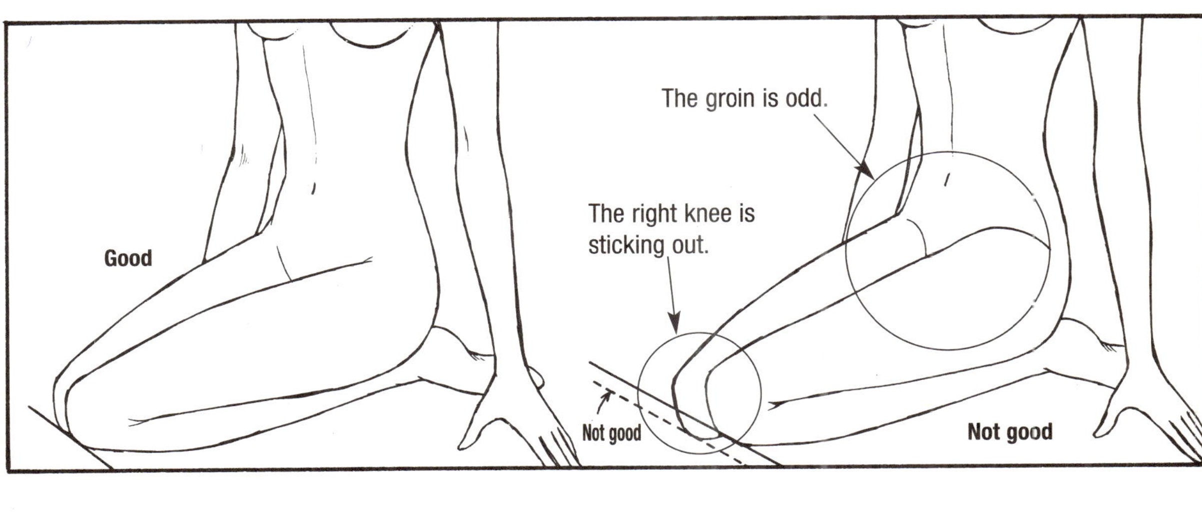

Textures of Clothing

The texture of clothing differs depending on the type of material. Actually touch clothing and look at magazines and photo collections for ideas.

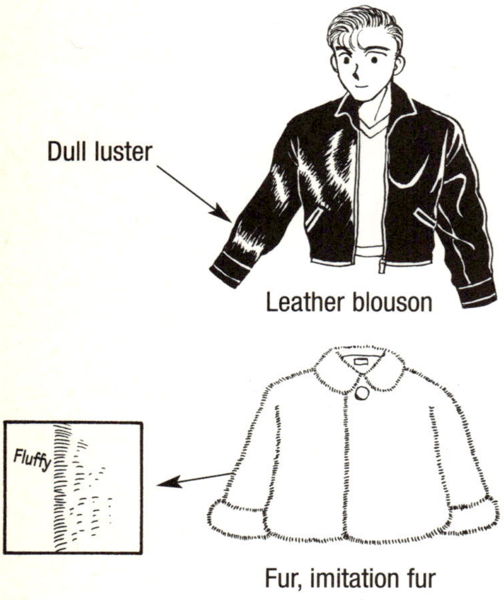

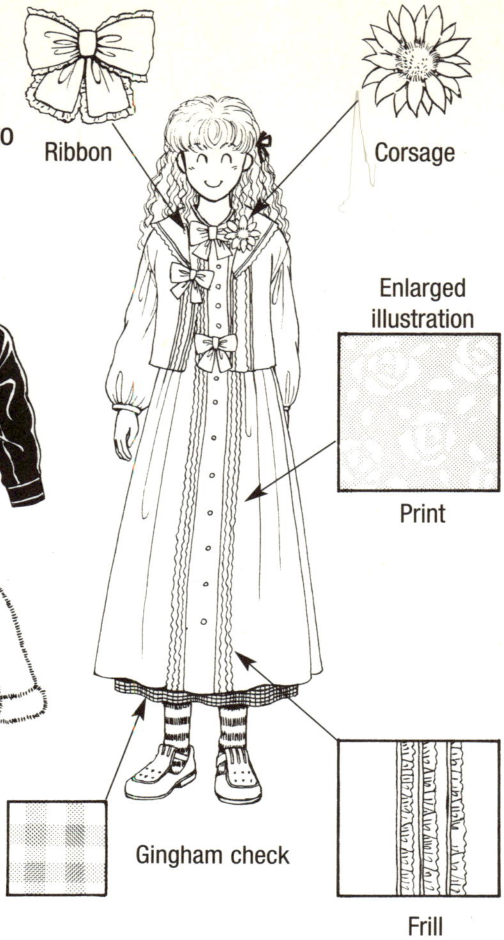

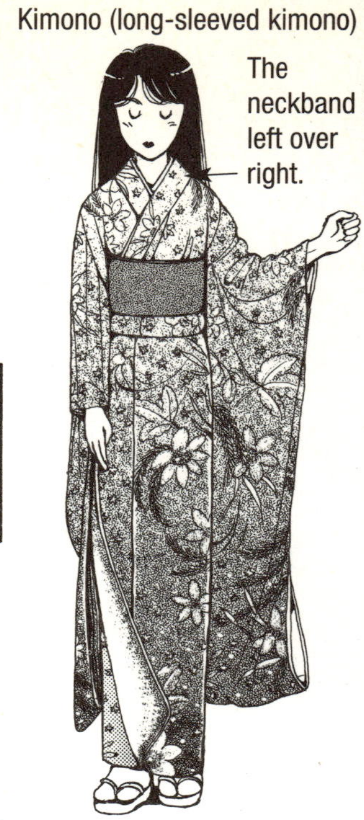

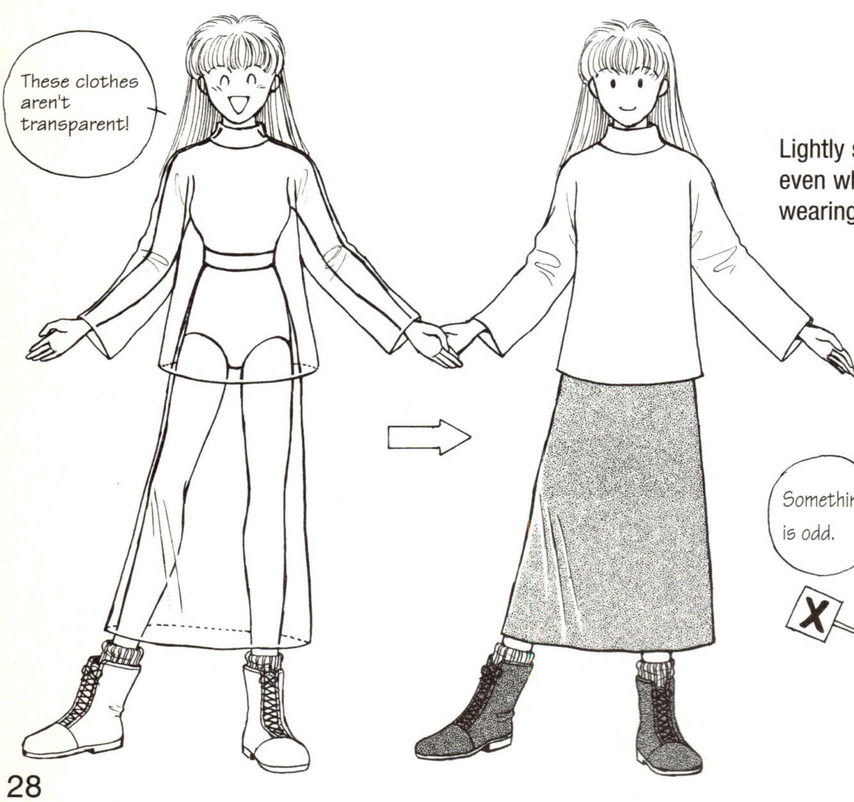

Lightly sketch the lines of the body even when the character will be wearing clothes that will hide them.

The position of the feet and the balance of the character will be off if you draw just the clothes without thinking about the lines of the body.

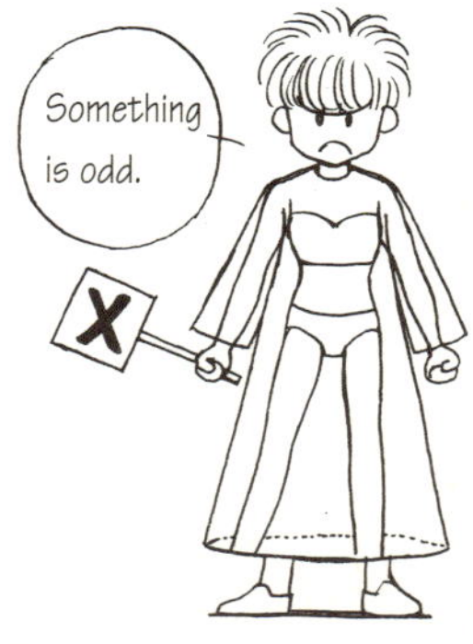

Jackets

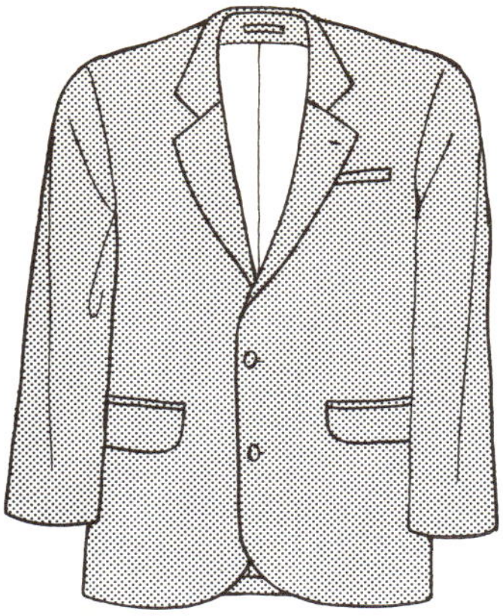

Men's jackets (left over right)

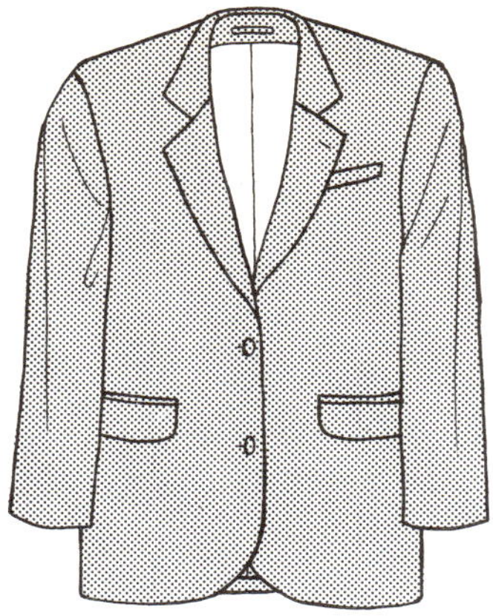

Ladies' jackets (right over left)
⁕ Some ladies' jackets are left over right.

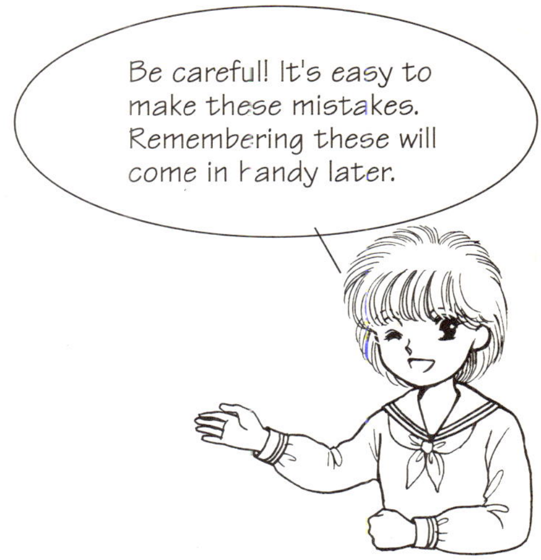

Sleeve 1

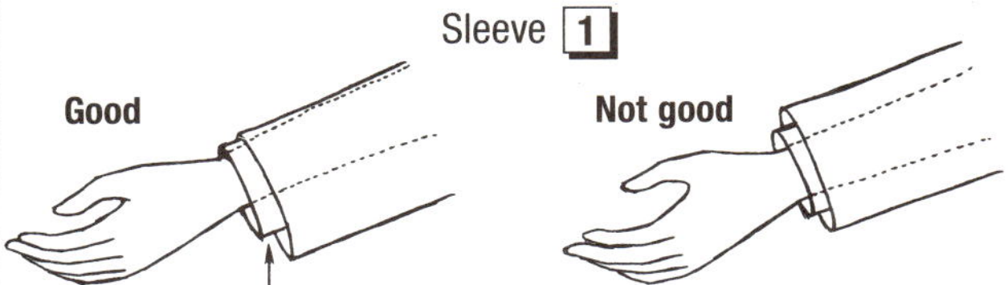

The sleeve falls when the arm is raised.

Sleeve 2

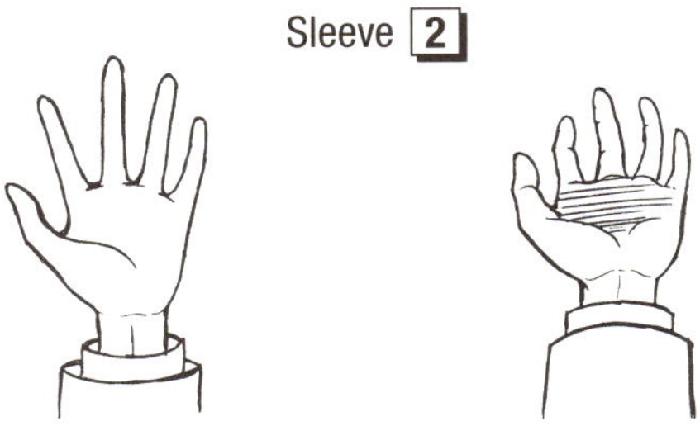

Jeans

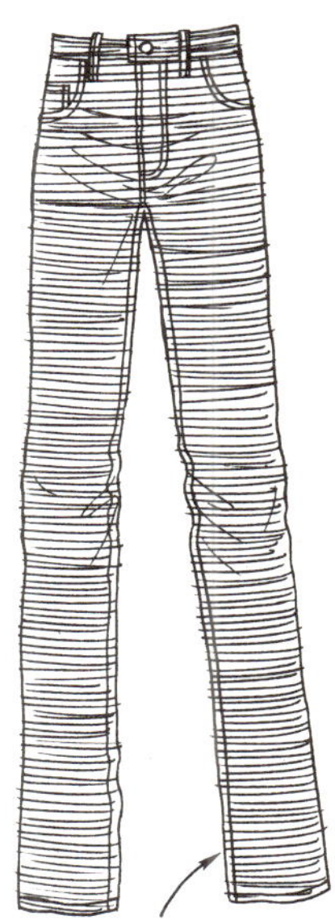

Jeans rendered with a pen.

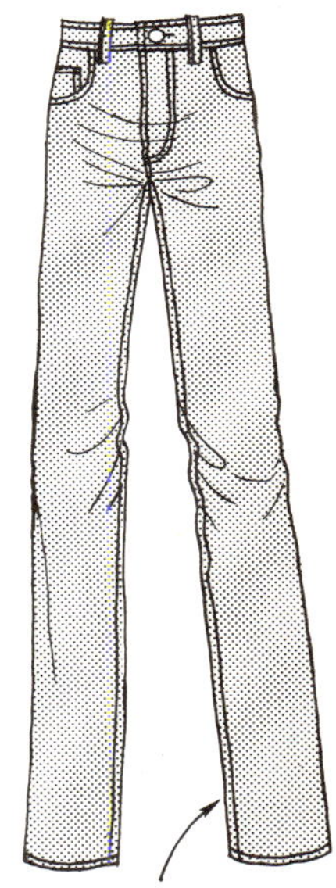

Jeans done with tone.

Striped T-shirts

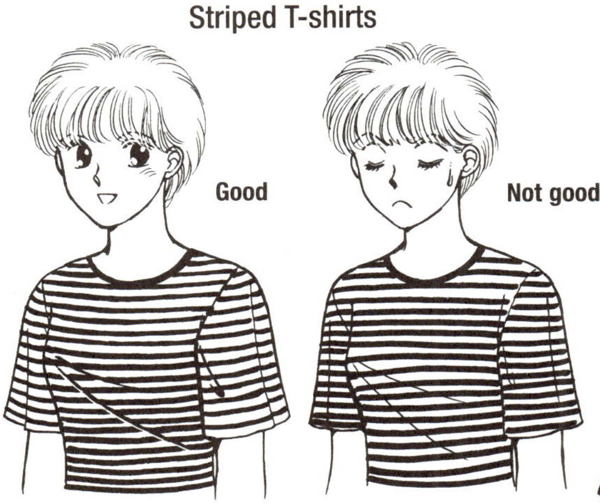

The stripes are unaligned at the creases.

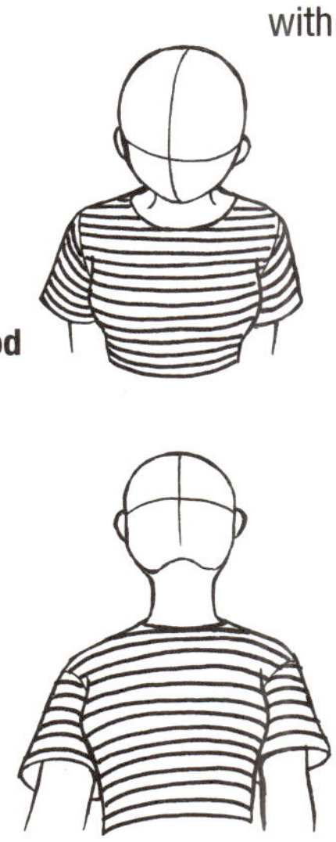

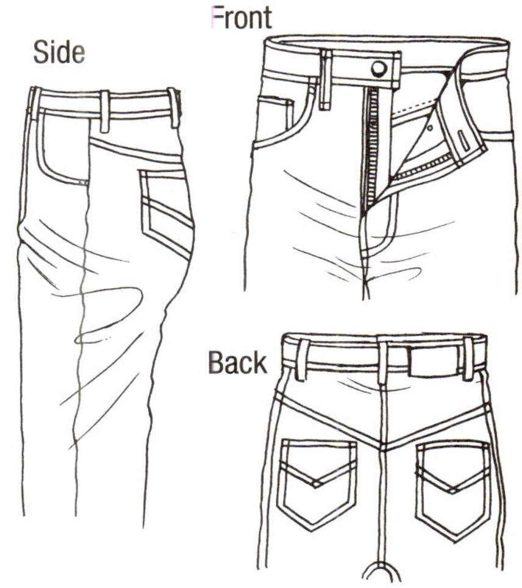

Wrinkles in Clothing

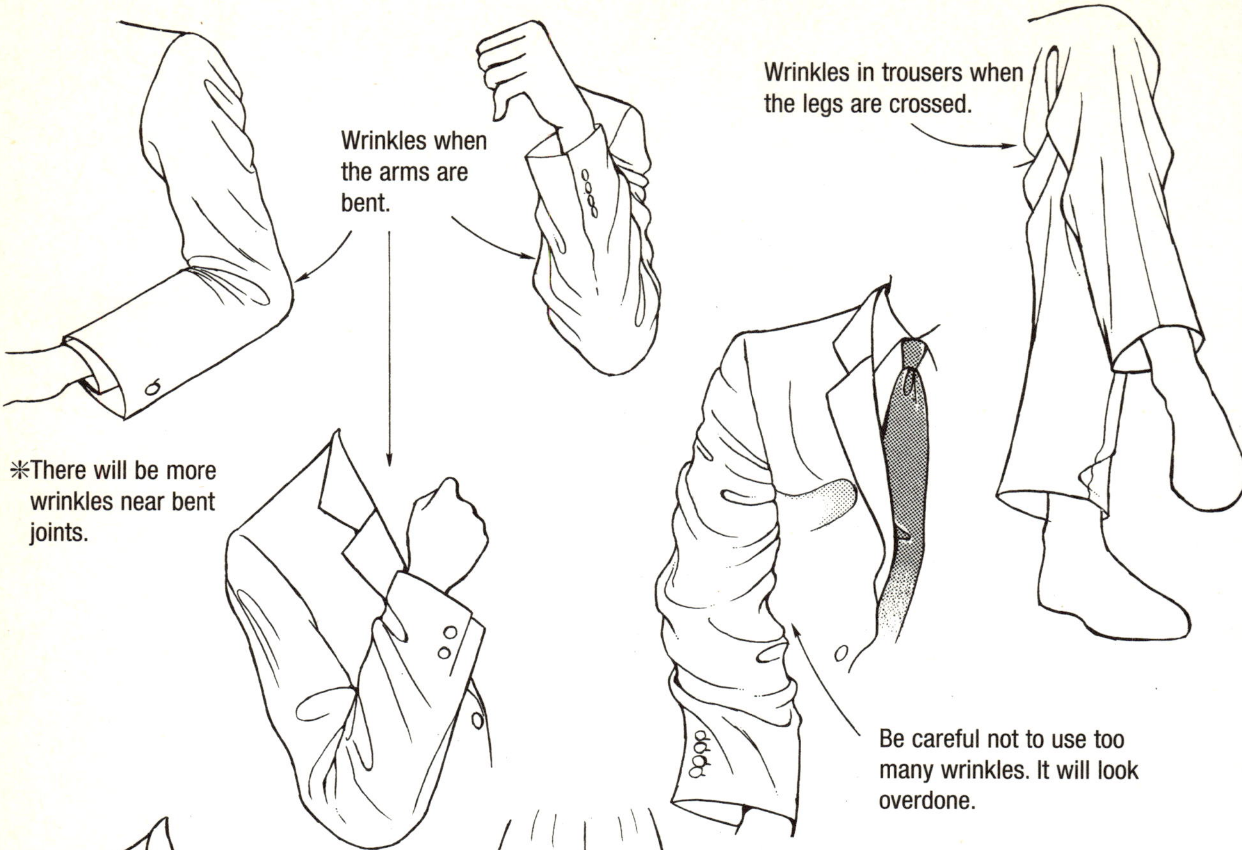

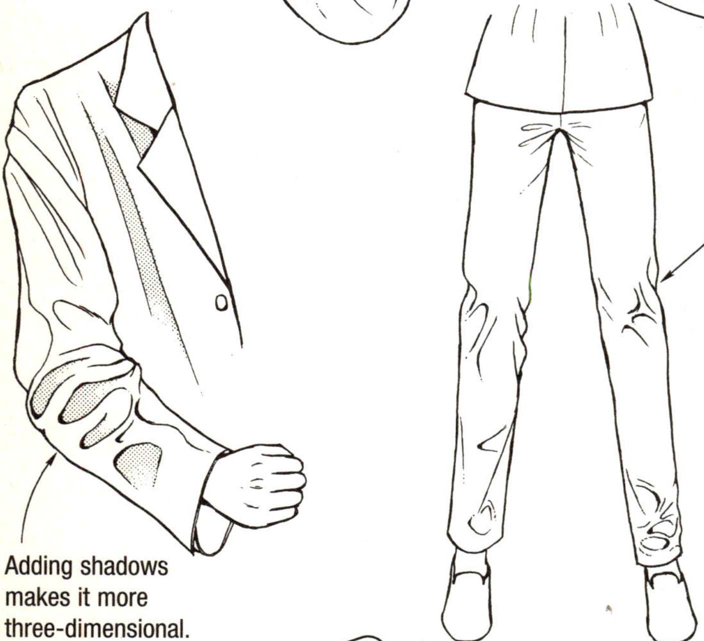

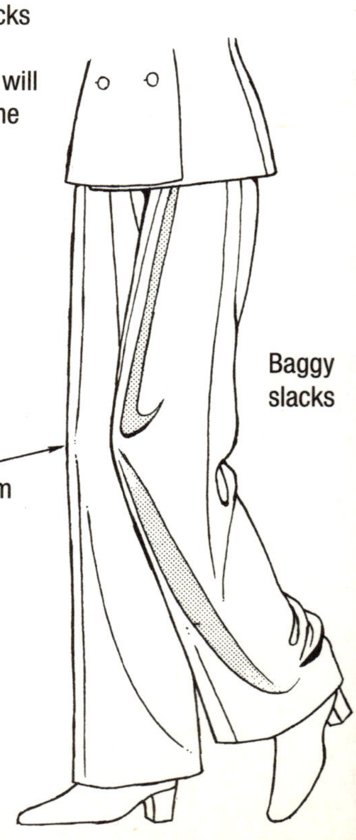

Key Point

- Loose-fitting clothes made of soft materials have more wrinkles.
- Tight-fitting clothes made of hard materials have fewer wrinkles.

Tight Skirts

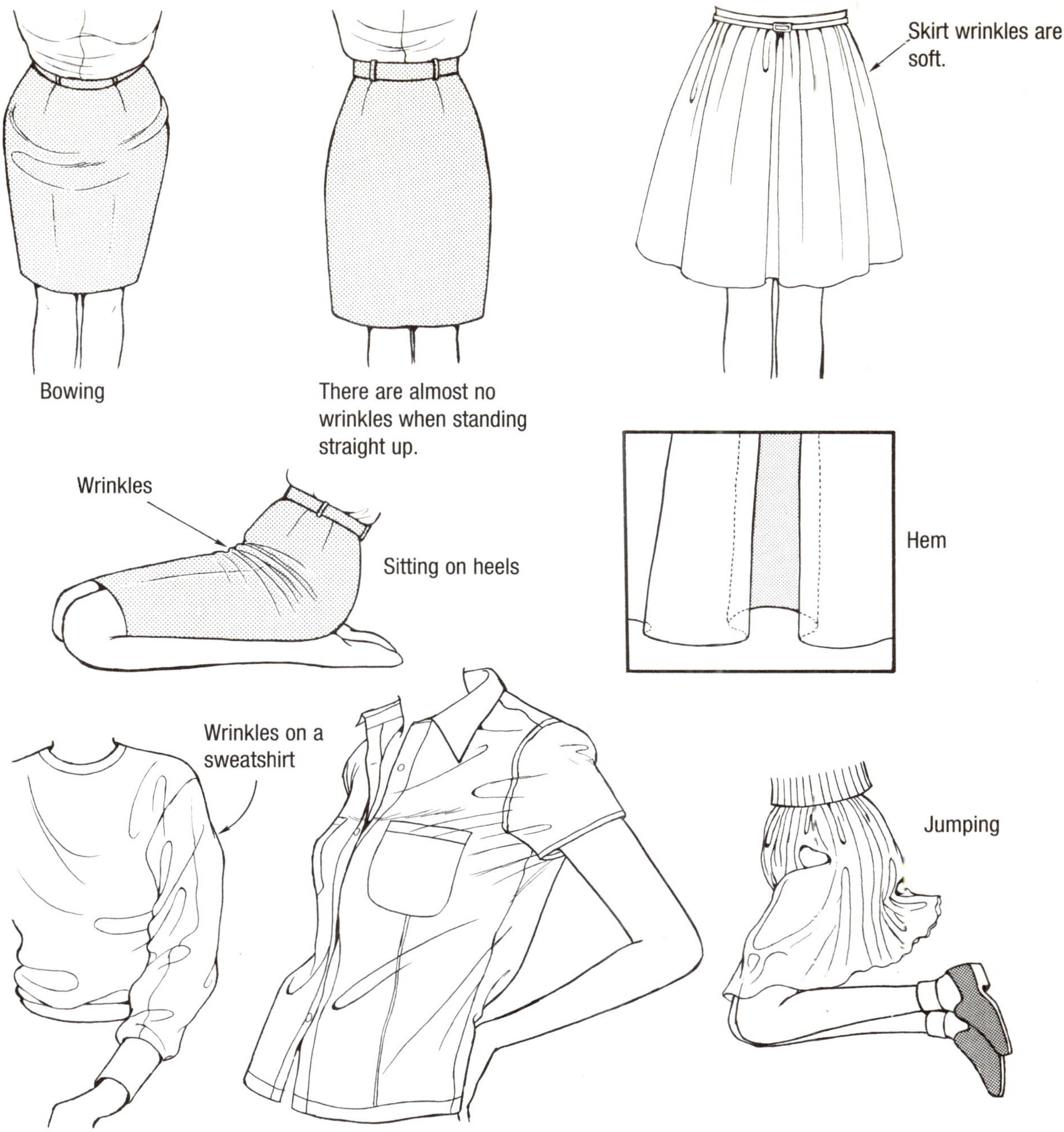

Sunglasses/Glasses/Caps

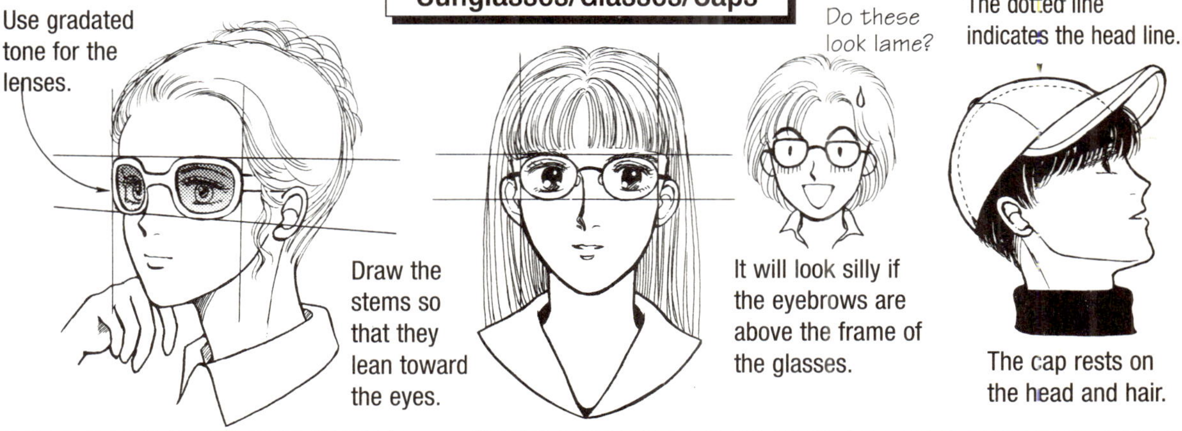

Chapter 2
How to Draw Backgrounds

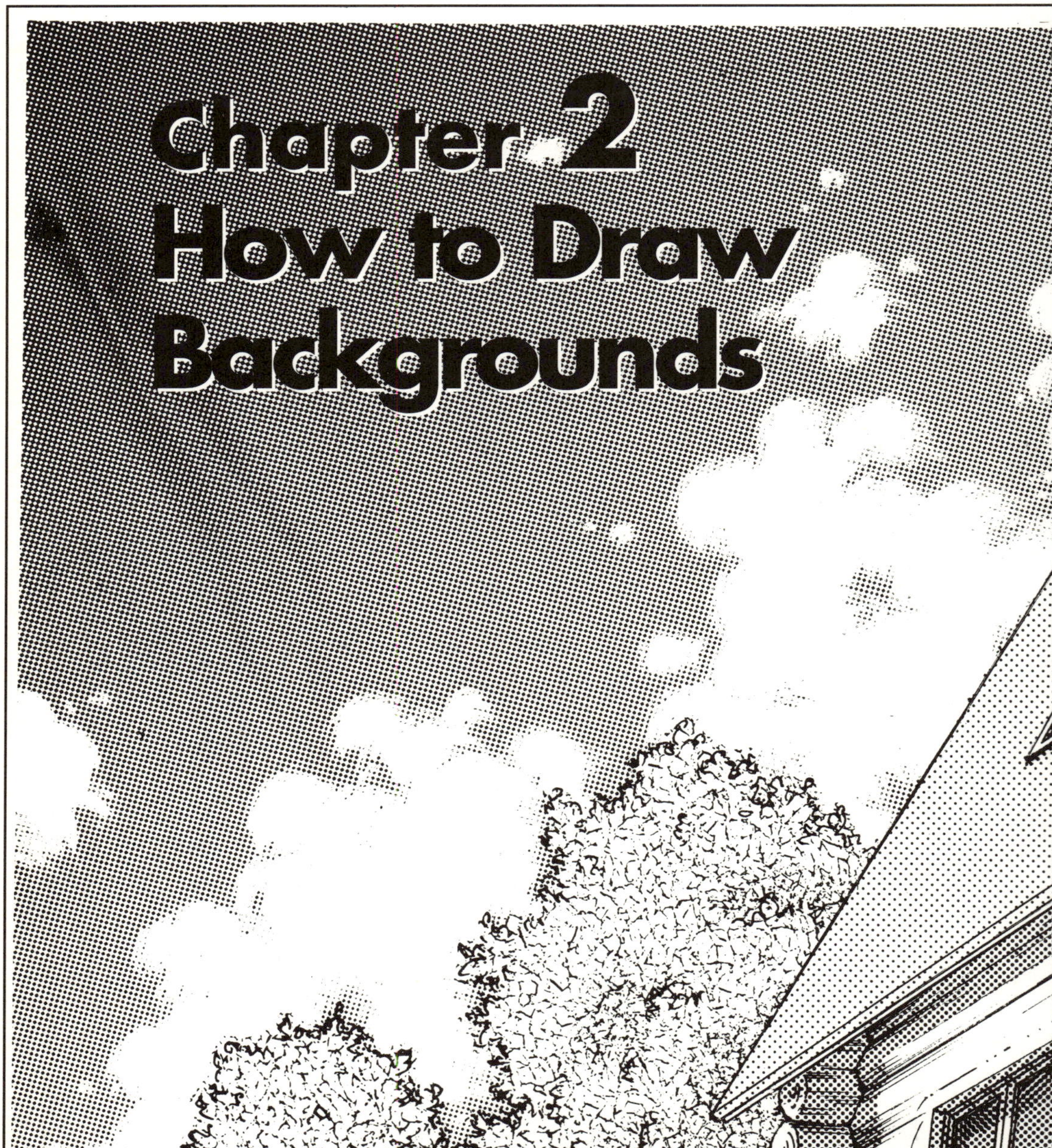

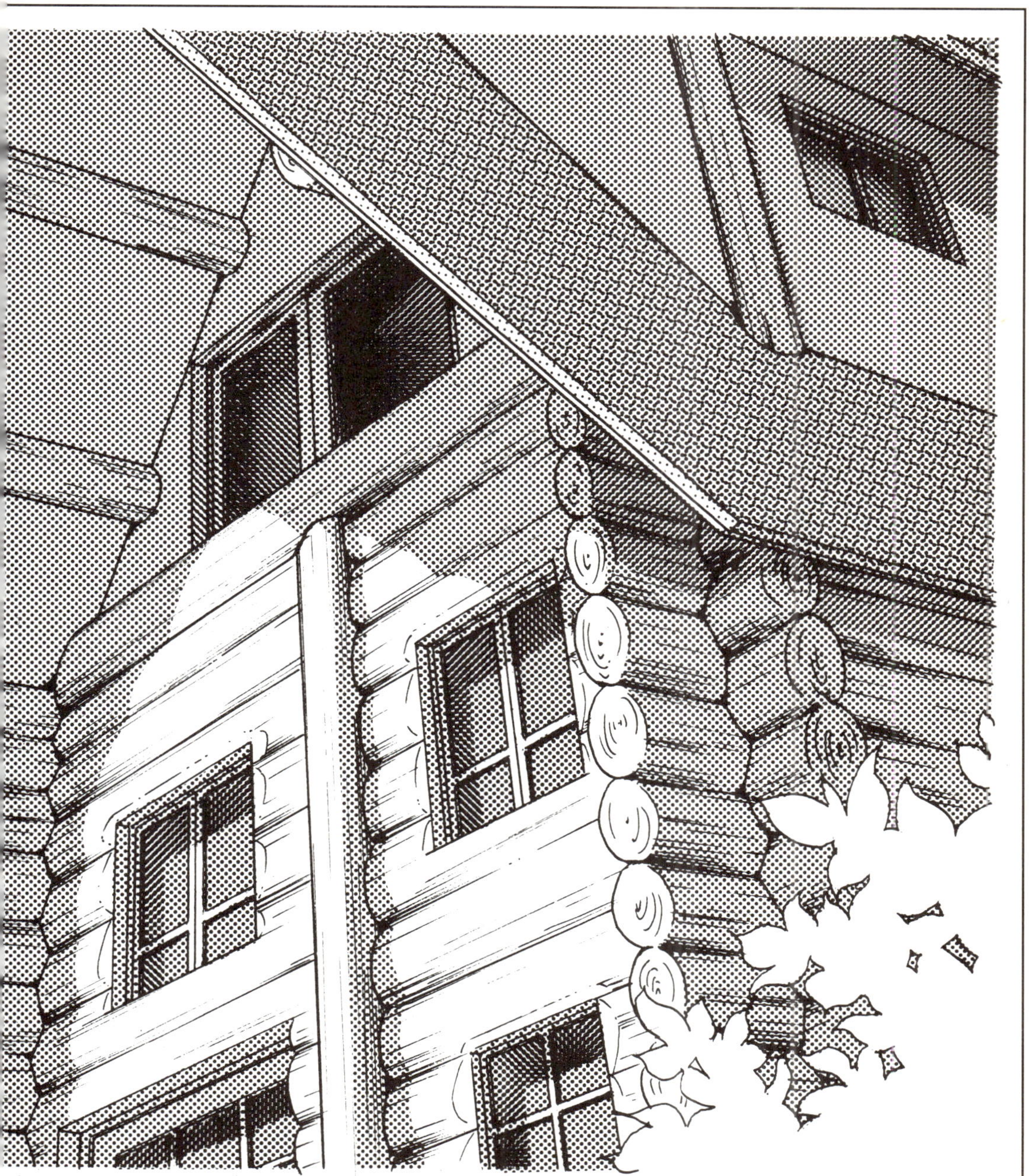

Backgrounds

Many of you may think that backgrounds do not have to be drawn clearly since it is a girls' comic. However, that is not true. If you know the basics, It will be surprisingly easy to draw any kind of background and it will be effective for the girl's comics. We hope that by all means you will give it a shot.

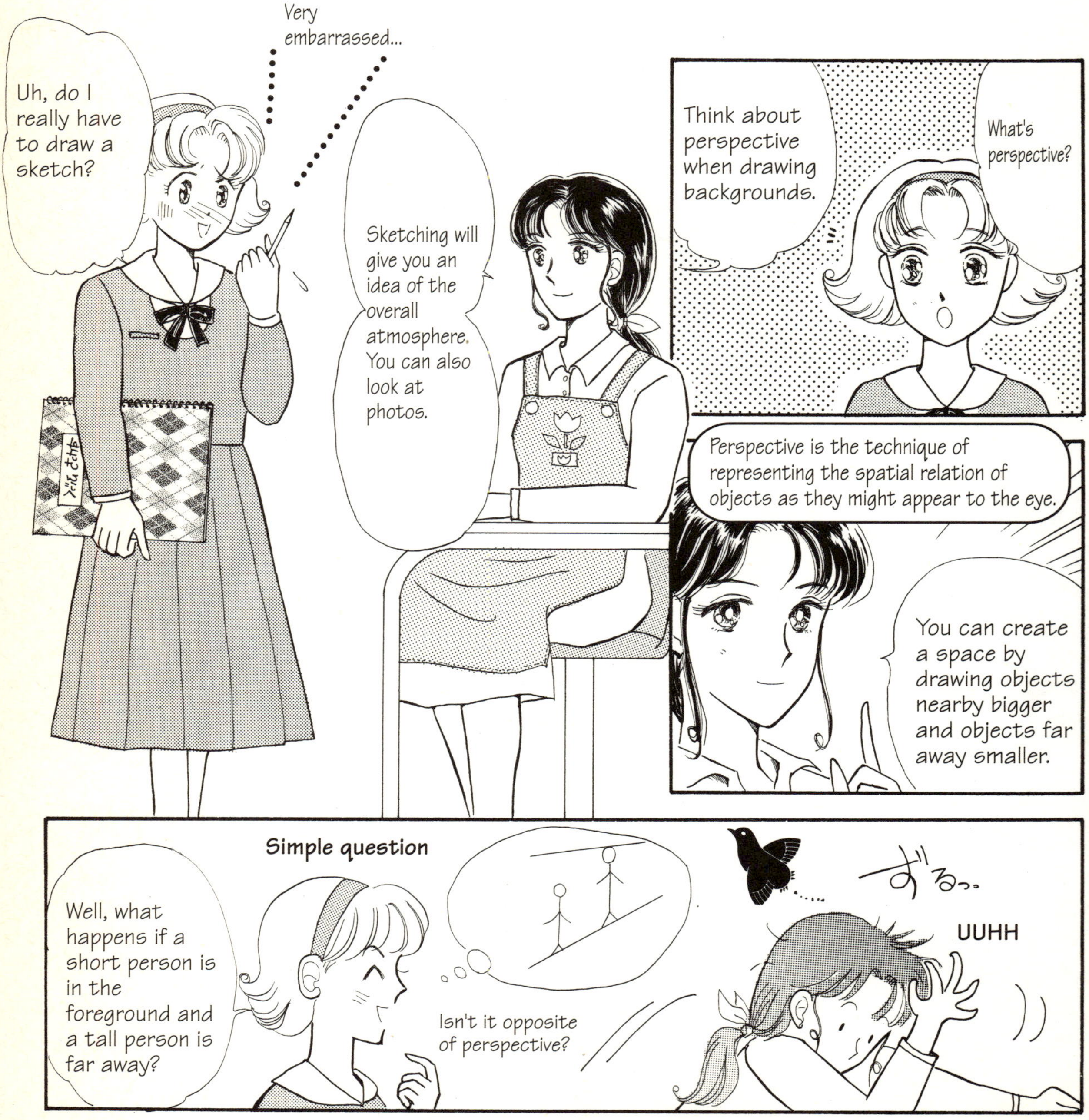

Figure A

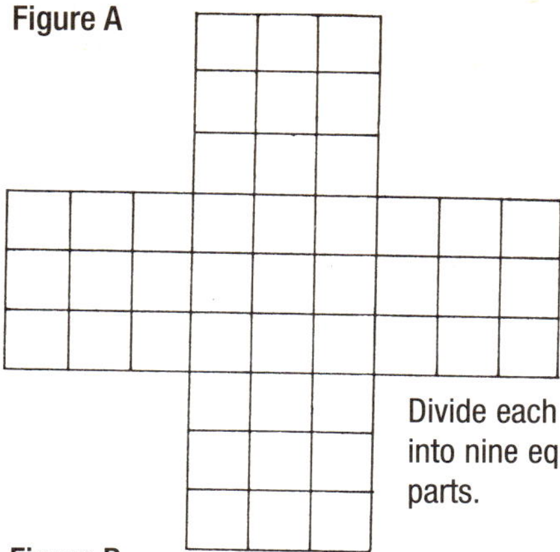

Spread out a box that is missing one side.

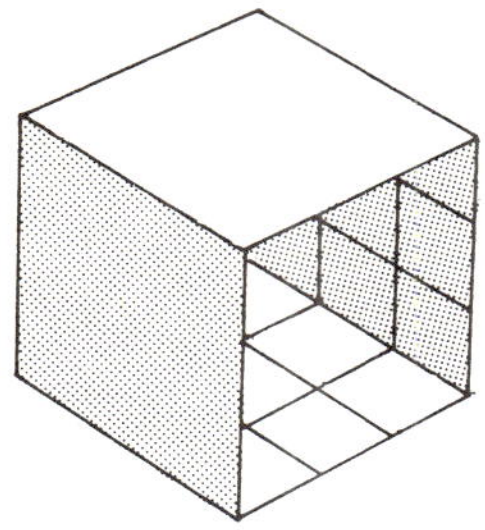

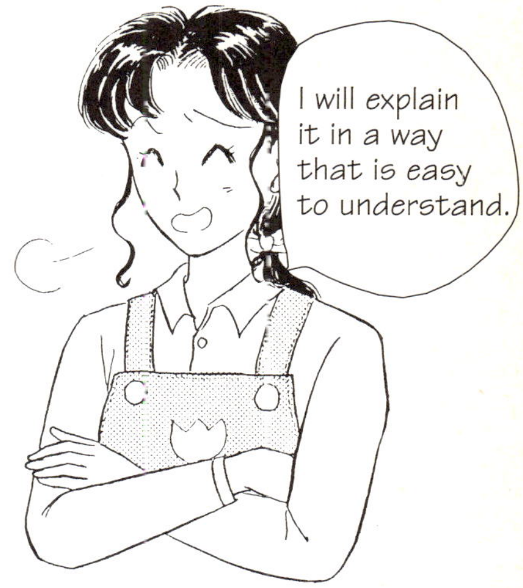

Divide each side into nine equal parts.

Figure B

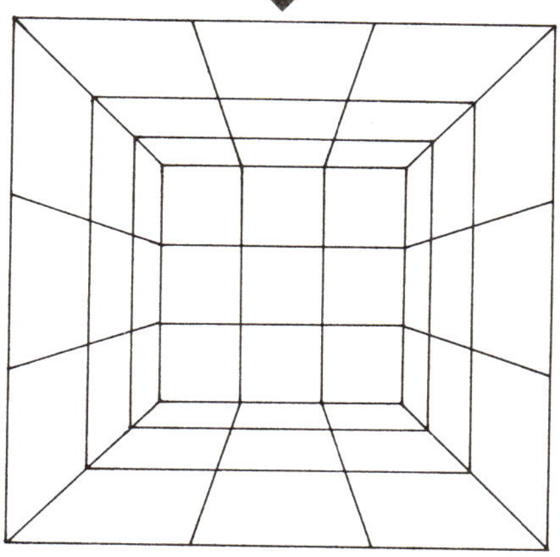

You can see in perspective when you put the box back together. Adding characters, a door, a table, and a window results in the next picture.

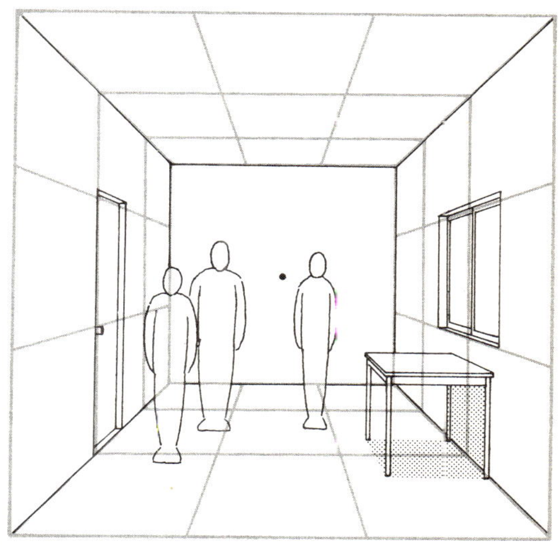

A tall person is in the back.

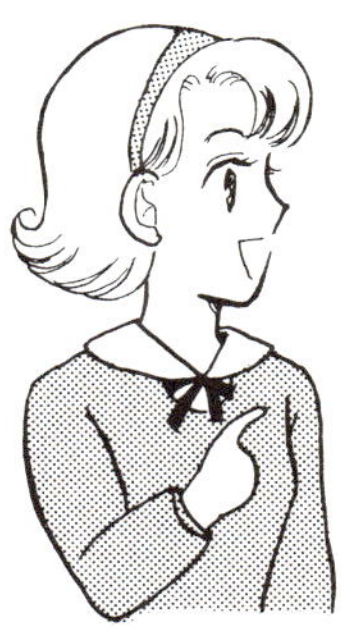

A point (this is called the vanishing point) is drawn in the middle to make it easier to comprehend.

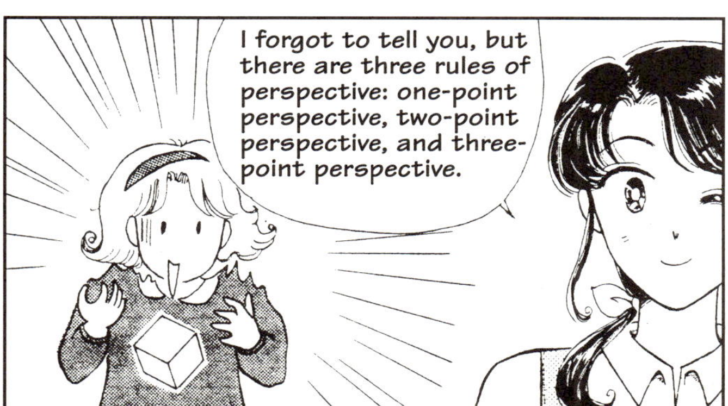

One-Point Perspective

This is convenient for drawing pictures that show depth. You establish one vanishing point and draw depth lines toward the vanishing point (it is called one-point perspective because the lines all converge on one point).

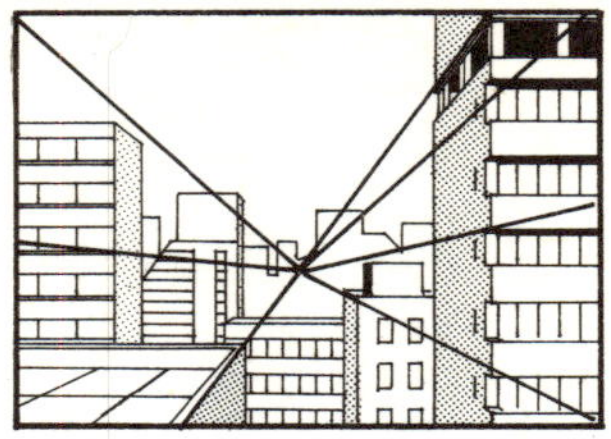

First, choose the vantage point of the camera. Eye level is the height of the eyes of the person viewing the picture or the height of the camera lens.

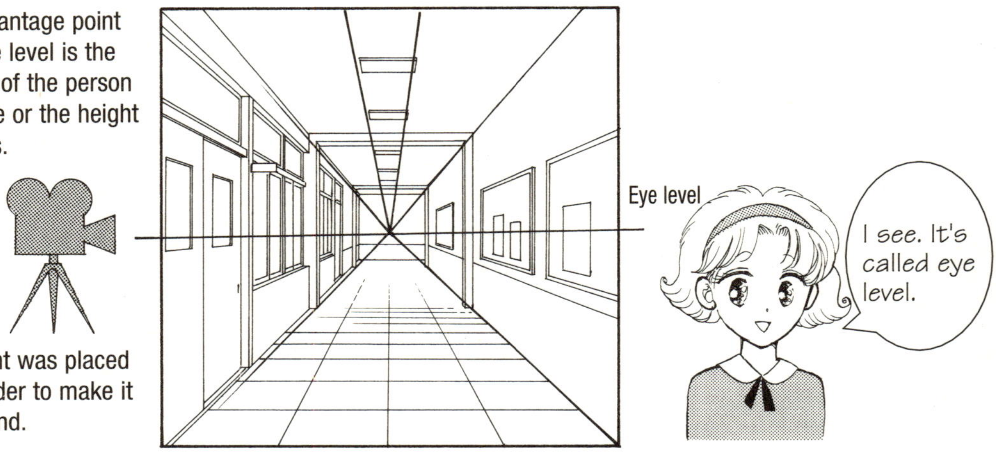

The vanishing point was placed in the center in order to make it easier to understand.

Let's try adding characters.

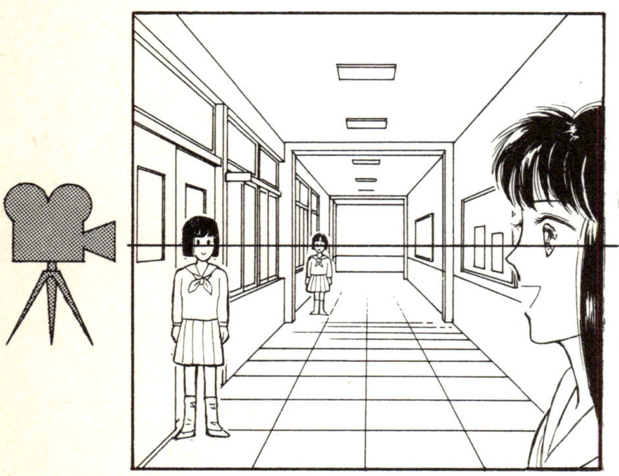

Good example
By way of experiment, draw characters in perspective with the eyes of the characters at eye level (assuming they are the same height). The position of the eyes stays the same no matter how small the character is.

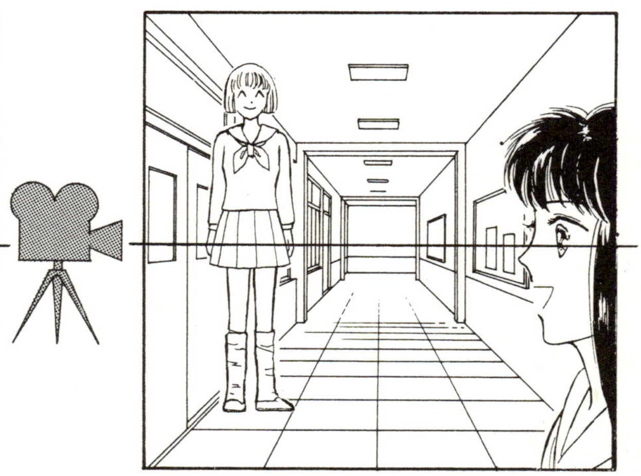

Poor example
If you draw a character in perspective relative to the hallway and eye level and the character do not go together, the character will look very tall.

Example

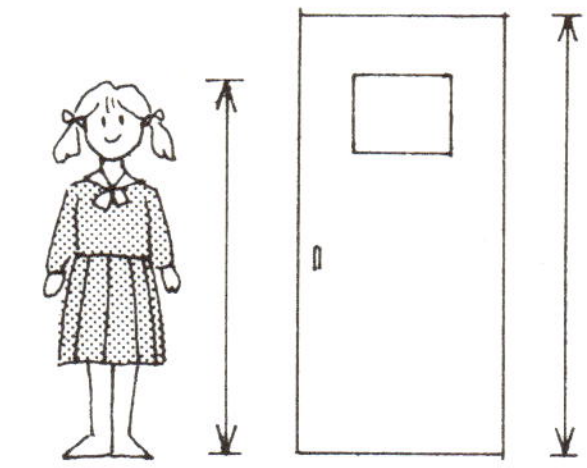

Girl: 154 cm (61.6 in.) Door: 180 cm (72 in.)

You need to be careful when it comes to the size of windows and doors. They should match the size of characters.

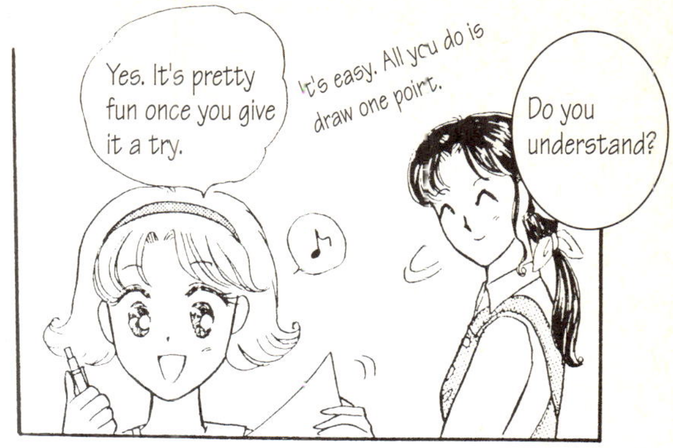

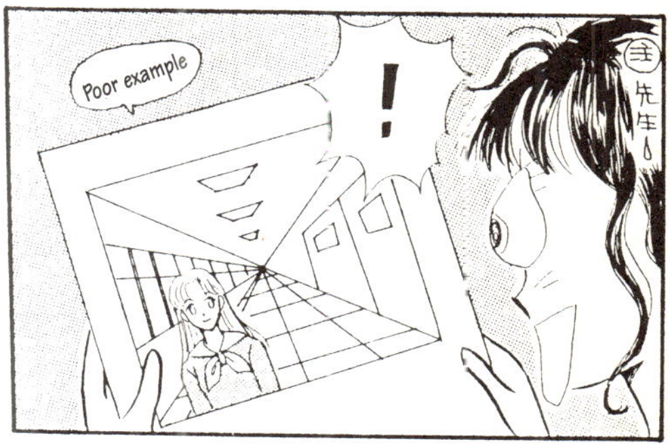

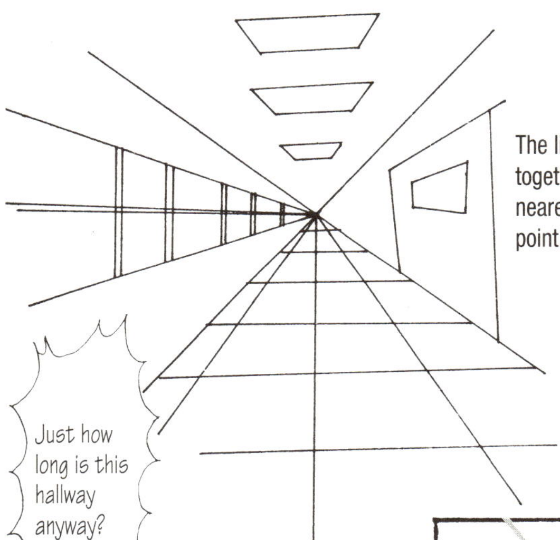

The lines will meld together as they get nearer the vanishing point.

Just how long is this hallway anyway?

Good Example

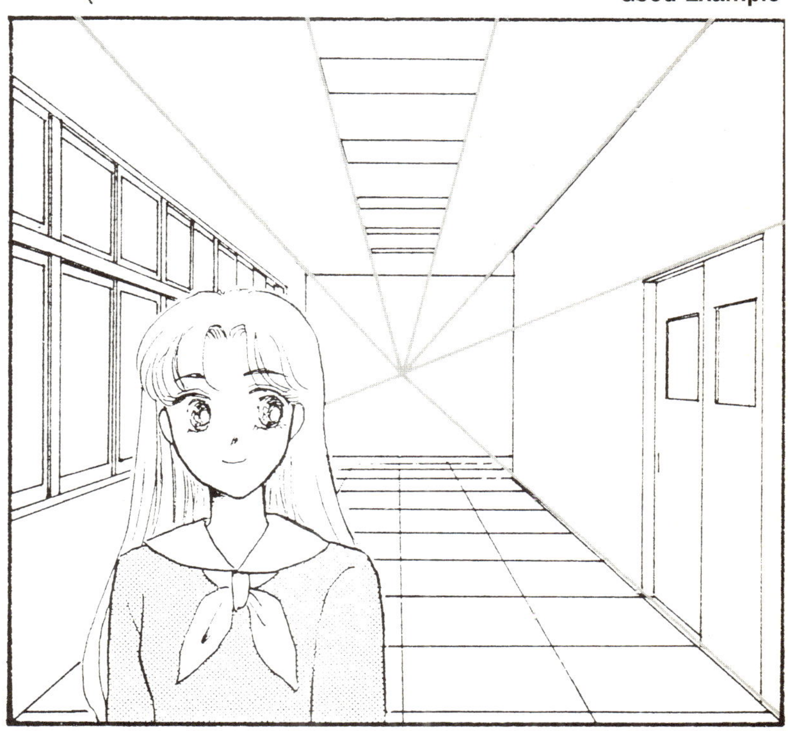

Ceiling Lights

Not good

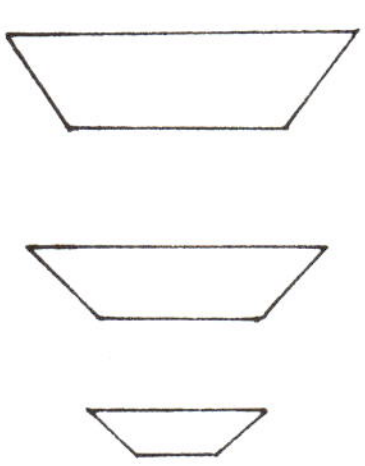

Good

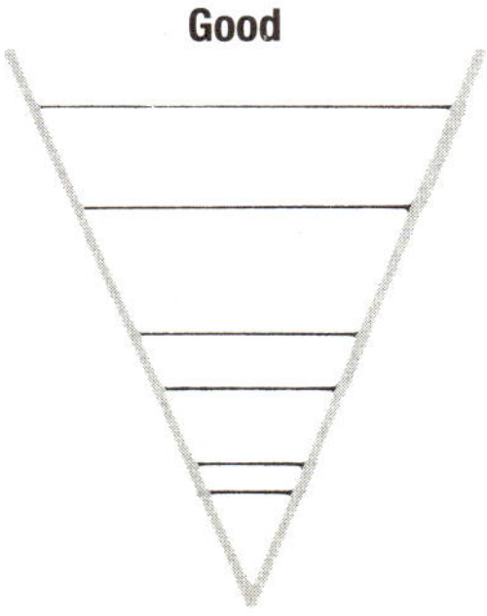

Even if a picture is drawn using one-point perspective, it will feel odd if it is taken too far.

Incorrect example (Figure A)

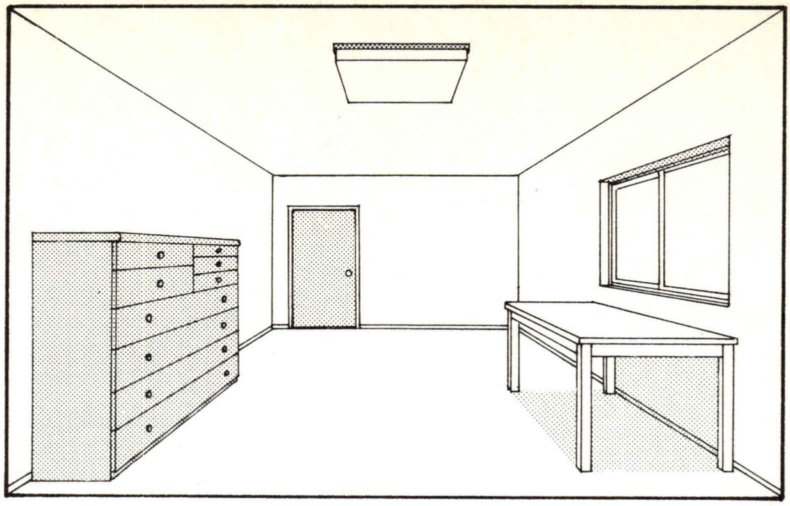

Correct example (Figure B)
It is close to how a human would see it.

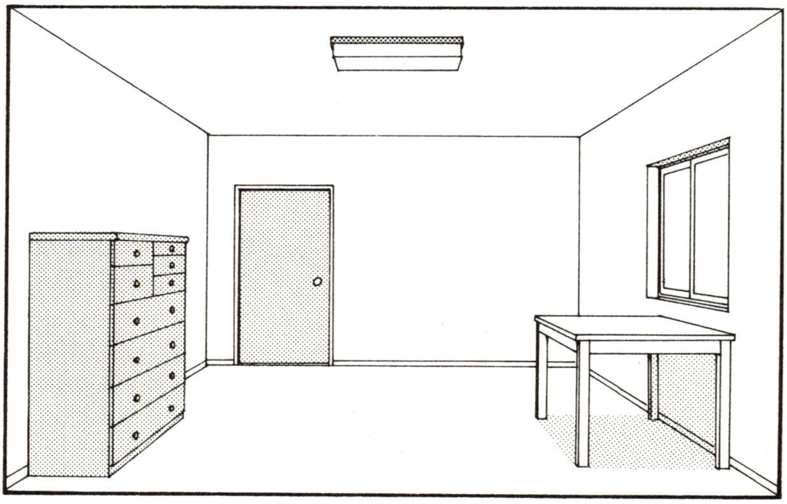

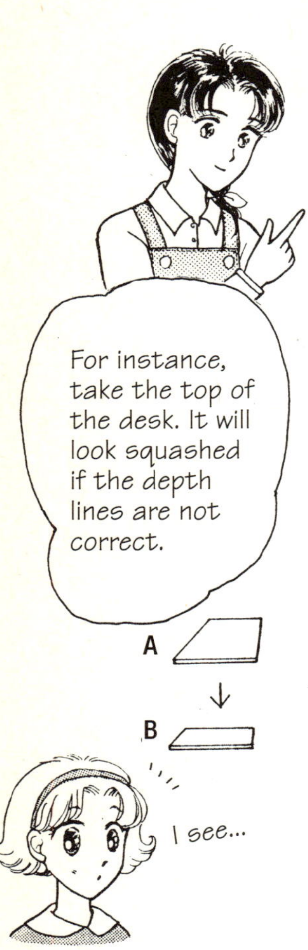

Low and High Angles

Before we move on to two-point perspective, let's familiarize ourselves with low and high angles.

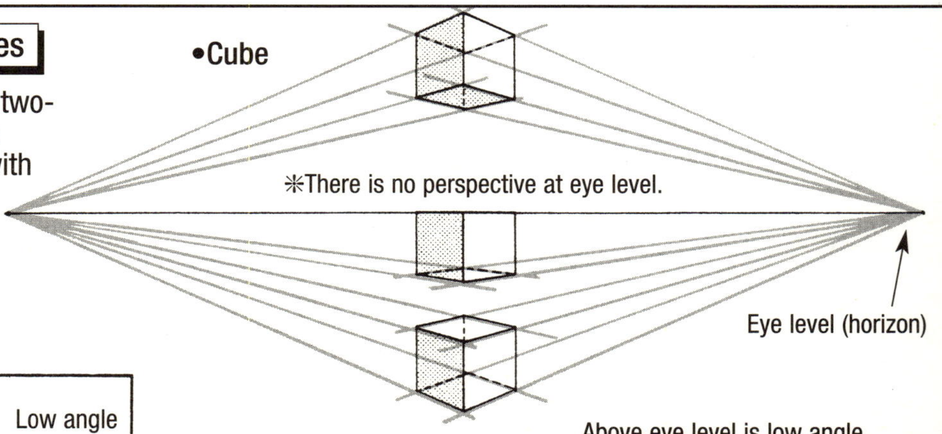

Above eye level is low angle (looking up from below) and below eye level is high angle (looking down from above).

One-point perspective

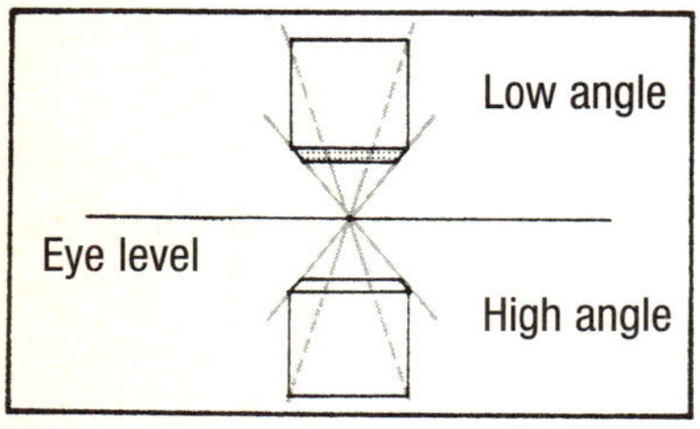

Let's try drawing using one-point perspective.

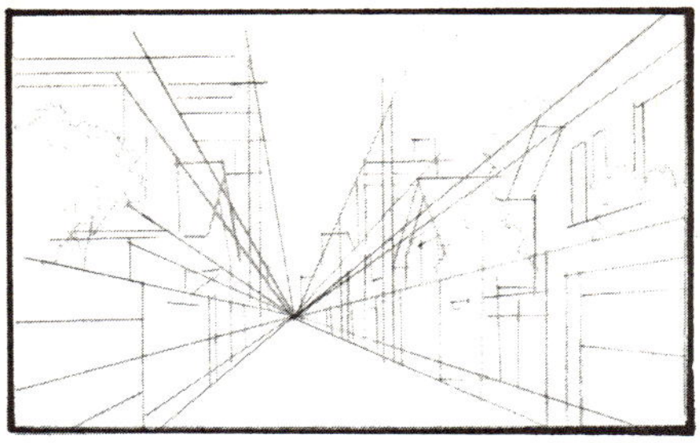

1

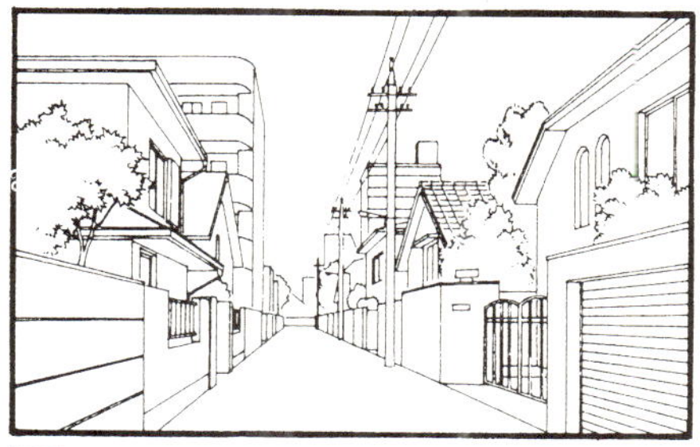

2

1 Perspective lines have been drawn on a rough sketch.
2 The drawing has been penned in.
3 Completed drawing (tone has been applied).
Letra 684, 1211, 61, and 62; C-124; IC 668

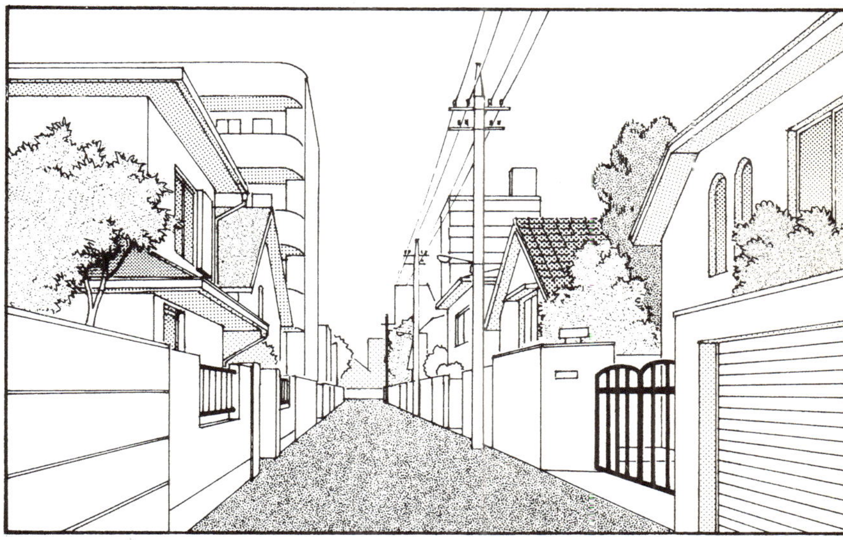

3

In the case of a cylinder, think of the surface as gradually being squashed as it goes around.

•Cylinder

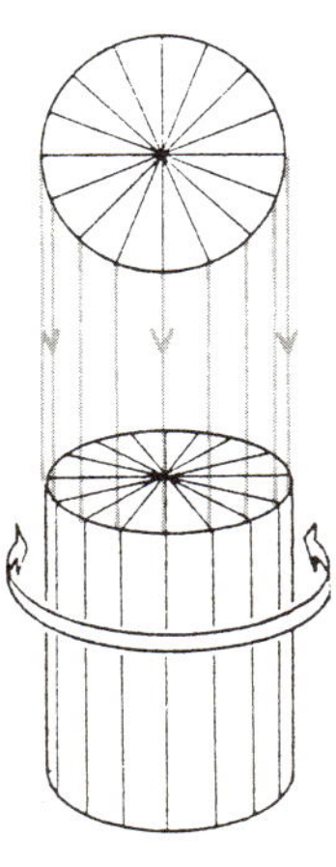

Eye level (horizon)

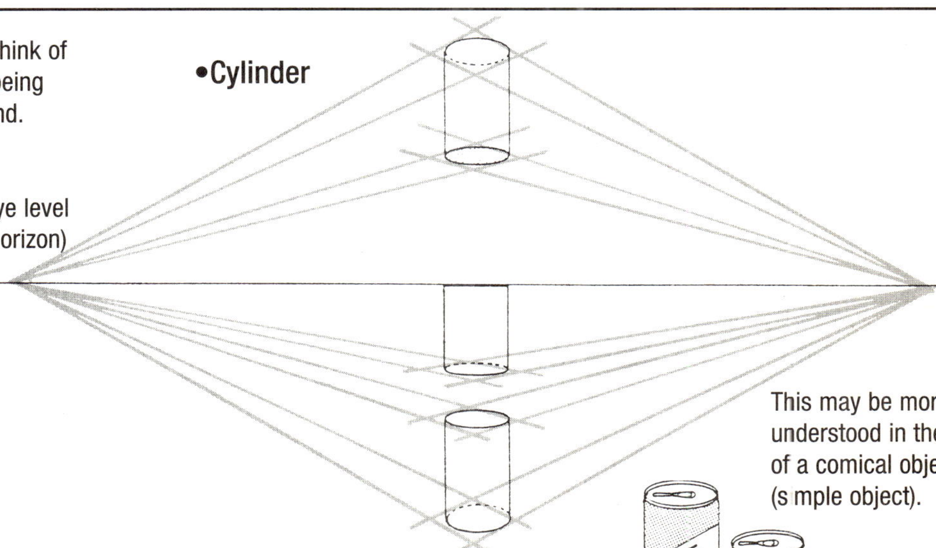

This may be more easily understood in the case of a comical object (s mple object).

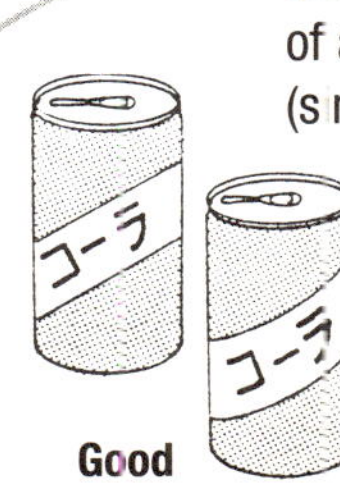

Two-Point Perspective

Two-point perspective is used the most when drawing pictures. It is used when you want to show two sides of a building, and it is often used for the exterior and interior of buildings. It is called two-point perspective because there are two vanishing points.

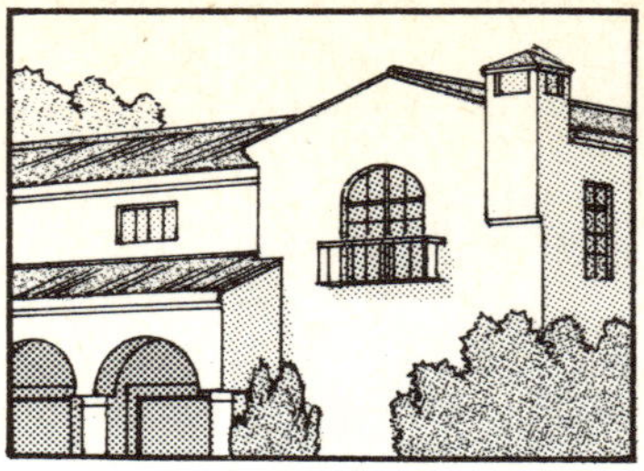

Good example

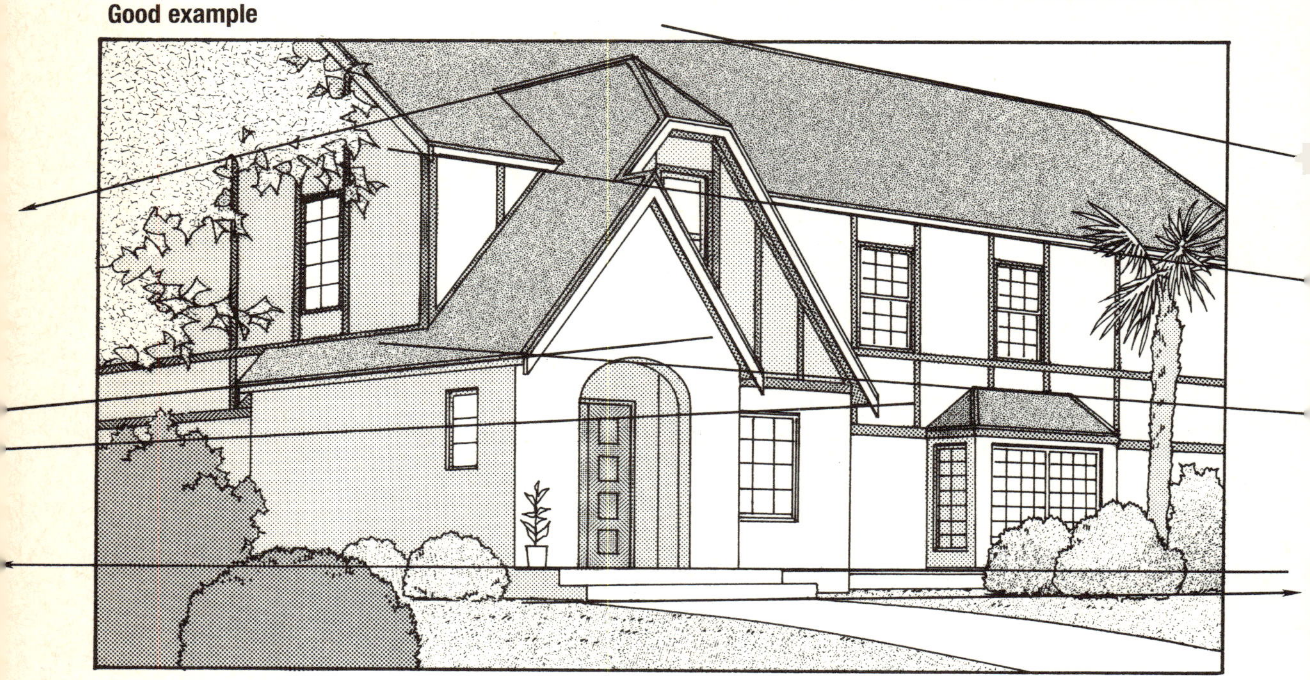

Poor example

In the case of two-point perspective, there is a tendency to want to include two vanishing points in a frame, but if you do so the drawing will look very different from what the human eye would see.

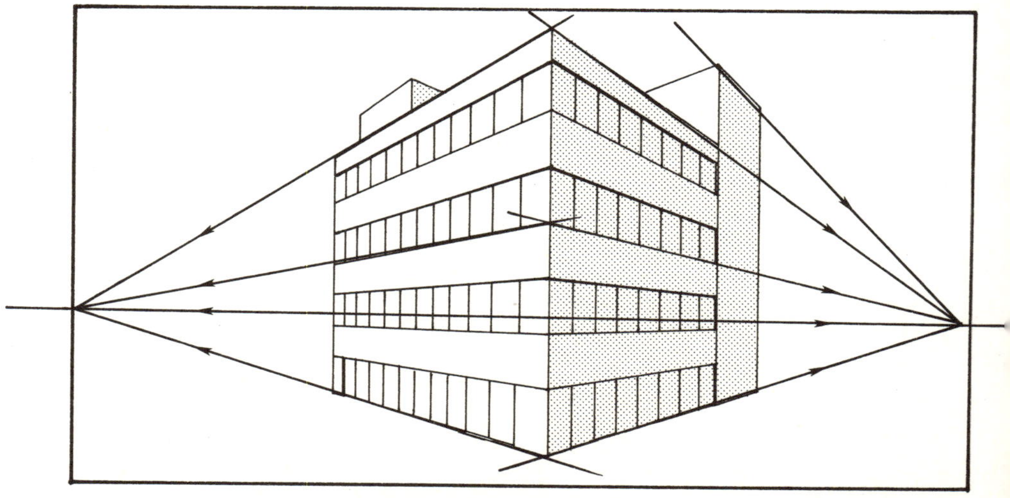

Please note that this is not a mistake. This can intentionally be used to make it look like a wide-angle lens has been used (it is normally best for the perspective to look natural).

What to do when the vanishing points are far away.

When the vanishing points do not fit on the drawing paper, tape some sheets of paper to it and draw the vanishing points there.

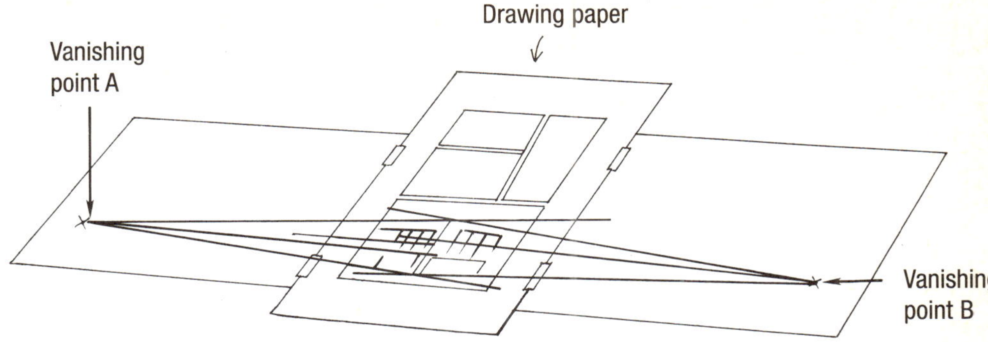

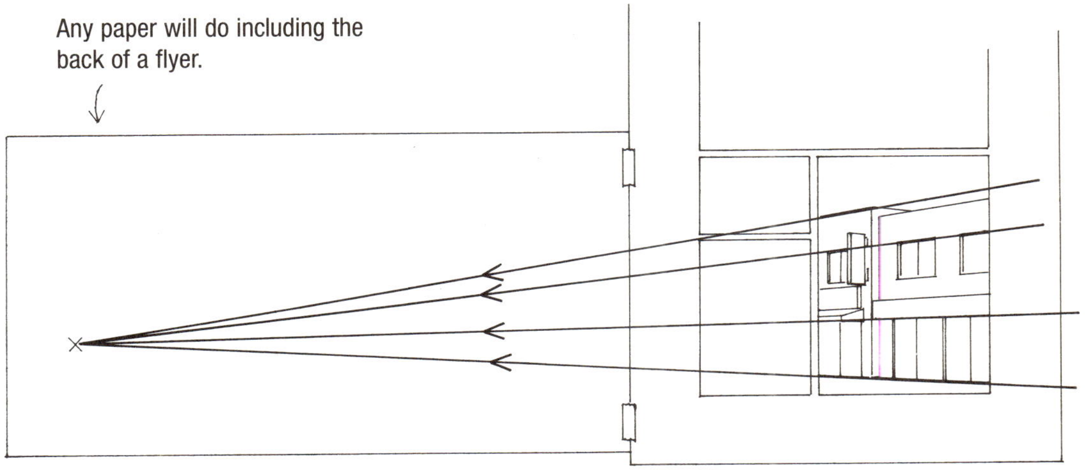

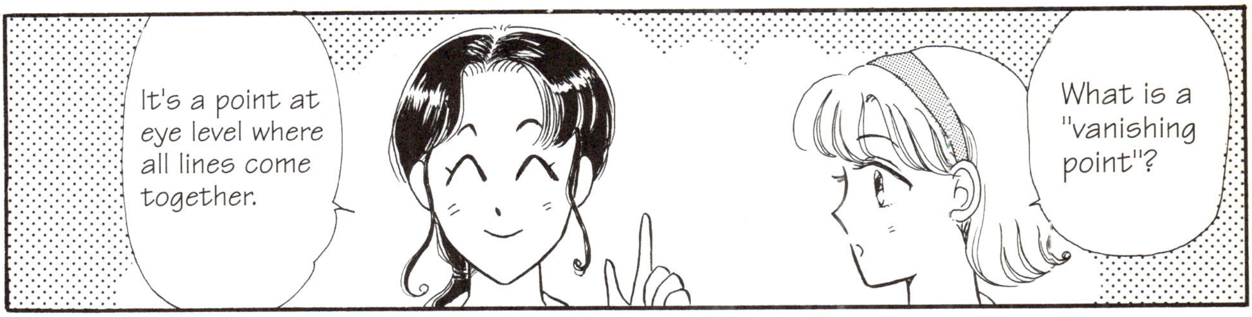

The two points (vanishing points) are always at eye level (eye level is the horizon).

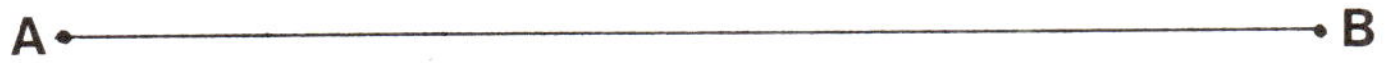

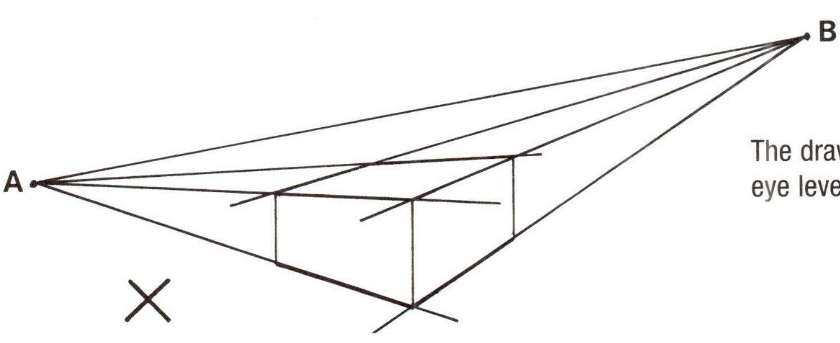

The drawing will be distorted if eye level is tilted.

Drawing a Room Using One-Point and Two-Point Perspective

Example of One-Point Perspective

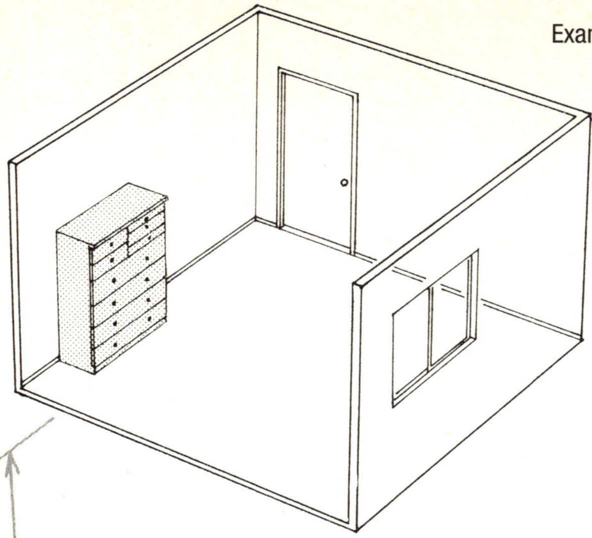

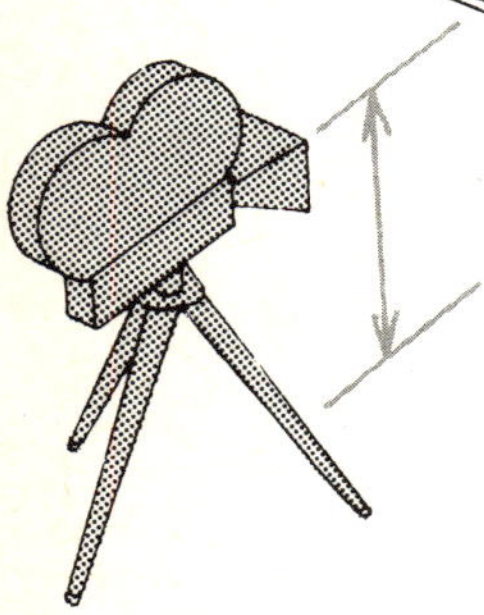

The height of the camera lens is eye level.

Eye level

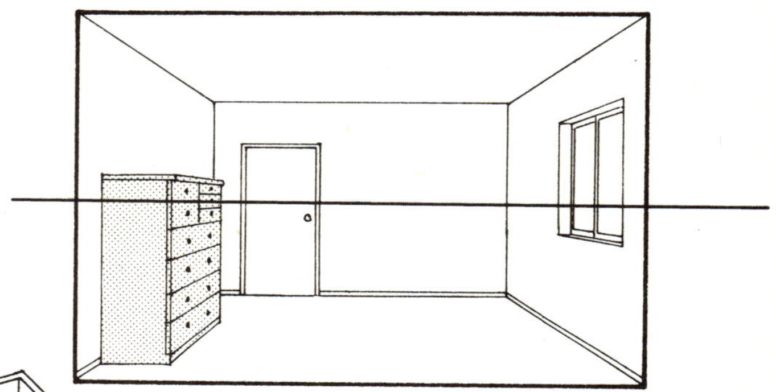

This is the image seen by the camera.

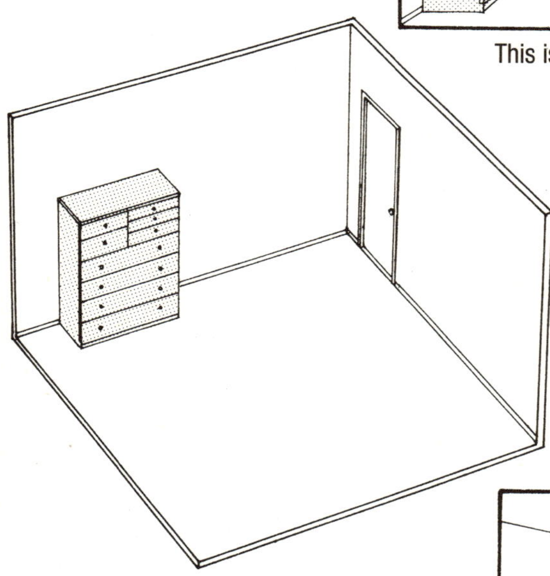

In the case of two-point perspective, the room is diagonal in relation to the camera.

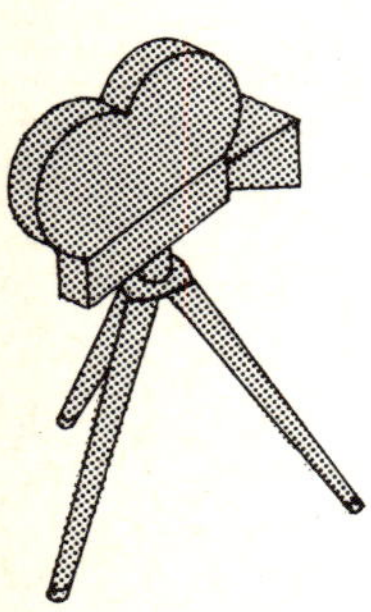

Eye level

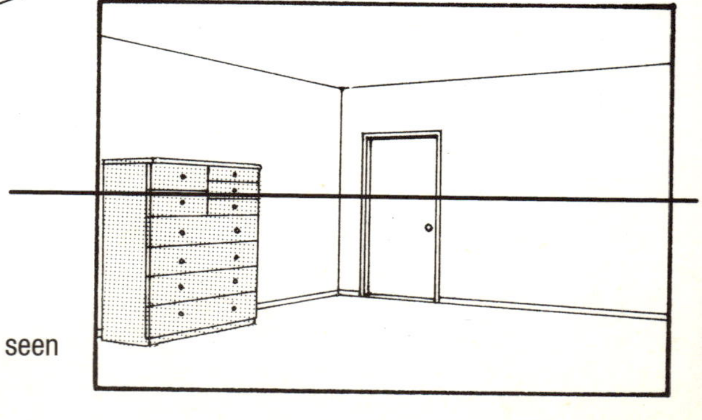

This is the image seen by the camera.

Drawing in Which One-Point and Two-Point Perspective Intersect

It is impossible to draw a table that is sitting askew using one-point perspective. In other words, one-point perspective can be used for objects located on a square that is parallel to the camera. Two-point perspective is used for objects that are located diagonally to the camera, and both vanishing points are located at eye level, just like in one-point perspective.

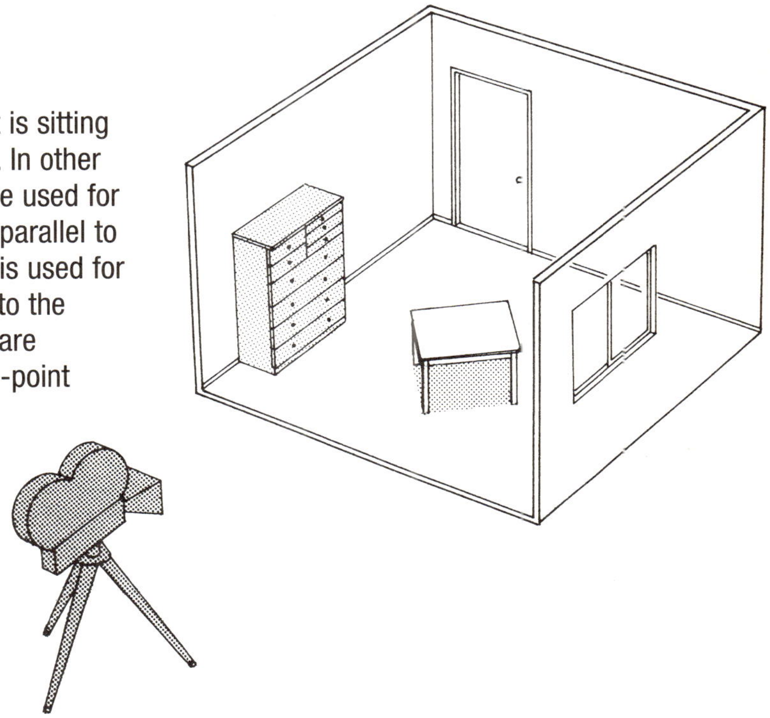

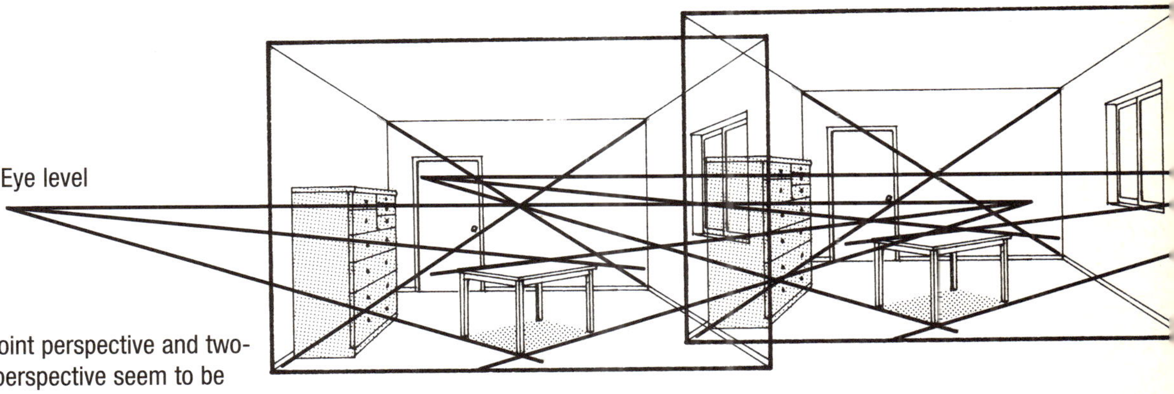

One-point perspective and two-point perspective seem to be discrete ways of drawing, but in fact they are both types of perspective drawing.

Drawing Characters the Same Height in a Room

When two characters are the same height, draw in perspective with the position of the eyes and shoulders aligned. When there is a height difference, draw in perspective after determining the height difference.

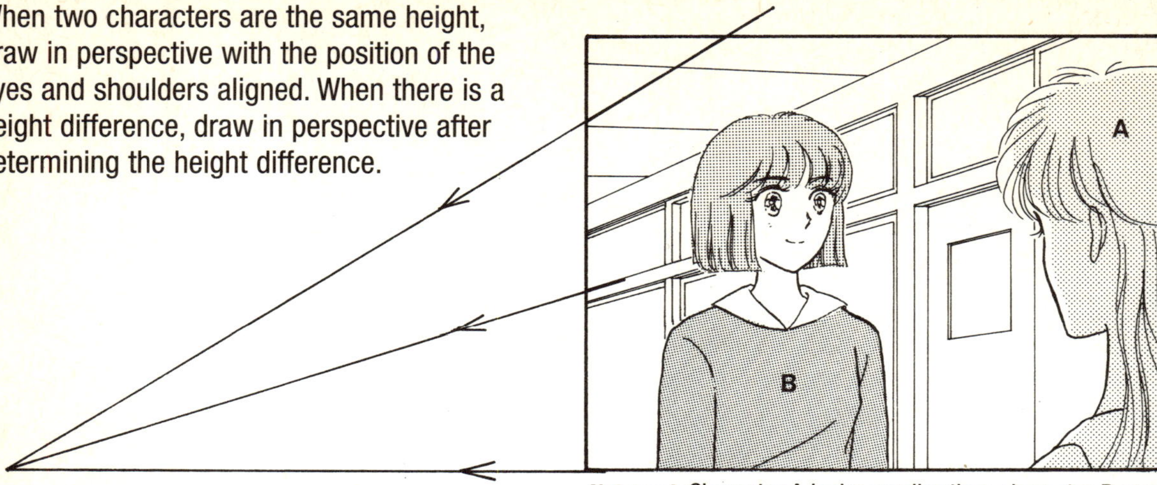

Not good: Character A looks smaller than character B even though they are the same height.

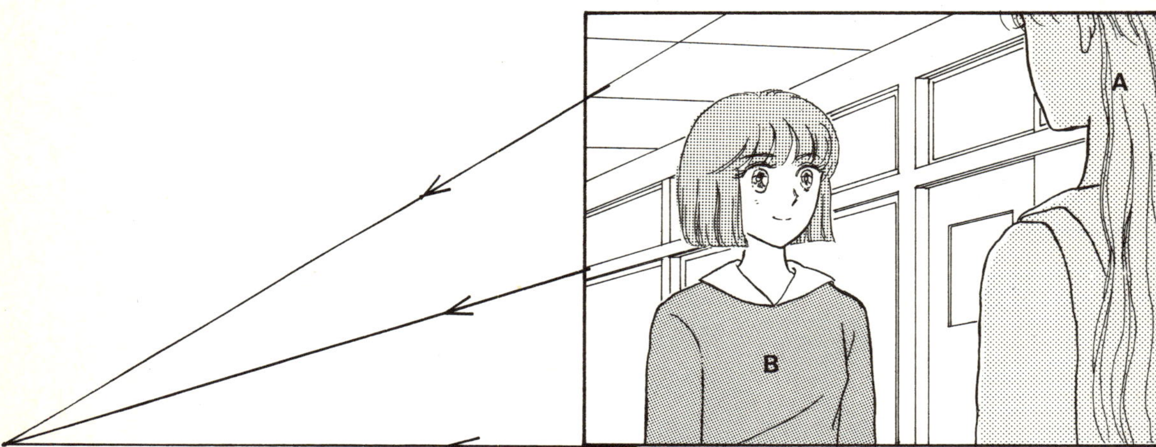

Good: Change the height of character A.

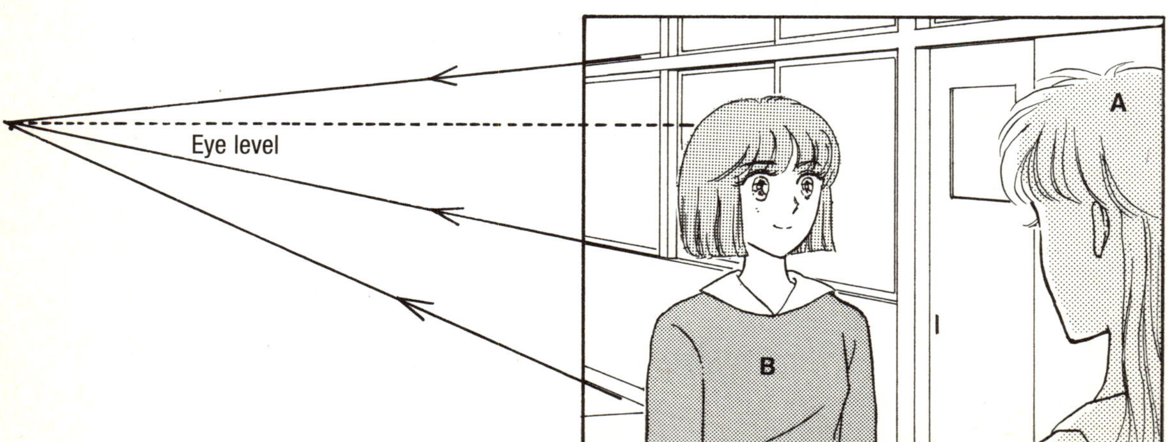

Good: Change the perspective of the background.

Window Frames

Correct Example

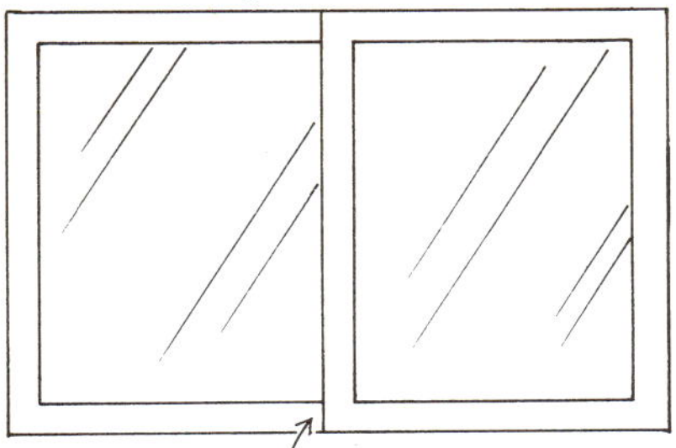

This part overlaps.

When the window is opened...

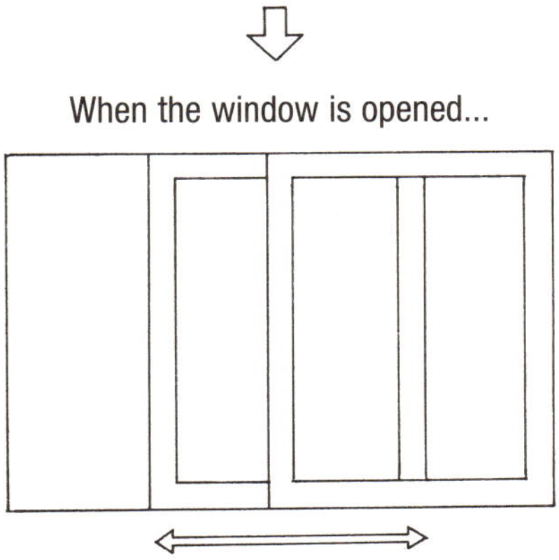

The window is the same width even when overlapping.

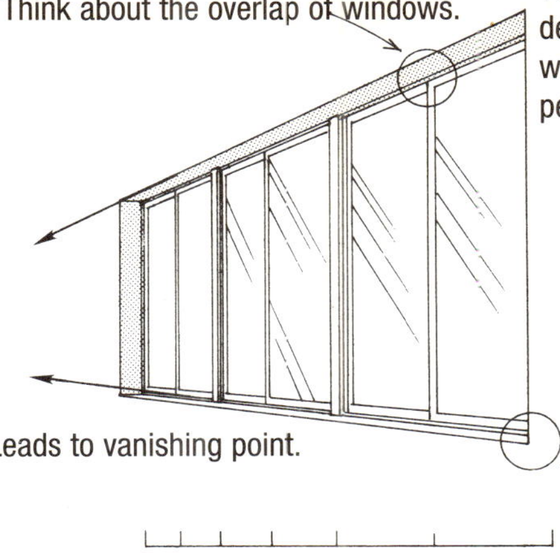

The window gradually narrows as it gets nearer the vanishing point.

Overhead View

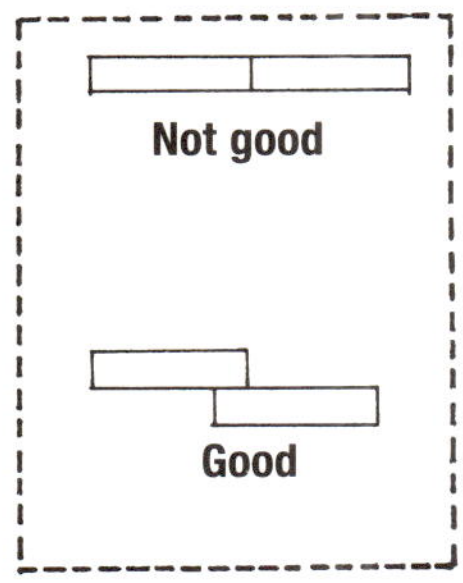

Incorrect Example

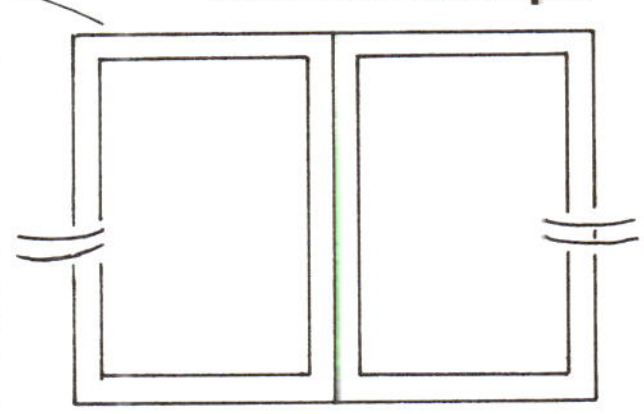

This looks like a casement window.

How to divide equally a window and other squares in perspective.

Divide into two equal parts.

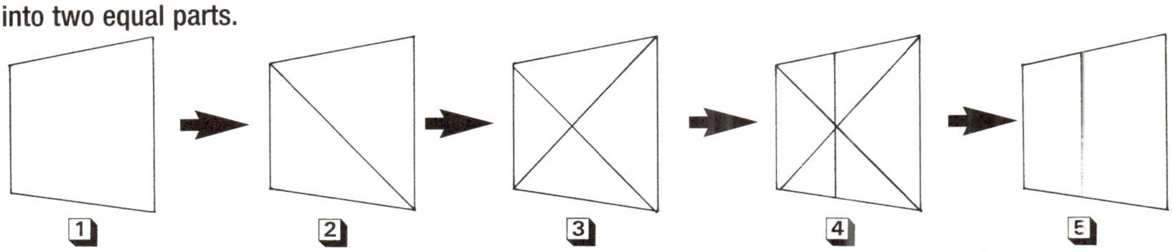

Divide into three equal parts.

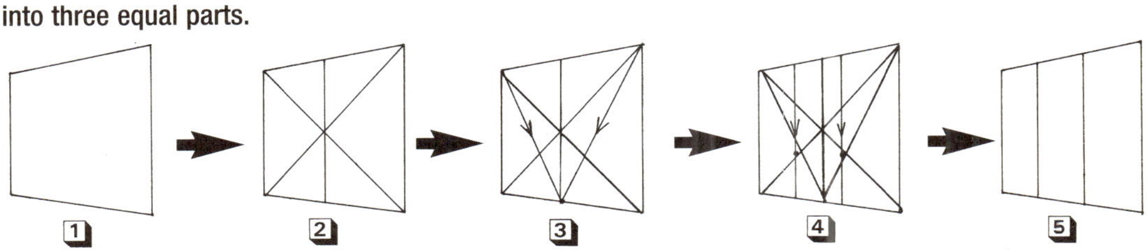

Divide into four equal parts or more.

Follow steps 1-4 above to get to this point.

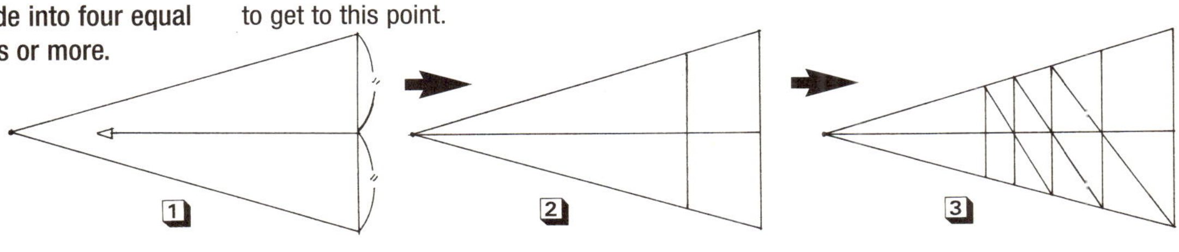

Three-Point Perspective

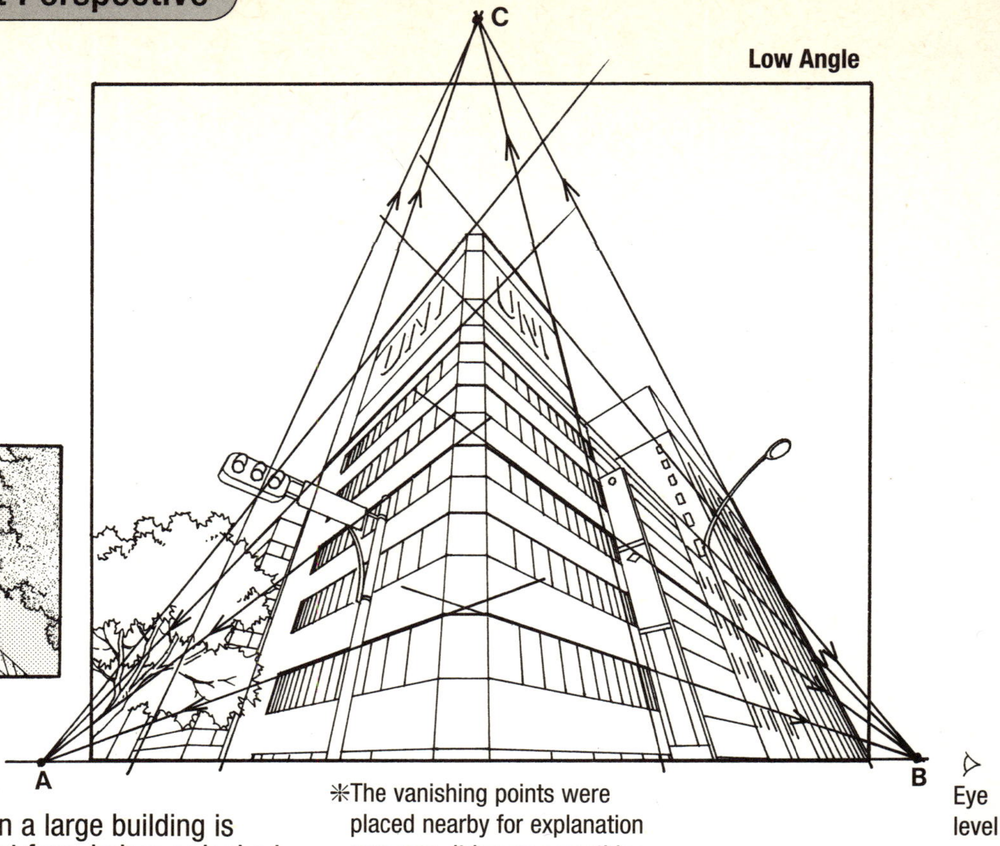

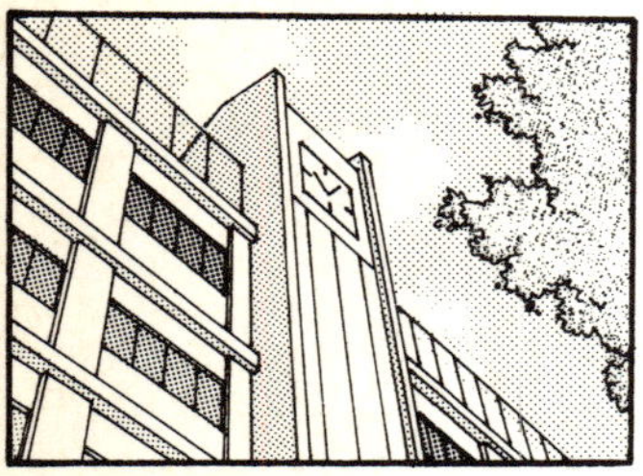

※The vanishing points were placed nearby for explanation purposes. It leaves something to be desired as a picture.

This is used when a large building is being looked up at from below or looked down on from above. It is called three-point perspective because there are three vanishing points. The picture will look unrealistic if the vanishing points are not far away.

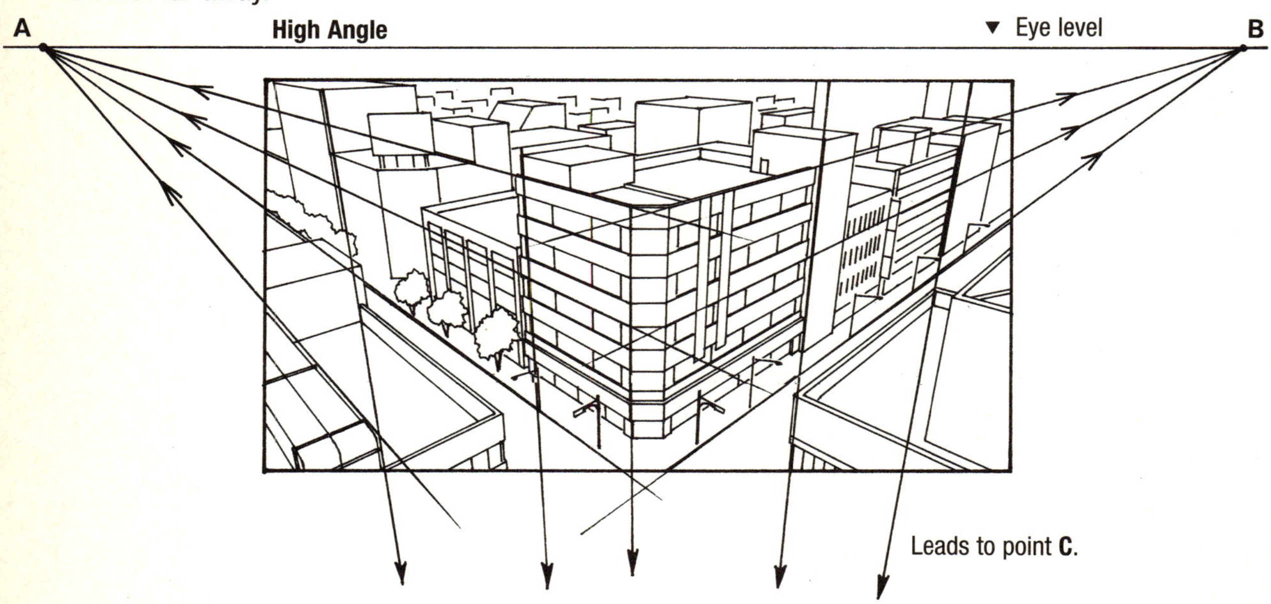

To make drawing easier, think of buildings as boxes lined up on squares. All the vertical lines of the buildings converge on point C (in this case off the page).

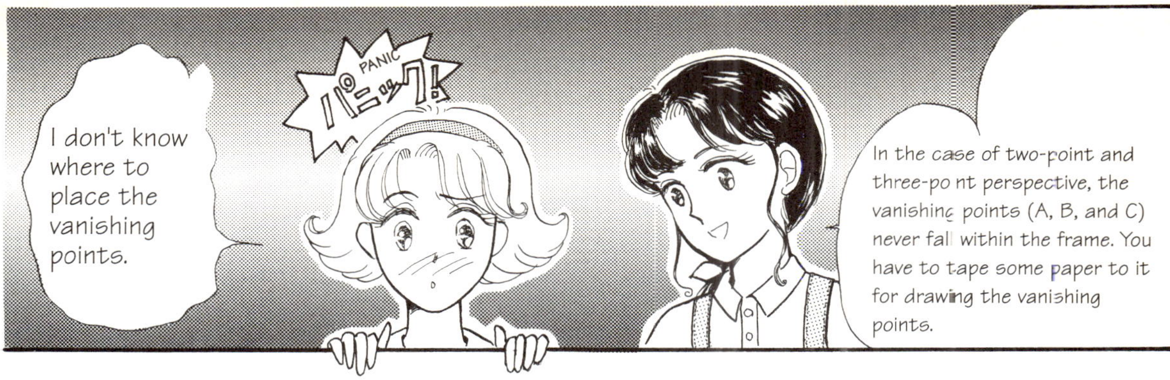

Two-Point Perspective

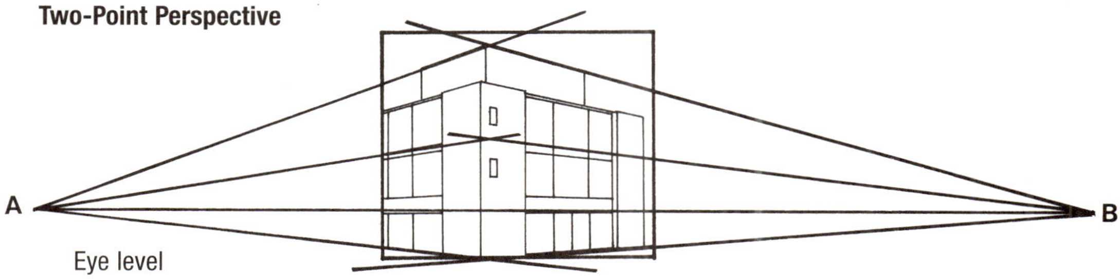

Three-Point Perspective
For a high angle, place point C far below the picture.

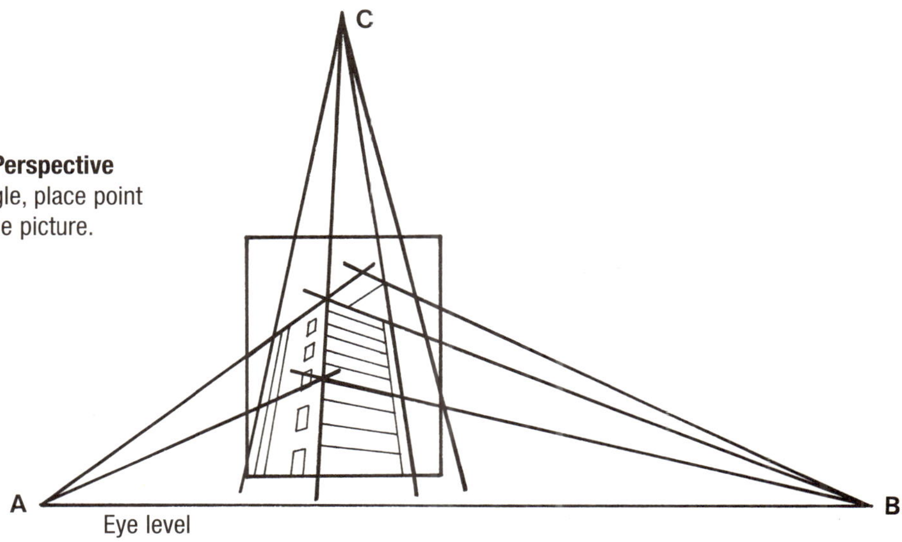

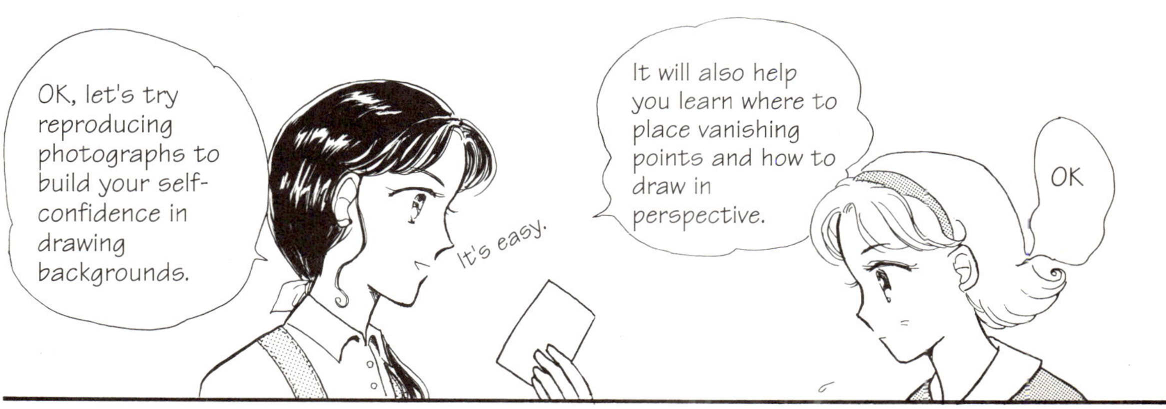

Let's Try Reproducing Photographs

Reproducing photographs in photo collections and magazines exactly will cause copyright problems, so think of photographs as a starting point for your drawings. Photographs you have taken yourself are the best.

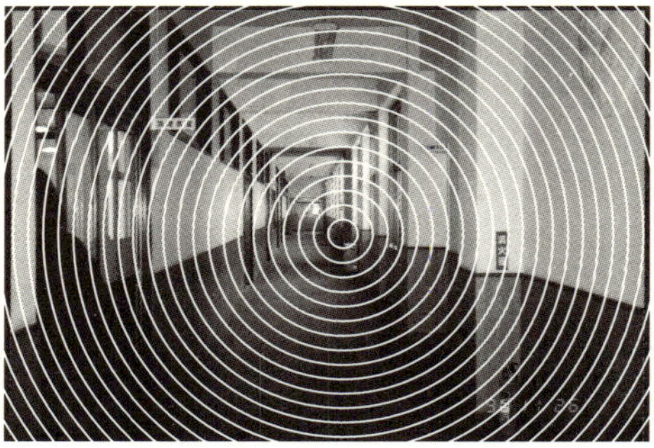

Completed Drawing

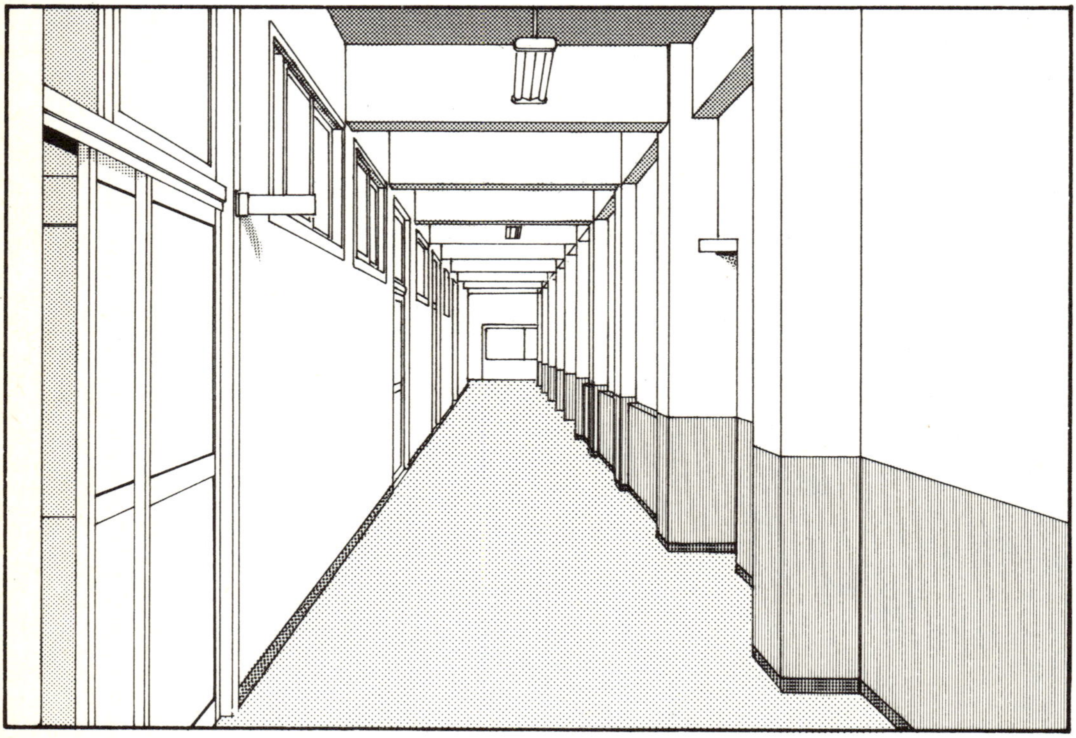

Tones used: Letra 61, 62, 1210, and 1021
IC 473

Process

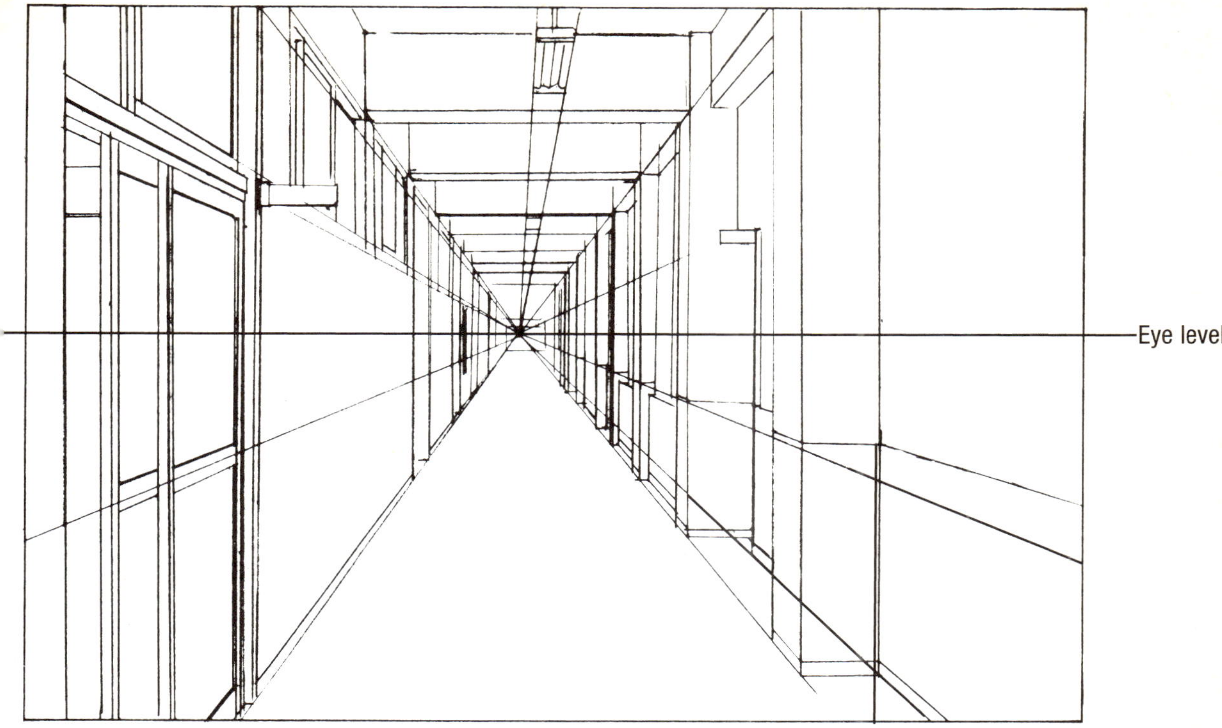

1 Rough sketch drawn using one-point perspective.

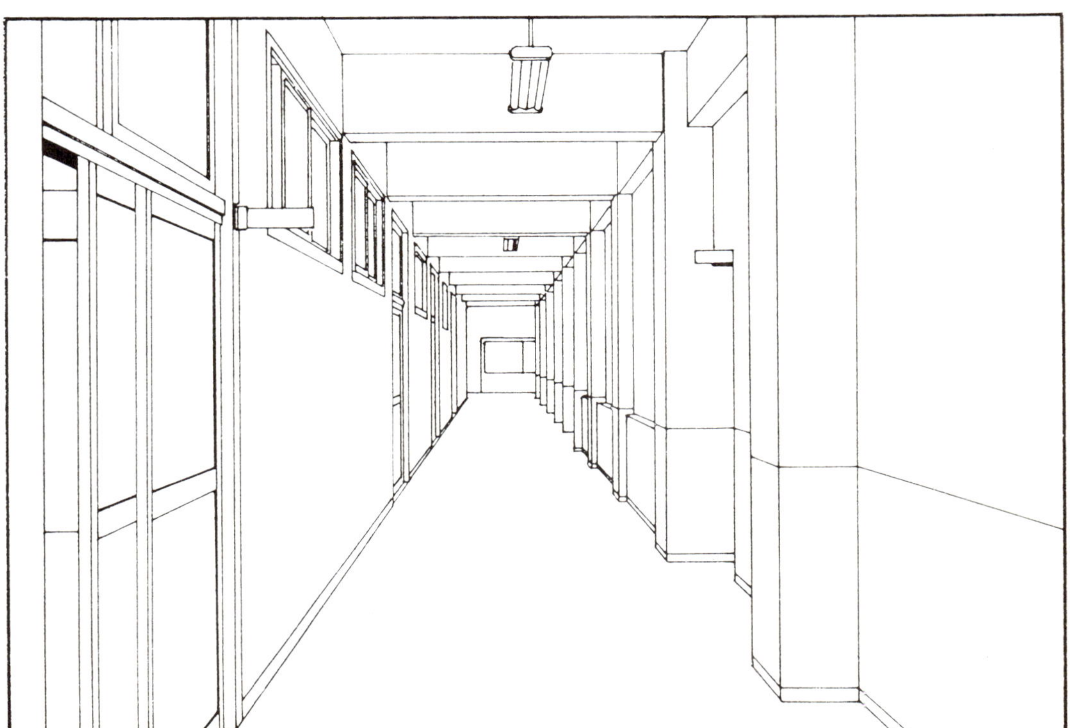

2 Pen in the lines, fill in the solids, and make corrections with correction fluid. Then apply tone and you are finished.

How to Abbreviate Classrooms

Drawing all the chairs and desks in a classroom will make the picture look cluttered and annoying. When there are no characters in the picture, decide what part of the classroom you are going to emphasize. In the case of peripheral characters, one approach is to draw them as part of the background using thin lines.

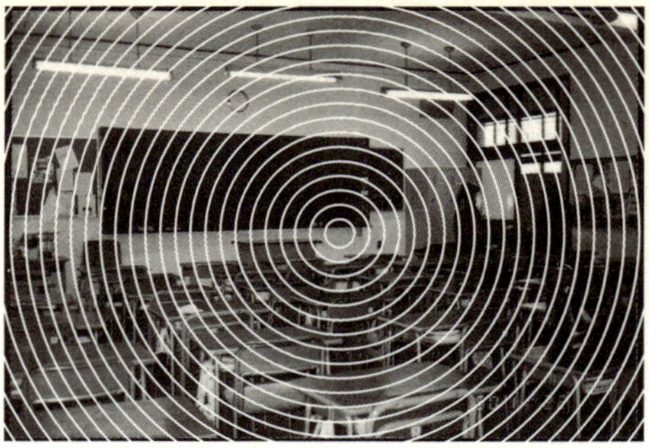

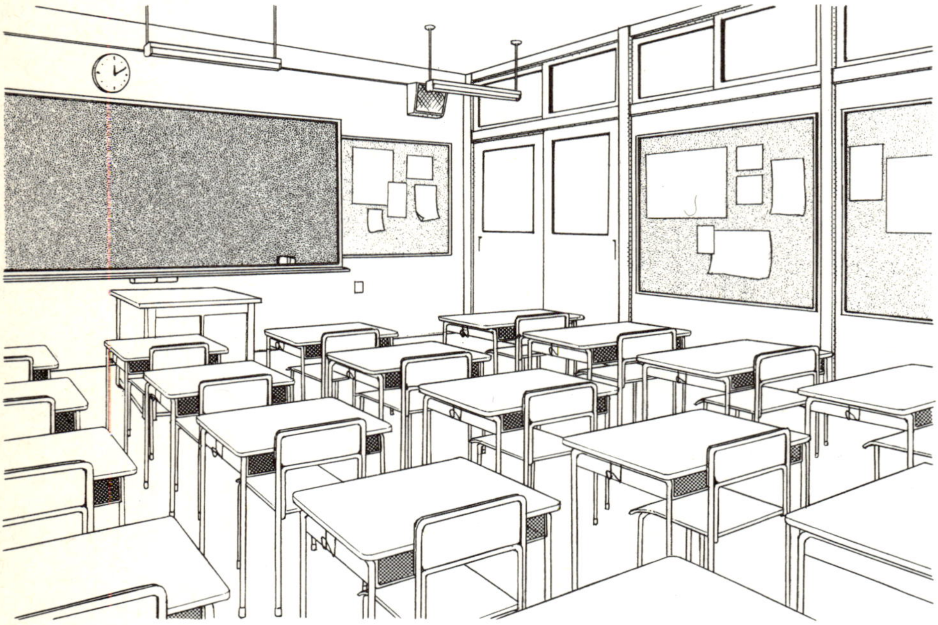

Drawn Exactly Like Photograph
Put enough distance between desks for people to sit and walk. Adding small objects such as messages on the bulletin board, speaker, and a blackboard eraser will make it look more like a classroom.

Upper Left (Direction of Vanishing Point) Blurred
When blurring one part of a frame, it is common to blur a part in the distance (direction of vanishing point) or blur the foreground (in the case of background alone with no characters). When there are characters in the frame, it cannot be summed up so easily, because the effect will differ depending on the part you want to show at any given time.

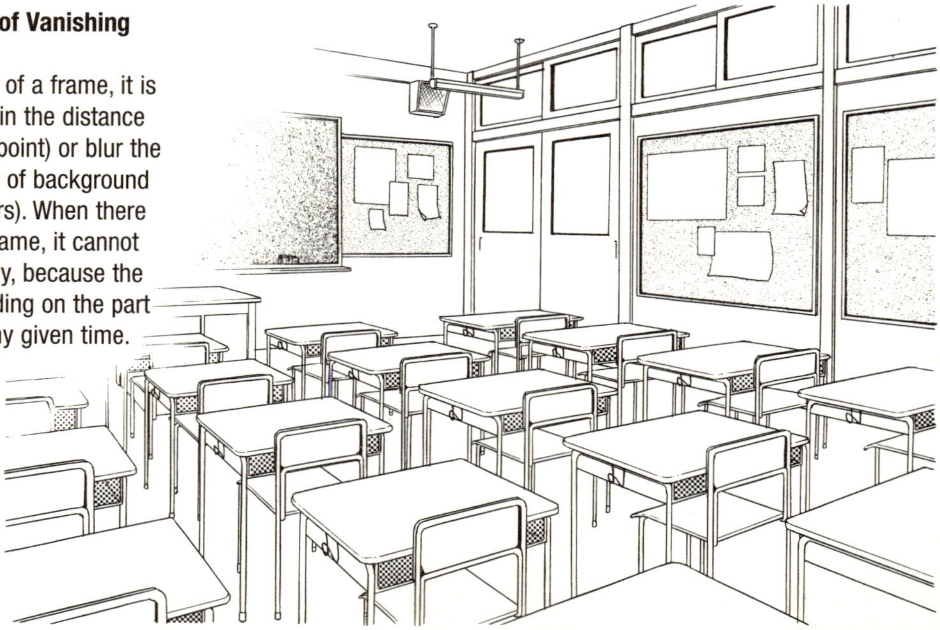

False Perspective (Parallel Perspective)

False perspective is often used for backgrounds in girls' comics. I will explain exactly what this means.

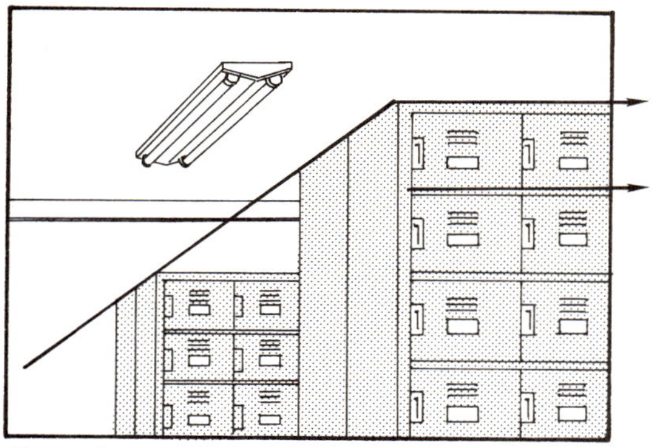

These lines do not converge on a vanishing point. They are parallel with eye level.

Figure 1

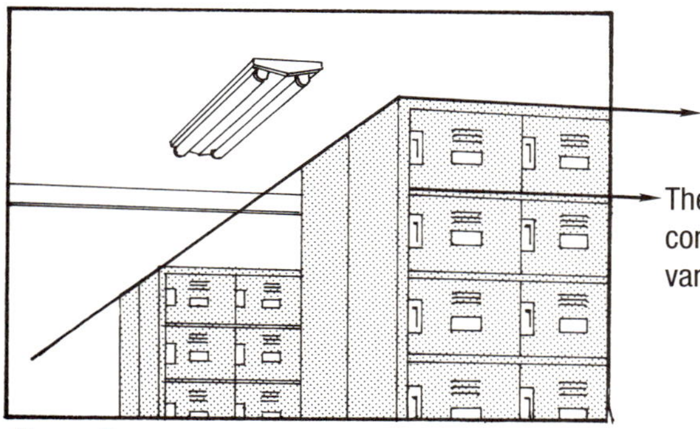

These lines converge on a vanishing point.

Figure 2

If you think of this section as being depicted in one-point perspective, it can be said to be the same as Figure 1.

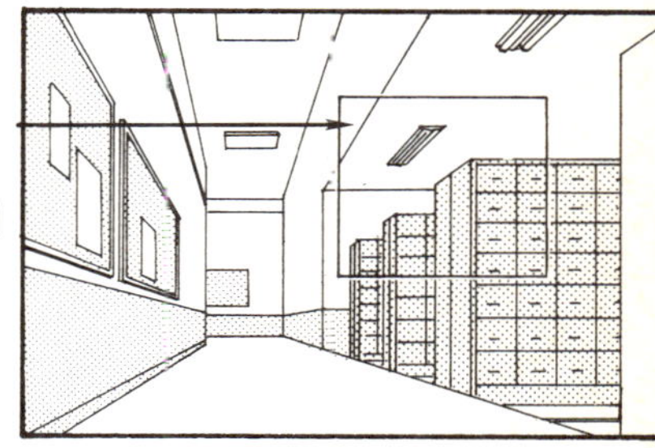

Figure 3

The drawing in Figure 1 may be odd from a theoretical standpoint, but visually it is more stable than that in Figure 2.
Why does the drawing in Figure 1 look more stable even though it goes against the theory of two-point perspective?
The truth is that, to the human eye, the drawing in Figure 3 looks like that in Figure 4.

When drawn in an extreme way, this is what it looks like (This occurs because the human eyes are lenses. They are similar to a fish-eye lens or wide-angle lens on a camera.). It looks like the drawing in Figure 3 to the human eye because the brain corrects it.

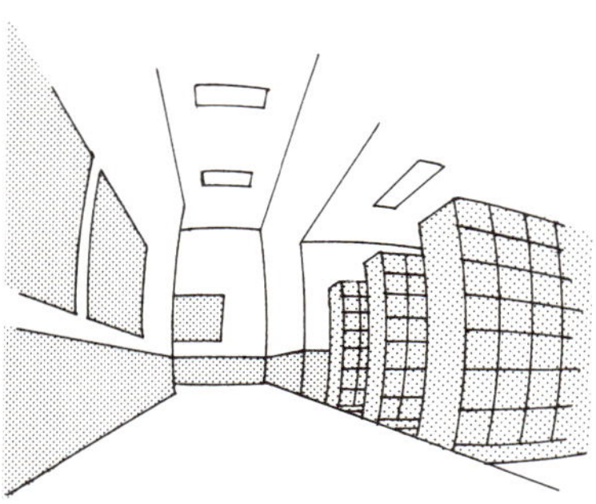

Figure 4

Let's say you stare vacantly at point A on the ceiling without concentrating (or focusing) on it.
The line with point B on it should look curved like in Figure 5. If you shift your gaze and focus on point B, however, it will look like a completely normal straight line.

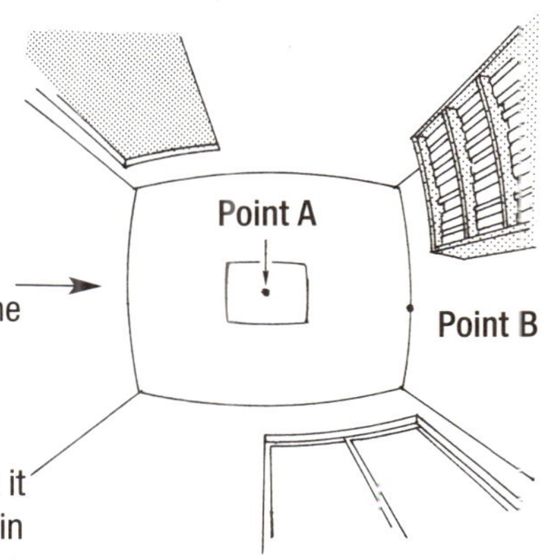

Figure 5

Try lying face-up on the ground and looking up at the ceiling.

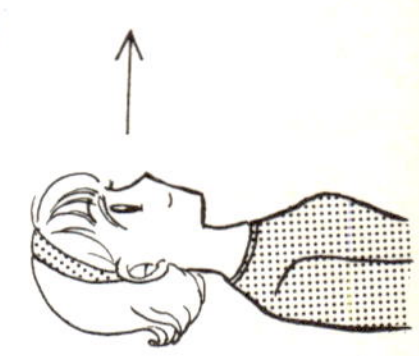

Consequently, in reality the drawing in Figure 1 looks like that in Figure 6. The theory of perspective was originally created to make a drawing look more like what the eye would see, so there is nothing to worry about as long as it looks natural.

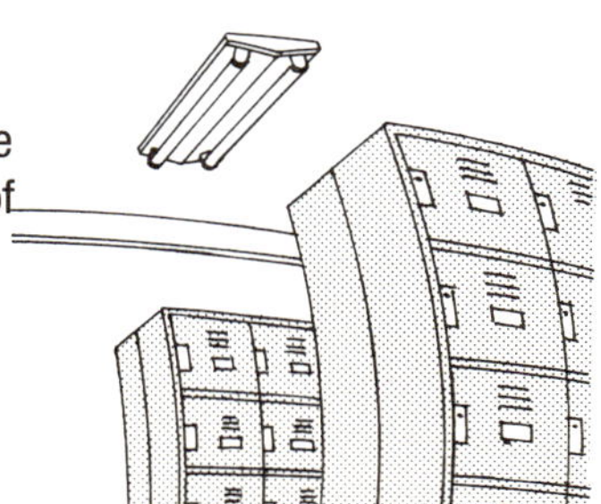

Figure 6

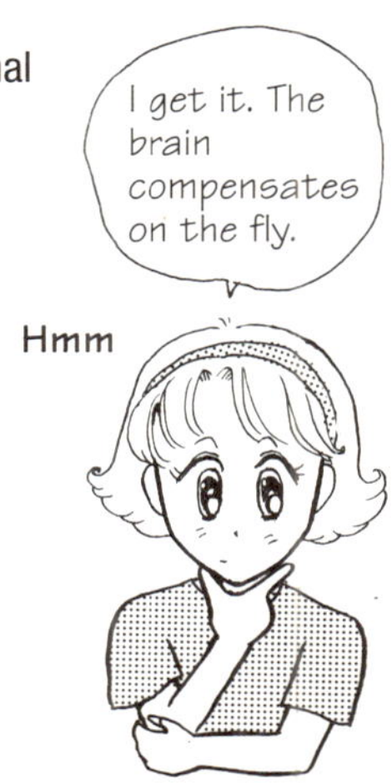

Perspective of Circles

There seems to be a surprisingly large number of people who cannot draw a circle in perspective. Try drawing with an understanding of the concept.

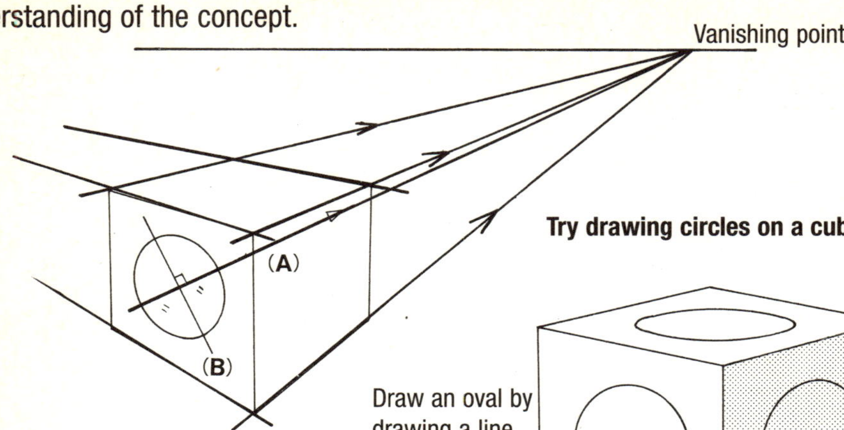

Try drawing circles on a cube.

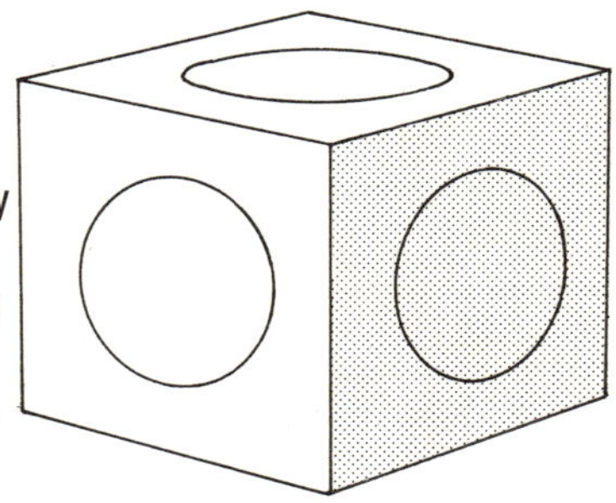

Draw an oval by drawing a line (B) that crosses at a right angle the perspective line (A) that leads to the vanishing point.

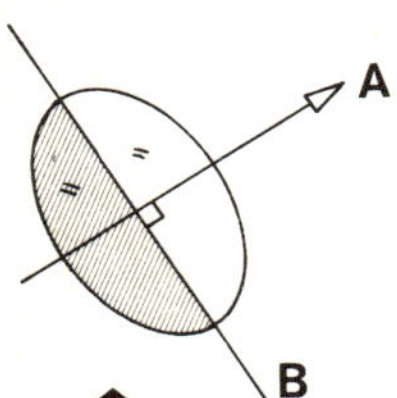

Make the oval symmetrical with the line (B) in the middle.

The best way to flatten an oval in perspective is to draw a square and work from there.

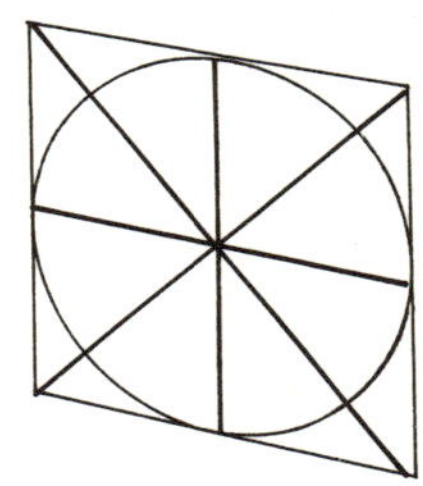

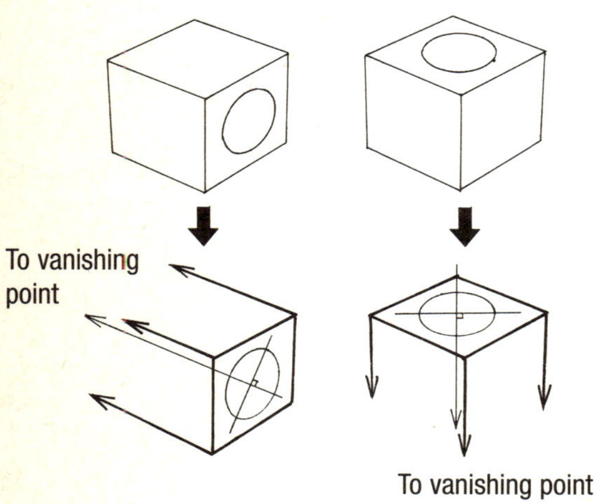

Poor Example

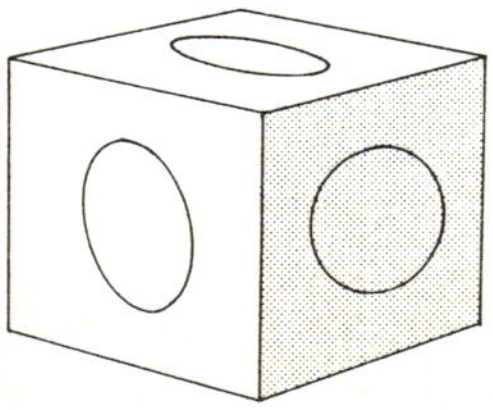

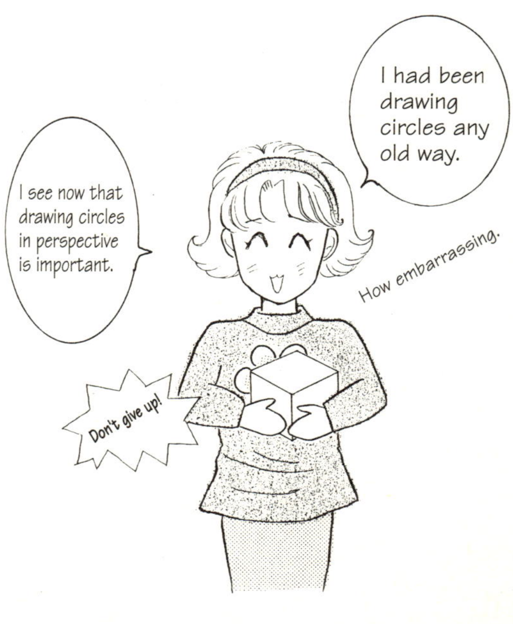

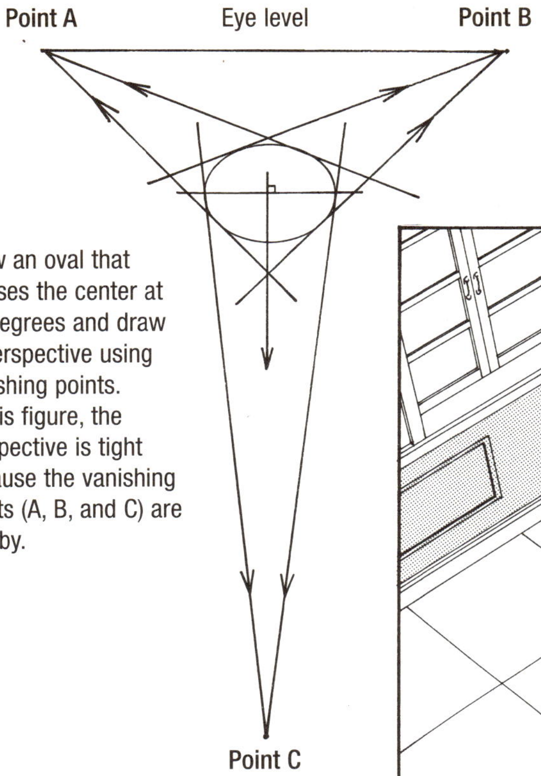

Draw an oval that crosses the center at 90 degrees and draw in perspective using vanishing points.
In this figure, the perspective is tight because the vanishing points (A, B, and C) are nearby.

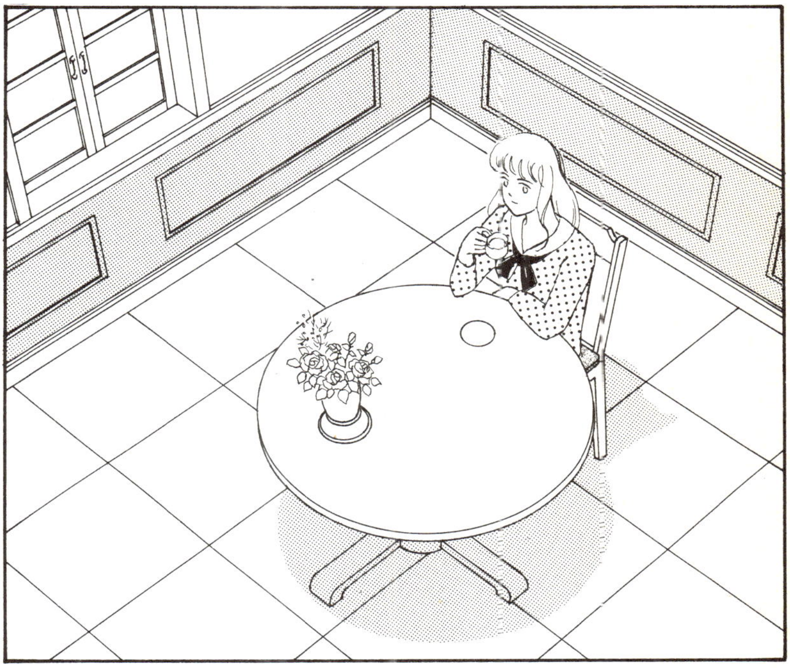

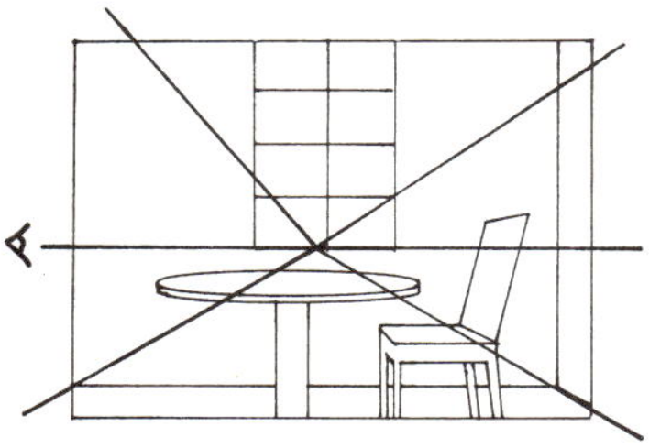

Flattening a Round Table

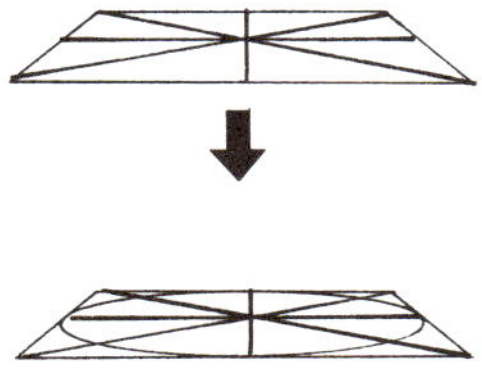

It is easiest to first draw a square in perspective and then draw the circle.

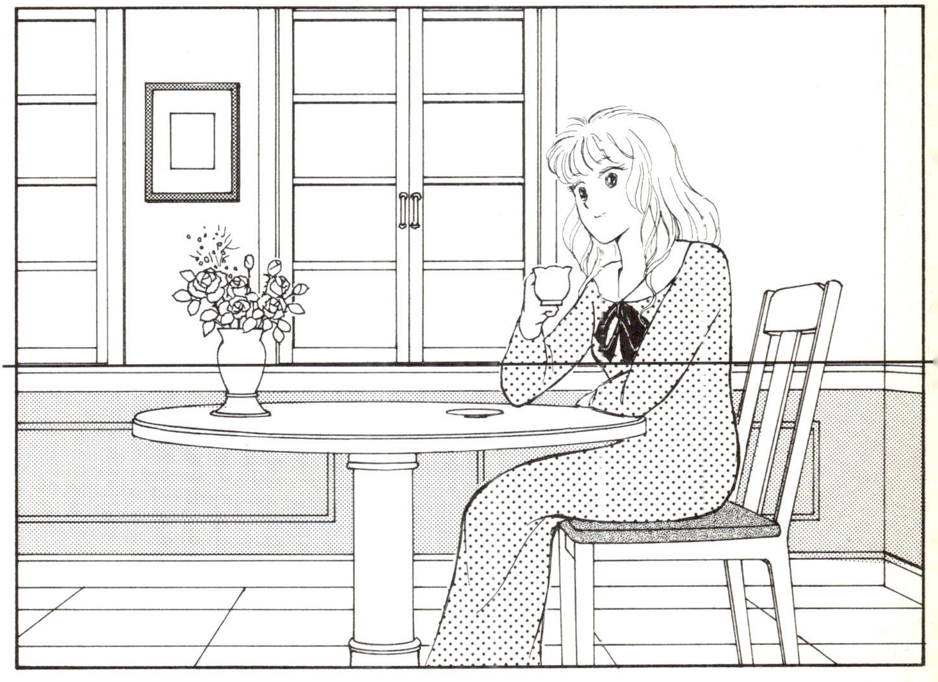

For side views, make the vertical lines completely perpendicular.

Background Techniques 1

Round Arch-Shaped Windows

There appear to be many people who can draw square windows but few who can draw round ones. Do not just copy what you see. Draw with a grasp of the concept.

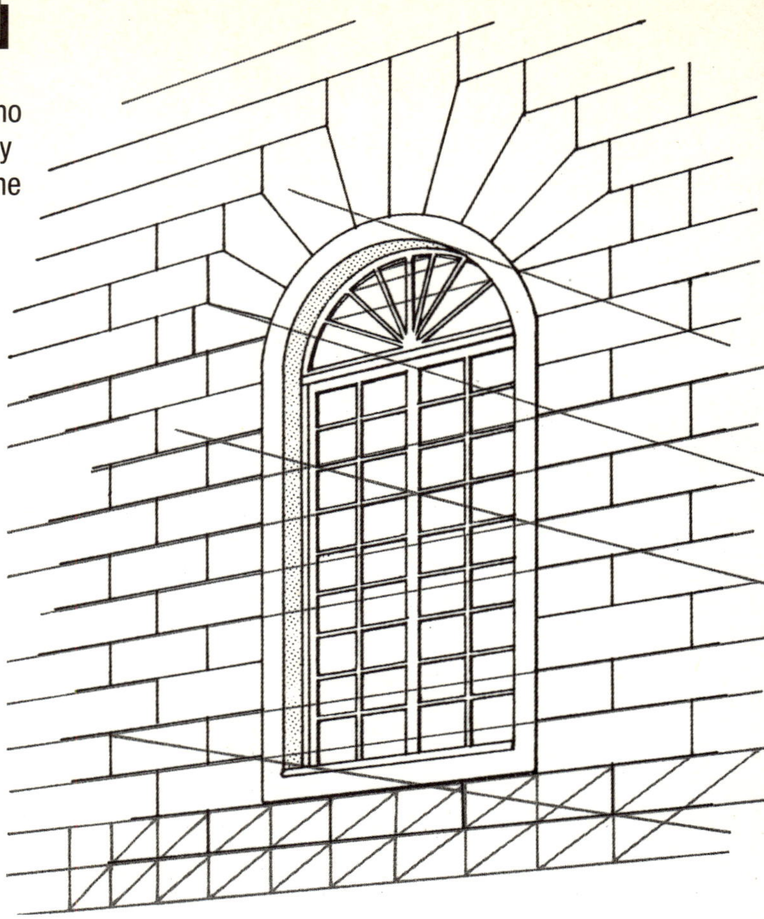

Incorrect Example

Many people cannot draw this curved portion.

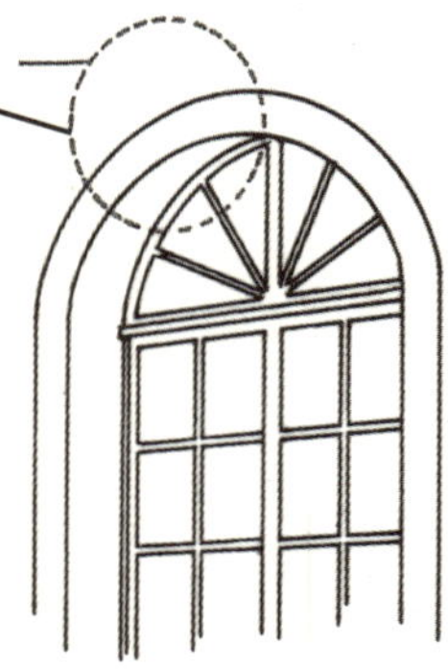

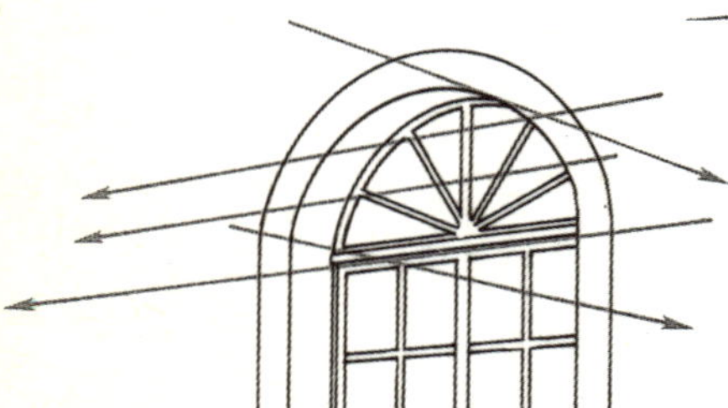

Correct Example

When drawing a rough sketch, it is best to draw the parts that are not visible as well.

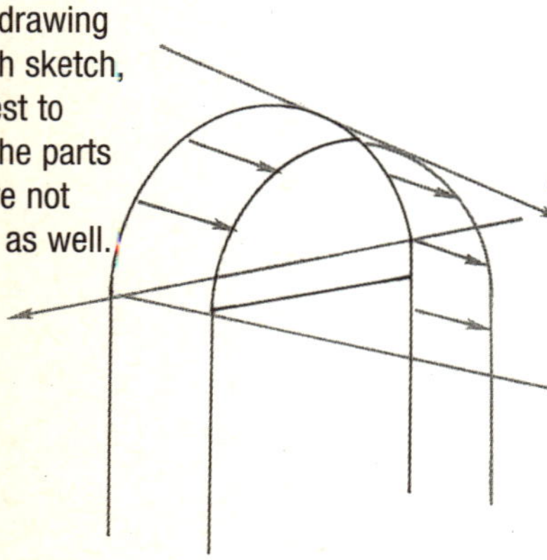

Required Tools

Templates come in limited sizes, but they make drawing easier if the size is right.

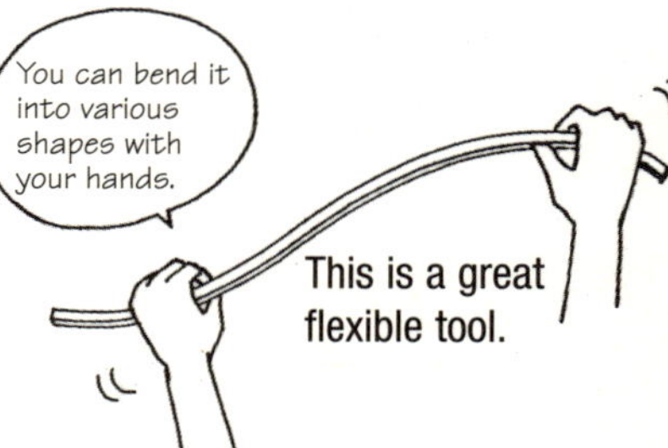

This is a great flexible tool.

A flexible ruler is easy to use once you get used to it.

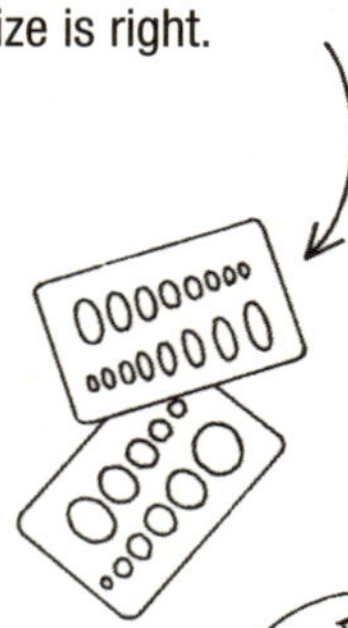

Circles, ovals, etc.

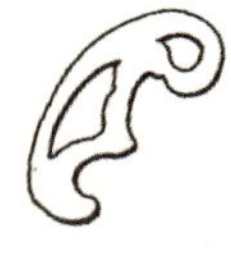

Draw using a curved rule. Those with the confidence can draw freehand.

☆Compare the height of the fence and the height of the characters.
☆If you draw the characters using lines that are bolder than those used for the background, they will appear to be in front of it.

Abbreviate or alter objects that are in the way, objects that have an intricate design, and objects that will look odd when reproduced exactly as in the photograph.

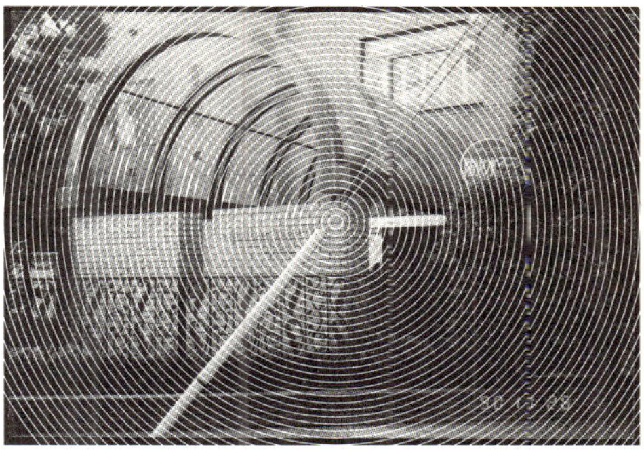

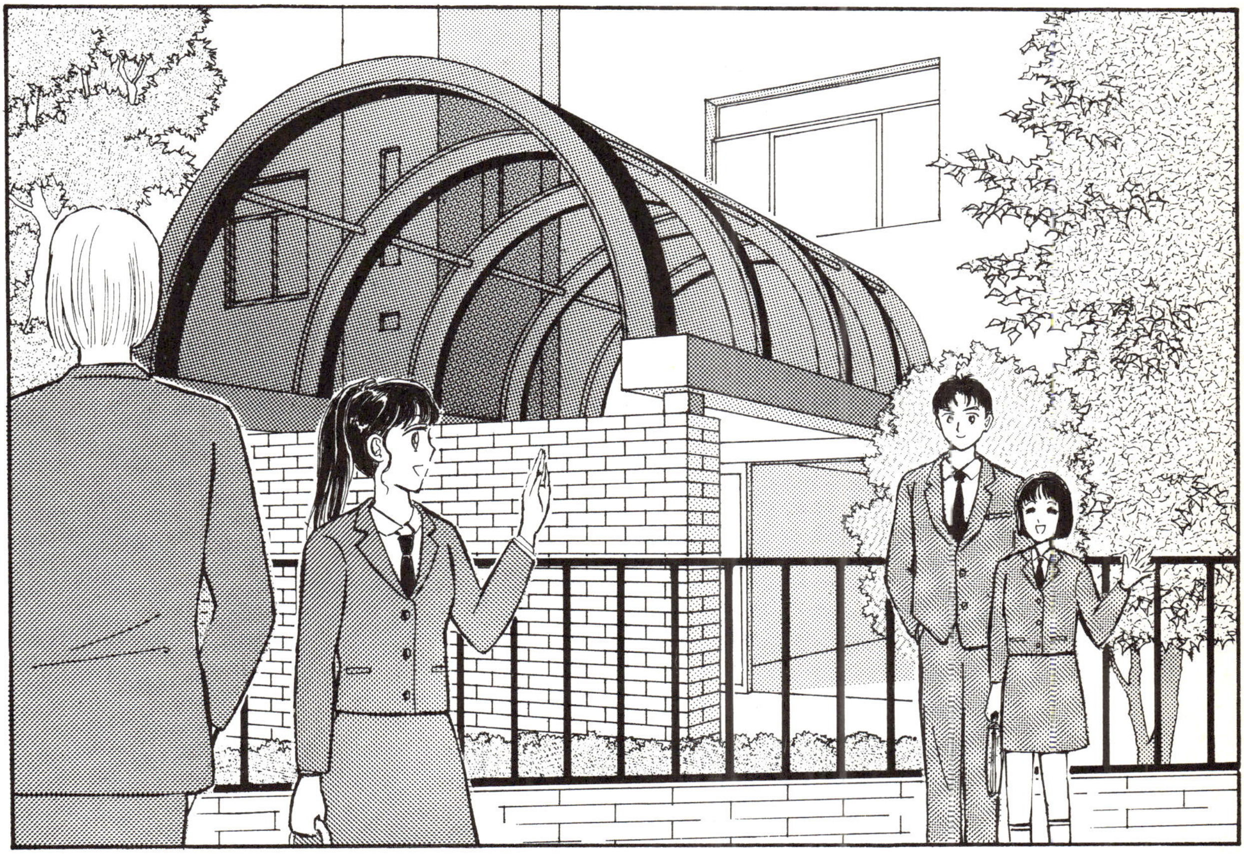

Background Techniques 2

Opening and Closing of Doors

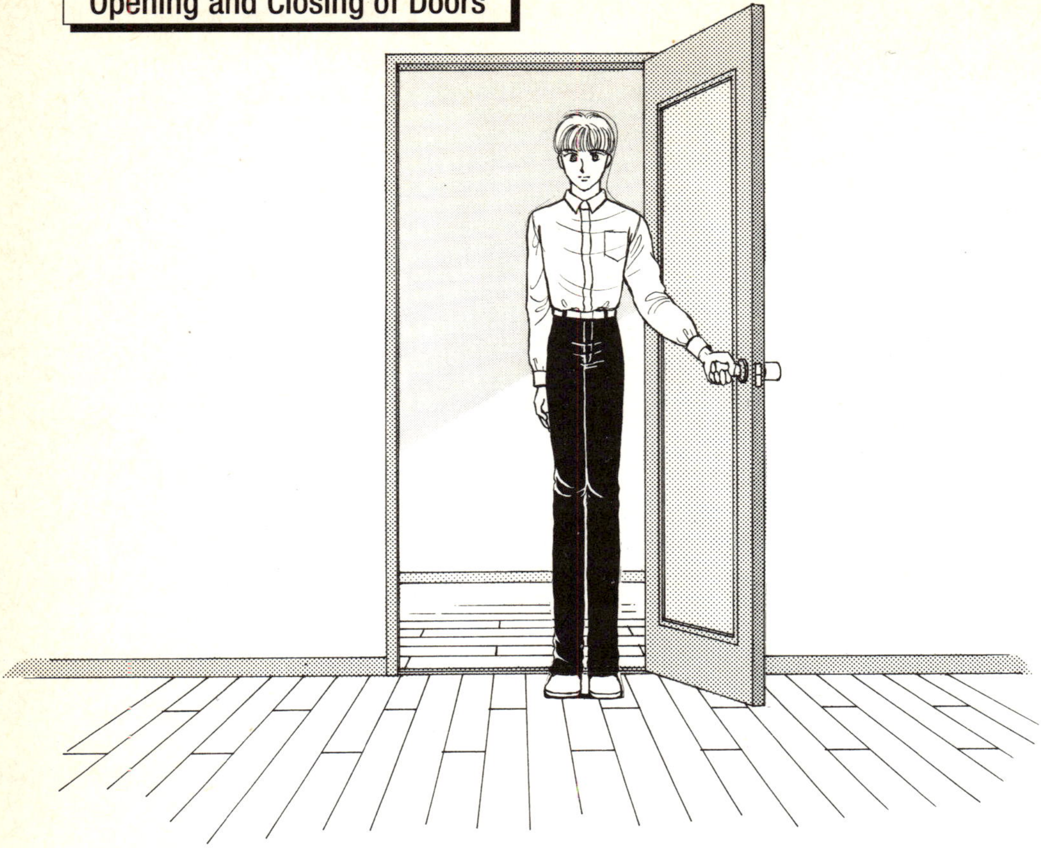

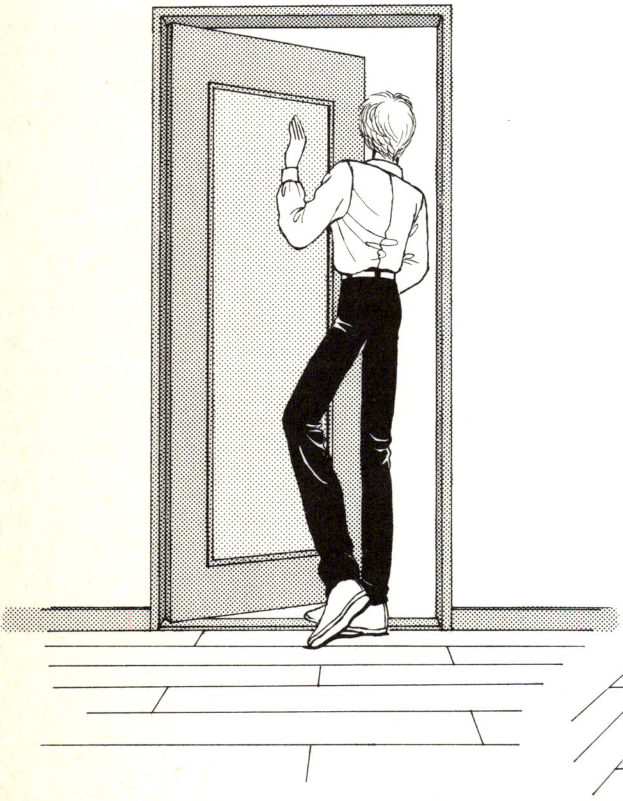

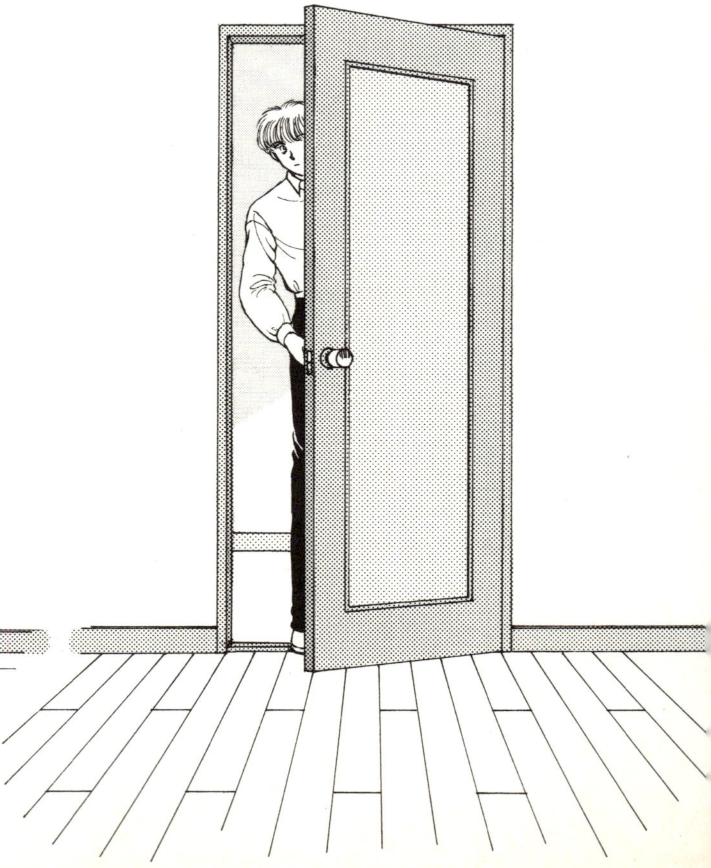

Drawing Doors From the Front

1 First, draw the floor, wall, and doorframe using one-point perspective (Eye level is always horizontal. Point A is the focal point.).

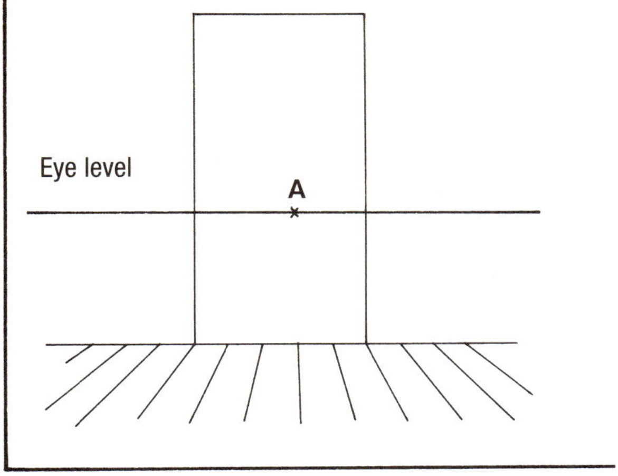

2 Next, draw an oval using the width of the doorframe (segment C) as the radius and the axis of the door B (▲) as the center.

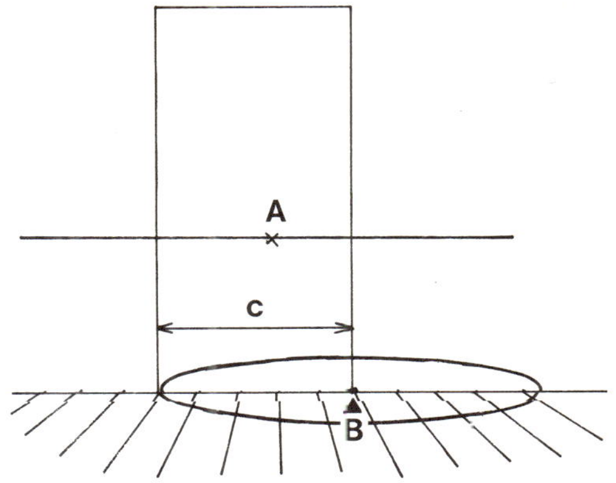

Short Advice

The center point of a circle will retreat slightly because of perspective. (It will deviate from the center of a drafted oval.)

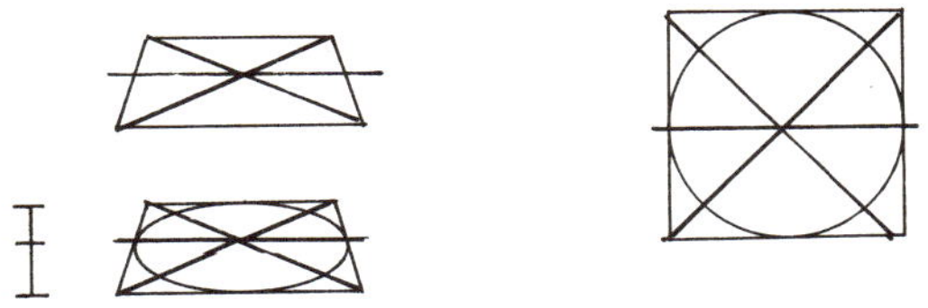

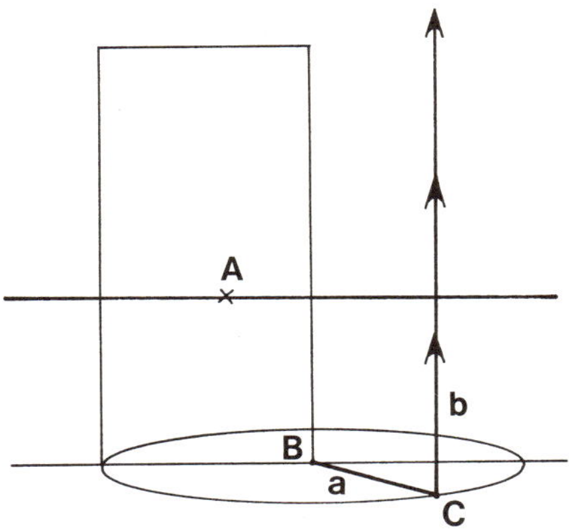

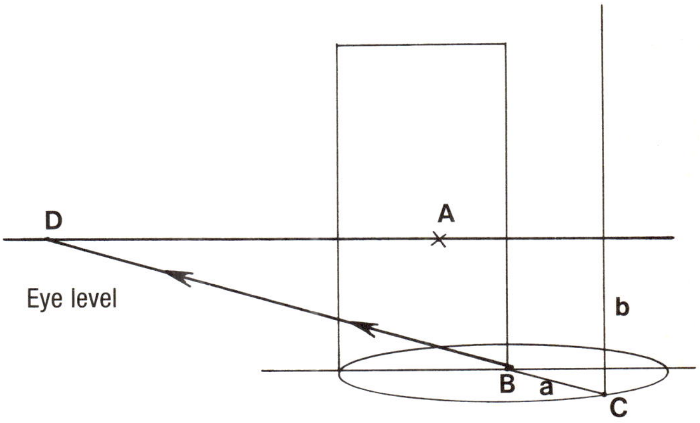

3 Establish the angle that you want the door to open and draw a line (segment a) from point B to the arc of the circle.

4 Draw a line (segment b) perpendicular to the horizon from the point (point C) the line touches the arc.

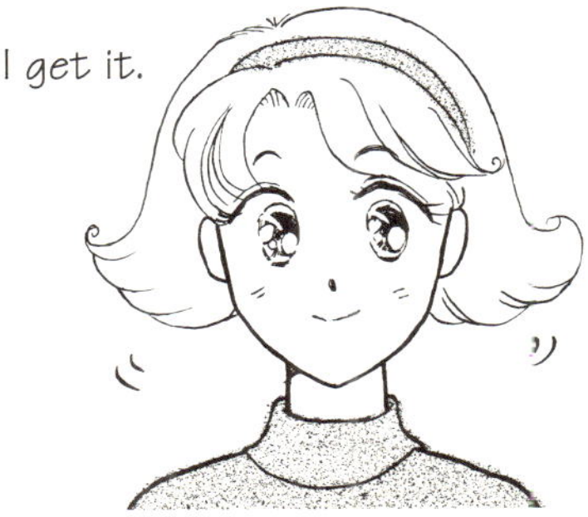

5 Next, extend segment a from point B to eye level. Call the point where the line intersects with eye level point D. Point D is the vanishing point for the depth of the open door.

6 Draw a line toward point B' from point D. Call the point where it intersects with segment b point E.

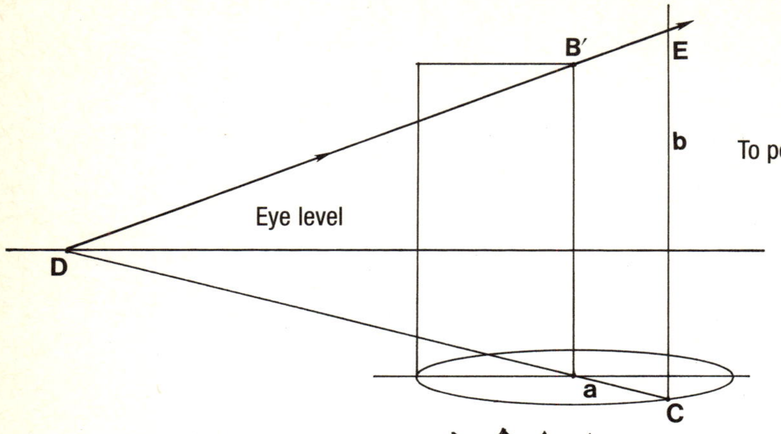

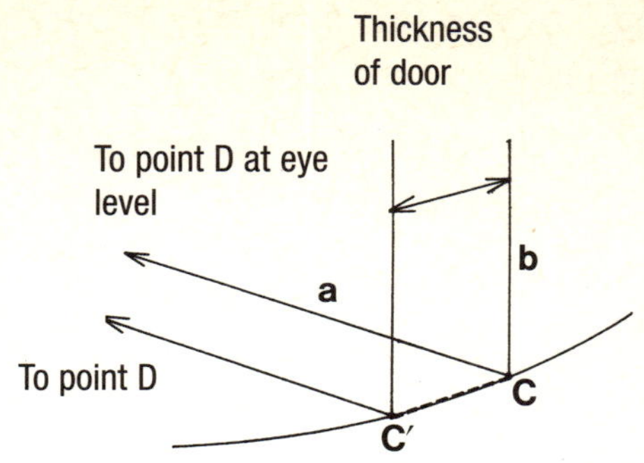

It has been exaggerated to make it easier to understand.

This completes the basis of the door.

7 For the thickness of the door and the angle of the thickness, using the circle drawn earlier makes things easier. A close-up is shown above. First, determine the thickness of the door (point C') relative to point C. Next, join point C and point C' with a straight line. This yields the angle of the thickness.

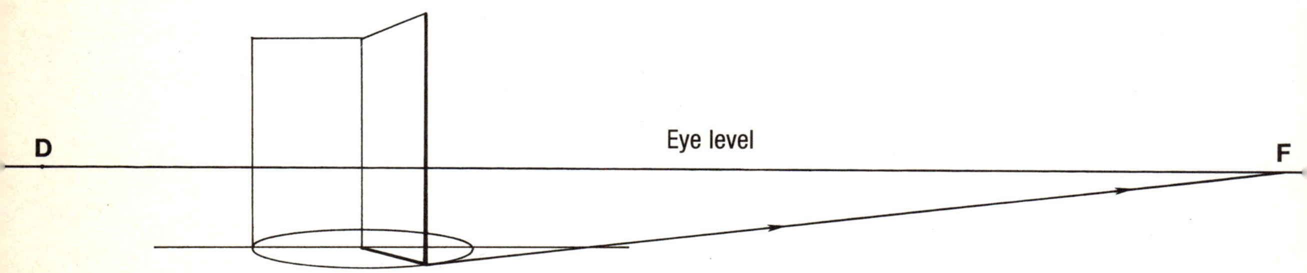

8 Extend the angle of the thickness of the door (C and C') sought earlier straight toward eye level. Call the point where the line intersects with eye level point F (this point is the vanishing point for the 90-degree depth relative to the surface of the door).

Once this is determined the rest is easy.

9 Respective thickness angles are sought from point F. The drawing will be complete once the doorknob has been added.

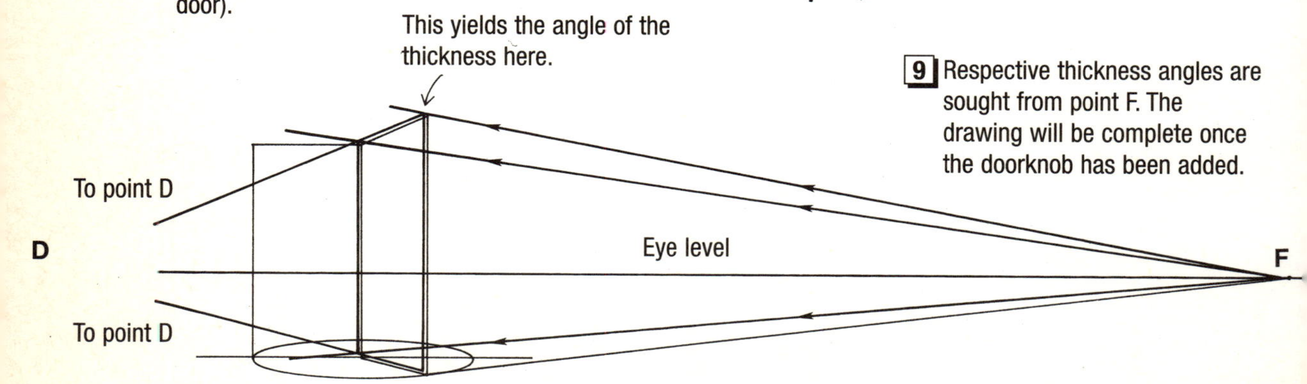

Doorknobs

Doorknobs (point G) should be slightly lower than half the height of the door (in the case of a door that is 180 cm =6 ft. high).

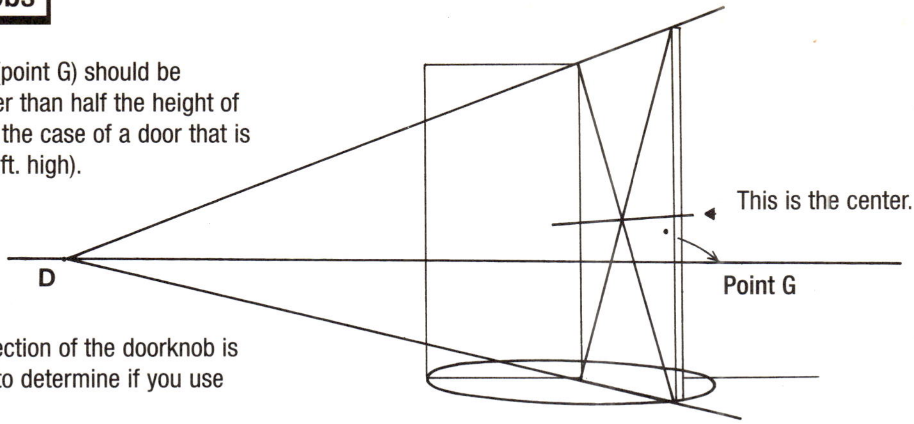

*The direction of the doorknob is simple to determine if you use point F.

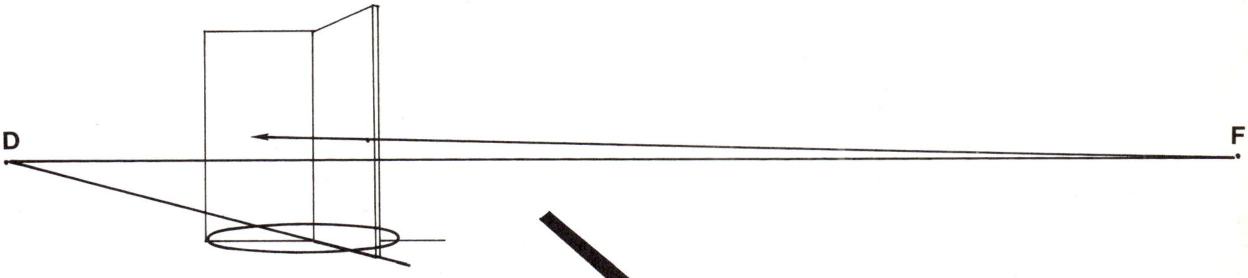

The knob on the opposite side is sometimes visible.

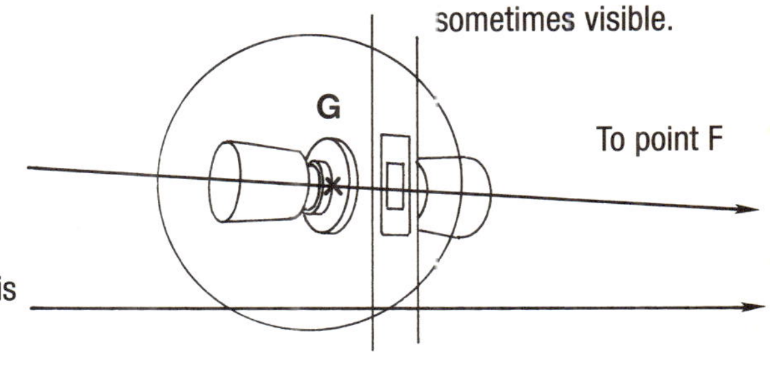

The doorknob itself is at a slight angle.

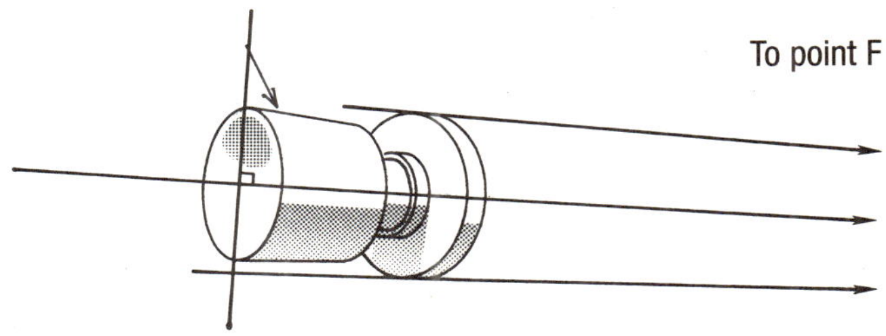

Doors in Japanese homes are between 80 and 90 cm (32 in. and 36 in.) wide. They may be narrower in some instances. Doors are usually 180 cm (6 ft.) high. In countries other than Japan, they are about 90 cm (36 in.) wide and two meters (6.67 ft.) high. Use your own house as a guide as well!

Background Techniques 3

Stairs

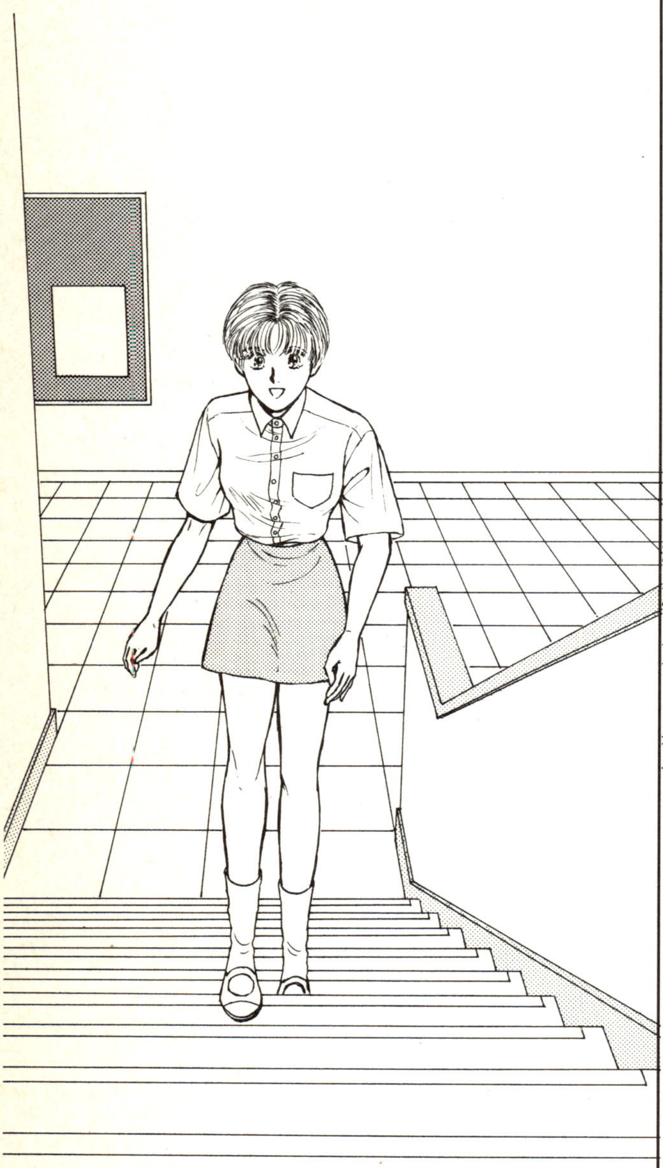

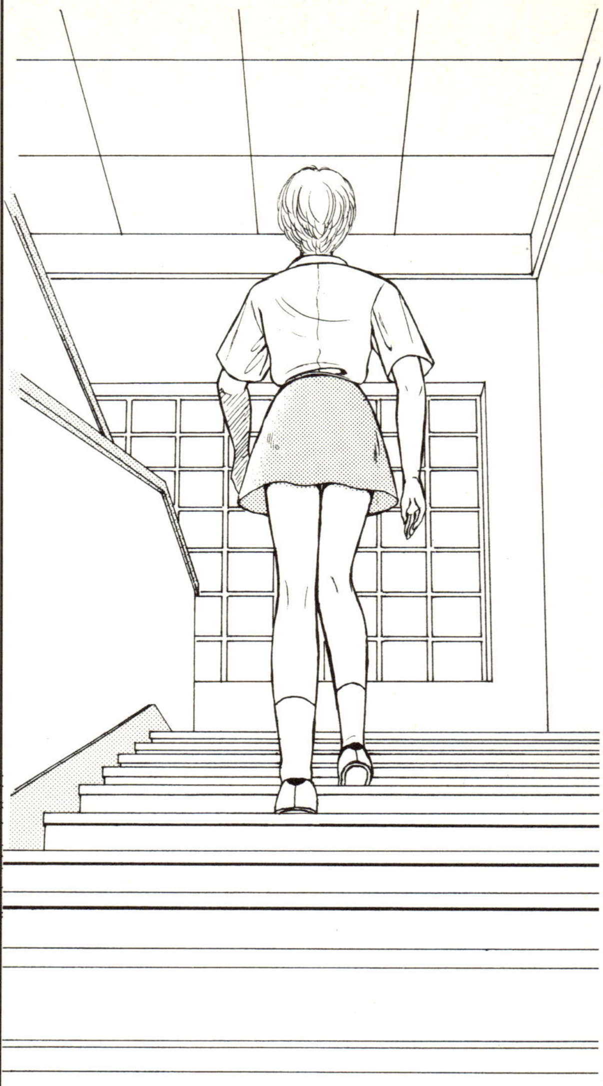

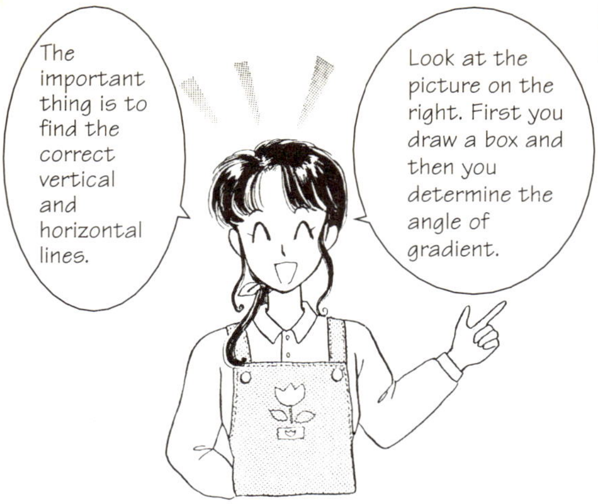

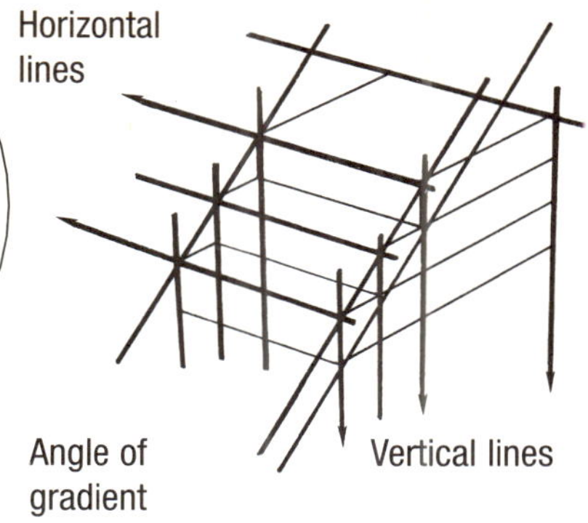

You can easily draw stairs if you think of them as one rectangular parallelepiped on top of another.

Both low- and high-angle views are drawn the same way. Draw a hand rail and other parts so that they match the height of characters.

Low-Angle Cross Shot

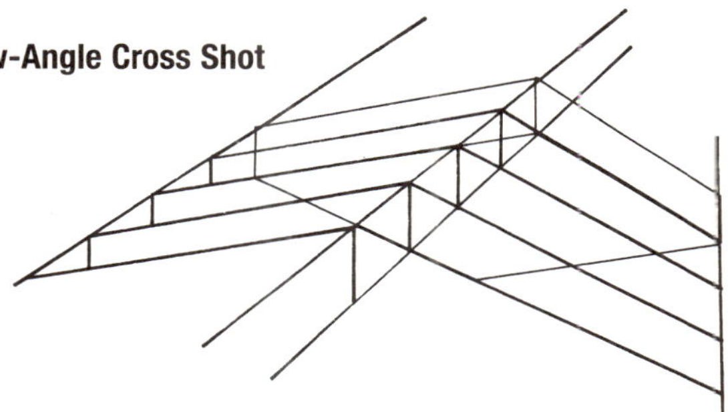

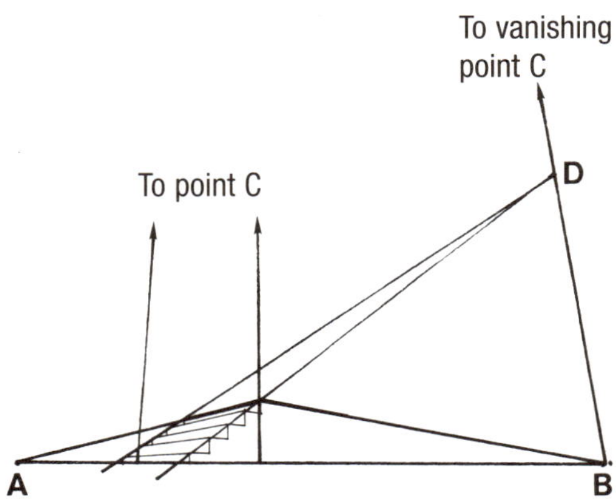

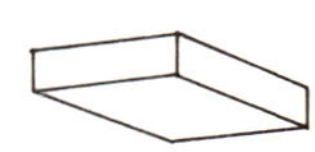

Identical sloping parallel lines converge on the same point (to point D). Point D is on the line that connects vanishing point B and vanishing point C.

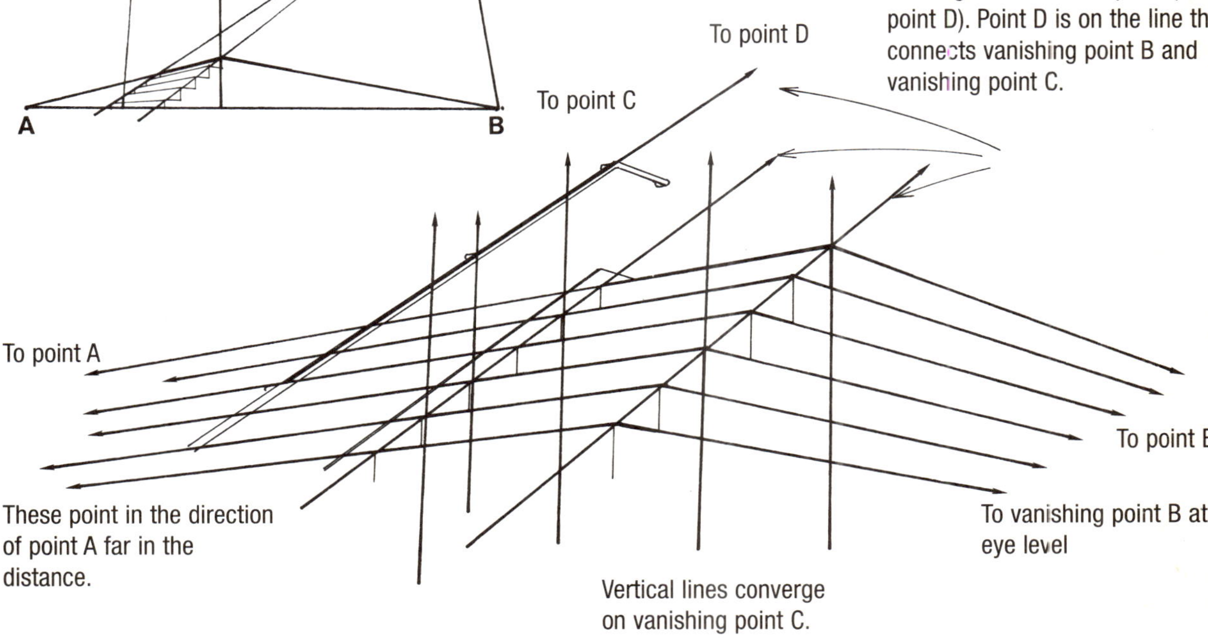

High-Angle Cross Shot

As in this example, you can also draw stairs by determining the vertical and horizontal lines from inside a large box.

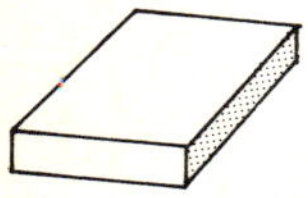

Boxes with the top surface visible are stacked on each other.

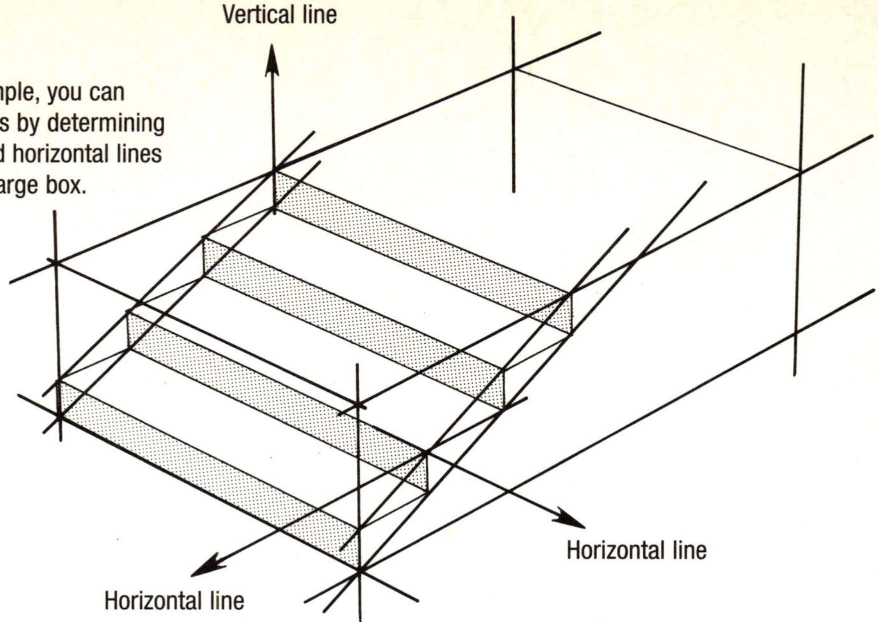

High-Angle Shot From Head On

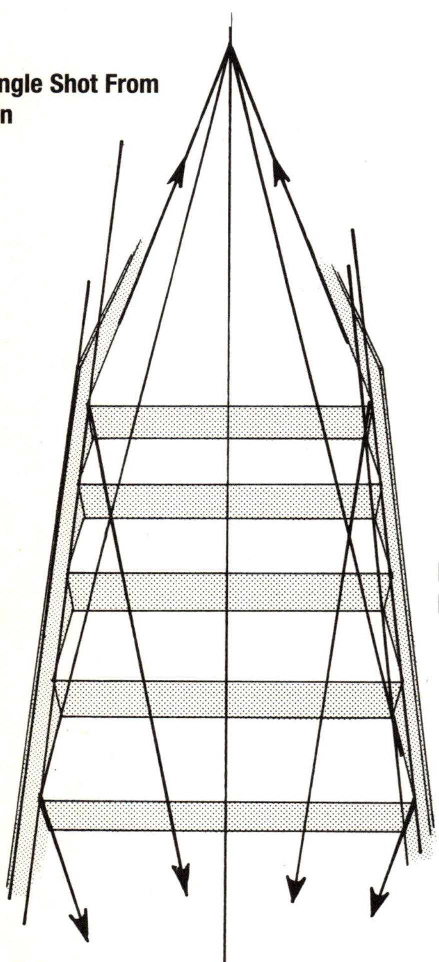

This surface gradually gets narrower and no longer visible.

The vanishing point is placed nearby, so the perspective is a bit tight, but it may make it convenient for observing changes in perspective.

Low-Angle Shot From Head On

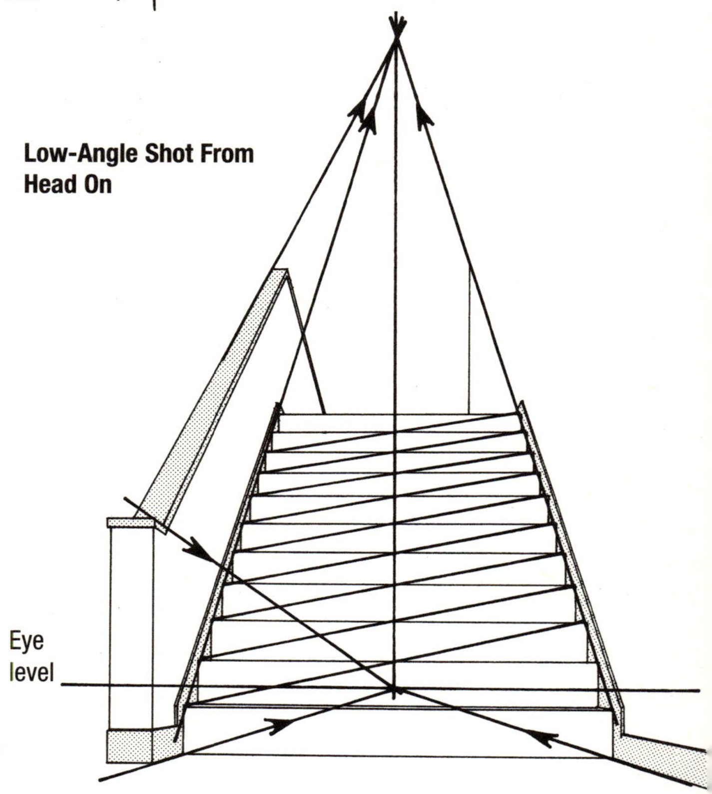

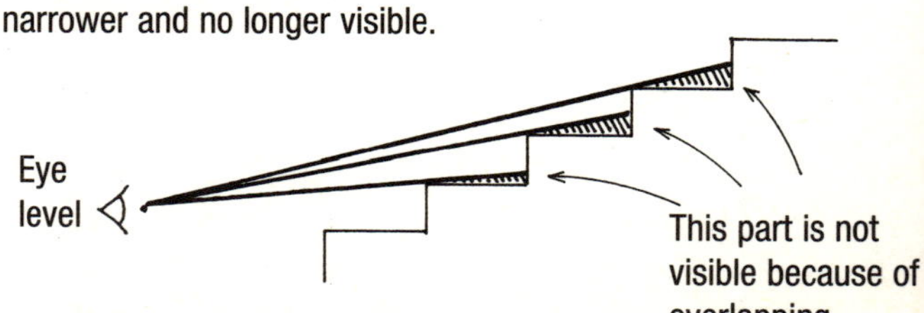

In the case of low-angle stairs, pay attention to the parts that are not visible!

Background Techniques 4

Buildings and Sloping Roads

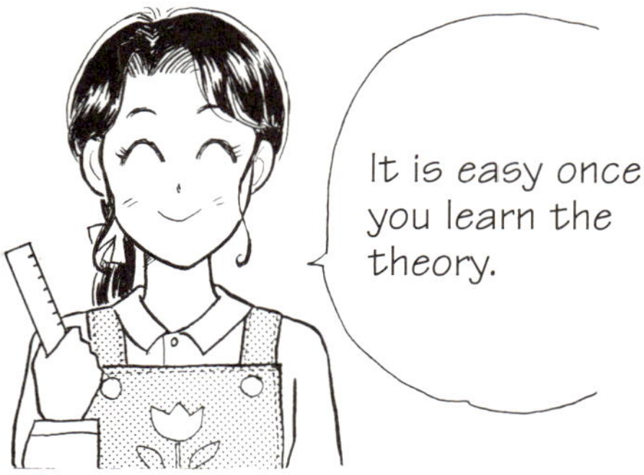

Both low- and high-angle views are drawn the same way. Draw a hand rail and other parts so that they match the height of characters.

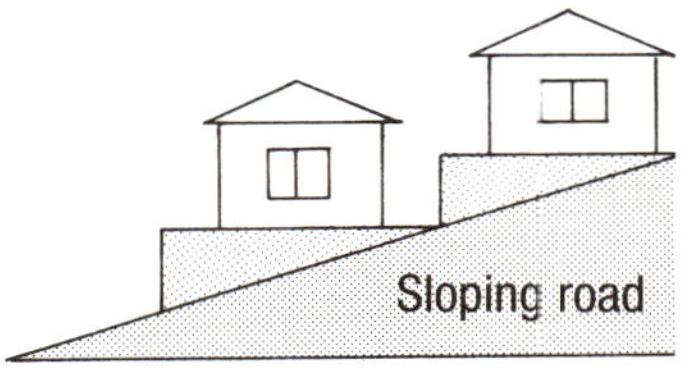

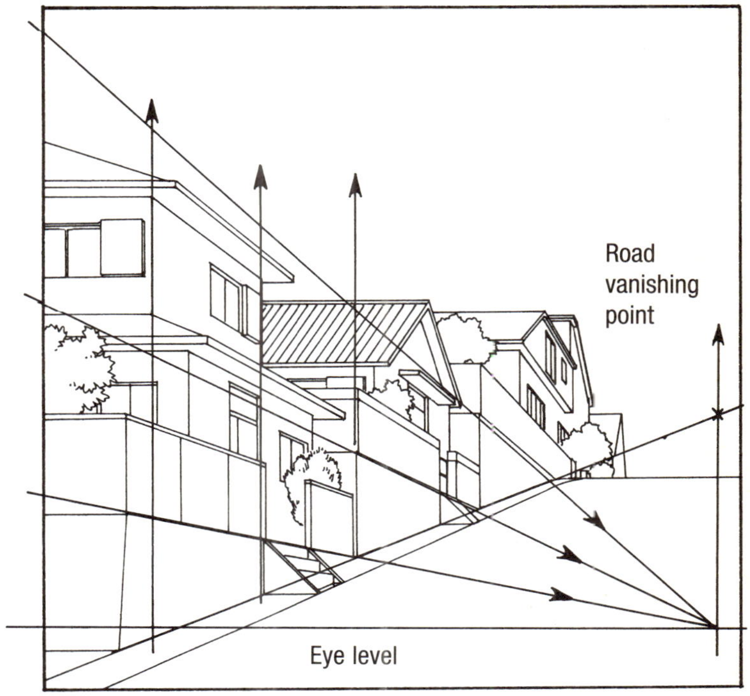

Vertical Lines (This drawing uses parallel perspective.)

You should think about the horizontal parts and the vertical parts when finding the vanishing point without being obsessed with the incline of the sloping road.

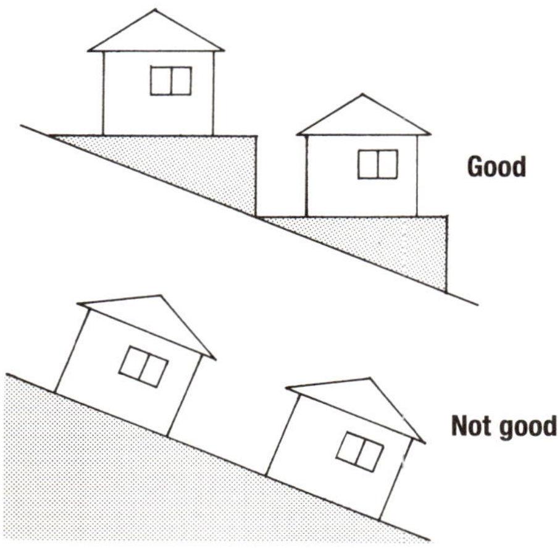

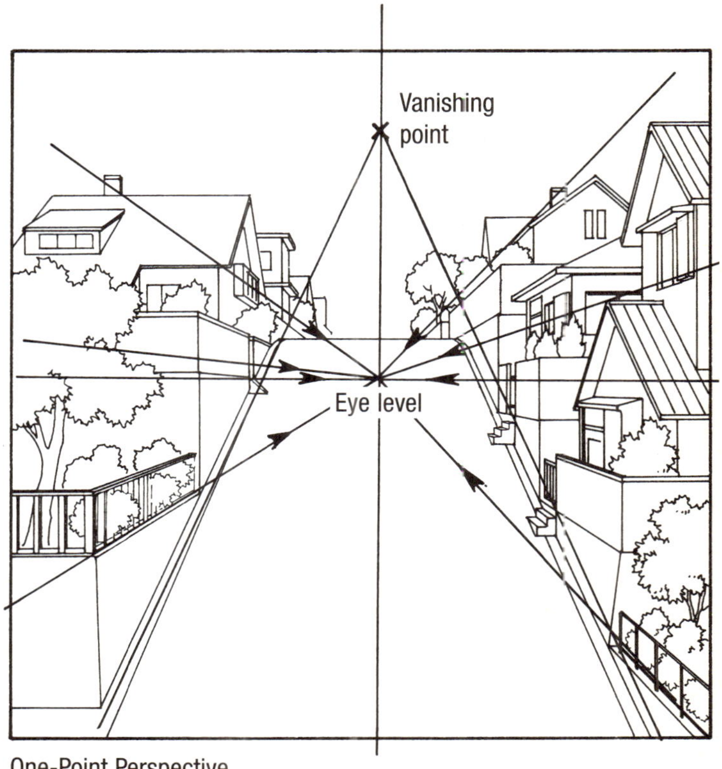

One-Point Perspective

How to Draw Natural Objects

When drawing natural objects such as trees, grass, and thickets, it is important to make sure that the lines do not become monotonous. Think about "simplification with variety" when drawing.

Comical Tree

Good

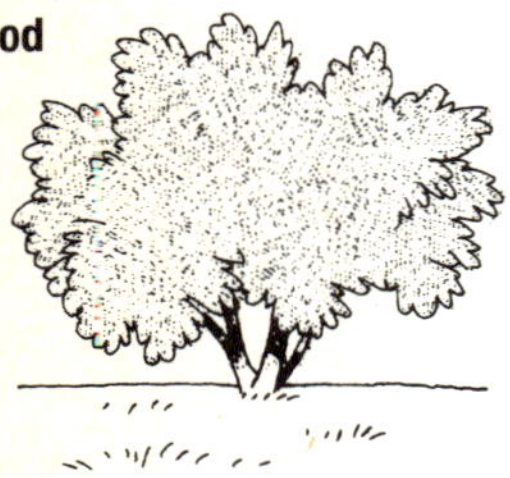

Not good

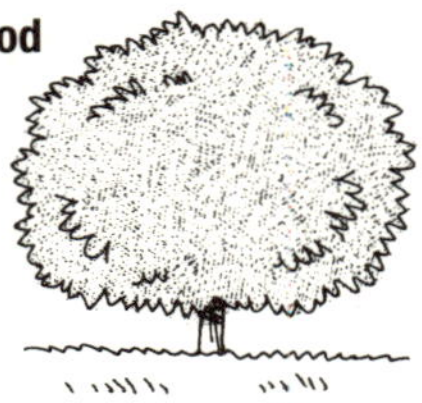

The same shape is repeated.
It is symmetrical.

Realistic Tree

Good

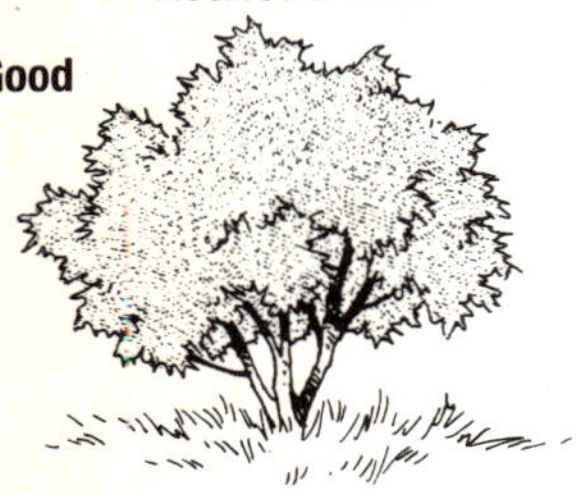

OK

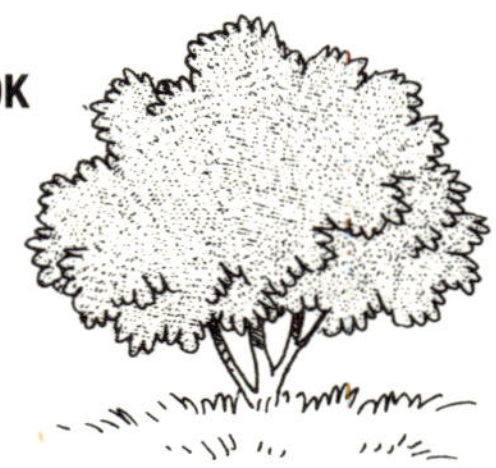

The shape of the leaves is monotonous, but overall there is variation.

Leaves Lacking Variety

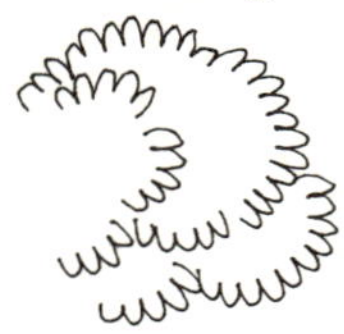

Not good

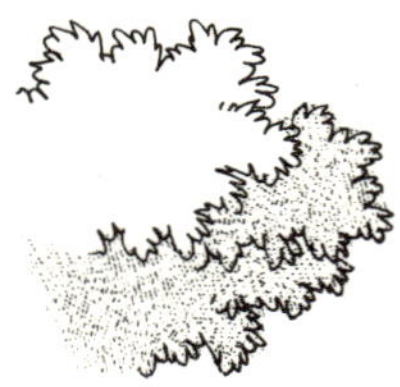

Good

Think of a thicket as a single mass while being aware of the leaves. Applying tone to the shaded areas will make it look three-dimensional.

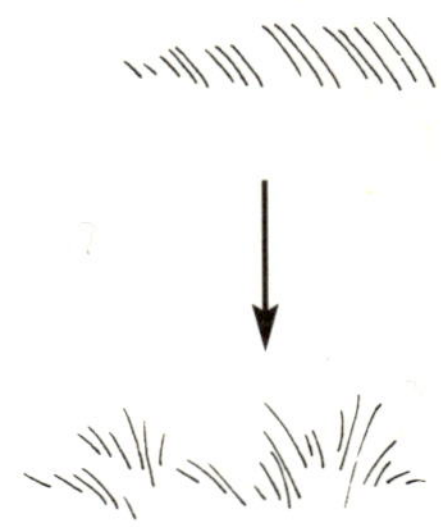

When drawing grass, adding rhythm and variation makes it easier to render softness.

Comical Style

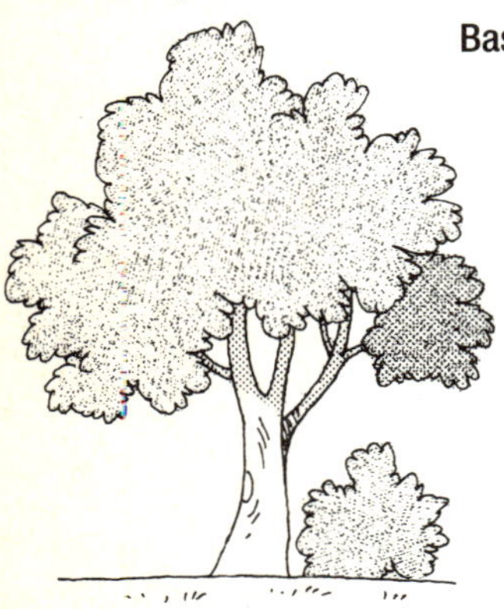

In order to bring the soft lines done in pencil into play, pen drawings in with a relaxed and natural touch.

Basic Drawing

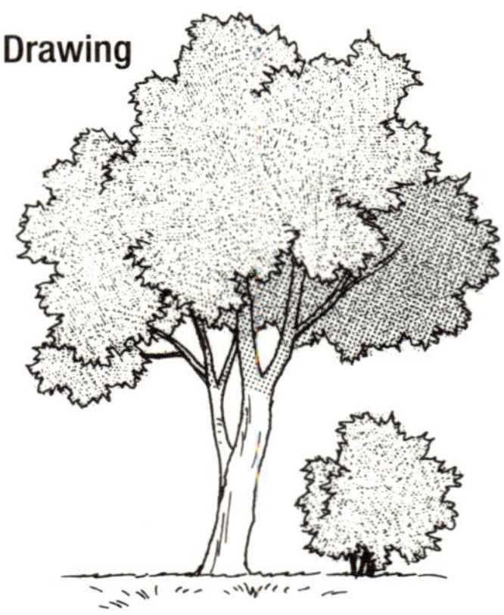

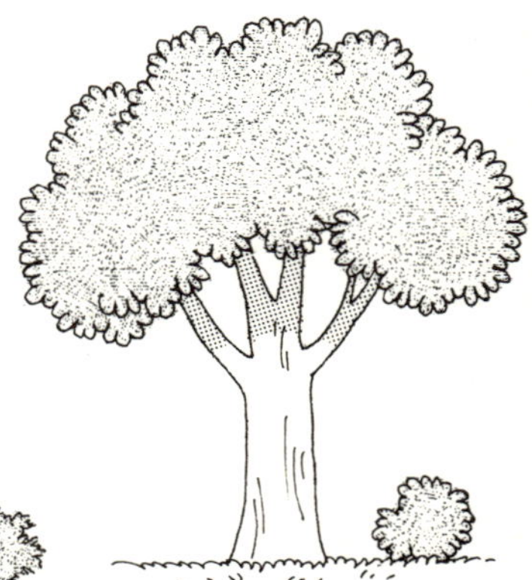

It is boring when it is symmetrical or the same shape is repeated.

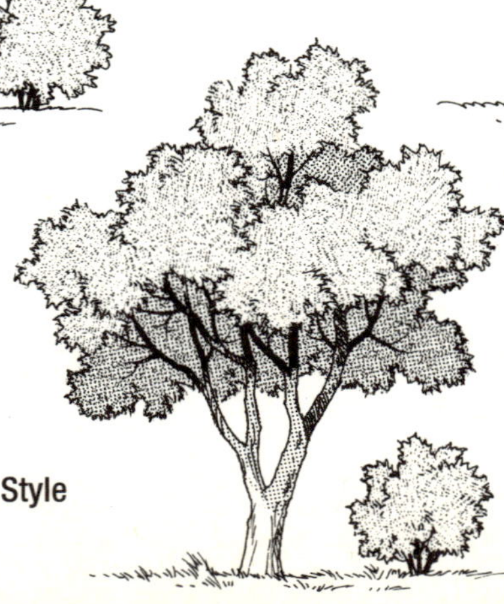

Realistic Style

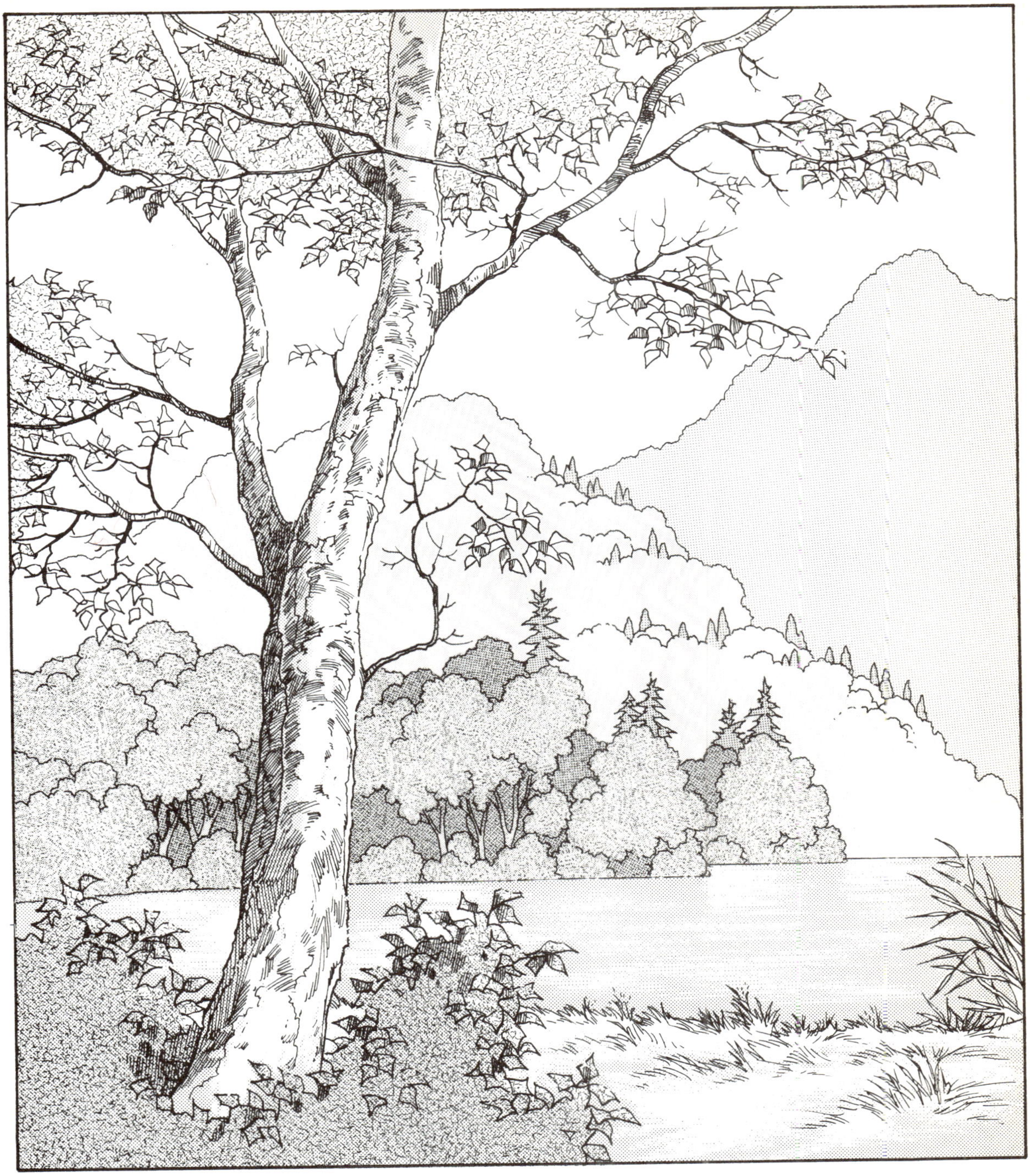

The tree and leaves in the foreground were done with a G-pen. The rest was done with a drafting pen (0.1).
Tone: Letra 1211 and 61
IC 676 and 668

Rendering Morning, Afternoon, and Night

When drawing natural objects such as trees, grass, and thickets, it is important to make sure that the lines do not become monotonous. Think about "simplification with variety" when drawing.

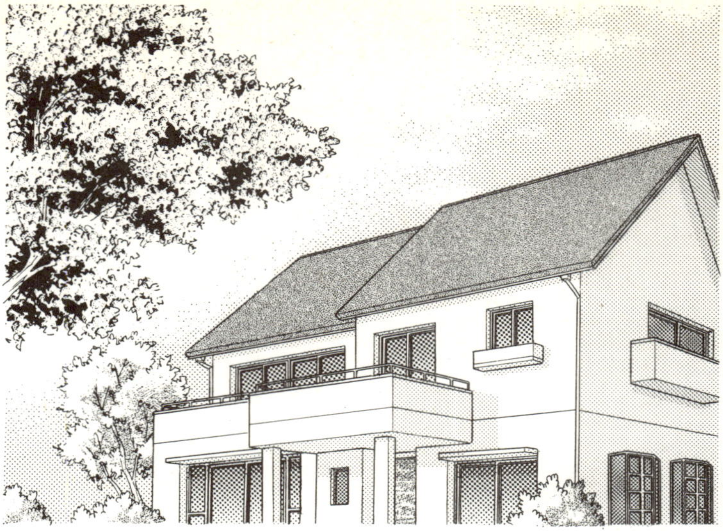

Morning — The clouds were scraped using normal gradation.
Letra 1210, 1211, 63, 684, 704, and 761
IC 244

In the morning and afternoon, it is darker indoors. Clouds reflected in window panes can be drawn by scraping.

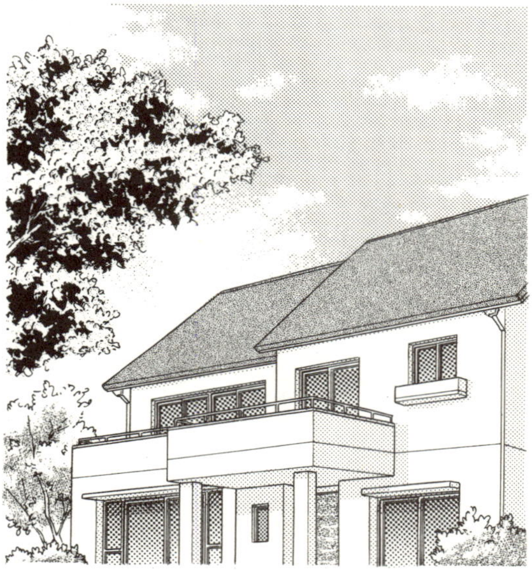

Afternoon — The clouds were scraped using the middle or back of the cutter blade.
Letra 1211, 61, 684, 704, and 761
IC 244

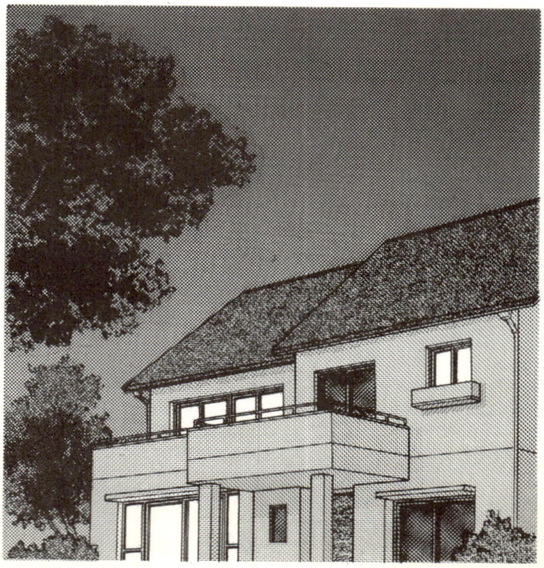

Night — Tone was used for the sky and dark windows, but you can also make them solid black.
Letra 1211, 63, 684, and 704
IC 244 and 477

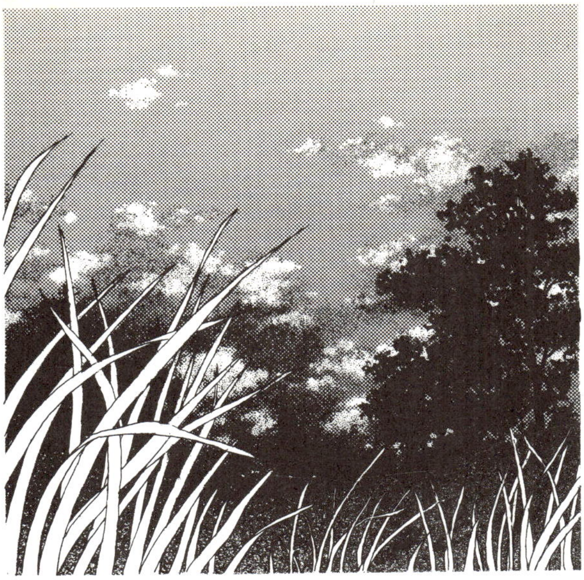

Natural Objects in the Evening—The sky is done by applying both gradation and sand gradation. The shadows are dark in the evening, so objects in the distance can just be silhouettes. If objects in the foreground are drawn in silhouette and objects in the distance are made whitish, it will have the effect of making it look designish. For evening skies, clouds are often rendered by applying overlapping gradated tone.
Letra 1538
IC 418 and 477

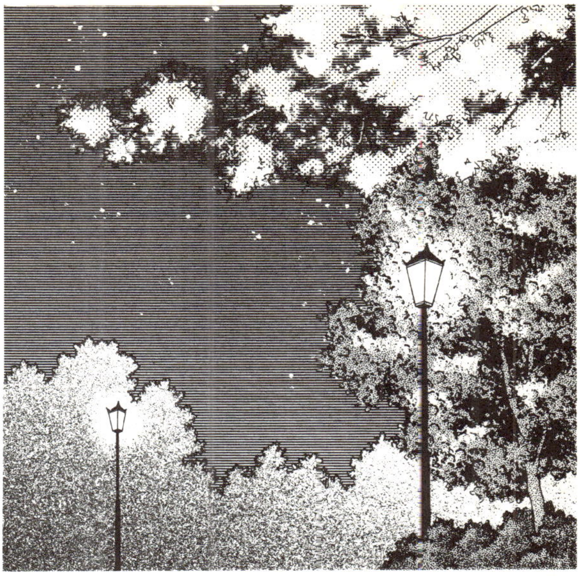

Natural Objects at Night—Like in the afternoon, vary the tone in order to give perspective to nearby objects using objects in the distance.
Near (dark)➡Far (light)
Or
Near (light)➡Far (dark)
Objects far away are often lightened when blurred.
Letra 1210, 684, and 754
IC 418 and 244

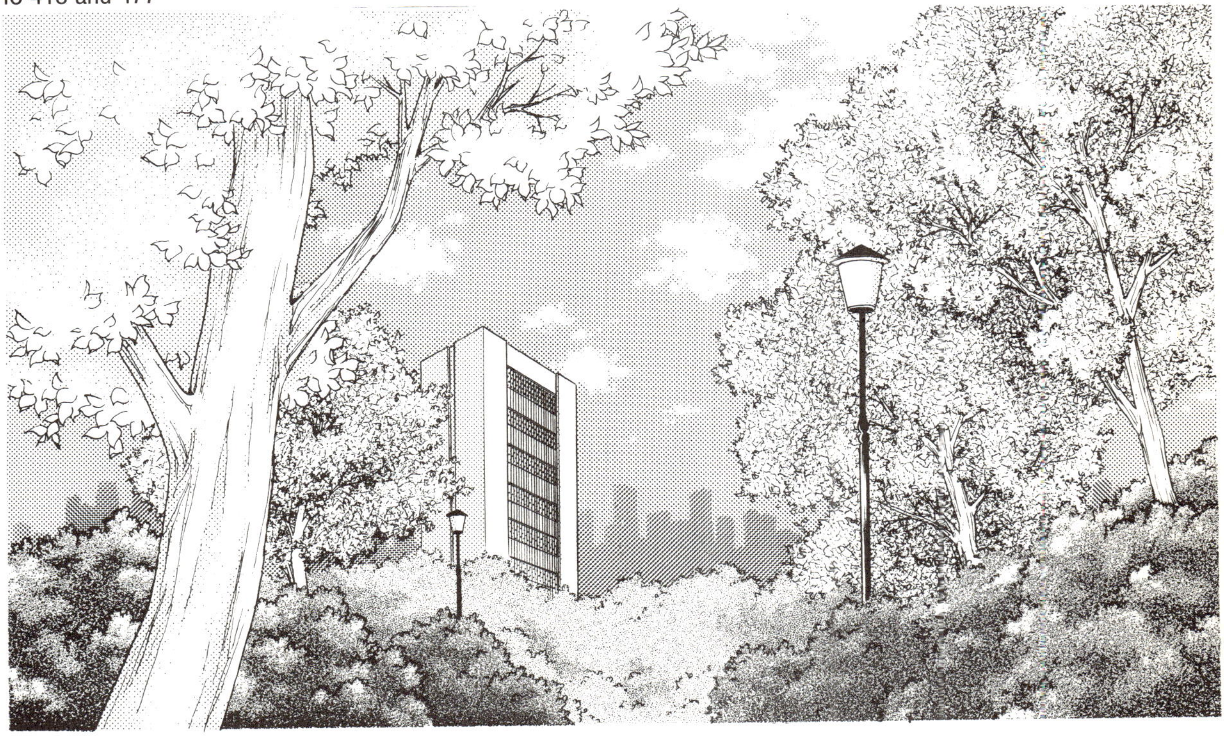

Natural Objects in the Afternoon—The group of buildings in the distance was done by applying double tone. The tone was placed in an orthodox manner. Nearby objects are clear while objects in the distance are light or blurred. Varying the tone gives a picture perspective. Objects very nearby were made light in this drawing, but it is alright to render them more clearly.
Letra 1210, 1211, 1538, 761, and 786
IC 676

Rendering Spring, Summer, Fall, and Winter

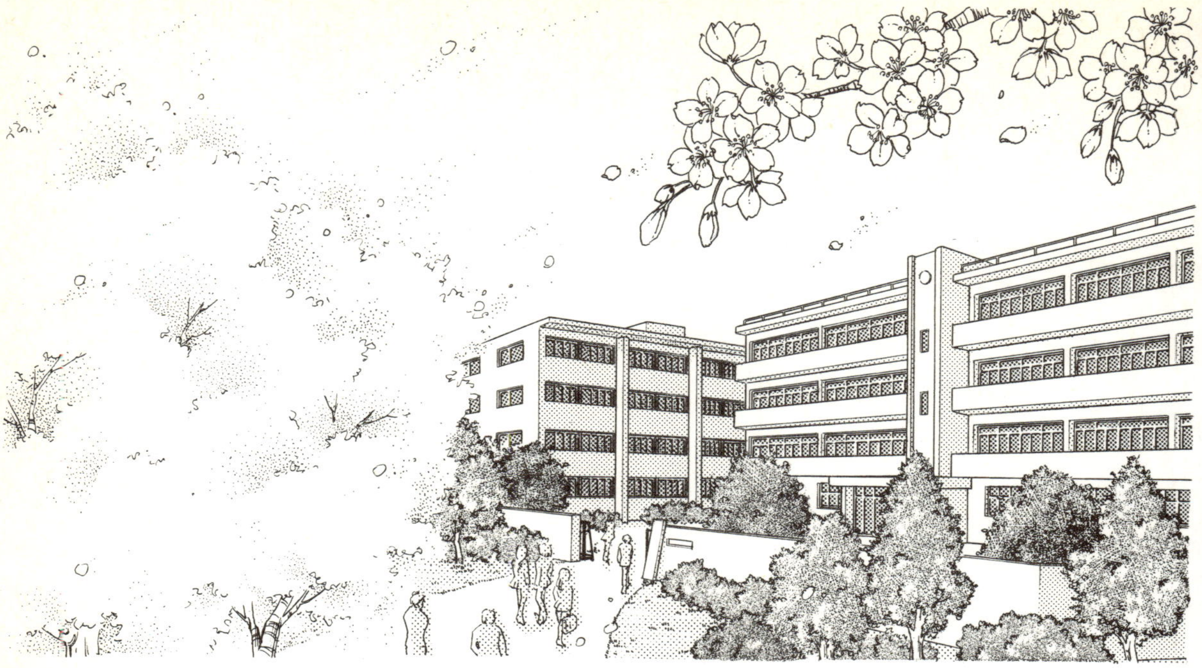

Spring

Using an orthodox background and placing branches of seasonal plants in the foreground will bring out the feel of the season. In this case, the lines of the windows of the school were abbreviated and whitened, and the thick parts in shadows were penned in.
Letra 1210, 1211, 62, 704, and 786

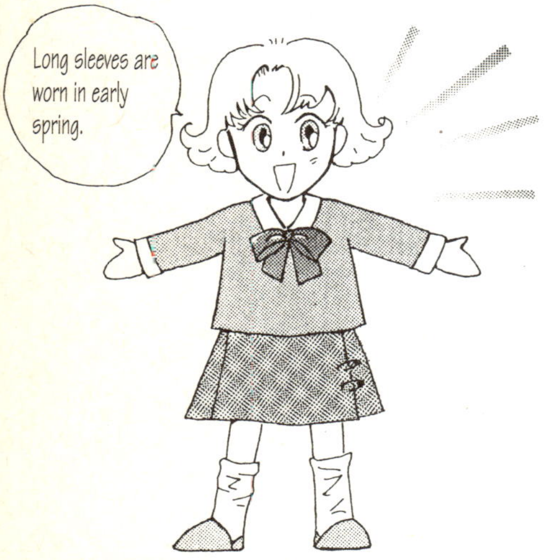

Note that throughout the year the clothing of characters and the background are intricately connected.

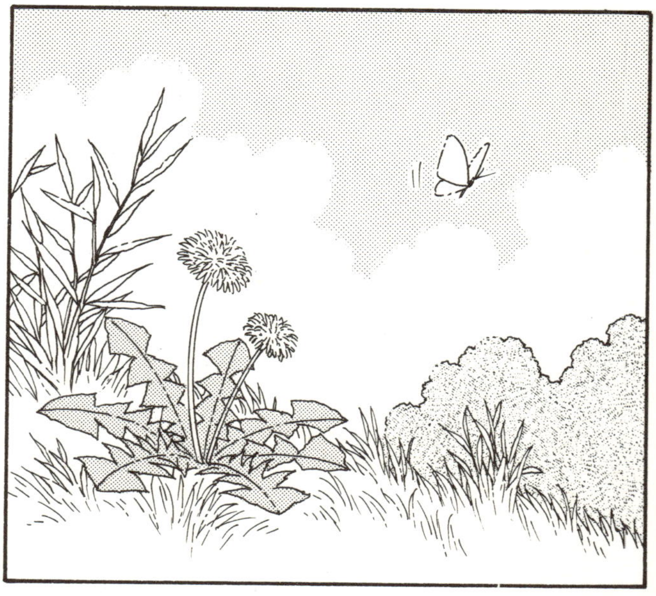

Dandelions and butterflies are typical of spring.

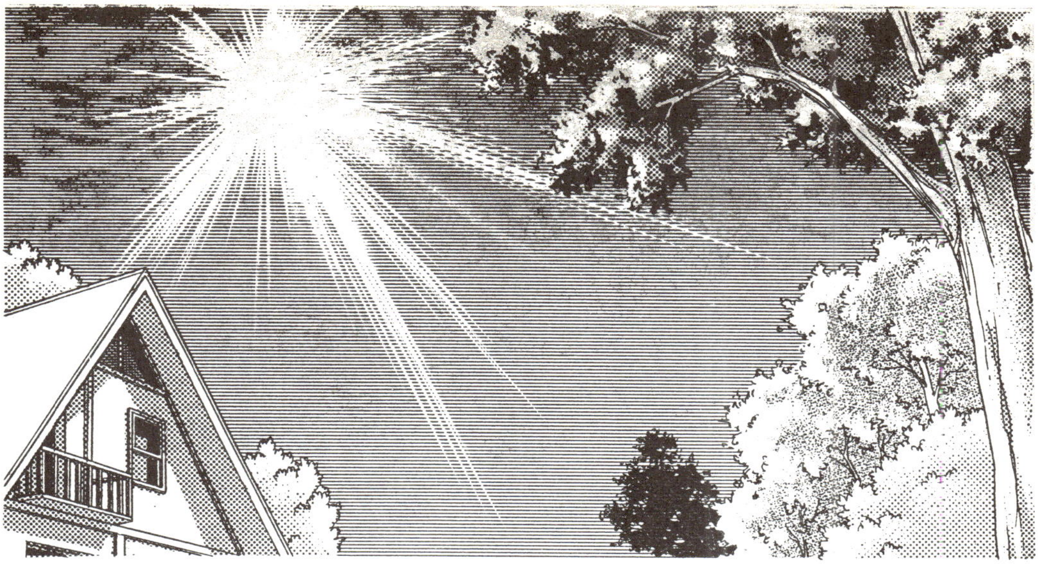

Summer

For the sun, a ruler was used and it was scraped to look like a flash. You can render the intensity of the sun's rays by using solid black for the dark shaded areas and silhouetting trees in the distance.
Letra 62, 63, 51, 704, and 754

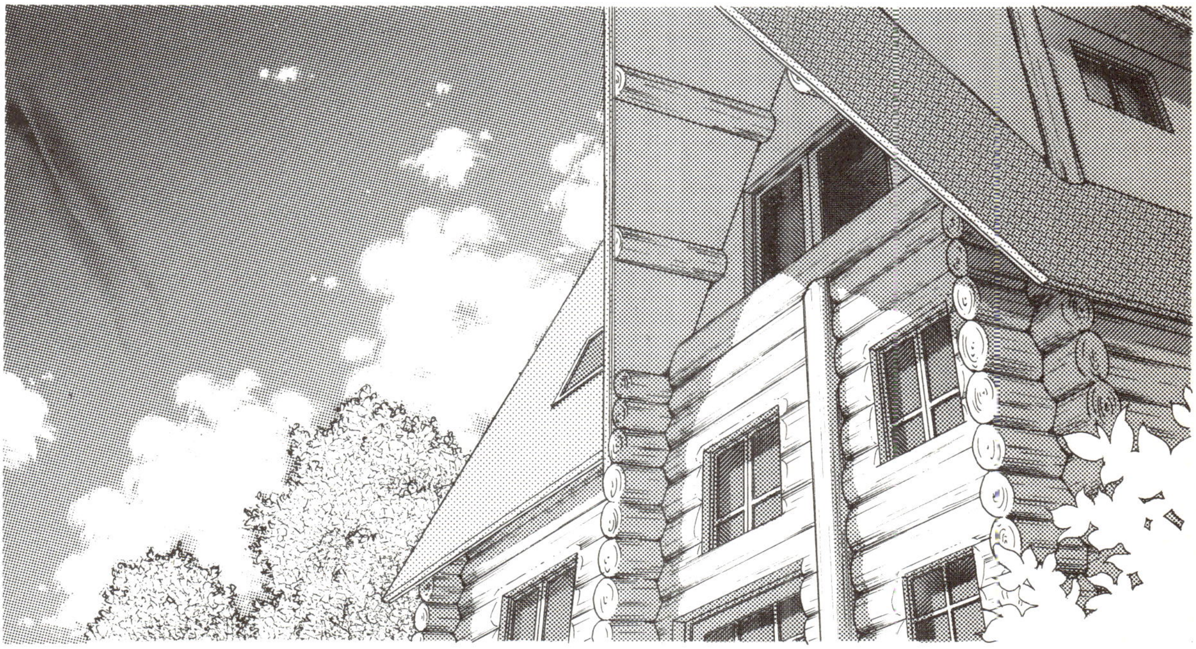

The sun's rays are intense in the summer, so make the shadows darkish. The sky is also dark. Clouds are white and clear. We wanted to make the sky high and spacious, so we used three-point perspective and a low-angle view.
Letra 61, 62, and 63
IC 477 and 676

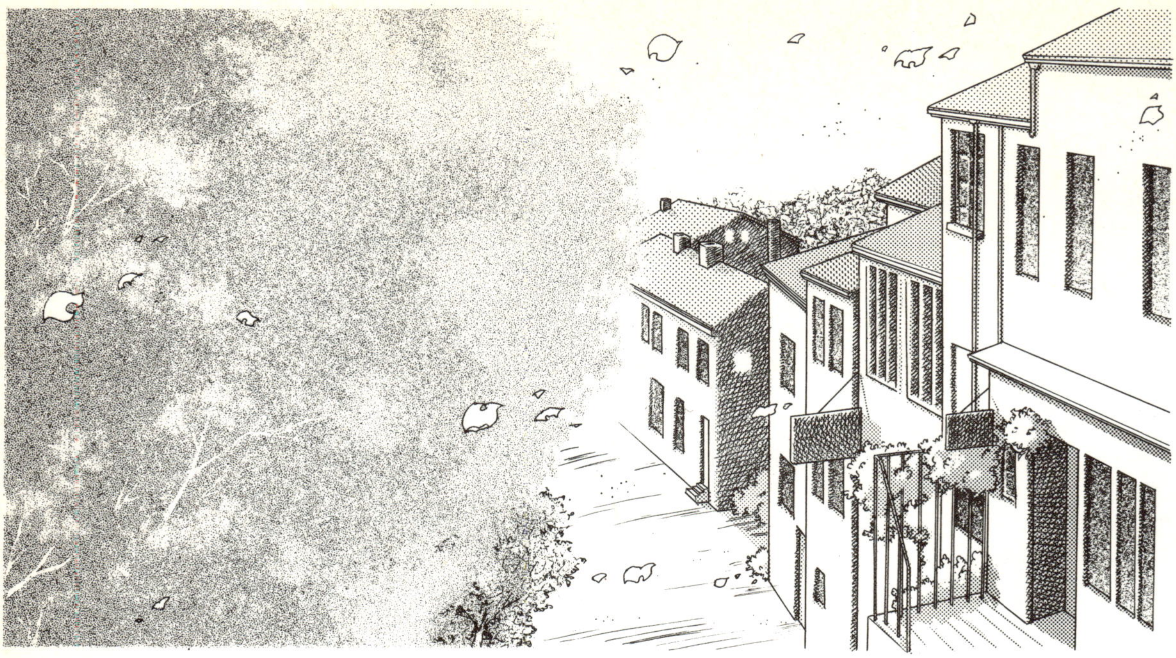

Fall

The sun's rays in the fall are soft and shadows are long. In this drawing, mesh was used for the shaded portions of the buildings to create a soft feeling.
Letra 1210 and 61
IC 418, 452, 477, and 676

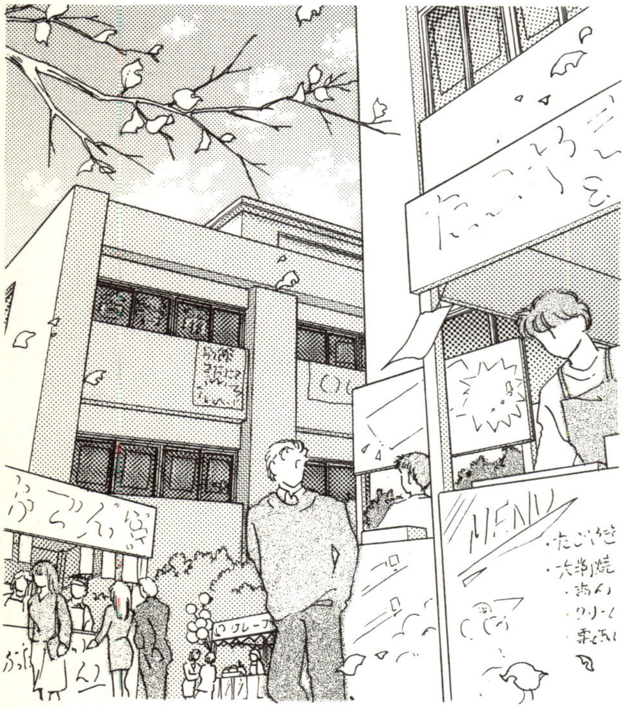

Three-point perspective. The feeling of fall was created by placing branches and dead leaves in the foreground. The crowd of people was made a part of the background.
Letra 1211, 63, 761, and 1538
IC 477

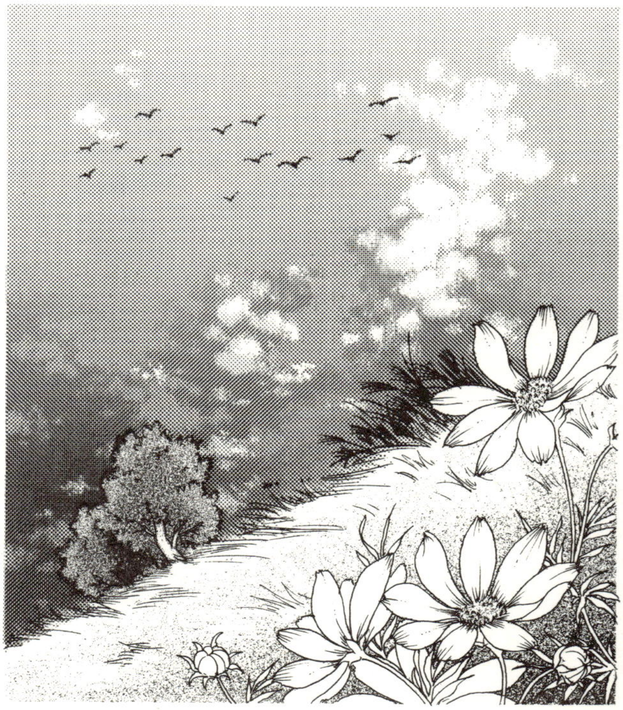

Double gradation was applied for the sky and clouds. Place a seasonal flower in the foreground.
Letra 786
IC 418 and 477

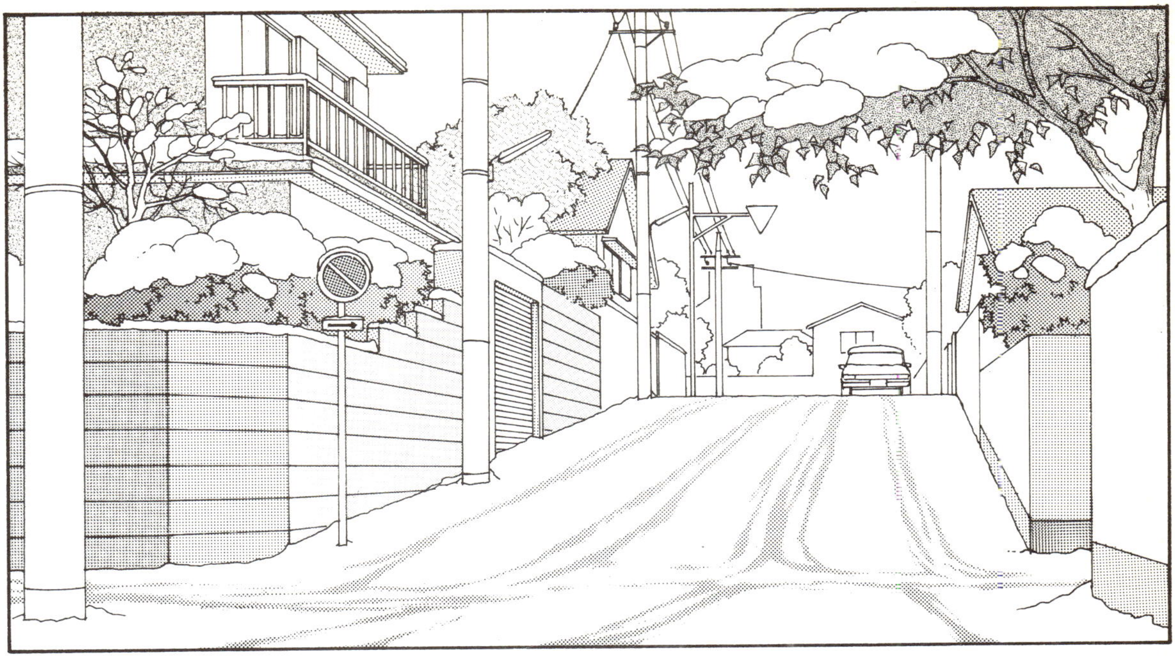

Winter

You might want to try using a slightly dark tone to emphasize the whiteness of the snow.

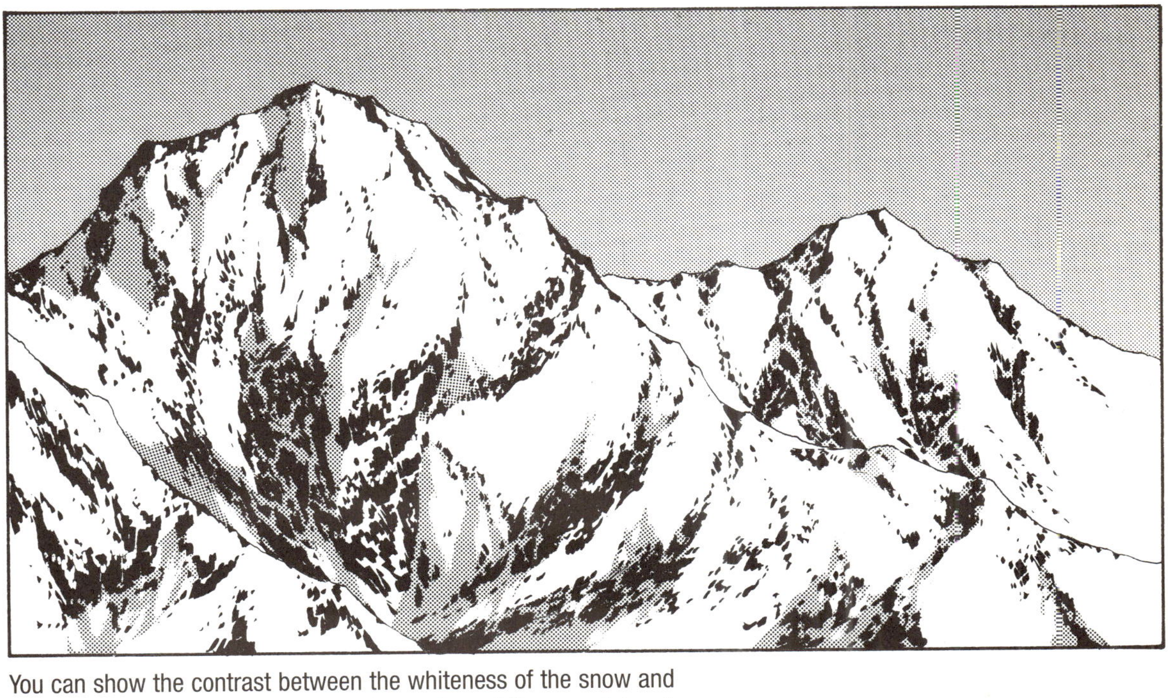

You can show the contrast between the whiteness of the snow and the black rock surface. Think about the surface of the mountain when applying the shadow tones.

Characters and Natural Phenomena

Whenever possible, it is best to depict rain, coldness, and other natural phenomena using pictures and not rely on dialog.

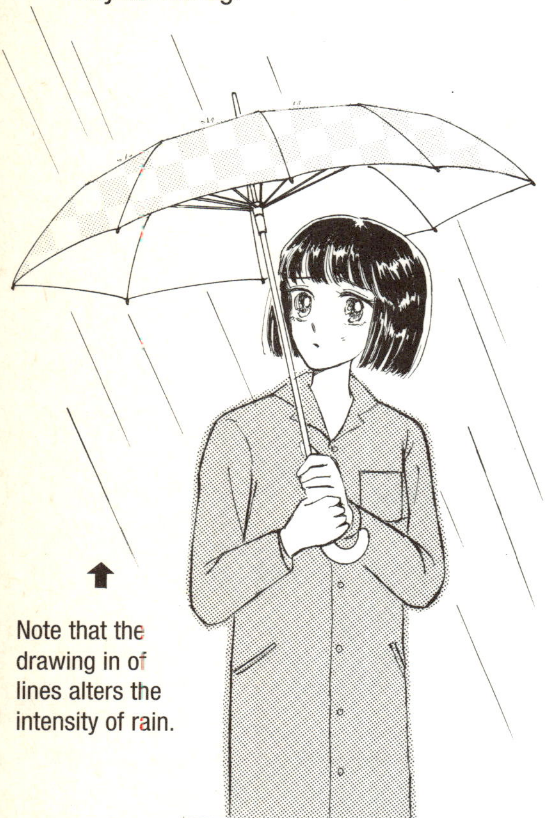

Note that the drawing in of lines alters the intensity of rain.

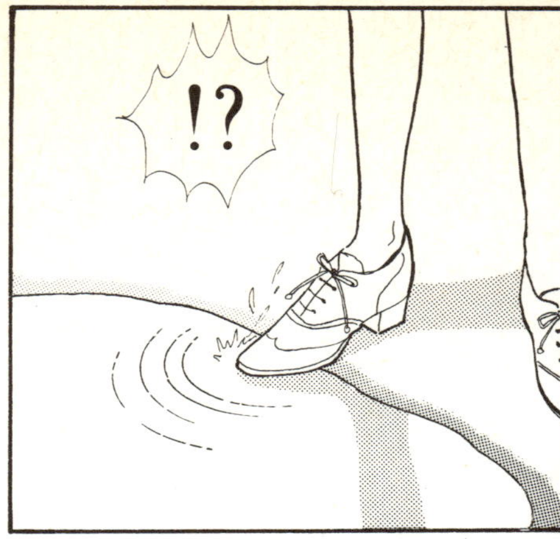

Ripples on water surface.

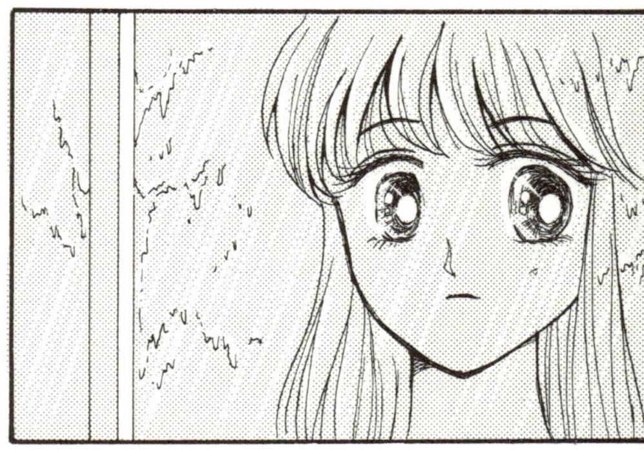

Rain on the other side of a window.

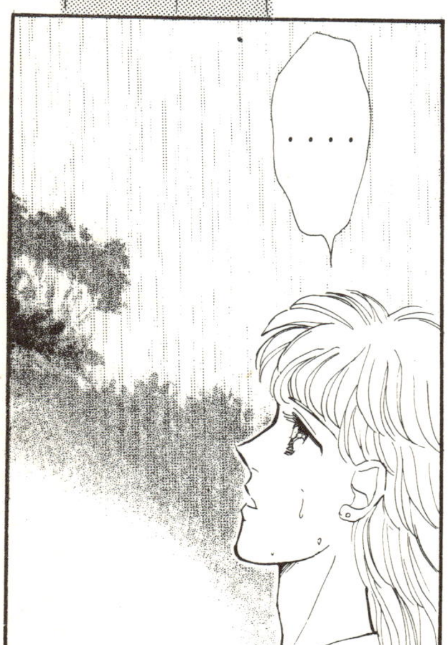

Rain created using tone.

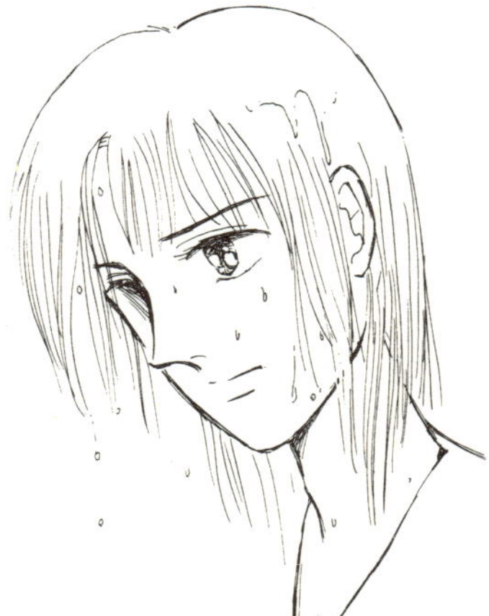

Wet hair

Depiction of someone drenched by rain.

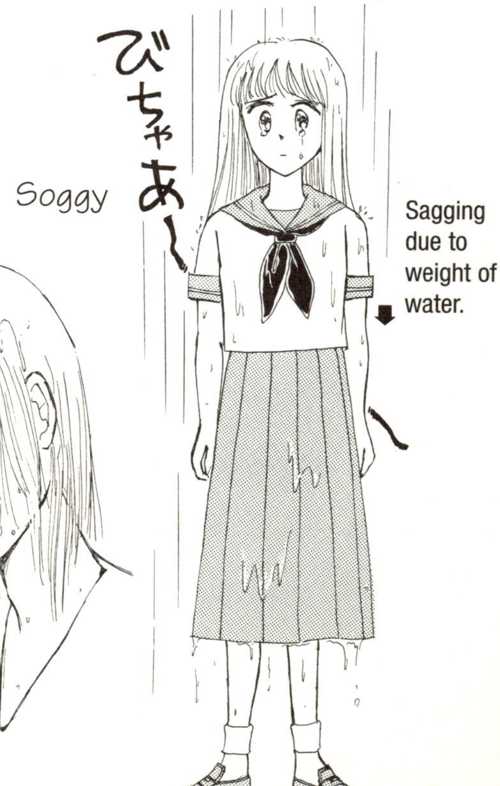

Sagging due to weight of water.

Depiction of State of Mind Using Wind
This is effective if used in a comic way for times when things do not turn out as expected or when a cold draft blows through the heart of the character.

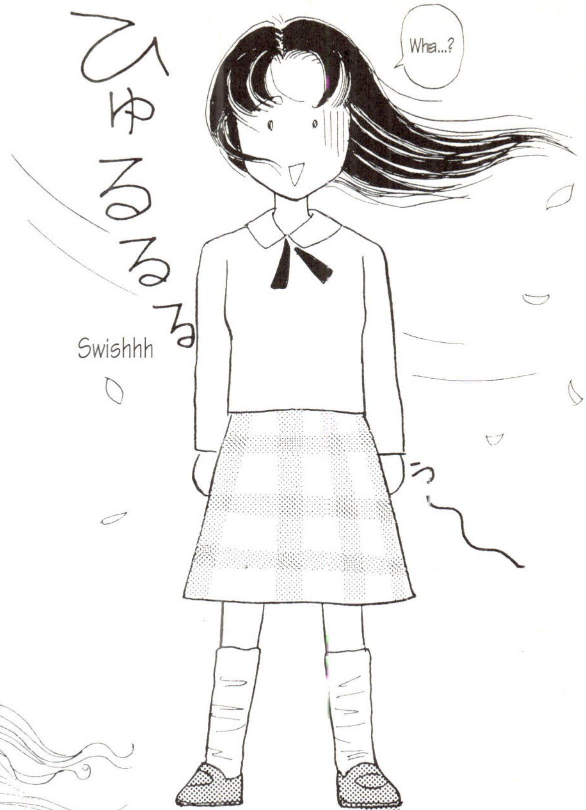

Winter Feeling

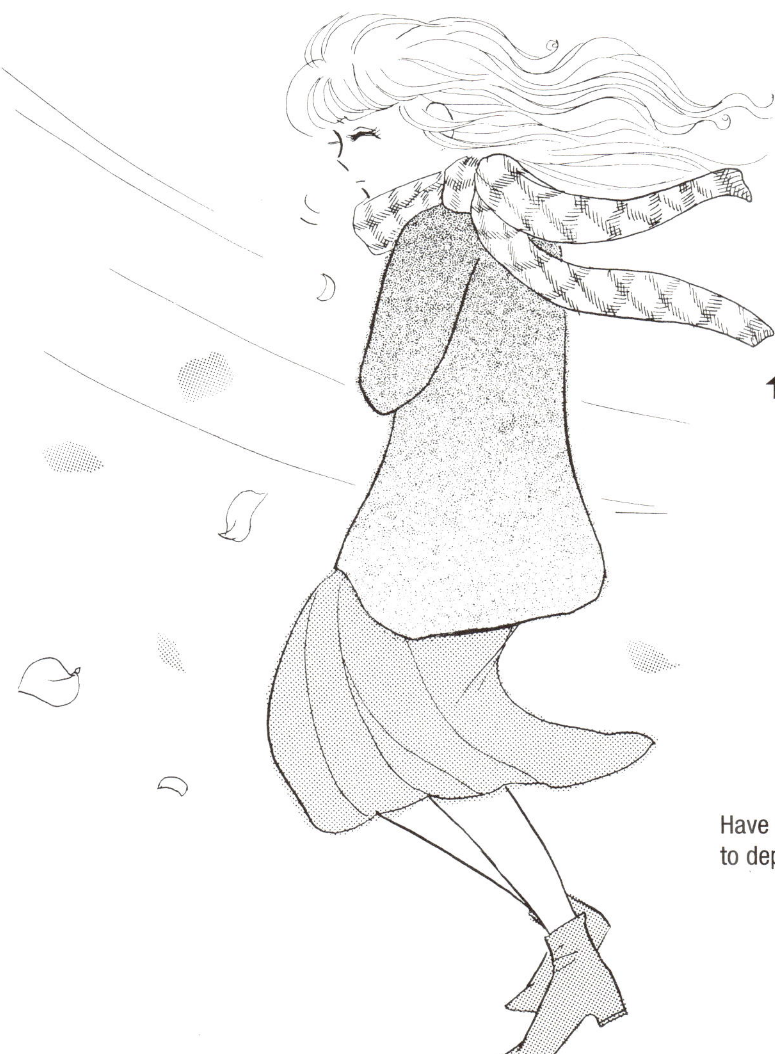

⬆ Make sure it does not look unnatural.

Have the character hunch over to depict the cold.

Effect Lines 1 How to Draw Mesh

We will present several effect lines that are used often in girls' comics. Some are drawn freehand and some are drawn with a ruler.

Tools Required

Pen holder for Round-pen nib

Round-pen nib

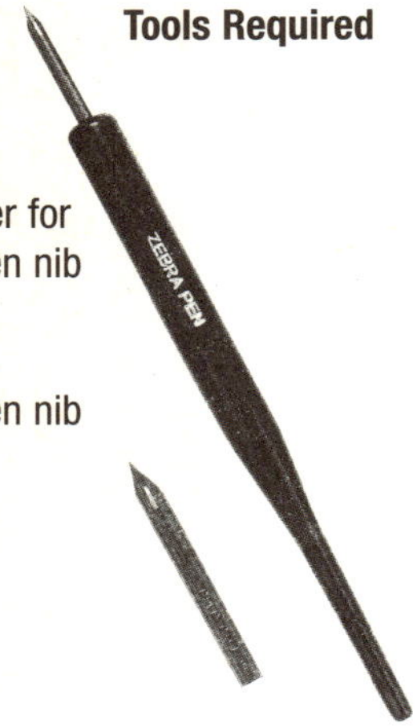

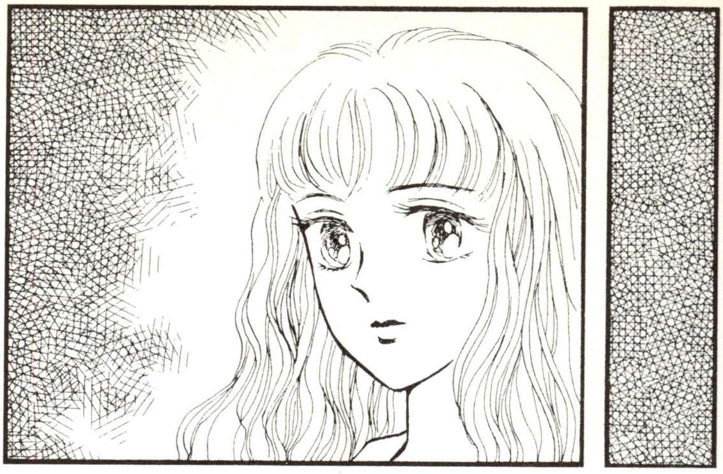

• **Triple Mesh**

How to Draw the Double Mesh

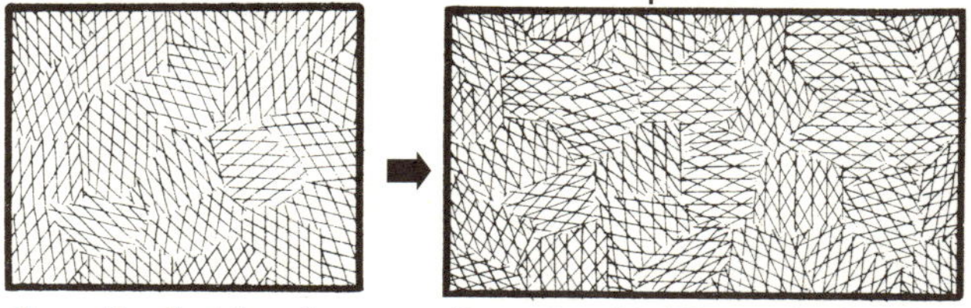

Draw the first two lines at a slight angle (so they look like diamonds) when you are going to draw triple mesh.

Completed Mesh

Draw the third lines, altering the direction from those of the first two lines.

• **Single Mesh**

Good Example

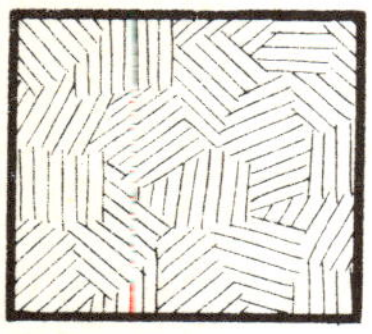

The lines should be parallel and an equal distance apart. The thickness of the lines should also be the same.

Poor Example

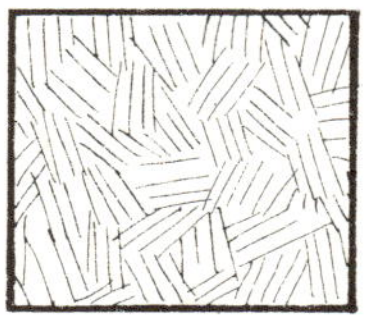

When you stagger the direction of the lines, make sure the directions are different, but do not forget to make the lines uniform.

• **Quadruple Mesh**

How to Draw the Double Mesh

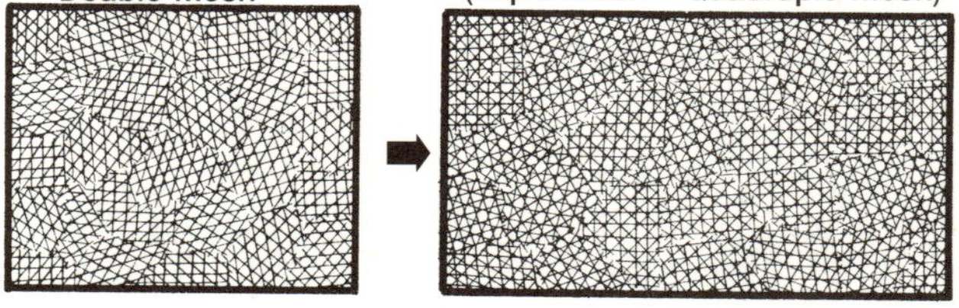

Draw lines at a 45-degree angle to the double mesh lines.

Completed Mesh (Triple Mesh→Quadruple Mesh)

Draw lines at a 45-degree angle to the triple mesh lines.

It should look like grains of rice!

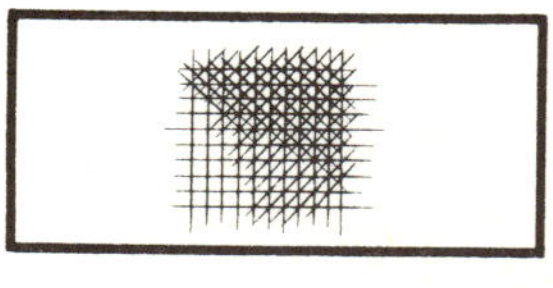

• **Double Mesh**

Good Example

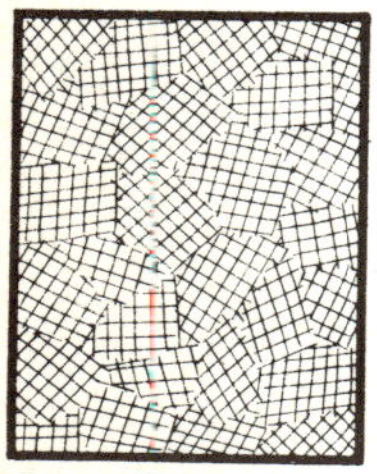

Draw lines at a 90-degree angle to the single mesh lines.

Poor Example

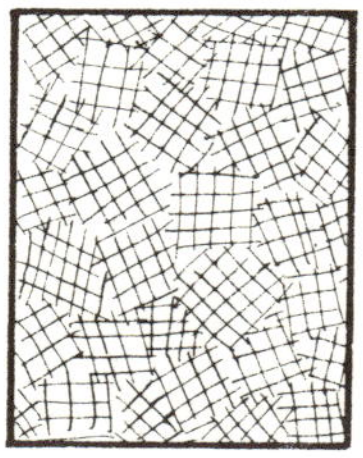

Draw so that you end up with regular squares.

• Using Solid Black and Blurring
Blur by going from solid black to a fine mesh and gradually to a coarse mesh. It is best to apply the solid black last.

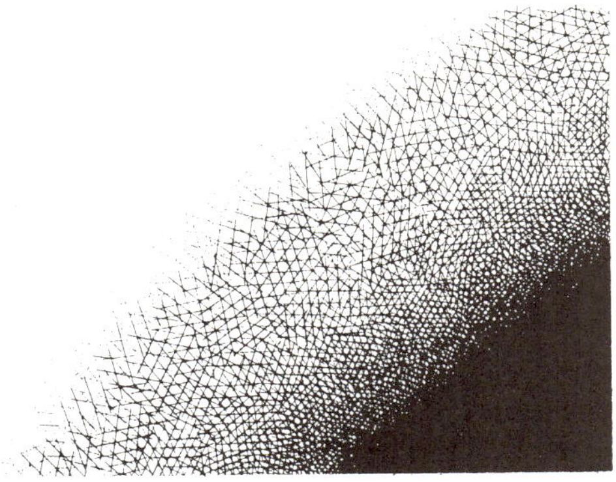

• Blurring Using Gradation
Blur by gradually going from a fine mesh to a coarse mesh.

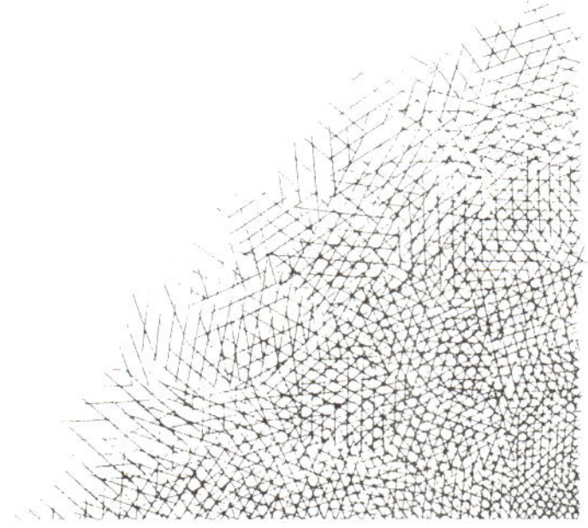

• Blurring Just the Edge of Mesh
Blur just the last mesh part of the mesh being done. You can also do it by whiting out lines with correction fluid. In this case, you should white it out as if you were drawing mesh with correction fluid.

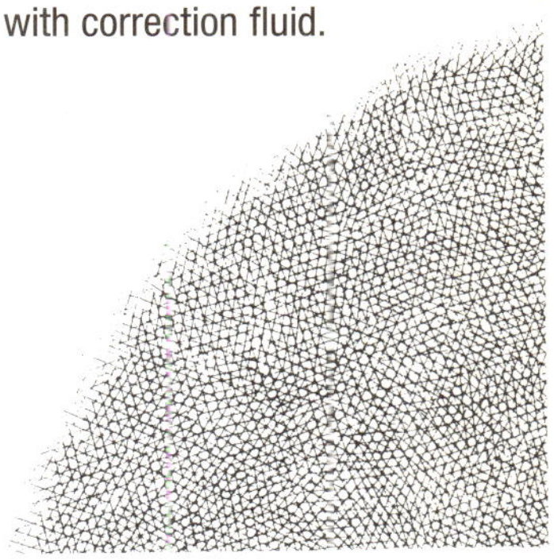

• Random Mesh

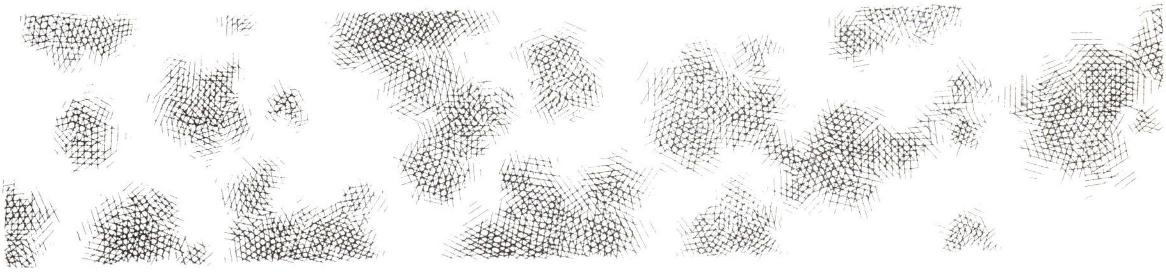

You can blur the mesh by gradually staggering each line. You can also make it irregular by varying the tone (tone is the same in this example).

Bad Example

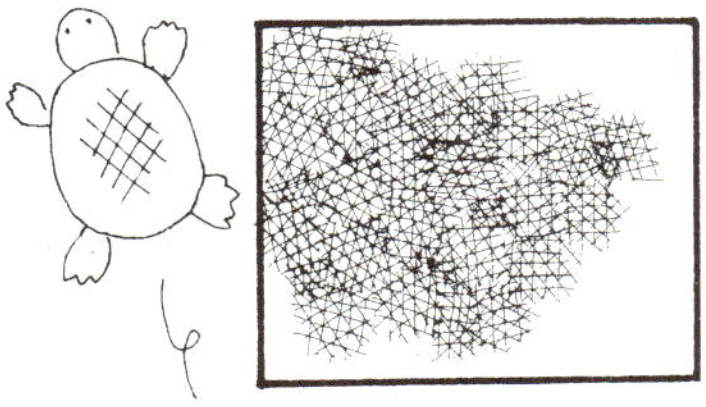

Beware that it will end up looking like the shell of a turtle as you add one block of mesh to another!

Trick to Making Mesh Look Good

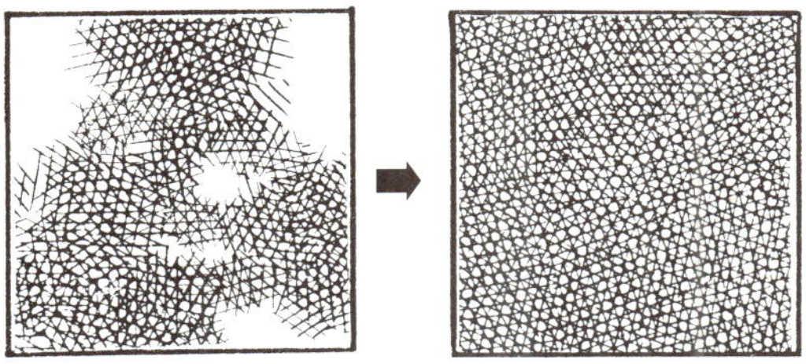

In this kind of situation, you should fill in the gaps between squares later.

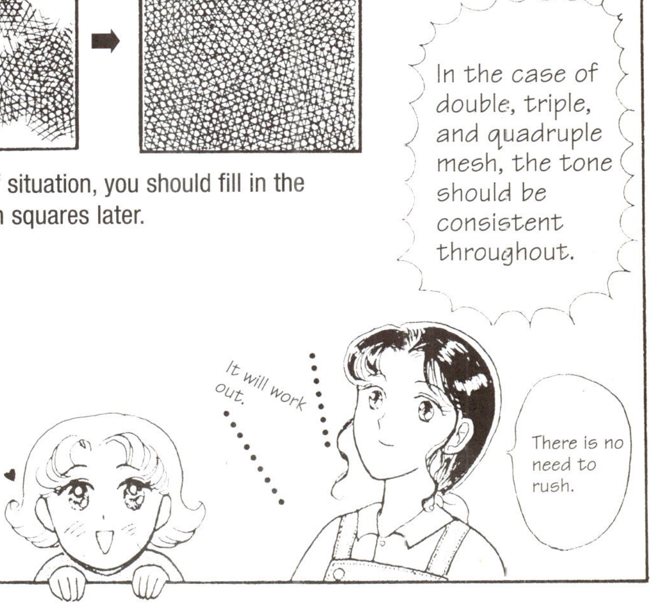

Effect Lines 2 How to Draw Rope

This effect emphasizes anxiety. It is drawn freehand.

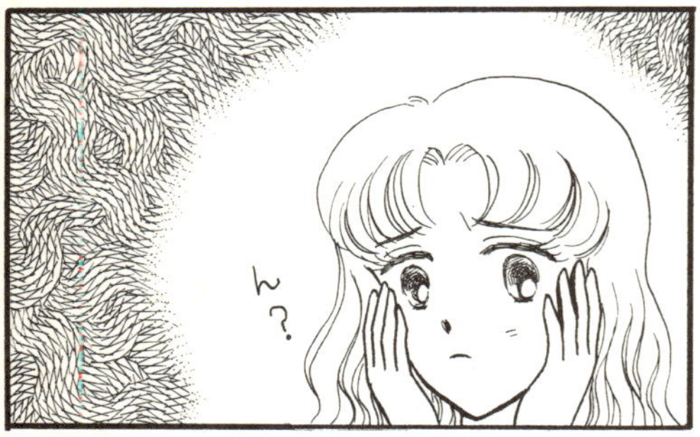

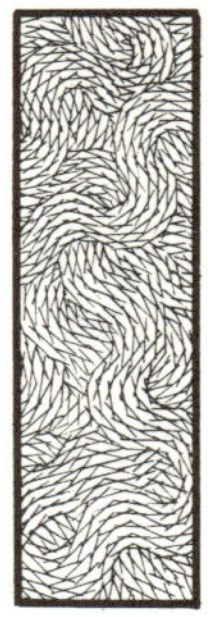

Make the lines the same thickness and as parallel as possible.

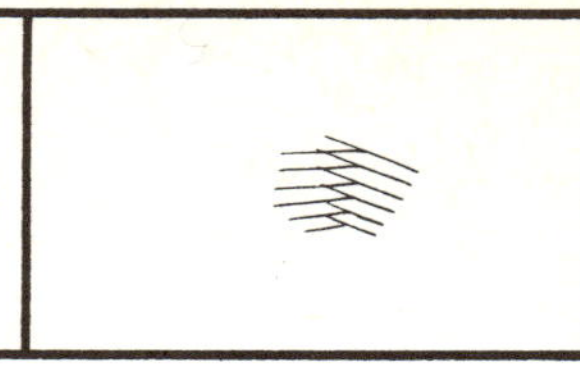

Draw by staggering lines lightly at an angle less than 45 degrees.

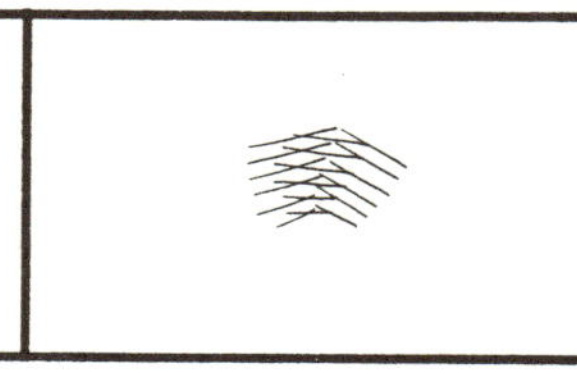

You are free to choose the flow of the rope pattern.

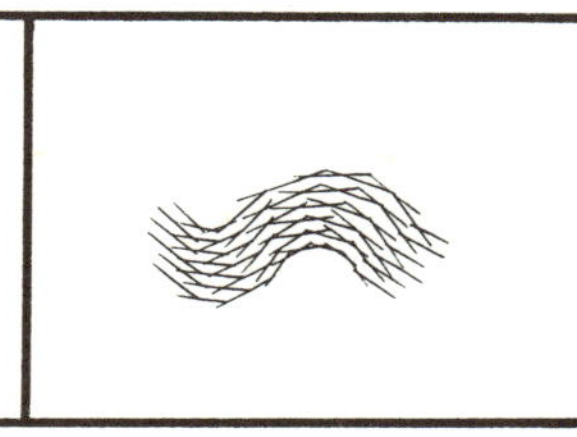

It will look nice if the tone matches throughout.

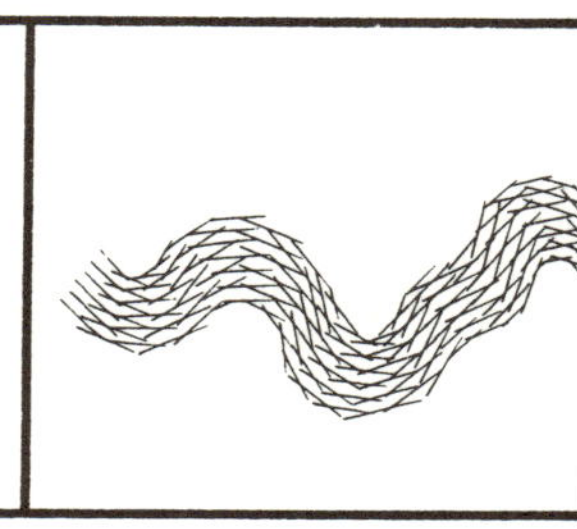

• **Gradation from Solid Black to Rope**

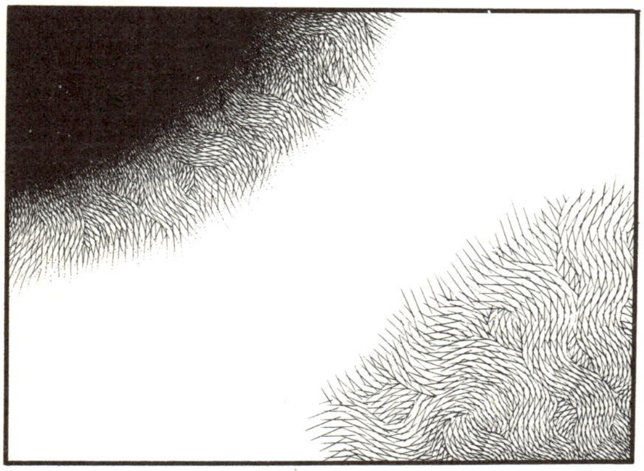

Use of rope. Gradually make it lighter by widening the gap between lines.

• **Irregular Ropee**

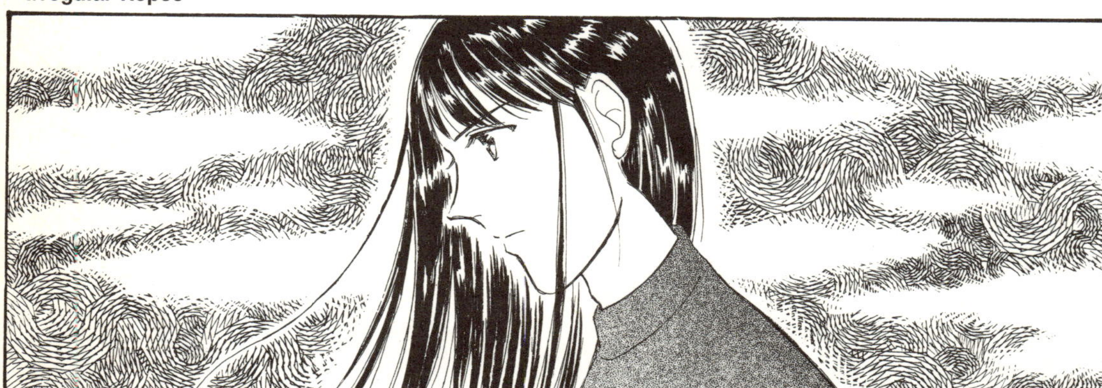

Draw irregular rope by mixing dark and light tones. Make sure that the color does not become solid black due to the gaps between lines being too fine.

Effect Lines 3 How to Draw Parallel Lines and Flashes (Converging Lines)

When drawing lines, any hesitation will immediately be reflected in the lines, so have confidence and relax when drawing lines. The key to drawing clean lines is to grow accustomed to using pens and to grasp the technique in your own way.

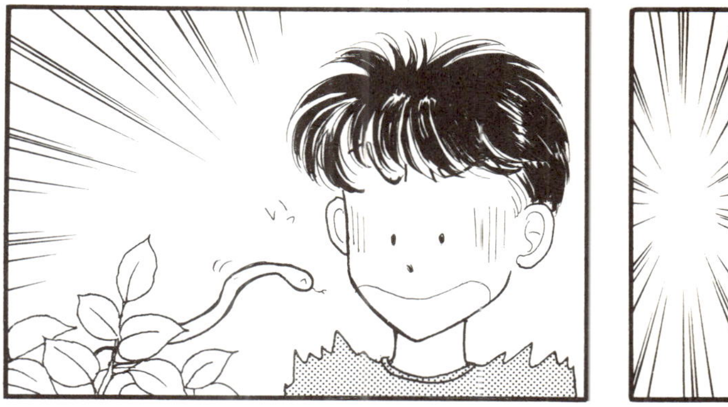

Draw using a ruler and a Round-pen!

• Solid Black Flashes
These are drawn in the same manner as flashes, but you should draw the lines in a swift motion in the direction of the center point, using as a guide an outline that is drawn first (the lines may deviate slightly from the outline). The flash will be complete once you paint the outer area solid black.

• Flashes (Converging Lines)
Draw a dot in the place where you want lines to converge and draw lines in the direction of the dot (draw in the same manner as when drawing parallel lines), moving the ruler a little bit at a time. If you are having a hard time keeping the lines going in the direction of the dot, you should poke a tack into the dot and draw with the ruler up against the tack. Patch up the hole with correction fluid.

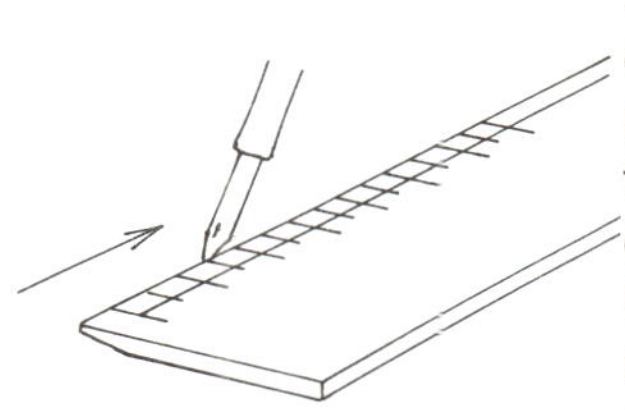

• Parallel Lines
Using a ruler with an edge and a Round-pen, draw a line from left to right (right to left for lefties) in a swift motion, tilting the pen slightly in the direction you are drawing.

Outline

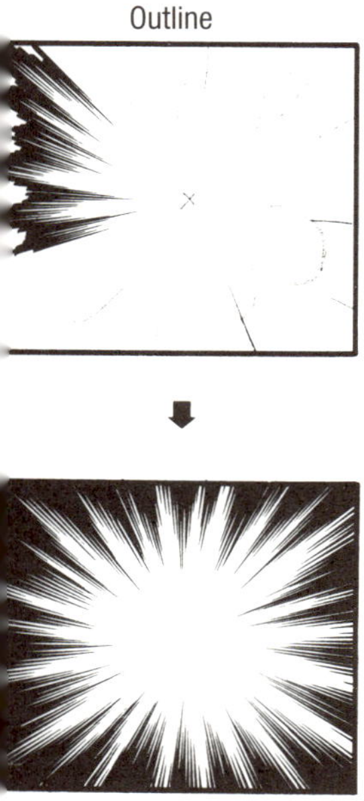

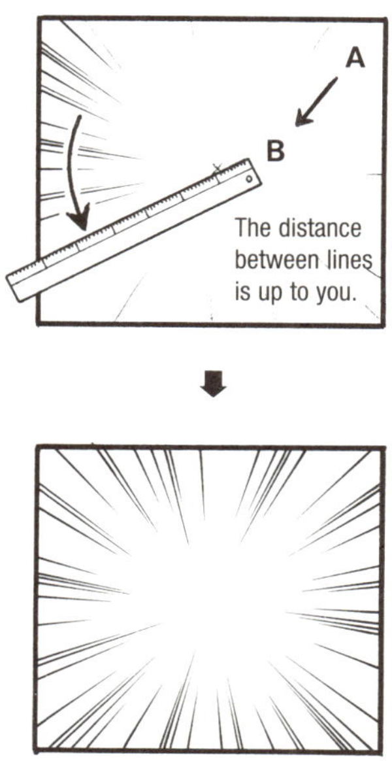

Relax at 1 and draw lines that appear to disappear naturally at 2.

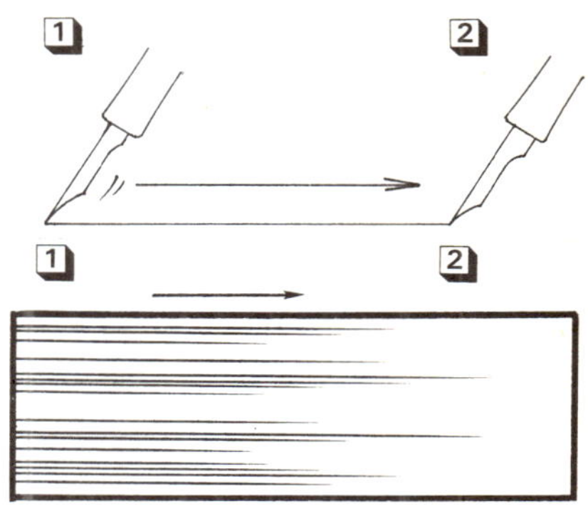

When you use a drafting pen or ink pen, always turn the ruler upside down (wipe any ink off the ruler often).

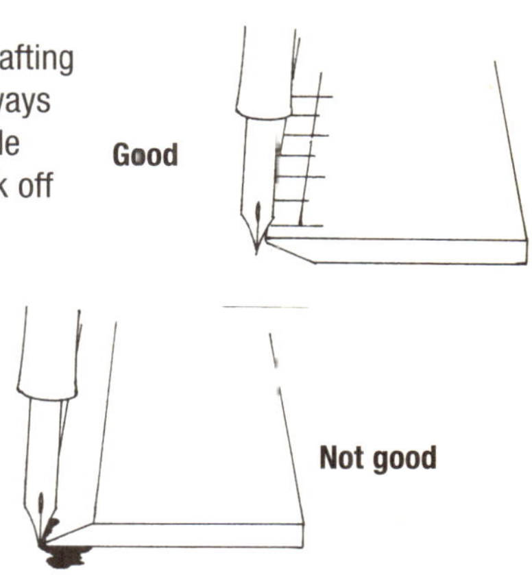

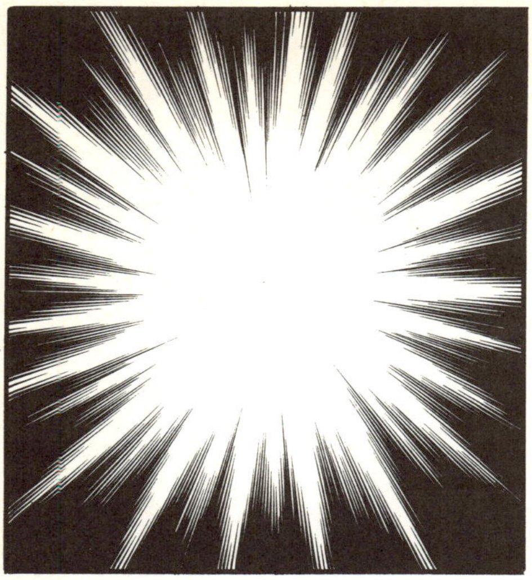

Solid Black Flash

Metamorphic Dialogue Balloon Using Flash

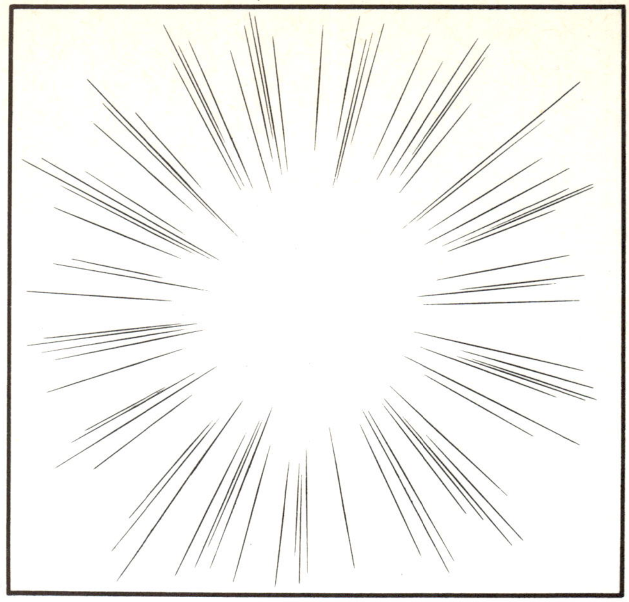

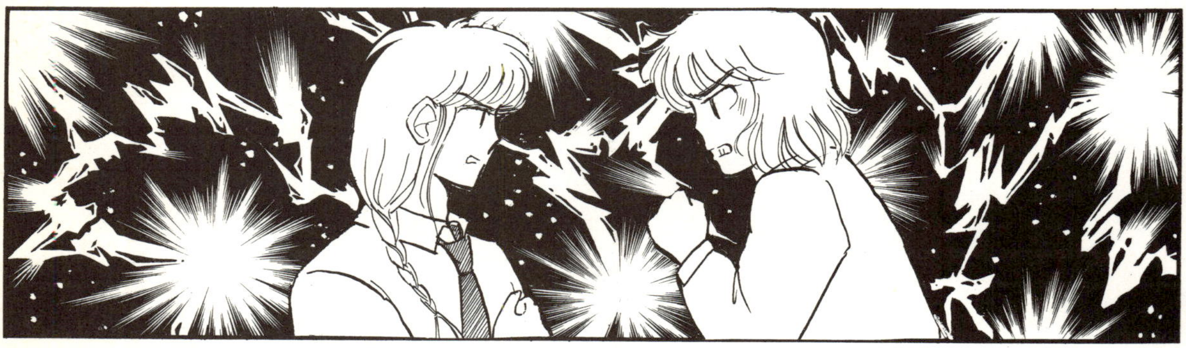

Lightning Flash (Variation of solid black flash. First determine the positions of the flashes and then add the lightning. You can also add them with correction fluid after adding the solid black.)

In the case of tone flashes, you should turn the cutter over when shaving the tone.

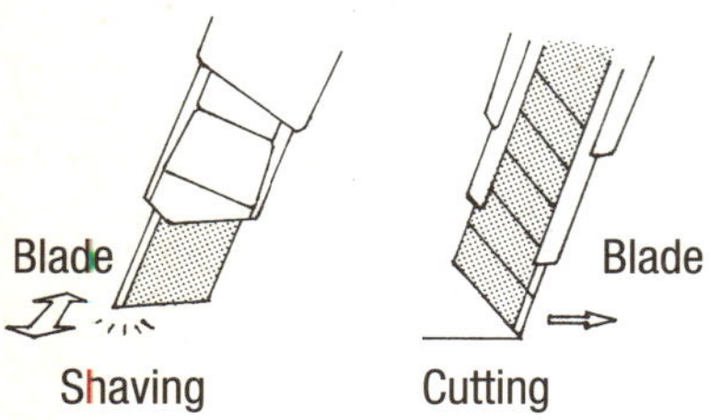

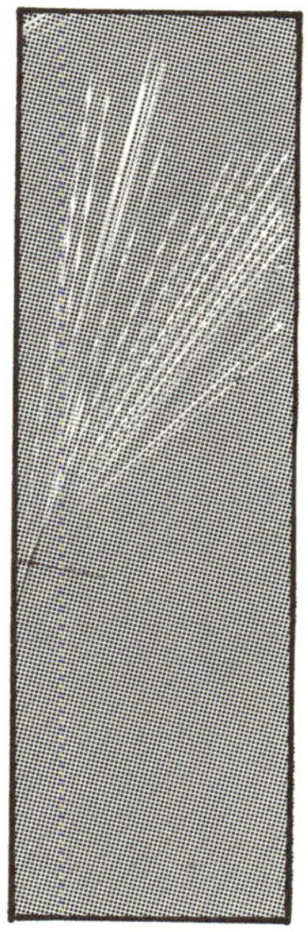

Bad Example

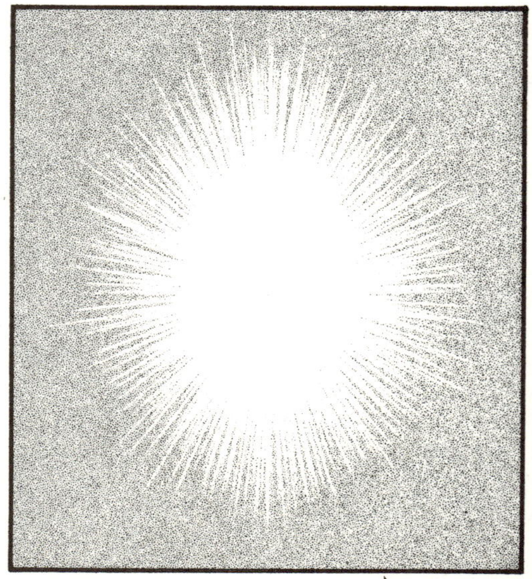

Tone Flash
(Scraped with Cutter)

You can use a stainless steel ruler too.

Effect Lines 4 Others

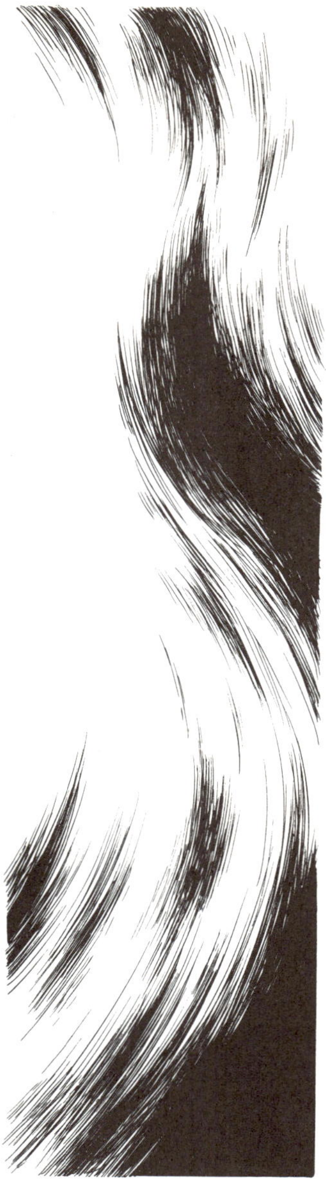

Think about where the solid black parts will be before starting and then draw freehand in swift motions. Apply the solid black last. Then look it over and add the details. Be mindful of the overall rolling flow.

A curved rule was used for this drawing. Make sure the width of the streamlines is not too orderly.

Good Example

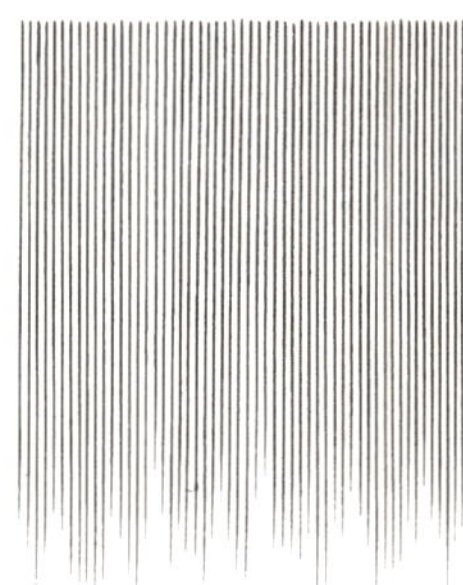

Poor Example

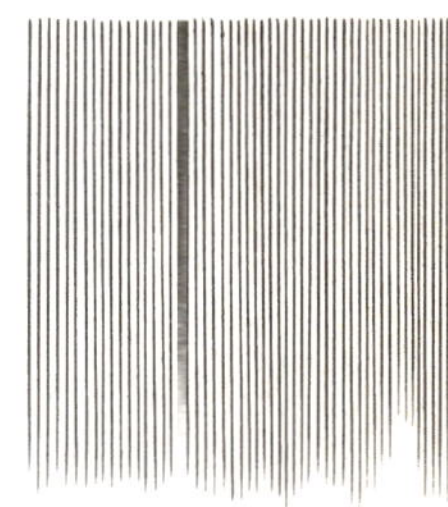

Make the distance between lines uniform. If you try too hard to align the ends of the line they will not fade cleanly. Have them fade in a natural manner.

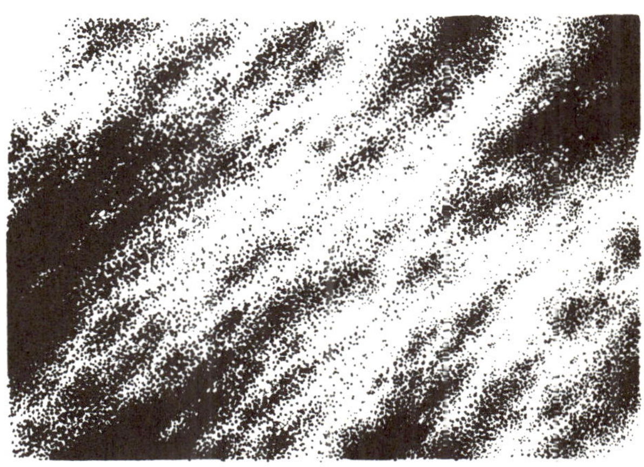

This effect was created using fine-tip pens (0.8, 0.3, 0.1, and 0.05). The solid black portion was determined in advance. We drew dots starting with a thick pen and gradually changing to thinner and thinner pens. The solid black was applied last. You can add correction fluid later if you want.

*See the following page.

Stippling

Stippling is not just a matter of drawing dots. Your pictures will look nicer if you think about rhythm and balance.

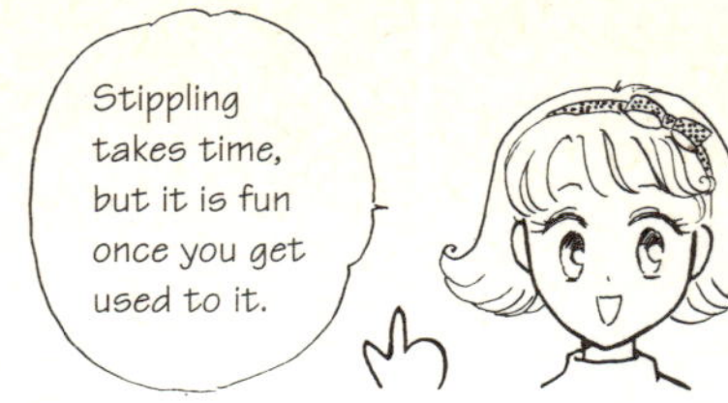

Things to Prepare

Round-pen-It takes a long time, but you can draw a very detailed picture.

Drawing Ink-It dries fast, so you have to wipe the pen tip often.

India Ink-The fluid is smooth, but be careful because it dries slowly.

Drawing Pen (0.05 - 0.1 mm)-You can draw relatively round dots in a uniform manner.

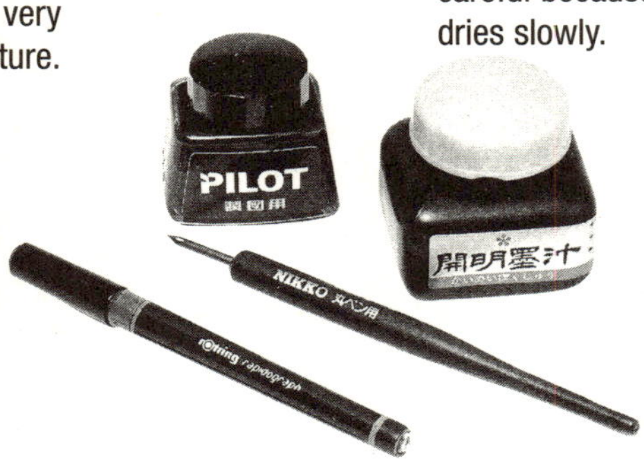

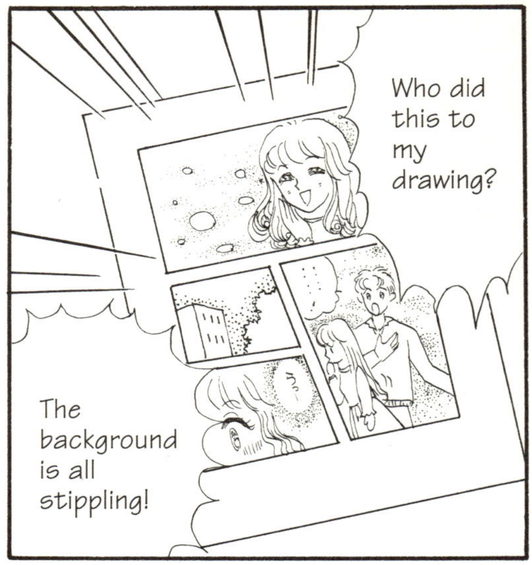

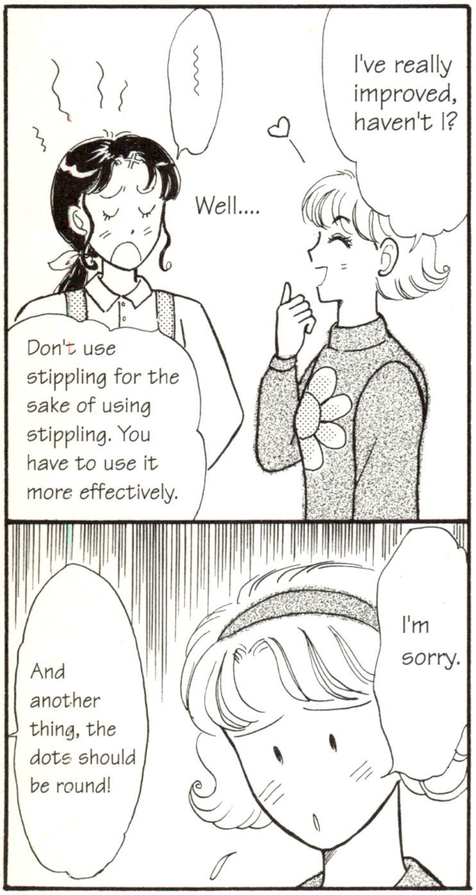

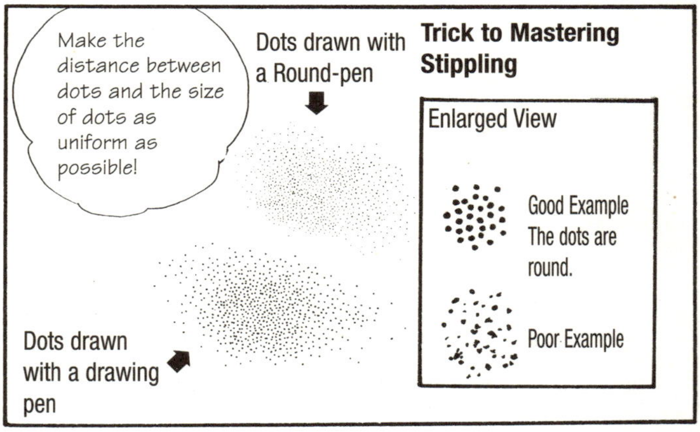

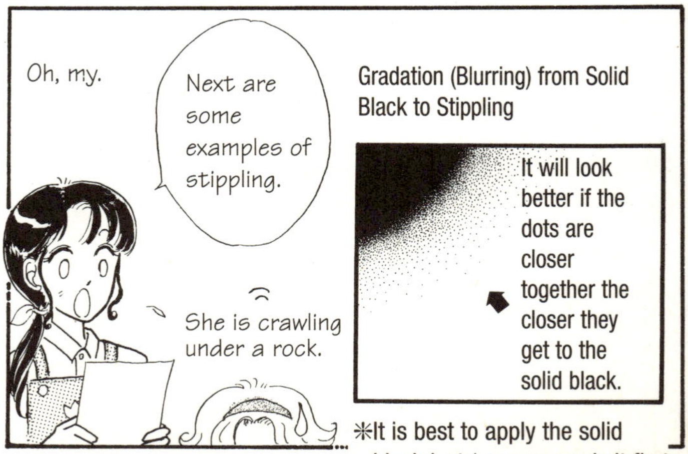

✻It is best to apply the solid black last (you can apply it first if it is on the small side).

Stippling is a special technique that is always used for depicting mental images in girls' comics. Depending on how it is used, it is an effect that creates dreamy, beautiful, and delicate images.

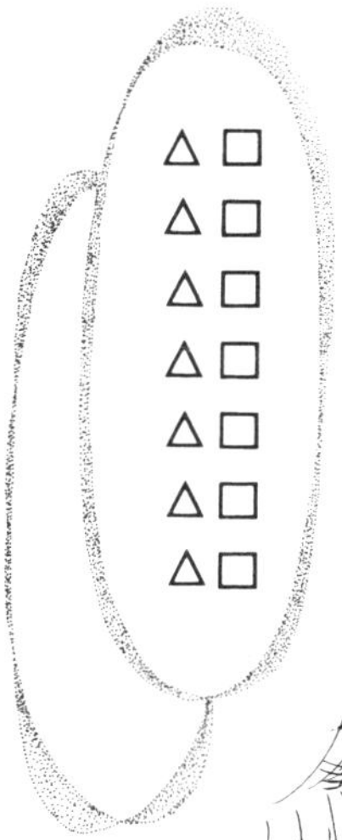

It makes interesting dialogue balloons.

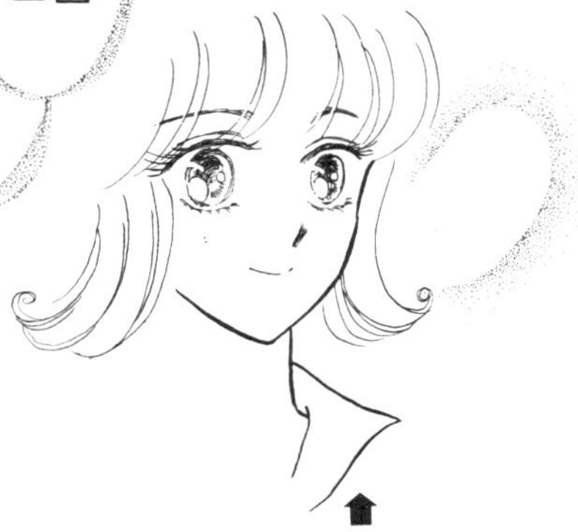

It was used as an accent in this example.

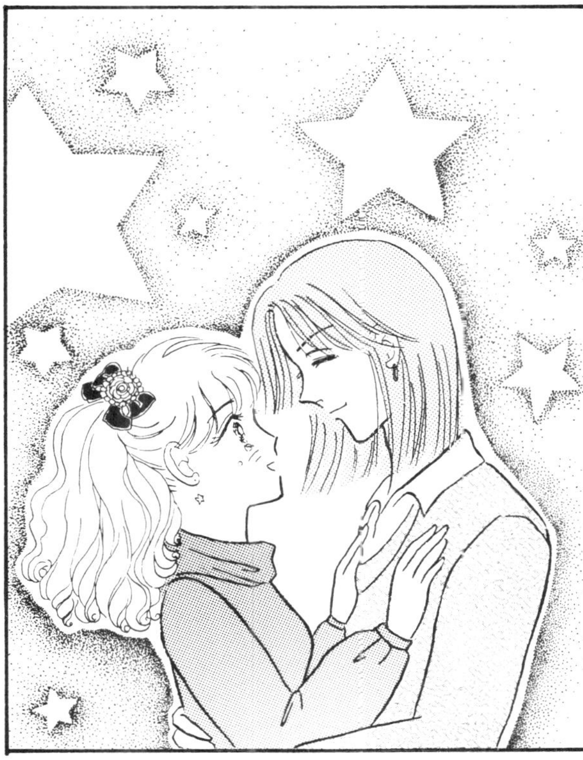

A Round-pen was used.

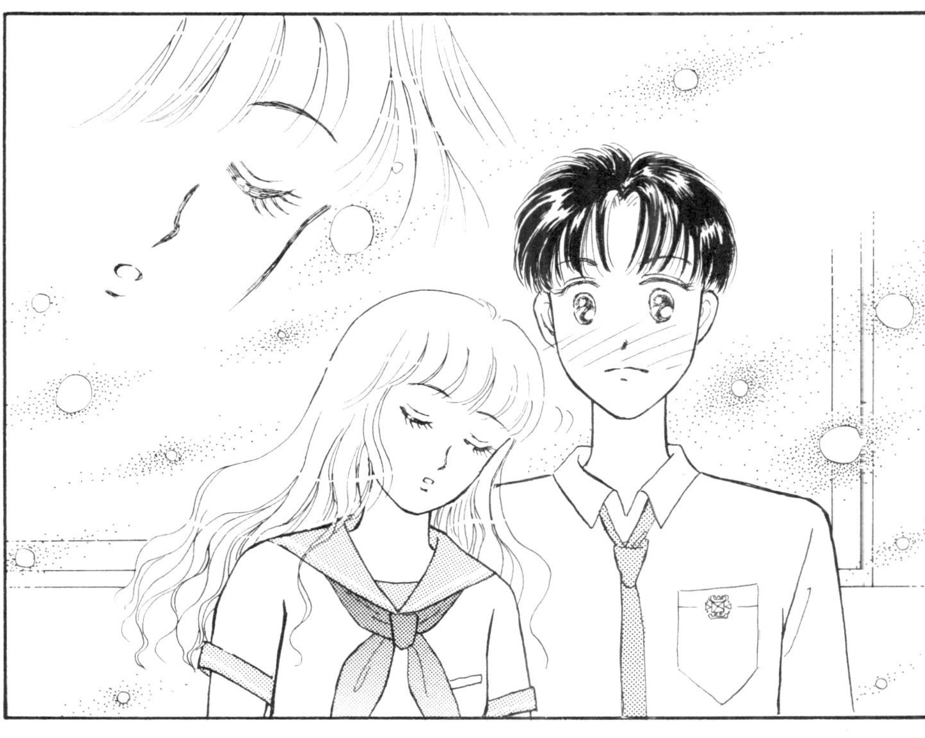

Stippling was used like mist in this example. (A drawing pen was used.)

Solid Black and Whitening

India ink and other types of ink are brushed to create solid black.

Whitening is used when you want to correct something or add a highlight.

Good Example

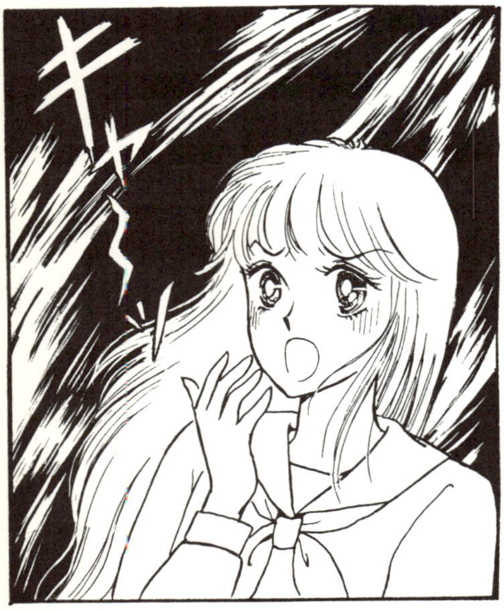

Use correction fluid when the background and drawn letters overlap and are difficult to see.

Irregular black is no good. Apply ink evenly.

Solid black (the white letters are painted over the black with a brush)

Poor Example

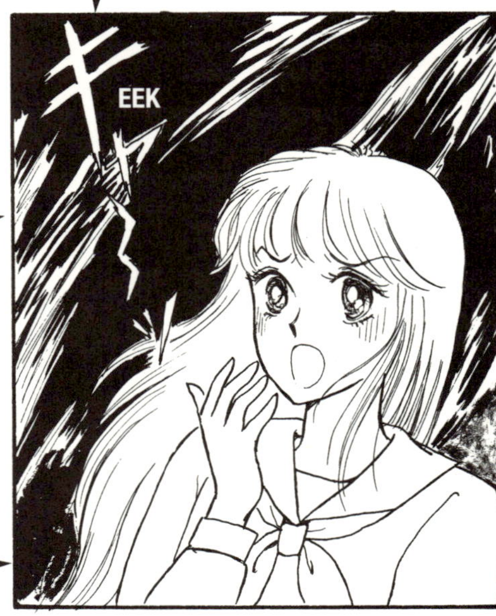

Watch out for parts that you forgot to completely filled in with black.

Use correction fluid for an ink that has spilled over into another area.

Oil on your hands repels ink.

How to Apply Solid Black

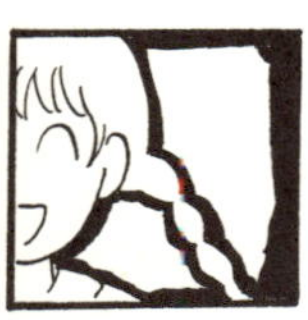

Paint the edges with a thin brush.

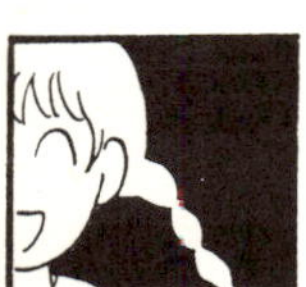

Paint the rest with a thick brush.

When painting solid black, it will look nice if you paint the edges first with a thin brush and then paint with a thick brush.

Precautions Regarding Tools

Do not use old India ink. Use it up quickly, because the ink will settle on the bottom. Correction fluid dries easily, so always replace the cap after use. ➡

Note
Add a little water often and store after mixing well (mix with a glass rod).

Prepare separate brushes for ink and correction fluid (You may think that you have washed the ink brush well, but the ink sometimes mixes in with the correction fluid if you use it for whitening.). ➡

Note
In order to extend the longevity of brushes, wash them well after use.

How Much Water to Add to Correction Fluid

Not good

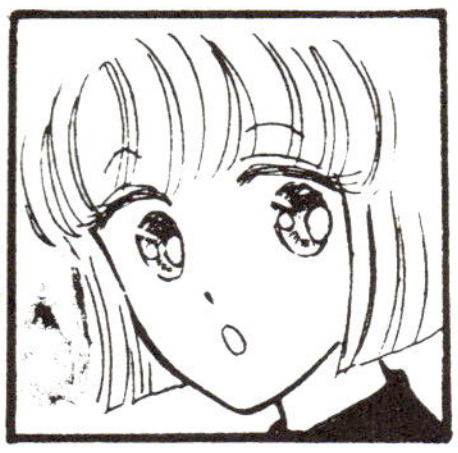

When applying correction fluid, wait until the ink has dried completely first. Wait for each layer to dry before applying correction fluid, because even if the ink is dry, the part of the ink where lines have been penned in will break up and get mixed in if you rub it persistently.

Good

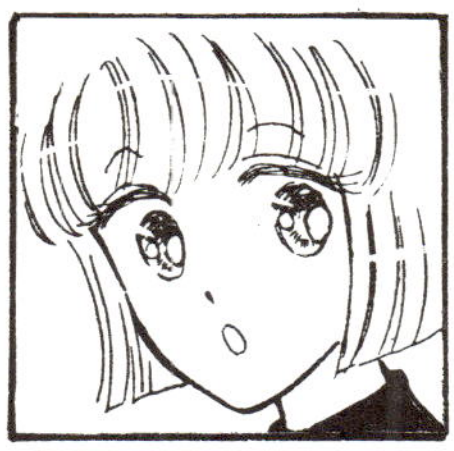

Daub correction fluid on a plate with a brush and thin with water until the part underneath is barely visible.

Not good

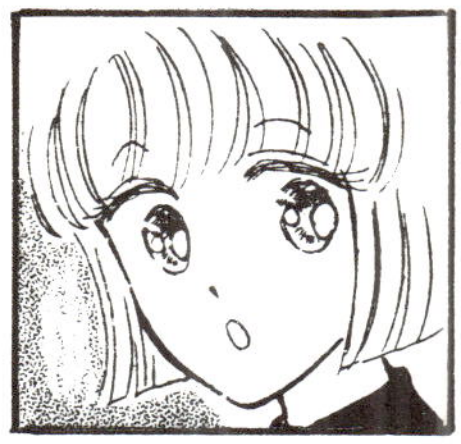

The correction fluid stands out because it is too thick.

Good

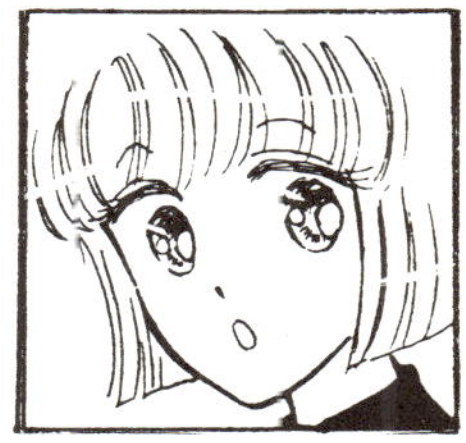

The picture underneath stands out because the correction fluid is too thin.

Materials and Tools for Solid Black and Whitening

Solid Black

Choose an ink to which correction fluid can be applied.

Lettering sol (It dries quickly.)

Kaimei India ink (It is a very smooth liquid that it easy to use.)

Line brushes (thin/thick)

Brush pen

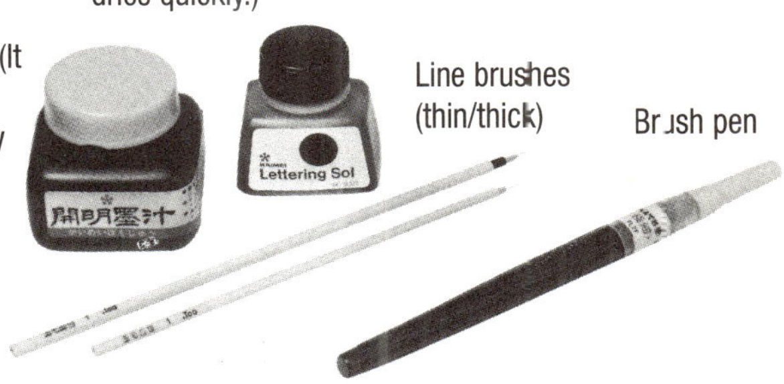

Whitening

Correction ink (It is designed for manga artists, so it is easy to use.)

Glass rod (This is convenient for mixing correction fluid, transferring it to a plate, and kneading it.)

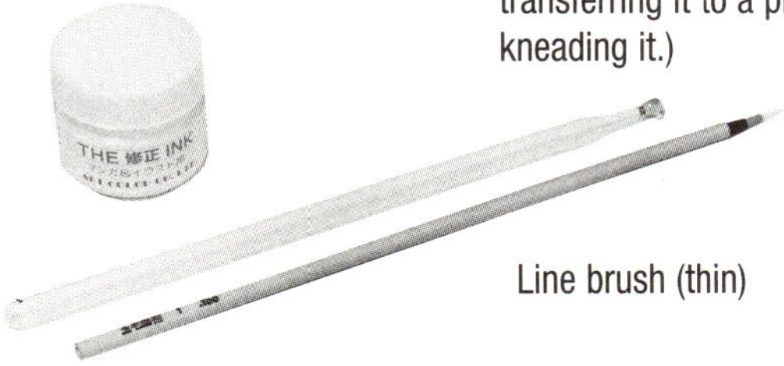

Line brush (thin)

When you apply correction fluid to tone, the tone will repel it if it is applied as is, so rub the surface of the tone with an eraser first.

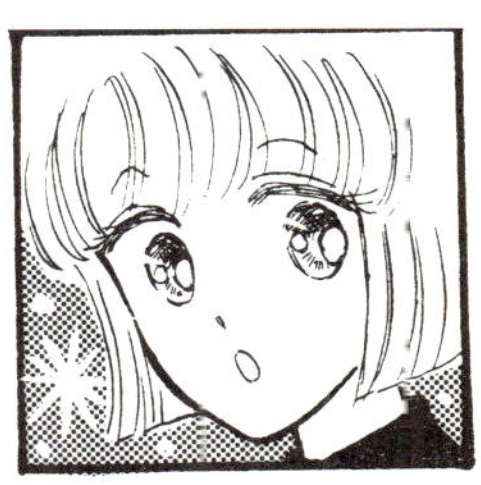

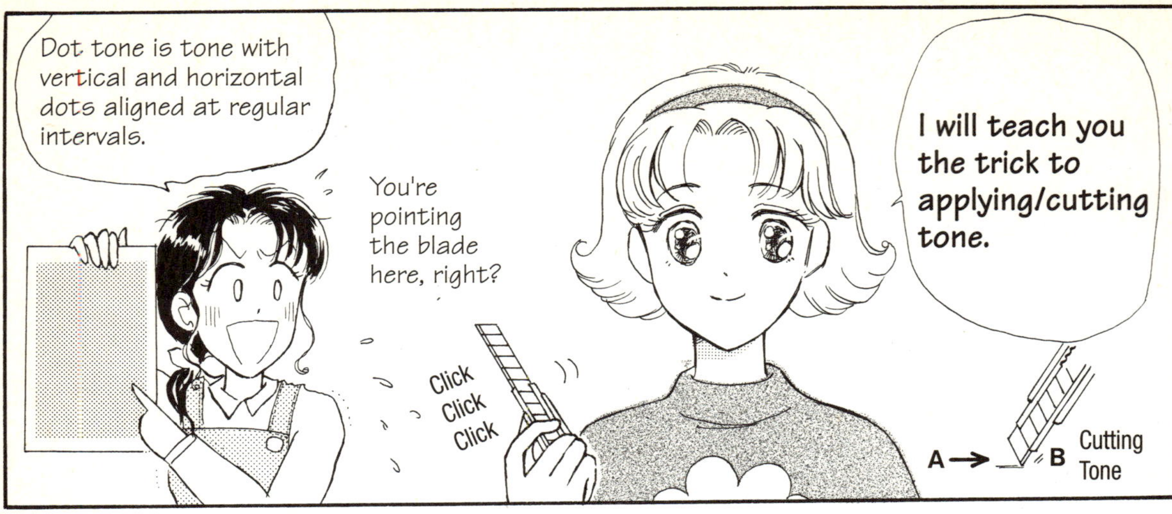

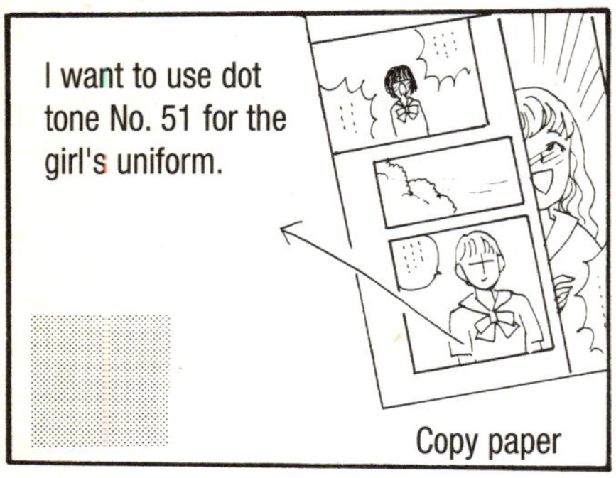

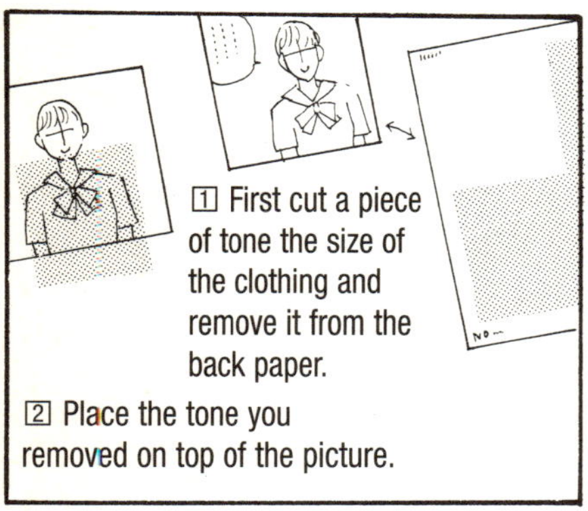

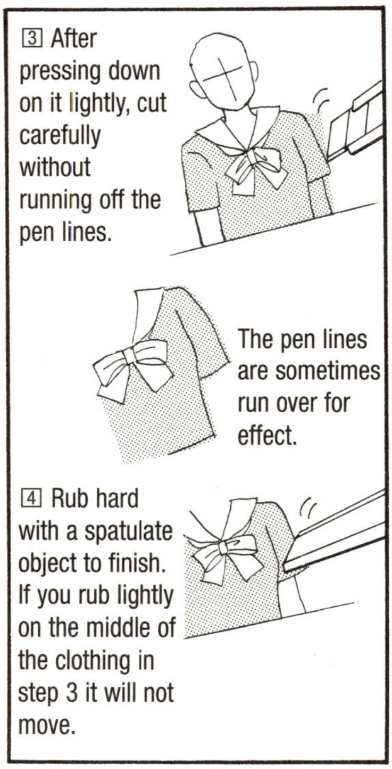

Attention

Do not remove all the tone from the back paper. It will wrinkle and get dirty.

Not good

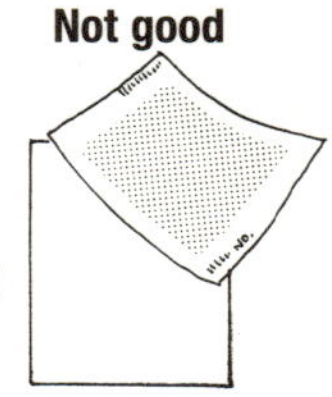

If you accidentally get dirt on the back of the tone...

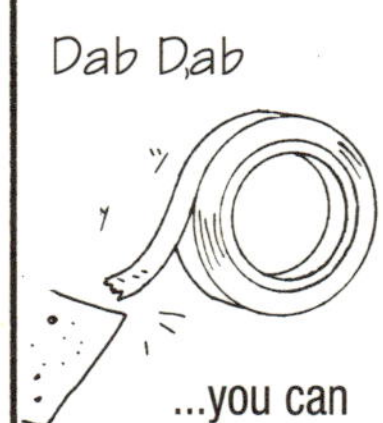

...you can remove it using adhesive tape.

Applying Multiple Layers of Tone

Try using both depending on the artwork and your tastes.

- This is what happens when you overlap two or more sheets of tone at the same angle.

This is called moire.

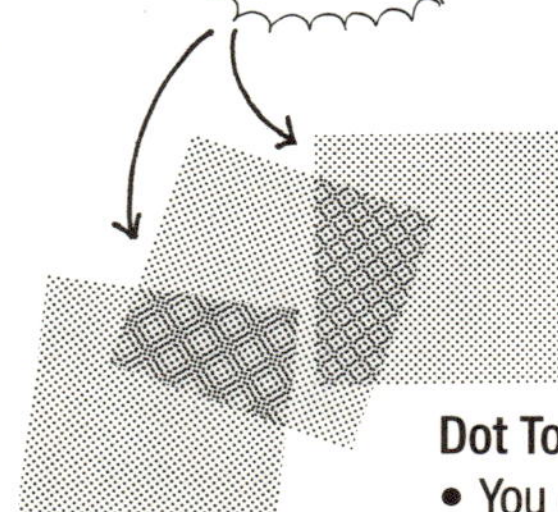

Letra 51

Dot Tones

- You can create interesting effects using the same tone by altering the angle.

Points to Note when Scraping Dot Tone

You can see that the dots are arranged uniformly.

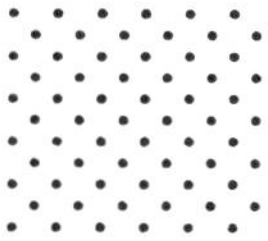

Enlarged View

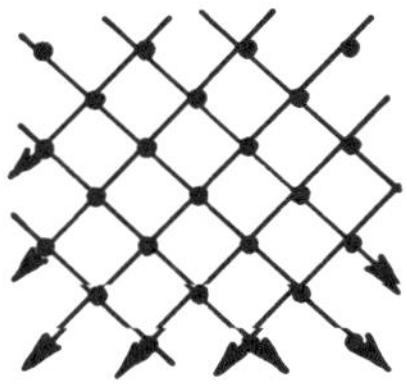

Dots will disappear if you cut horizontally.

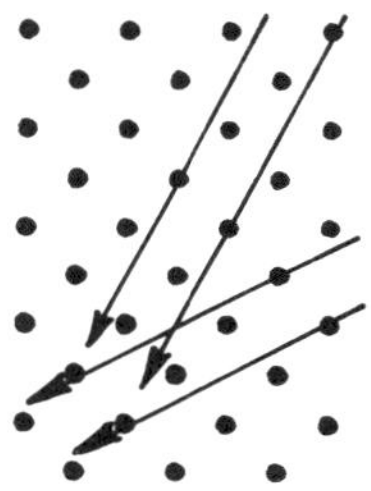

At an angle of 20-30 degrees, cut in this direction while looking closely at the dots (an angle of 45 degrees will be the same as the above figure).

For blurring, cut diagonally just like mesh at about an angle of 20-30 degrees. The mesh gets finer as it nears the white area.

Cut crisscross at about a 30-degree angle. The key is for them all to be in a uniform direction. The crisscross gets finer as it nears the white area.

Guidelines for applying and cutting tone should be drawn with light blue colored pencil directly on the copy paper (will not be seen when printed). Dark blue and other colors may be visible when printed.

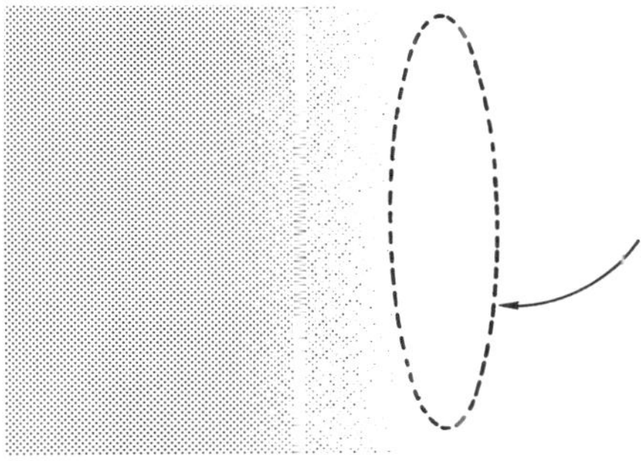

- **Points to Note after Tone Scraping**

The cut surface of this part will be printed, so always apply correction fluid.

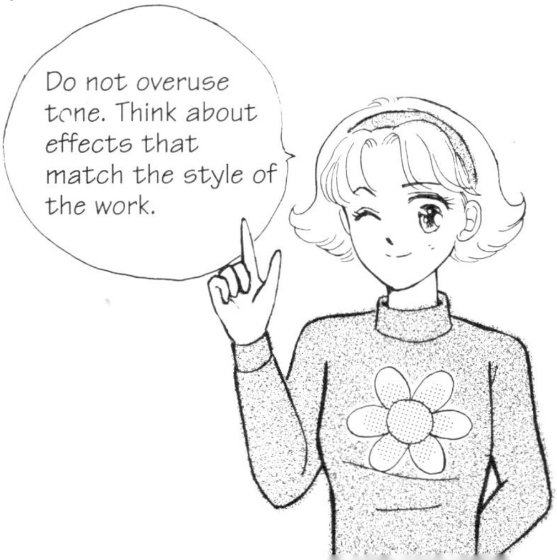

Be careful about pencil lines under tone. They will be seen when printed.

Various Uses of Tone

Here the middle of the cutter blade or the wide back of the blade was used to scrape the tone. First, the general shape was scraped using wide strokes (at this stage there is no need to worry about unevenness). Then, using the back of the blade, it was finely scraped using a kind of hitting and scratching motion. Special attention was paid to the shape of the fluffy clouds.
Letra 61

Clouds

Water Surface

A double layer of tone was used here. As each layer was scraped, we thought about which portion would be thin and which portion would have a double layer. Whitening was done last. We paid special attention to the flow and softness of the water.
Letra 61

Handy Effects and Tone

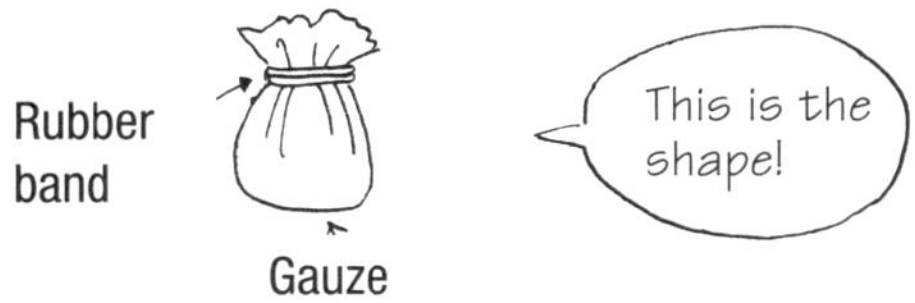

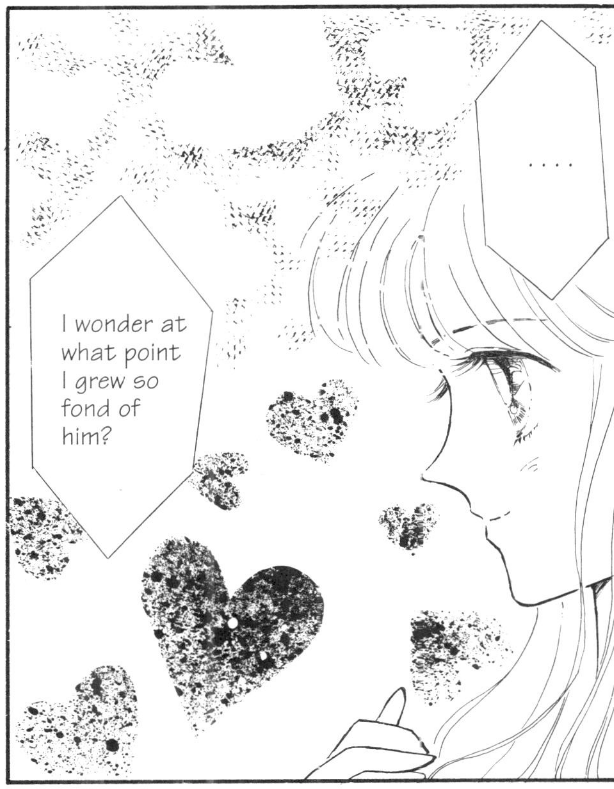

Cut masking film into the shape of a heart and apply. Lightly dab the area around the heart with balled up gauze (put on just a little India ink).

Apply masking film and cut out the shape of a heart. Put a little India ink on a toothbrush, spread it lightly with your finger, and cover with a tissue. Use paper when you have no masking film.

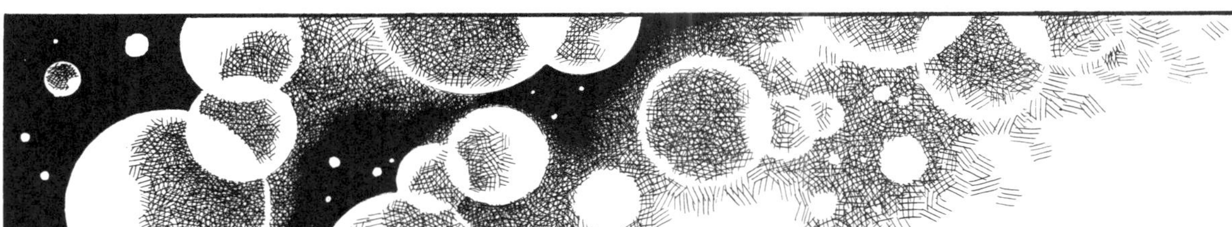

When drawing a rough sketch, use a template or a compass for the circles. Use gradation for the border between mesh and solid black (Note that greater use of solid black will result in a heavier picture.). Add correction fluid last.

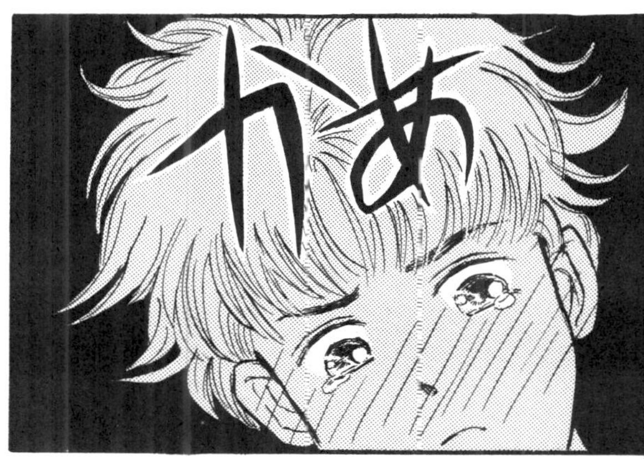

IC 61 and solid black were used. Always apply the solid black first and wait for it to dry completely before applying tone and cutting out the portion around the letters so it is white (together with the letters).

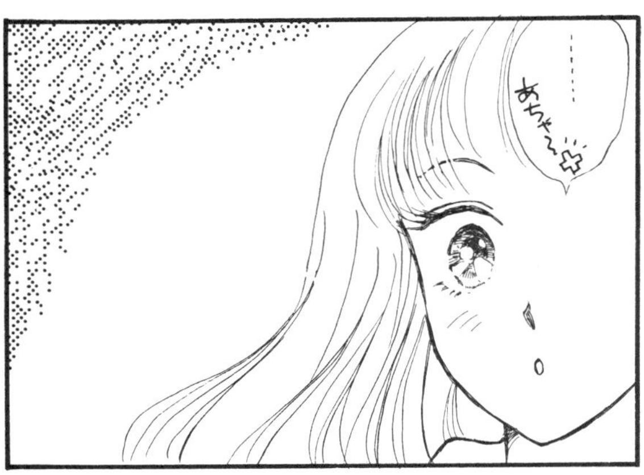

Letraset, Instantex Midi 34
It transfers to the spot of your choice when rubbed. Use it effectively.

Effect of Light and Shade

Light and shade are always together and inseparable. How effectively they are used in a girls' comic depends on the drawing style and the work.

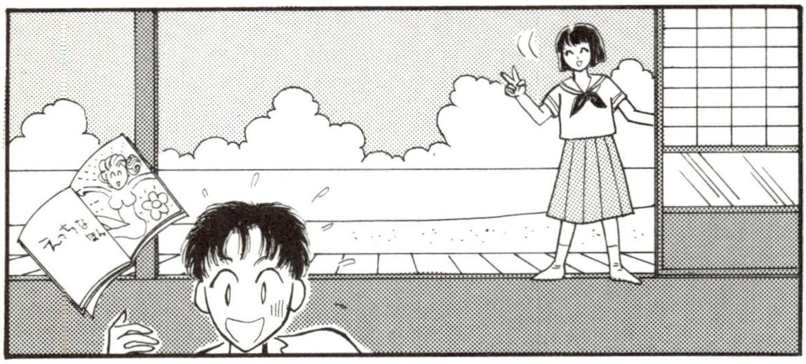

Make the inside darker when you want to make the outside look bright.

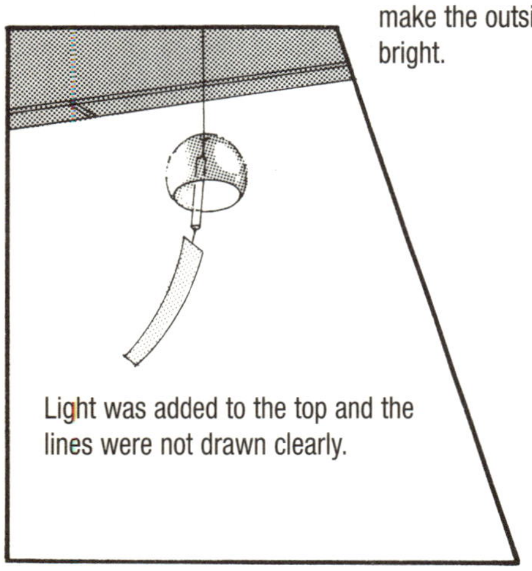

Light was added to the top and the lines were not drawn clearly.

Put tone for shade over the tone of the clothing.

There is shading under the chin.

In this case, light is shining down from the upper left.

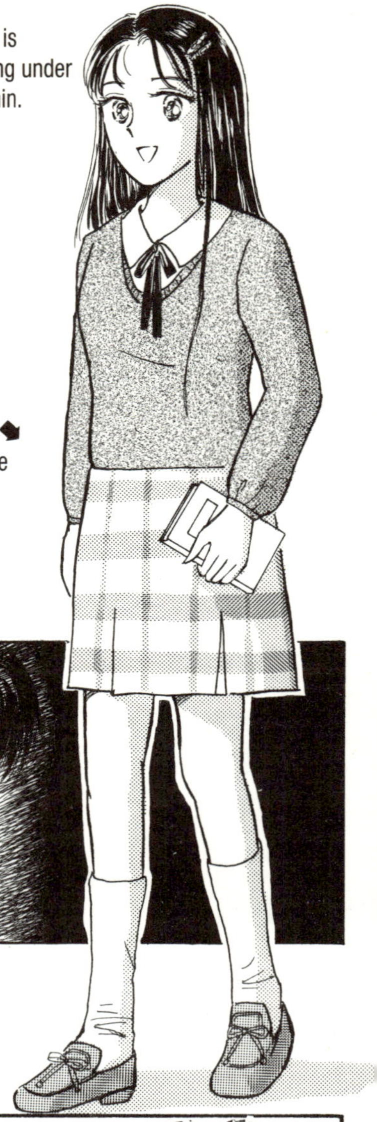

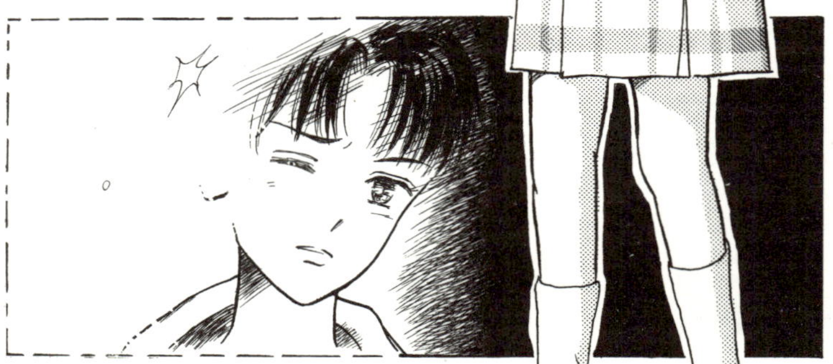

Here the borderline was broken up minutely. Solid black for the background makes it look brighter in comparison.

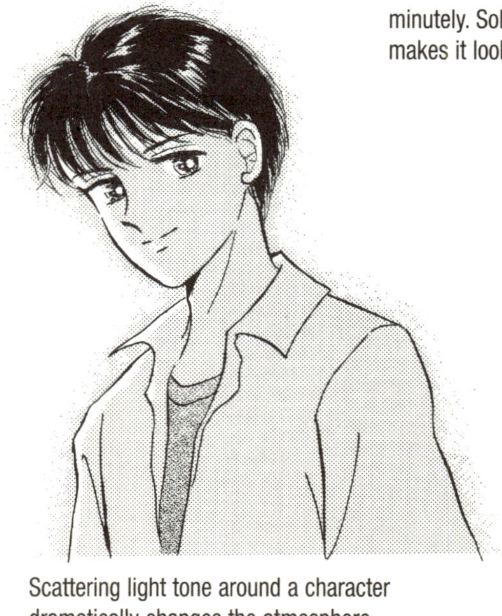

Scattering light tone around a character dramatically changes the atmosphere.

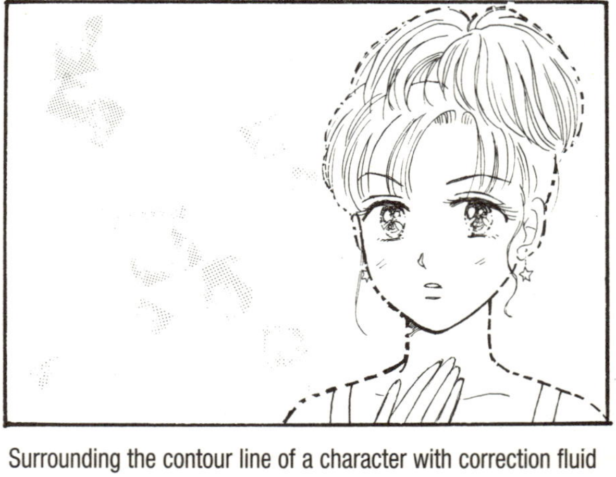

Surrounding the contour line of a character with correction fluid creates the sensation of light.

Flowers

Flowers make a work more cheerful and colorful. Make them fluffy or scatter the petals, whatever matches the image of the work.

Marguerites

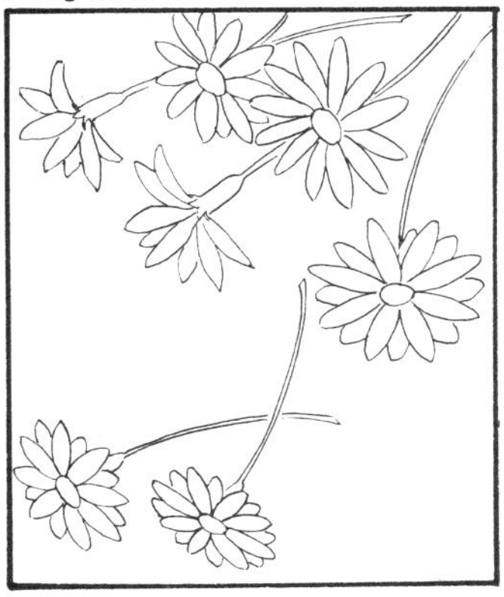

Roses

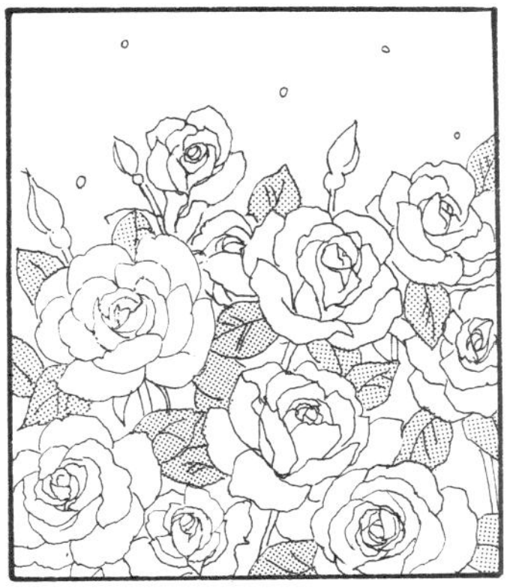

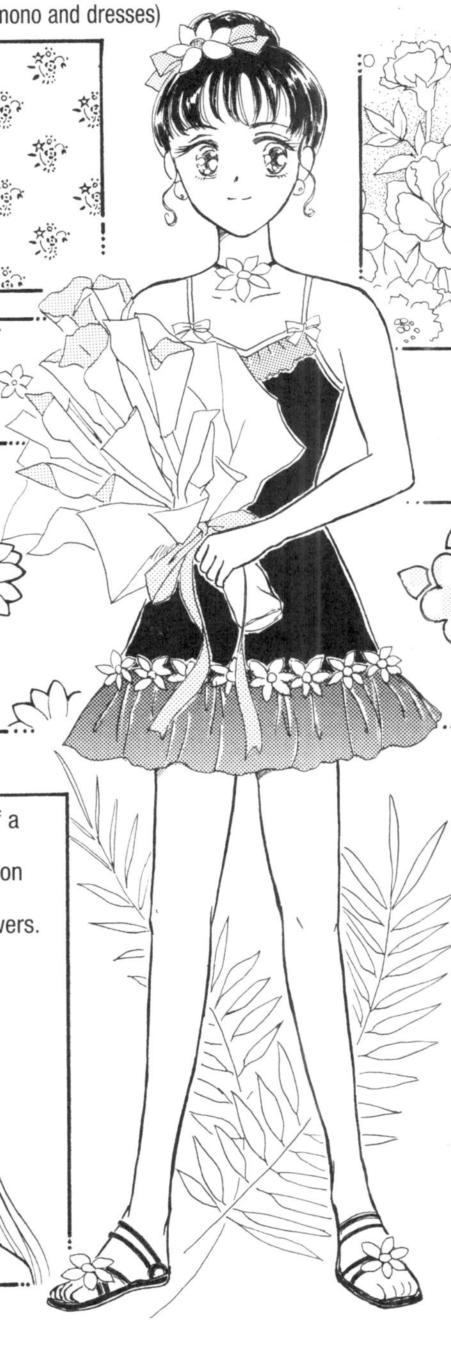

Flower patterns (fine ones can be used for kimono and dresses)

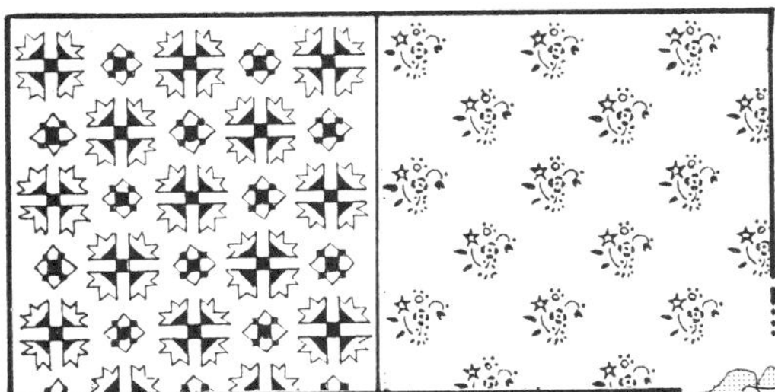

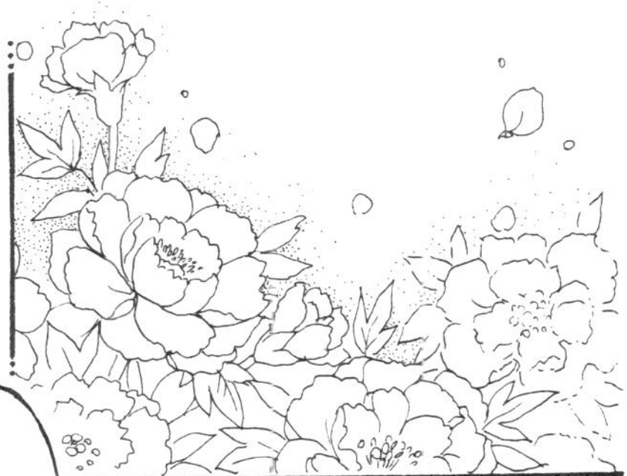

Peonies

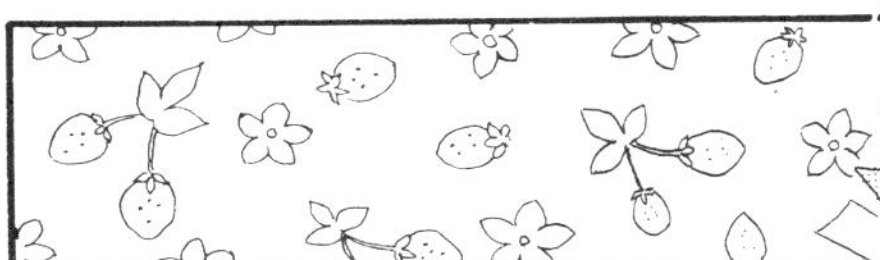

They can be combined with fruits.

Flowers with tone
IC S-679

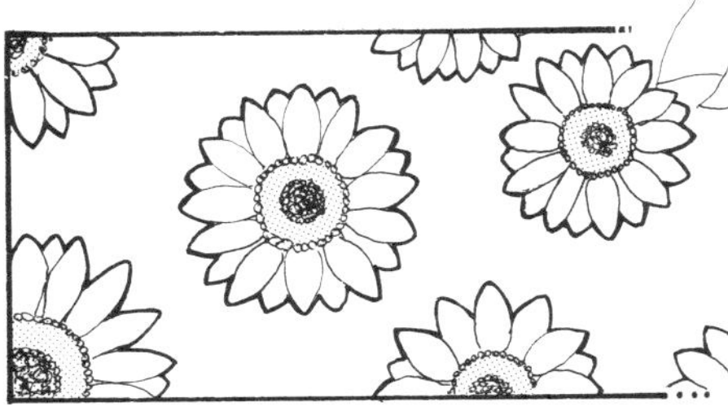

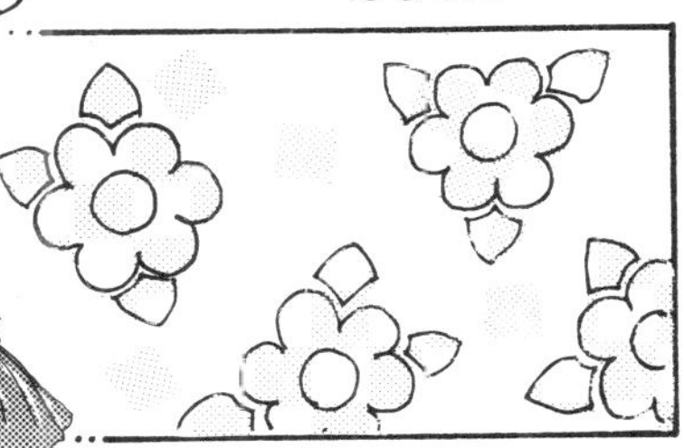

Flowers depicted in a comical way.

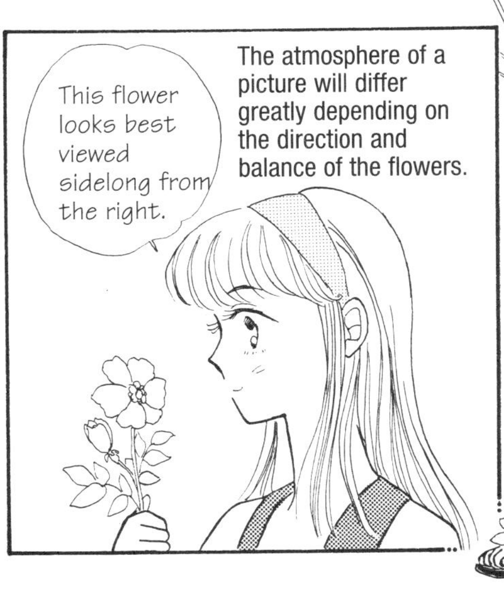

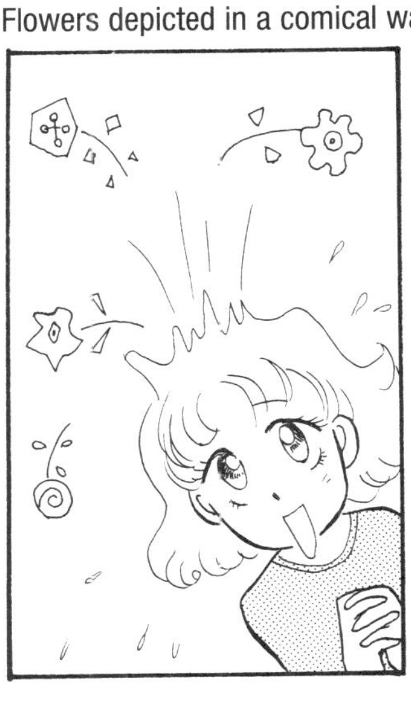

Chapter 3 How to Create Stories

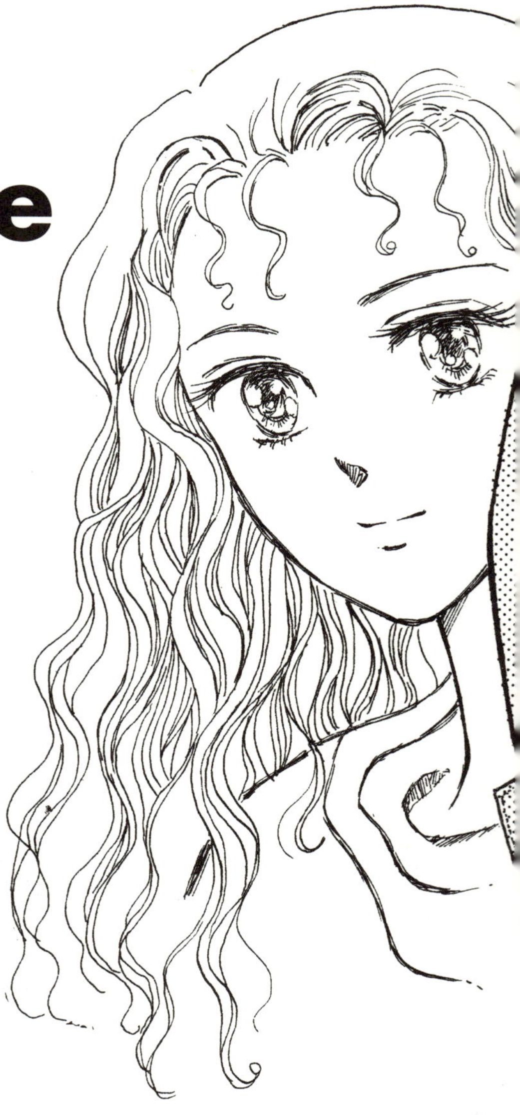

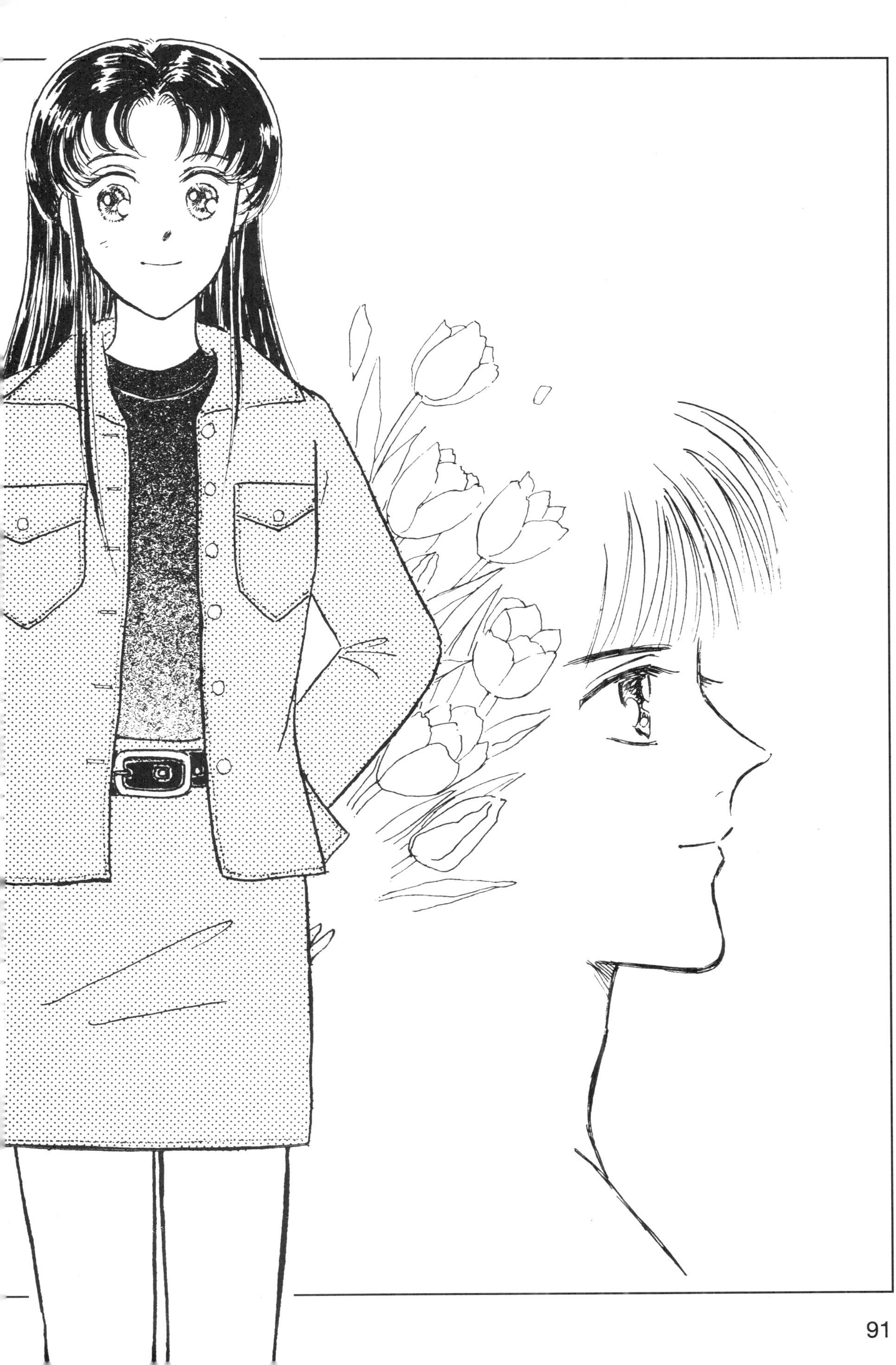

Begin with something you are interested in!

You can start with any of the five below.

Dream worlds are possible in the world of girls' comics. What kind of world exists in your mind? If you have just one thing you want to draw, try making your dream come true on paper.

1 Characters

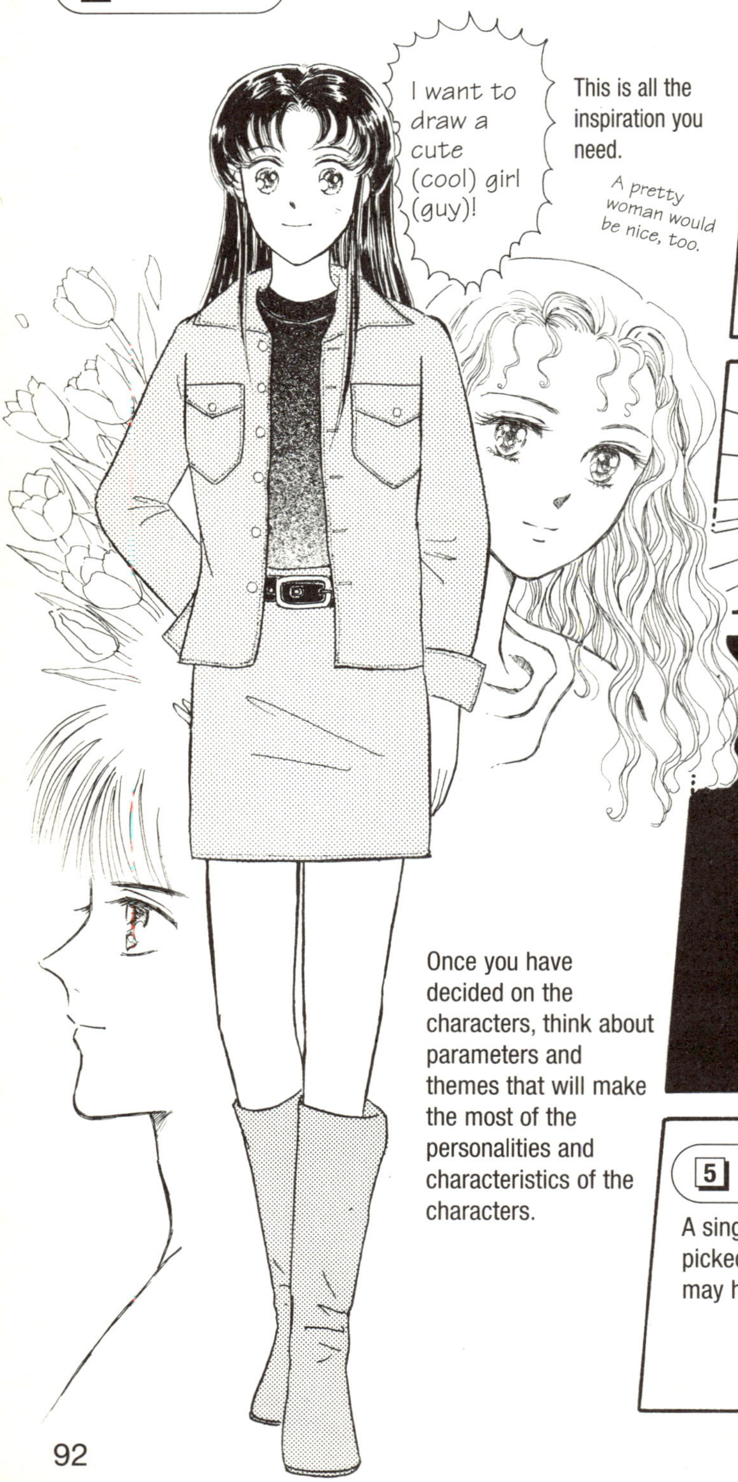

Once you have decided on the characters, think about parameters and themes that will make the most of the personalities and characteristics of the characters.

2 Theme

Love story, overcoming adversity in sports, human love, campus story, animal story, etc.

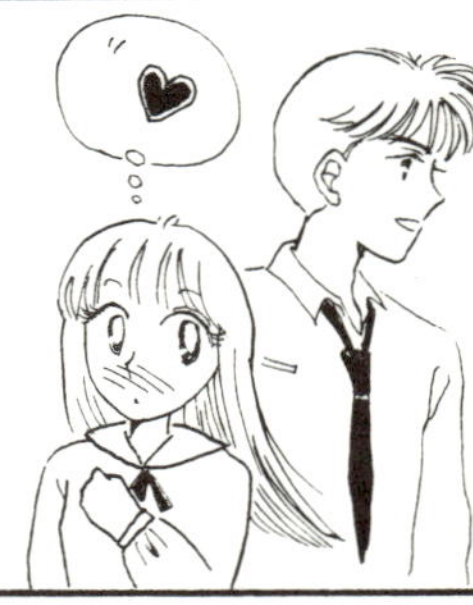

3 Story

Think of characters and parameters that match the theme.

4 Scenes

You may come up with the climax scene first or you may have a scene that you are burning to do. You can also try doing a surprise ending.

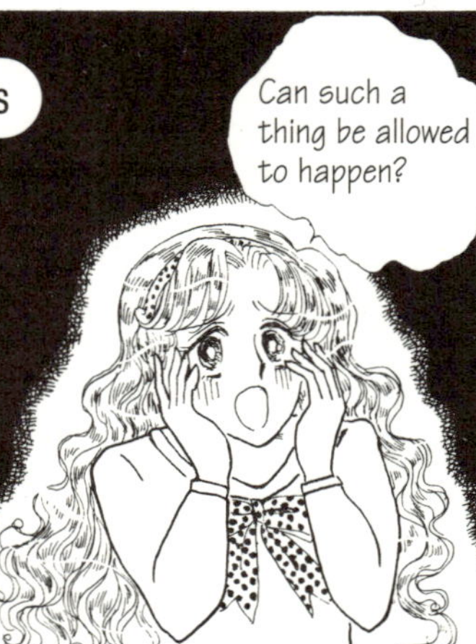

5 Props

A single shell (prop) picked up off the beach may hold a memory.

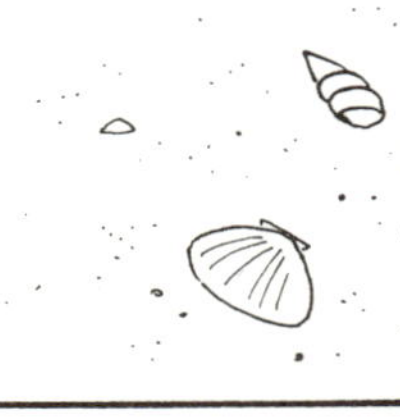

1 Set character parameters.

Any kind of character can be made the leading character. To start with, generate a character that you really like. Draw a distinctive character that only you can draw.

Example of Girl

Name: Miss A (8th grade)
Personality: She is earnest and shy.
Problem: She cannot make regular friends because on the outside she looks flashy and tawdry.

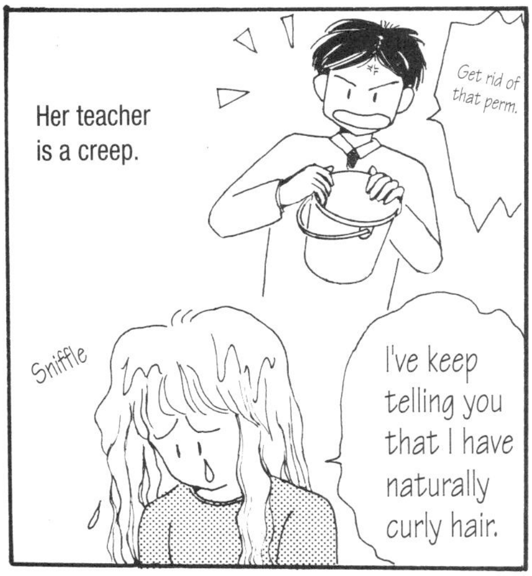

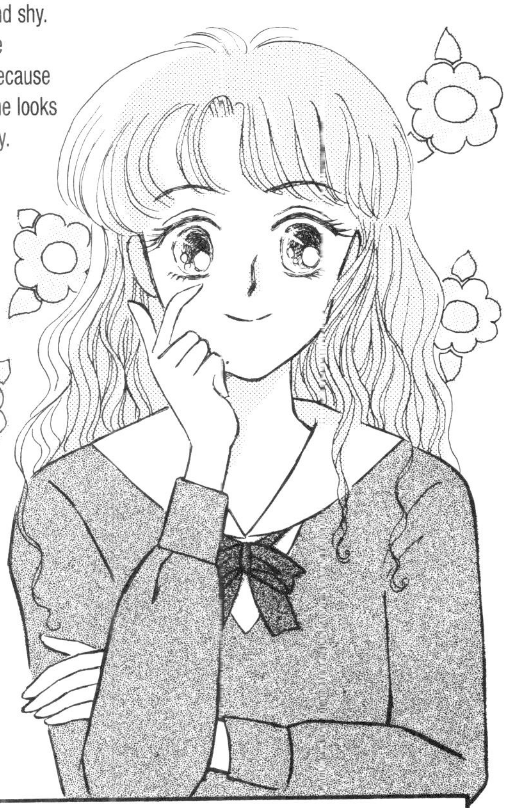

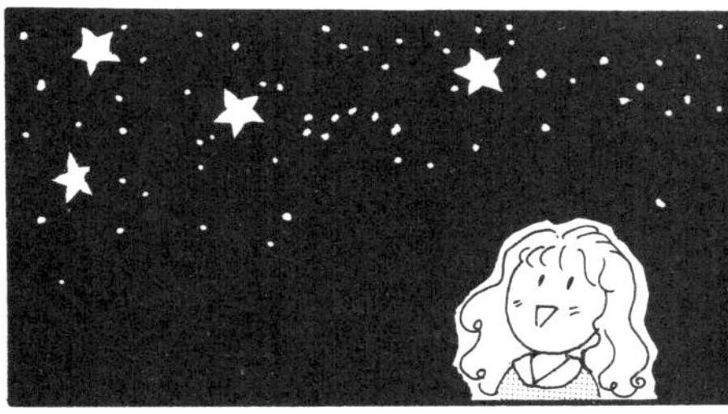

Hobbies and Dreams
She wants to live in an astronomical observatory because she likes to look at the stars.

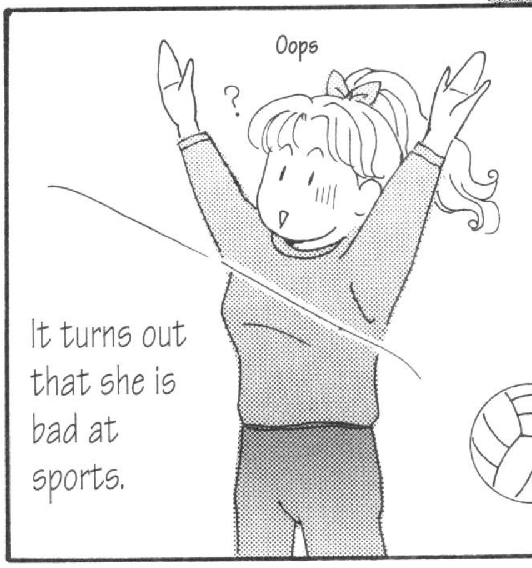

Element of Surprise
The element of surprise can involve the dreams, personality, hobbies, or environment surrounding a character. Making use of one of these areas in the story will bring out the element of surprise (Using all of them may be comical.).

If you go overboard with character parameters, the story will end up just being a narrative. Do not use any more parameters than are necessary to the story.

Example of Boy

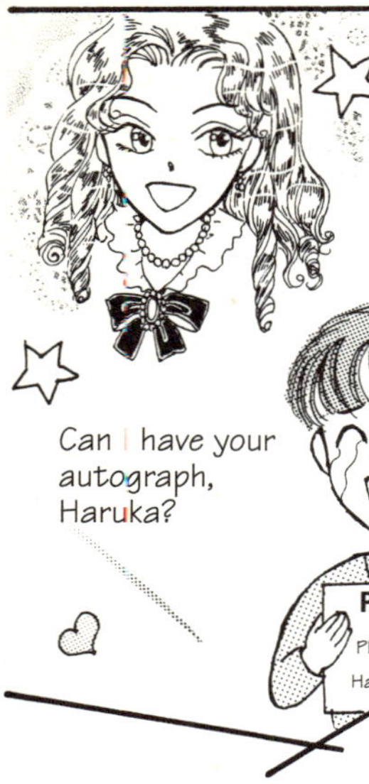

Element of Surprise
He is a fan of the Takarazuka Revue.

Name: John Doe
Personality: He is energetic and cheerful. On the outside he appears optimistic, but in truth he has a nervous disposition.
Problem: His parents may be divorcing.

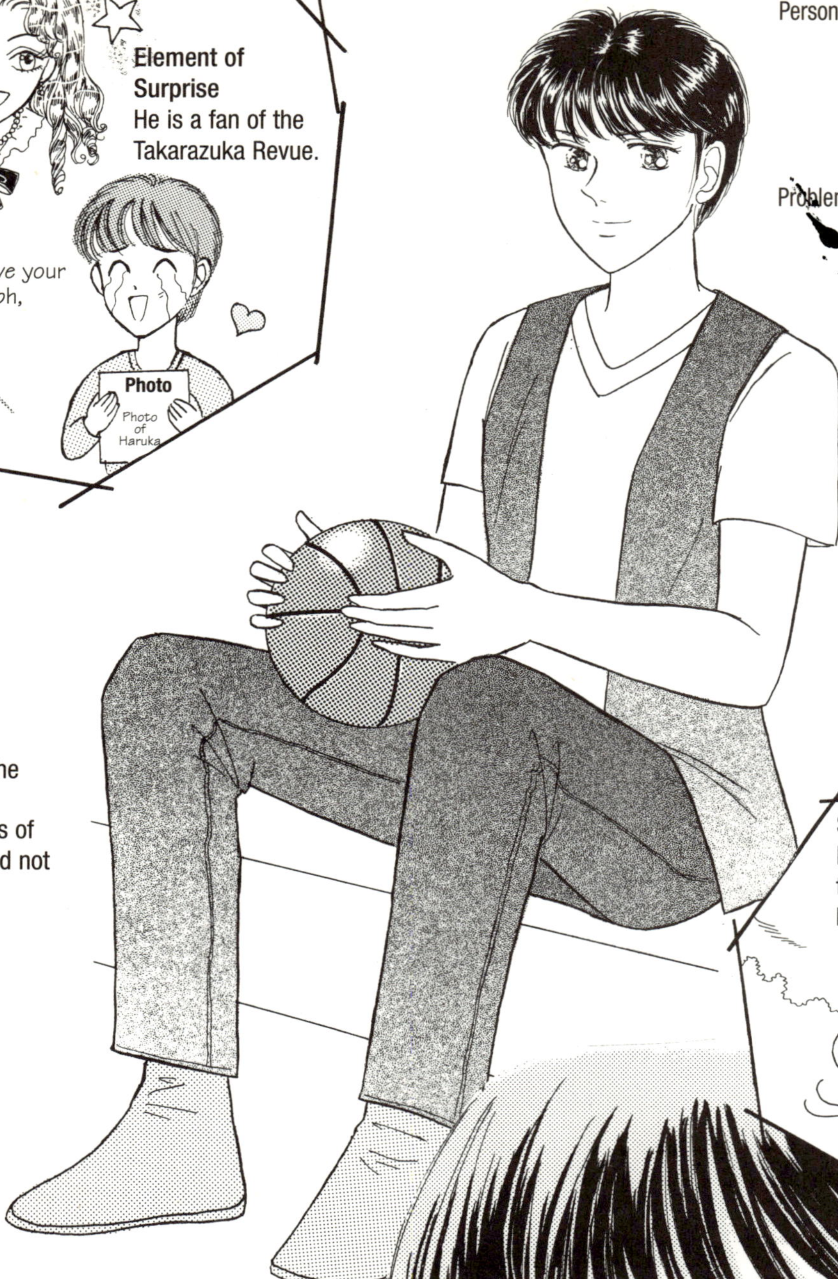

Depicting Characters
Think about the inner characteristics of characters and not just physical attributes.

Special Skills
He likes all sports to the point of being obsessed.

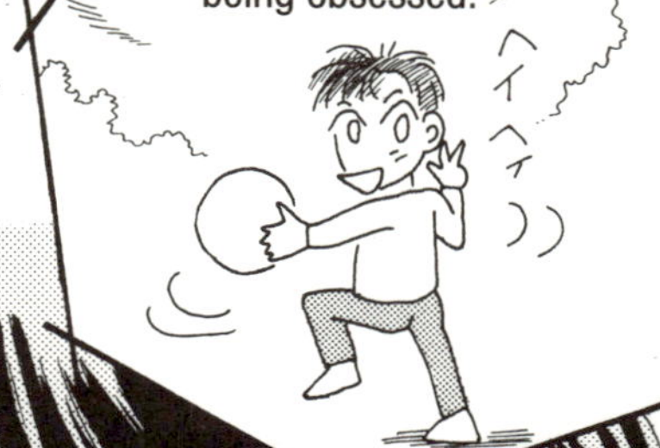

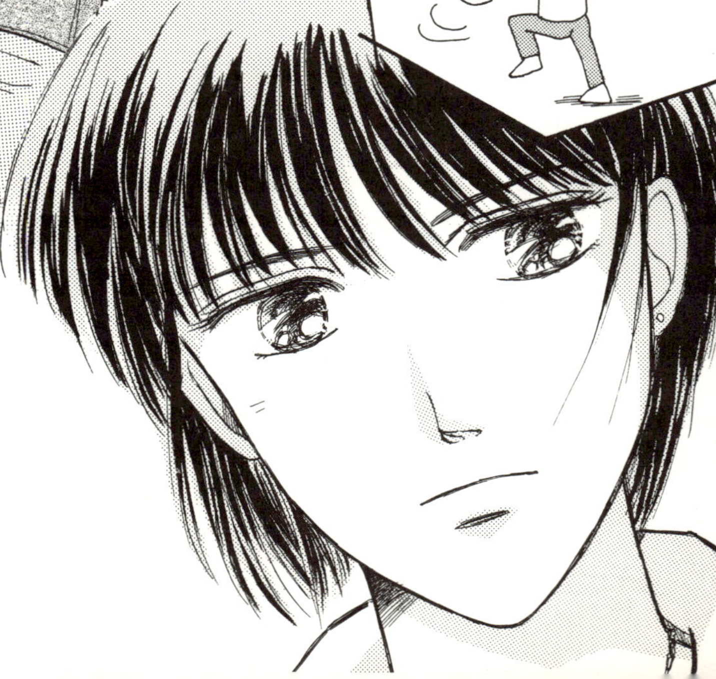

The above is just one example. The element of surprise is important for both characters and the story. Just make sure that the personality of a character does not change with every scene change. Make it clear to readers that it is the same character.

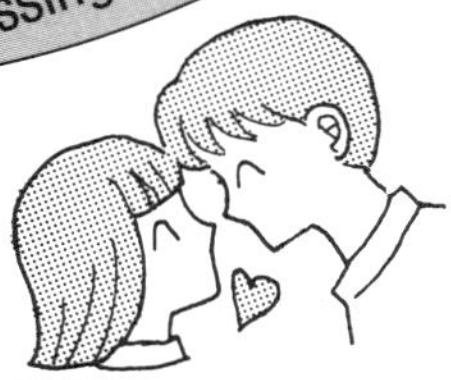

Special Effects Used in Girls' Comics 1

These are special techniques used in girls' comics such as campus stories and love comedies. They live or die by the characters and story.

Forced Kiss
No matter what the angle, with this type one party is pinned down and cannot move.

The male is daring and aggressive. He is confident and does not think about the other person's feelings.

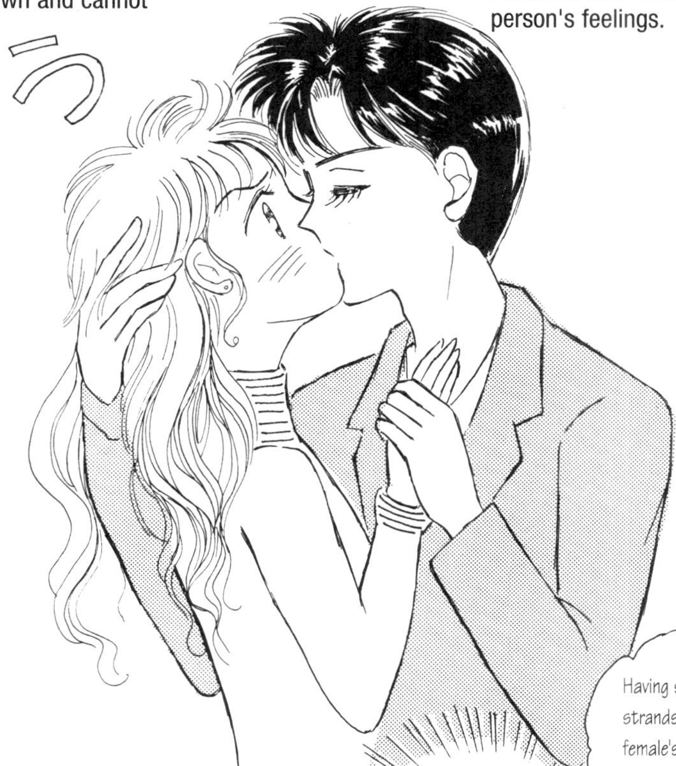

Kiss of Confirmation

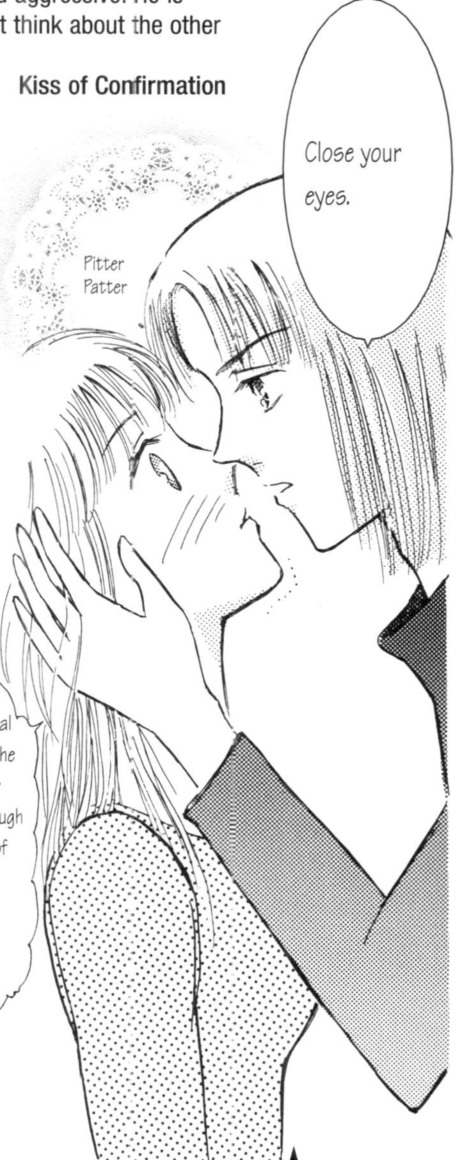

Having several strands of the female's hair running through the fingers of the male is effective.

Importance is placed on the mood, so awareness of the other party is enhanced. You will win over readers even if the kissing scene goes to a wide-angle shot after this.

Kissing in any Location
With this type, the kissers have no qualms about kissing at school or another location where people can see.

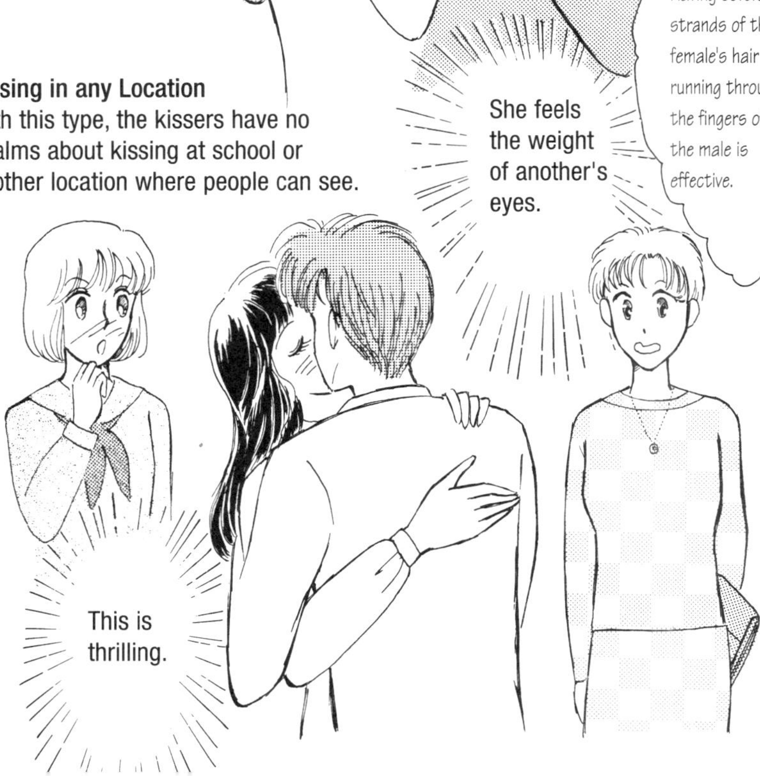

Appeal of Characters

Once you have set simple parameters for a character, think about the appeal of the character. Appeal lies in the personality and actions of the character.

■Orthodox Type
This type is good at sports, gets good grades, and is popular with the girls. He understands the feelings of the leading character. He will protect only one person.

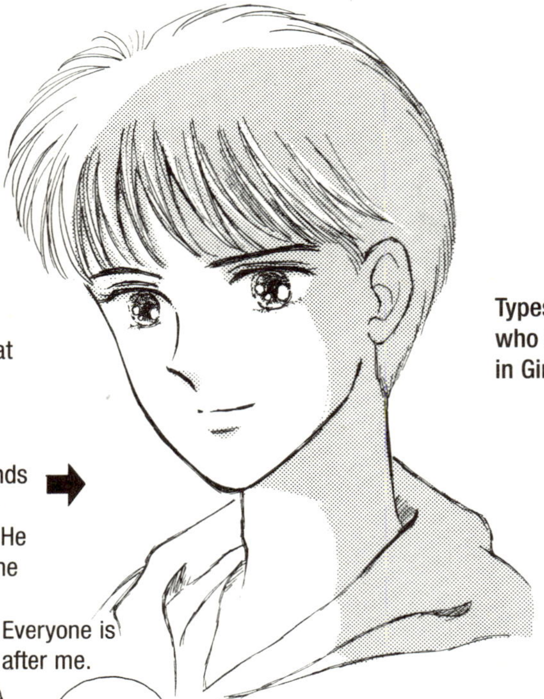

Everyone is after me.

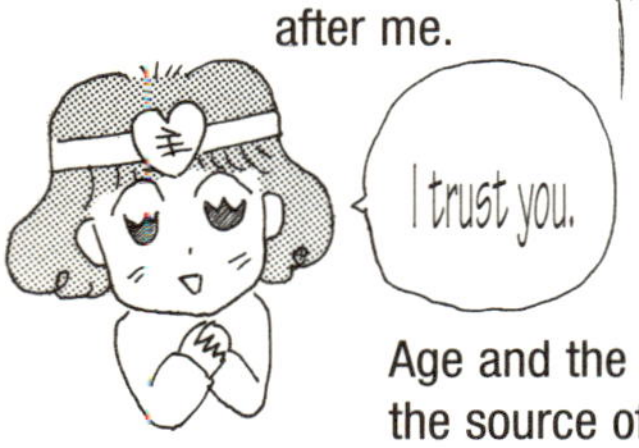

Age and the surrounding environment can be the source of a variety of episodes.

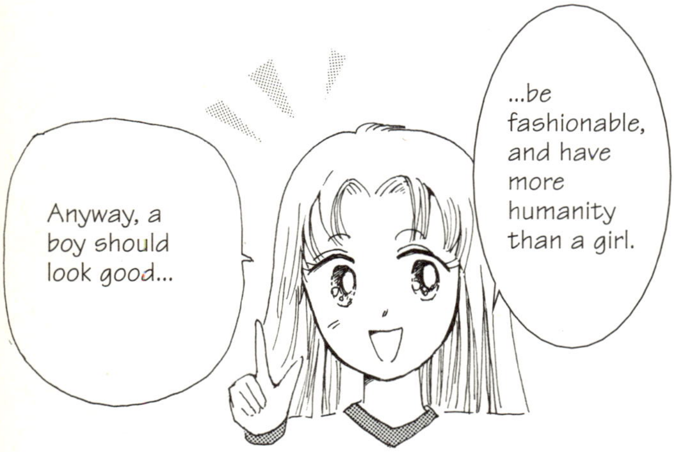

■Juvenile Delinquent Type
There is always a reason why someone acts like a delinquent, i.e., quiet, cold, playboy type, and a little melancholy. Readers will be alienated if you go overboard. Naturally such a character will use foul language. The orthodox type of character will also use such language.

His way of life and ideas may be different, but...

Types of Males who are Popular in Girls' Comics

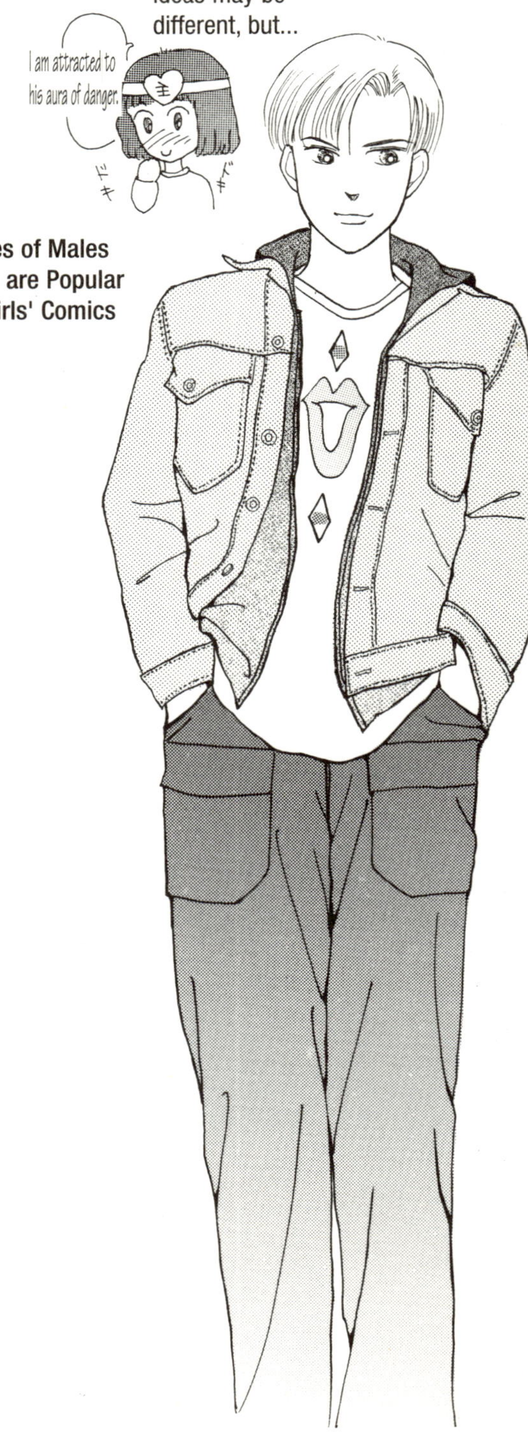

Something only possible in a girls' comic! Demand made on the boy!

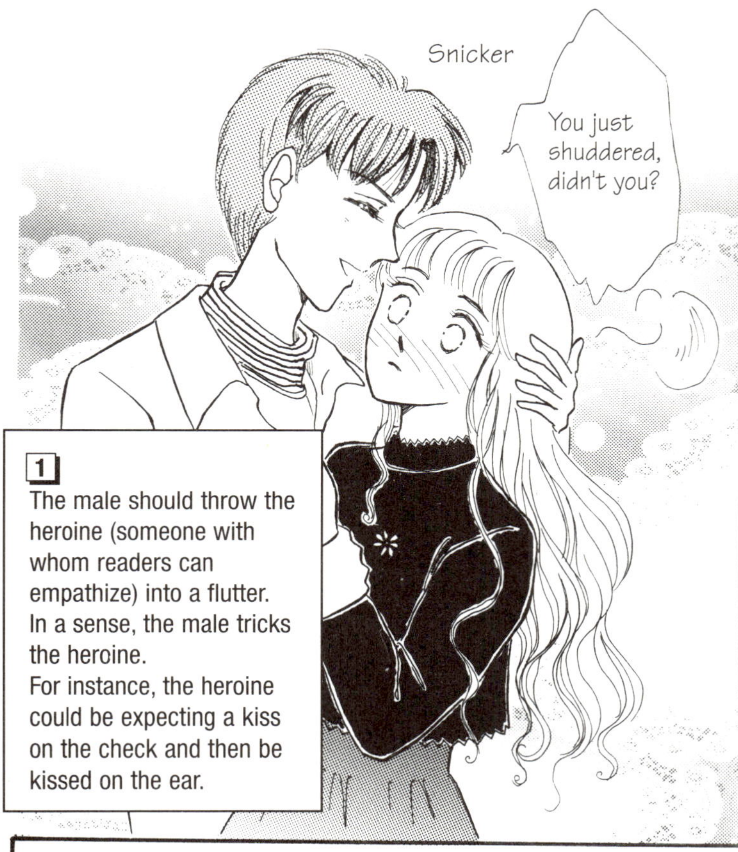

1
The male should throw the heroine (someone with whom readers can empathize) into a flutter.
In a sense, the male tricks the heroine.
For instance, the heroine could be expecting a kiss on the check and then be kissed on the ear.

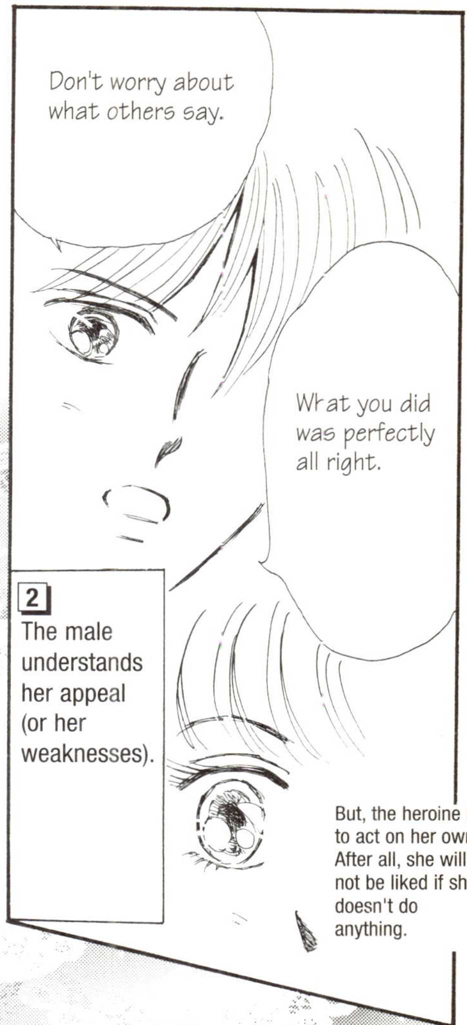

2
The male understands her appeal (or her weaknesses).

But, the heroine has to act on her own. After all, she will not be liked if she doesn't do anything.

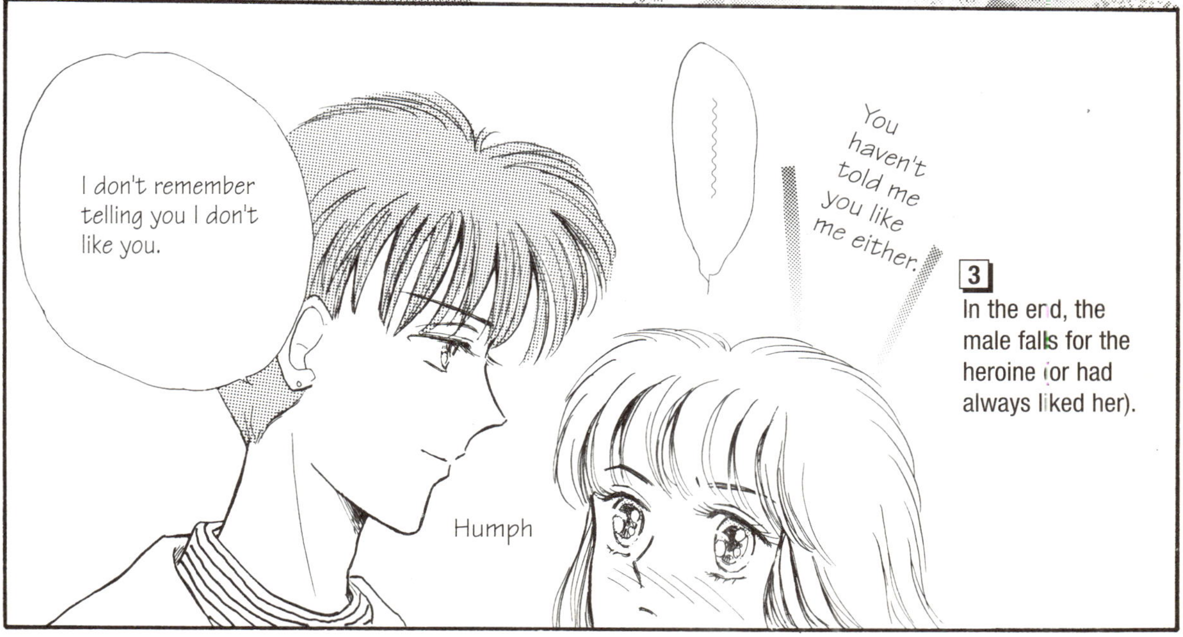

3
In the end, the male falls for the heroine (or had always liked her).

Psychological Characterization

Psychological characterization is an indispensable part of girls' comics. Characters live and die by their subtle emotional swings.

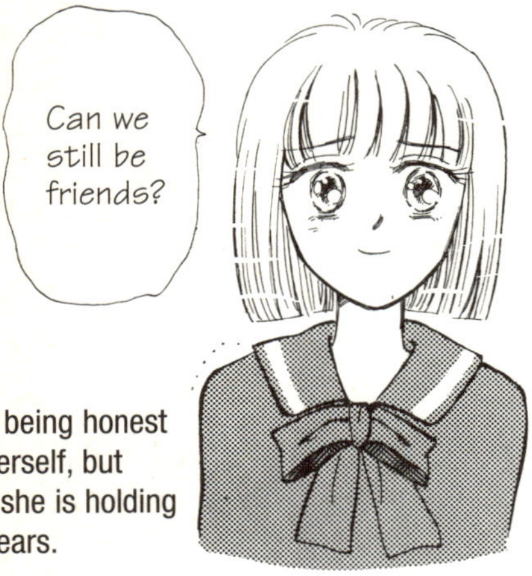

She is being honest with herself, but inside she is holding back tears.

Examples of girls confessing their love and being turned down

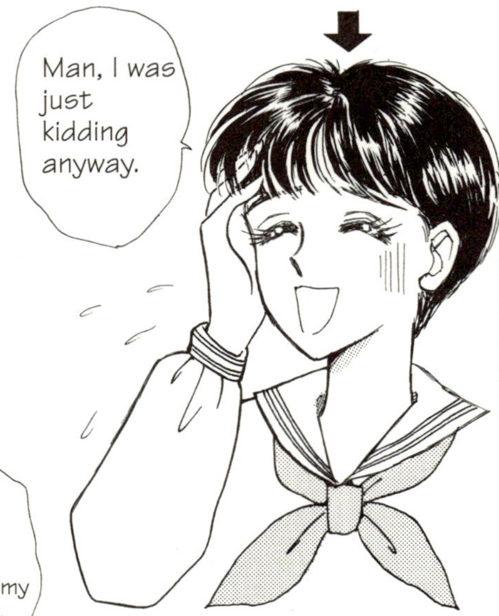

She blurts out something she doesn't mean and forces a laugh.

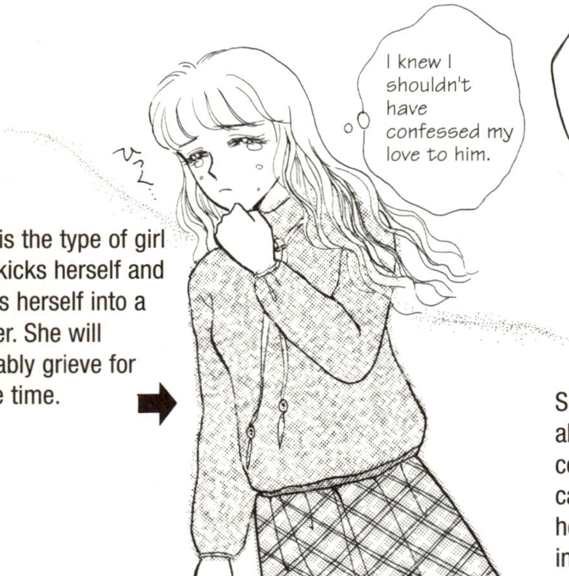

This is the type of girl that kicks herself and drives herself into a corner. She will probably grieve for some time.

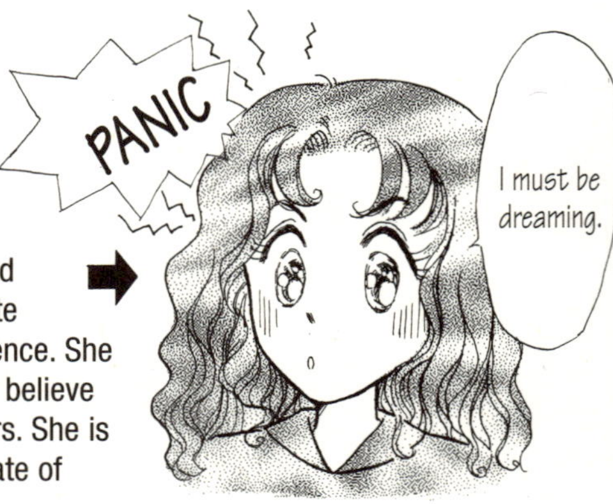

She had absolute confidence. She cannot believe her ears. She is in a state of denial.

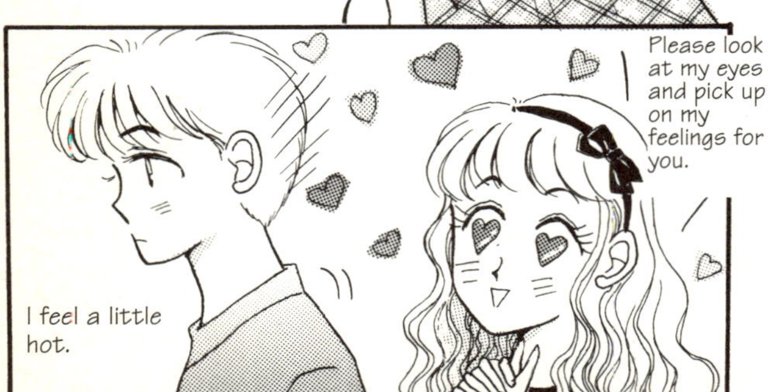

There are many examples like these. The psychological characterization differs depending on the personality of the character, so be sure to set clear character parameters.

It is best if you can depict the psychological state of characters using pictures and not words.

Psychological Characterization Process

1
For instance, let's say the heroine wants to confess her love to a boy. Different people fret in different ways. There is a mental conflict.

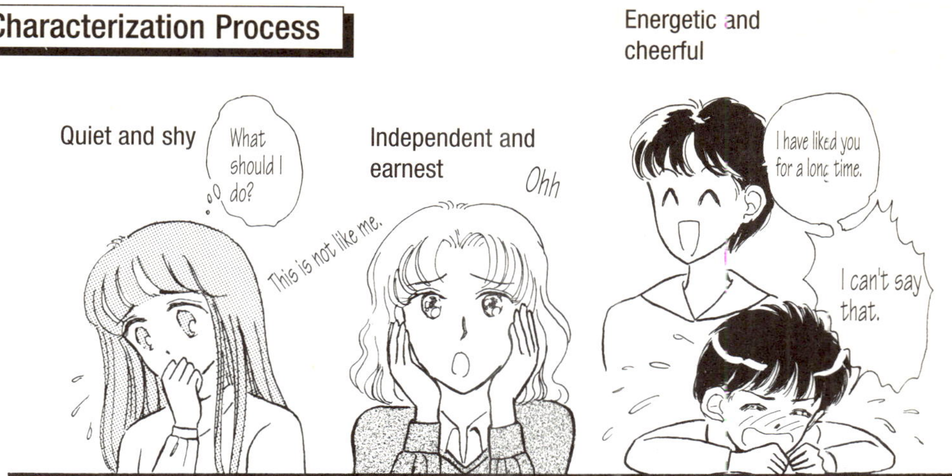

2
The heroine creates an opportunity to talk with the boy. Use of some props will make it look more natural.

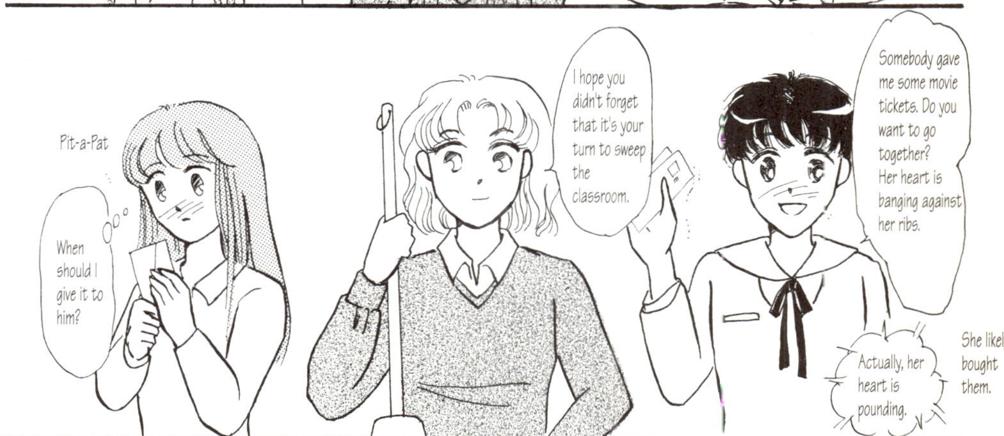

3
The boy likes another girl. The heroine sees the boy being friendly with the other girl and is shocked.

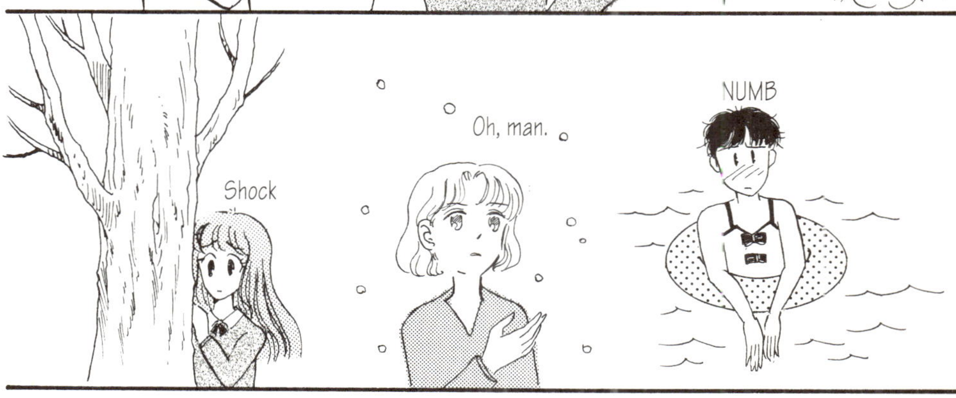

4
How characters think and their facial expressions will differ depending on their personalities.

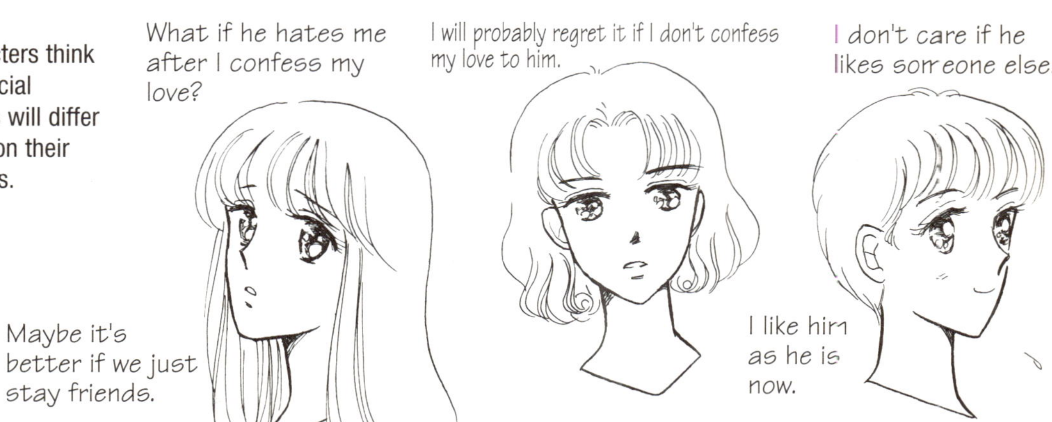

2 Choose a theme!

A theme is the objective for writing a comic. It is the ideas and opinions you want to convey to readers.

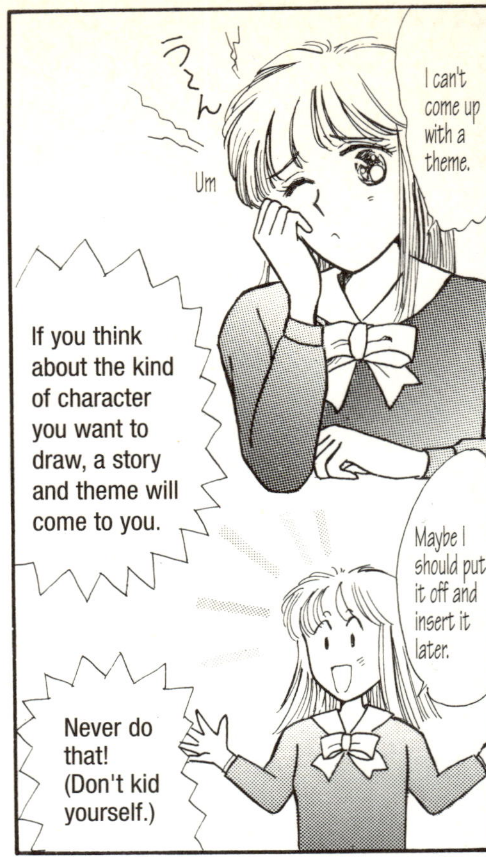

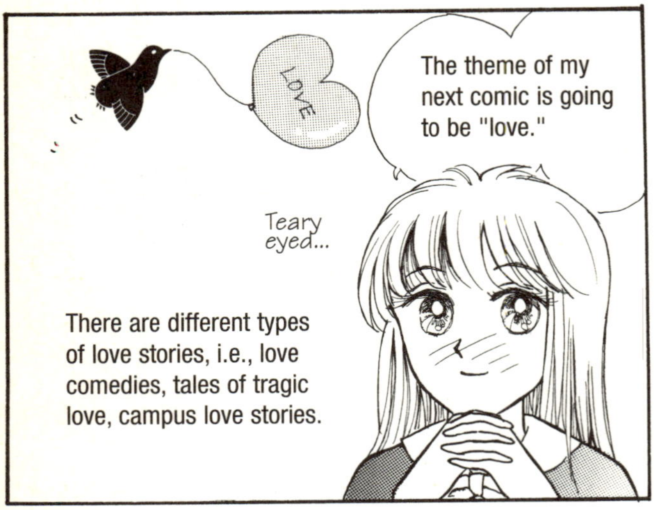

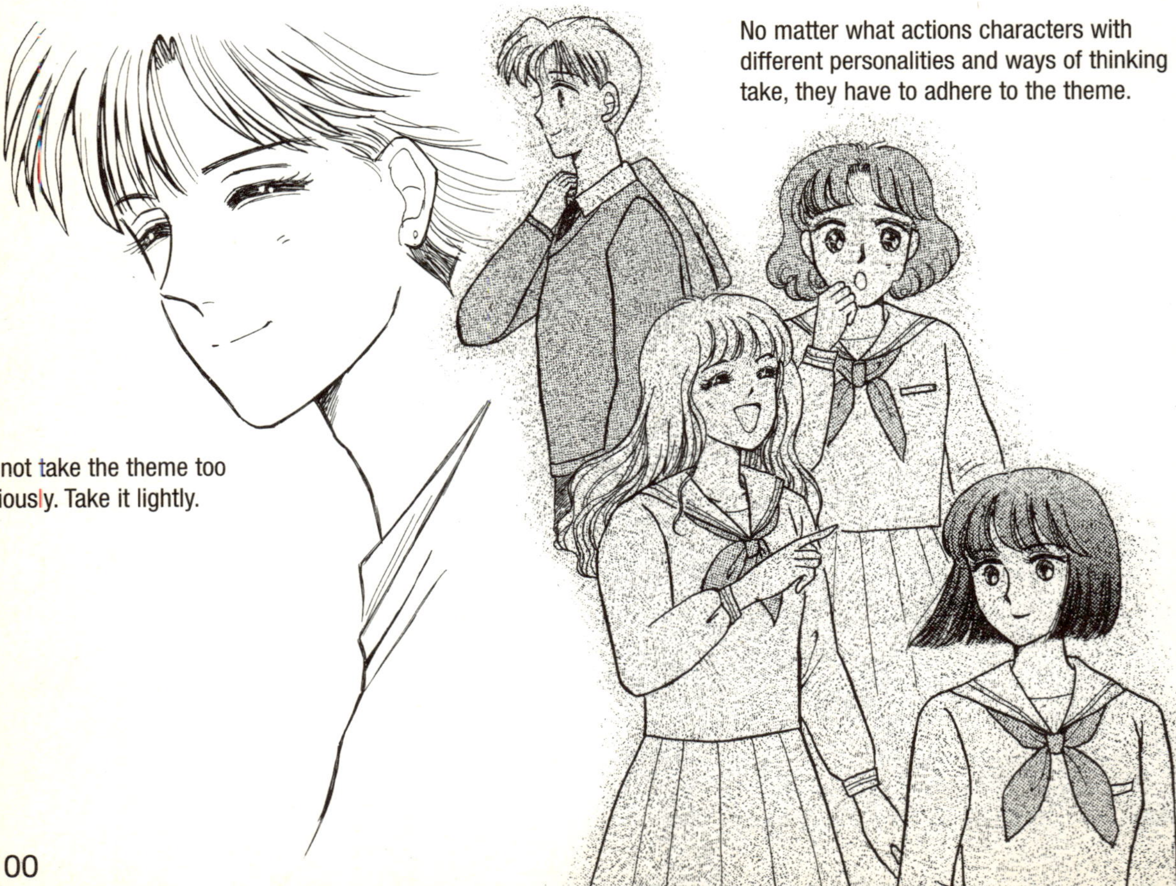

No matter what actions characters with different personalities and ways of thinking take, they have to adhere to the theme.

Do not take the theme too seriously. Take it lightly.

Special Effects Used in Girls' Comics 2

Surprisingly, blushing and sweating are often used together. Try coming up with effects that are only possible in girls' comics.

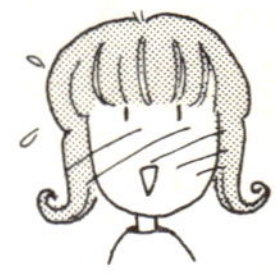

Blushing and Sweating

Slightly Troubled
The trick is to draw just one drop of sweat.

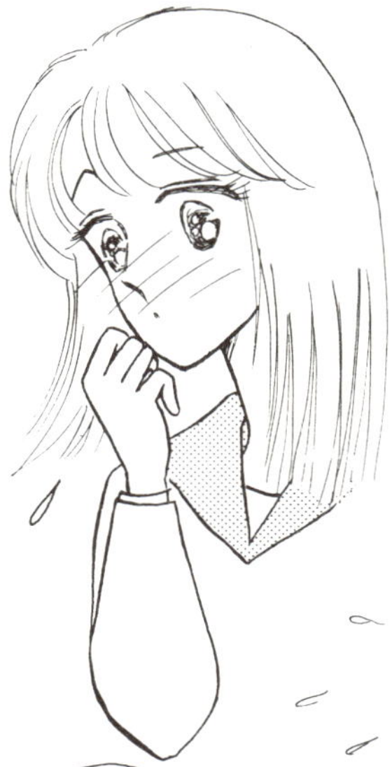

Cold Sweat

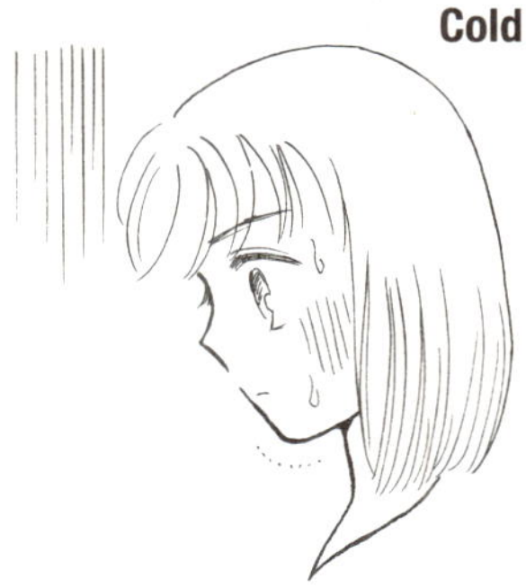

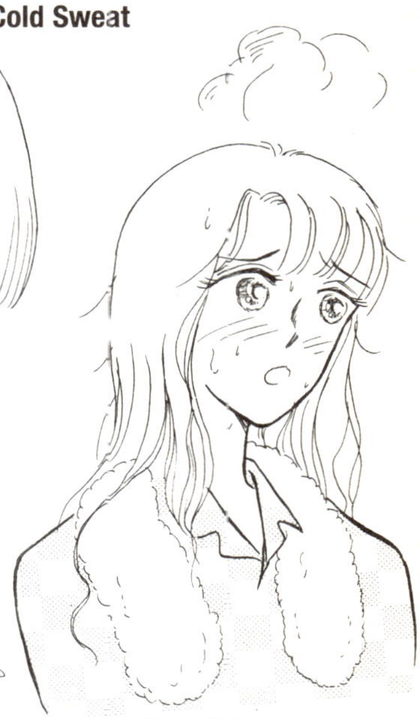

Feverish
Draw it so that sweat is springing forth from all over the body.

Pressured

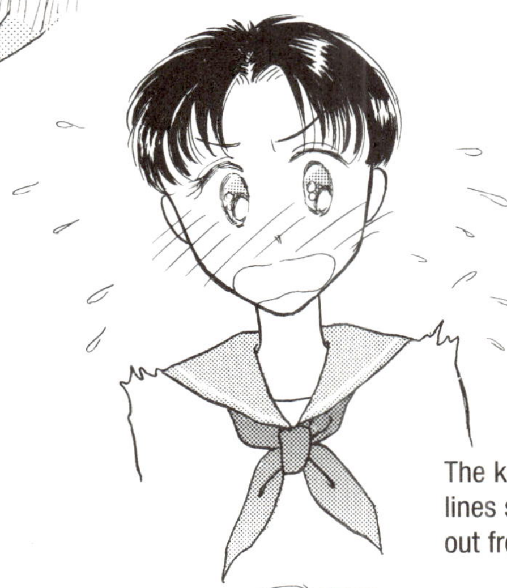

The key is to draw the blush lines so that they stick way out from the face.

Embarrassed
The back of the character and one large drop of cold sweat are effective.

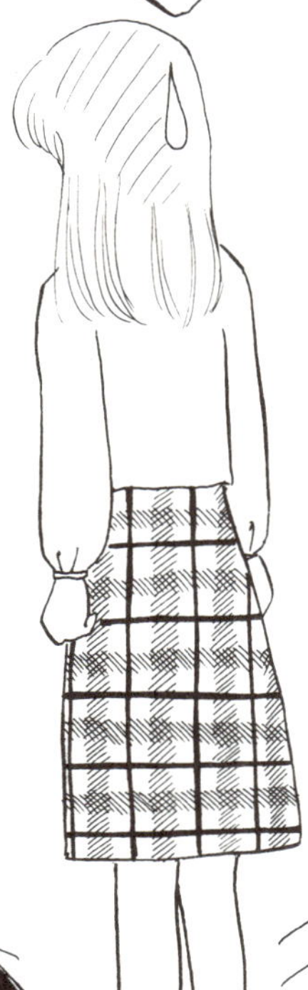

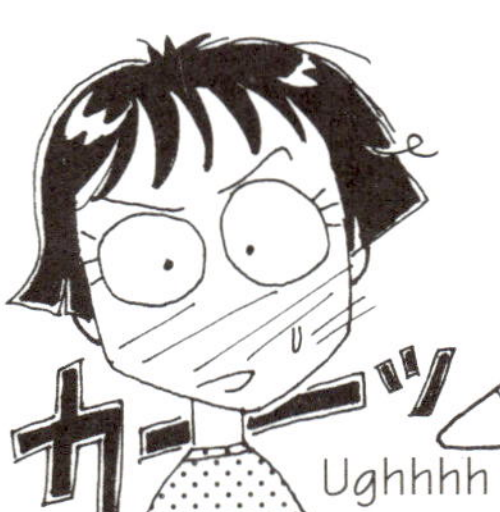

Using it comically is interesting as well. Drawn letters are also effective.

Really Hot

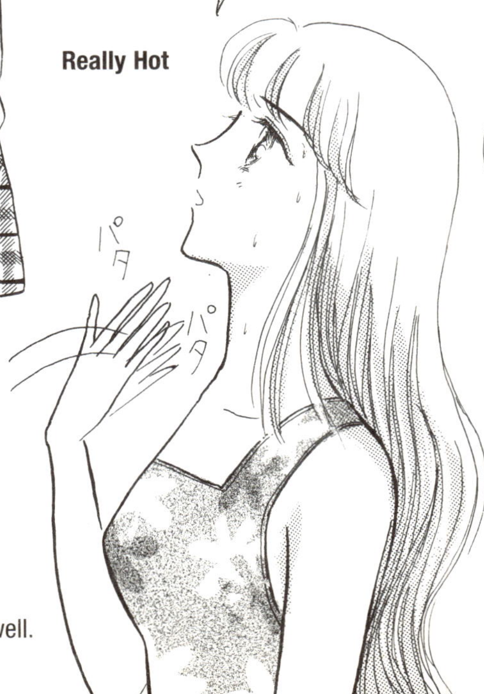

Giving Someone the Eye

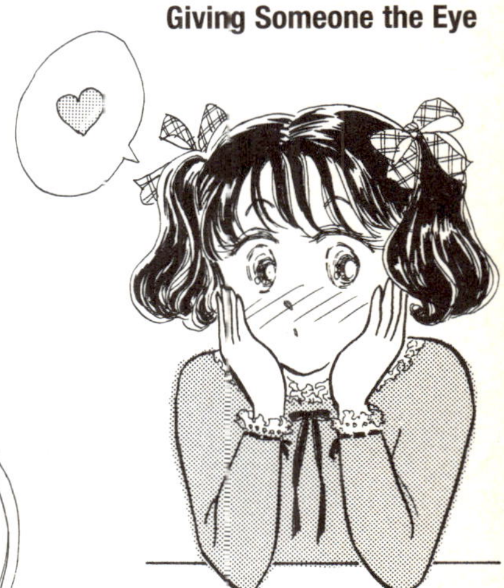

3 Write a story!

Even if the drawings are good, a comic is not going to be interesting if the story is not sound. It all begins with the logical process of introduction, development, turn, and conclusion.

Choose a subject (genre)!

Genres such as science fiction, fantasy, and history are more suitable for long comics, because the explanation of the setting takes up many pages. They are difficult to pull off in a short comic of about 16 pages that is going to be submitted.

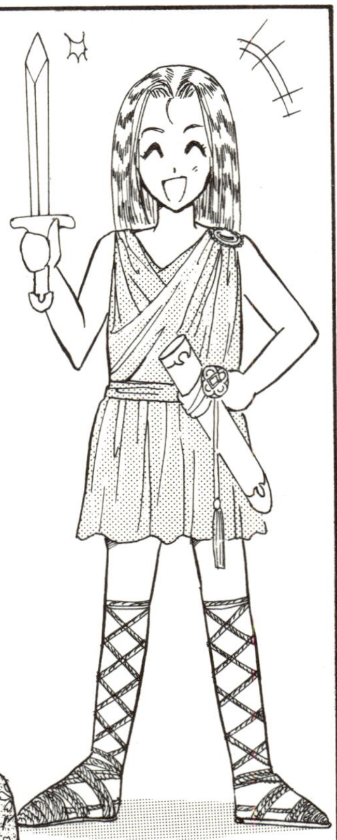

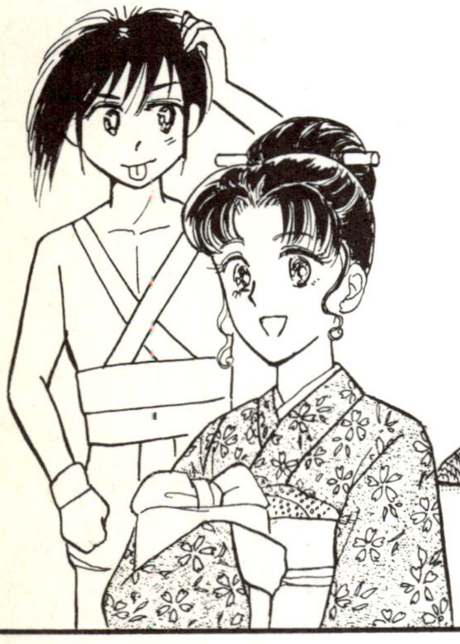

A campus story with a normal girl as the heroine is the easiest to do, but of course you are free to choose a genre of your choice.

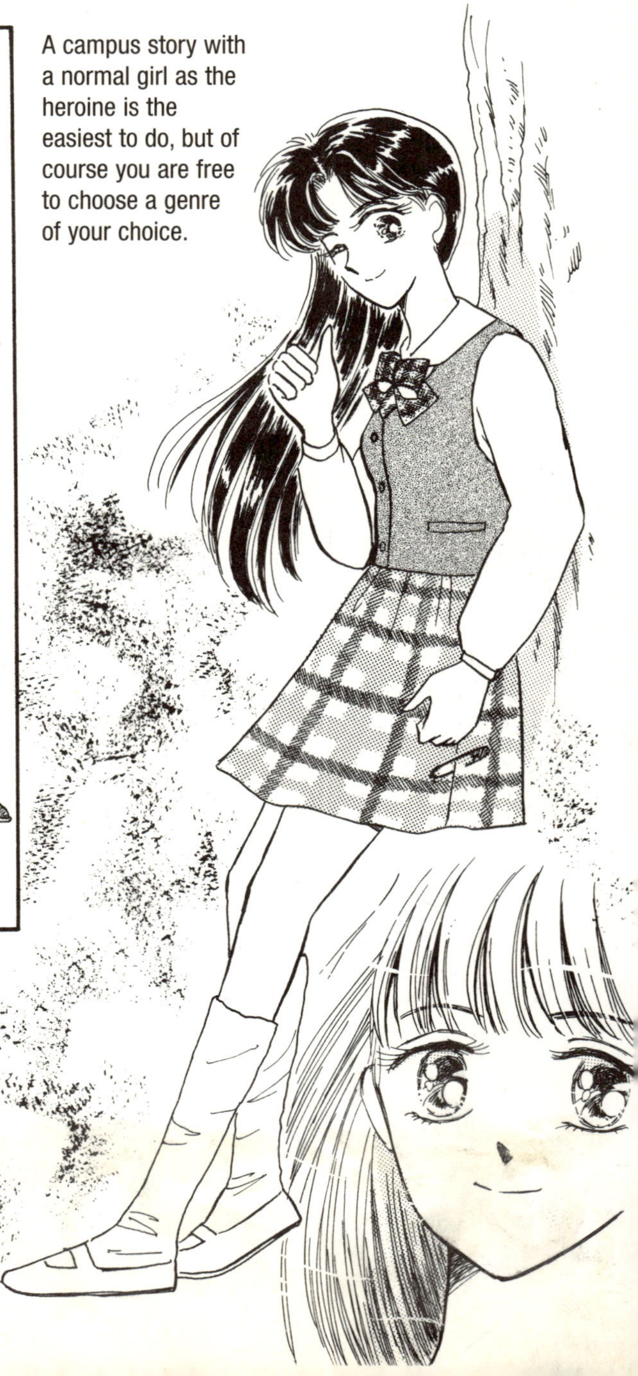

Even if the story itself is open and shut, it will be all right if the base is solid. You will be able to come up with several interesting episodes.

Example of Romance Comic

Introduction

The heroine is introduced.

Impress upon readers the name of the heroine and her relationship with those around here. Include the season, hour, and place.

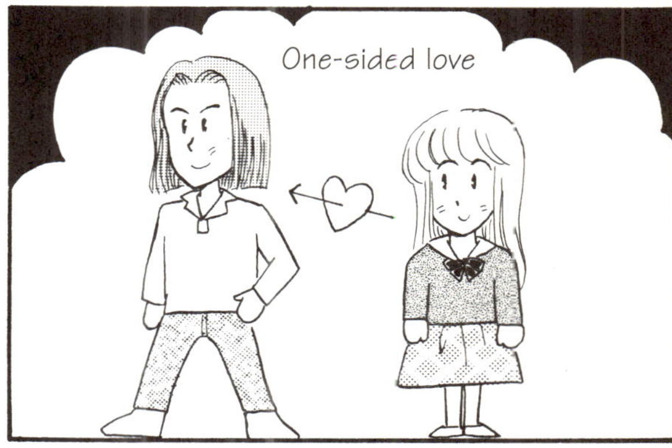

Development

The story is developed with different episodes (incidents).

Insert an episode where the heroine and boy become friendly with each other (catalyst).

⬇

Insert an episode where they have a falling out.

⬇

The two are unhappy and hit rock bottom.

⬇

They are happy (a large gap is more effective).

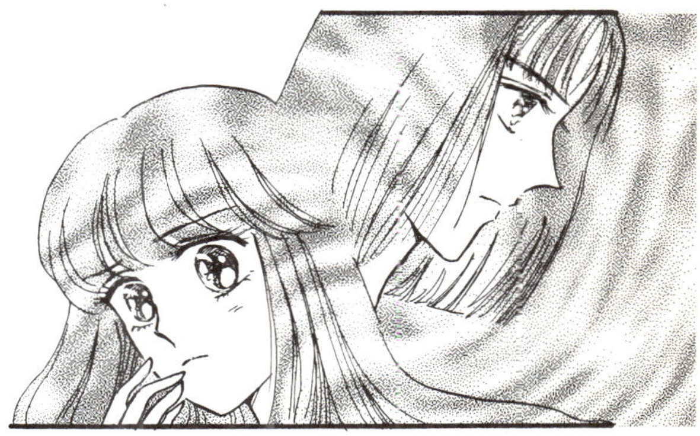

Turn

This is where the story reaches a climax.

Insert an episode where the two make up.
(The heroine can have no doubts about her feelings.)
There could be a change in hour or place.

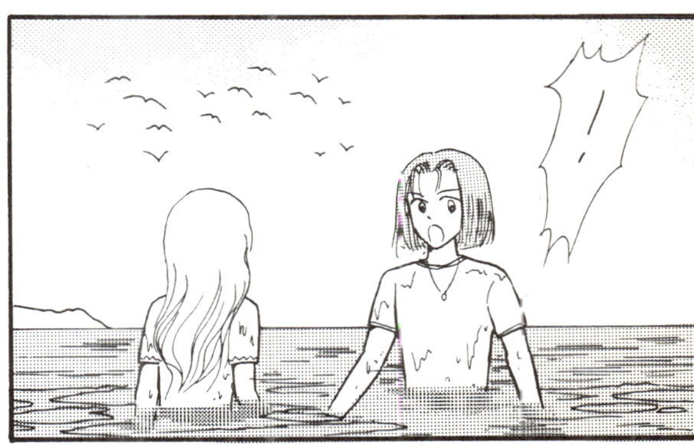

Conclusion

This is the last scene. The readers could be left hanging (by leaving something unsolved).

Make an impression by including a last scene that differs from that of others.

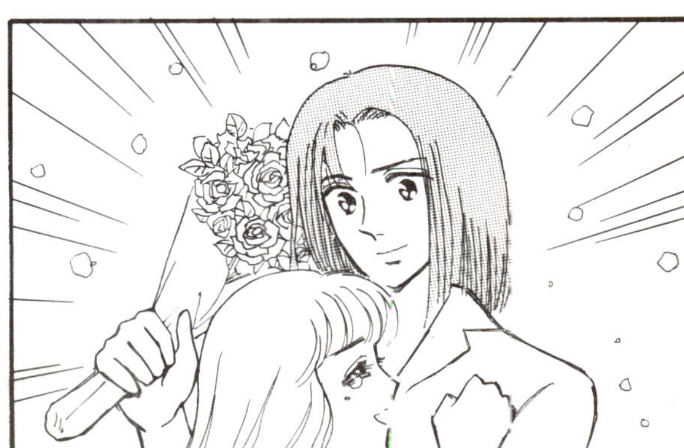

Hints for Stories

Everything about your existence can offer hints for comics. You will soon discover what you want to convey to people and what opinions you want to express.

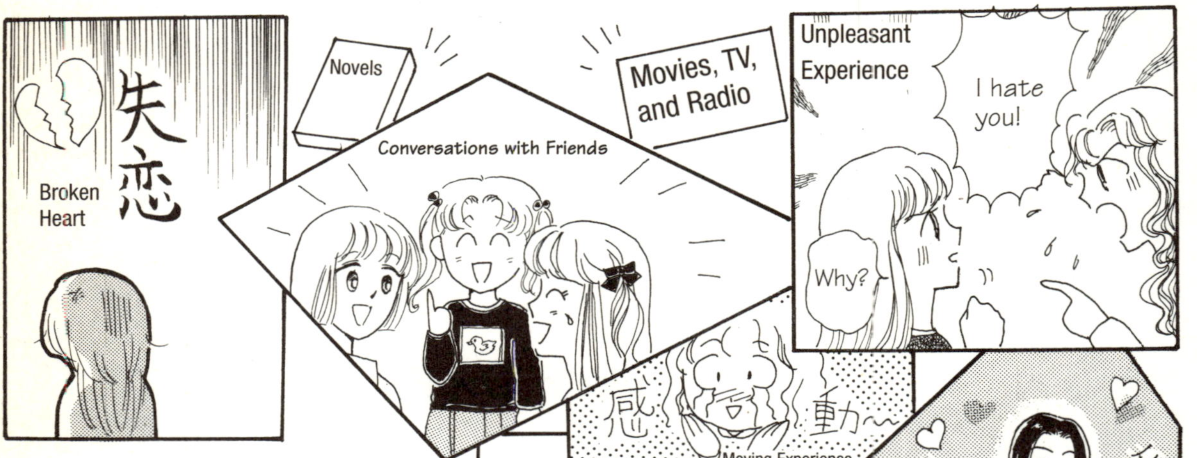

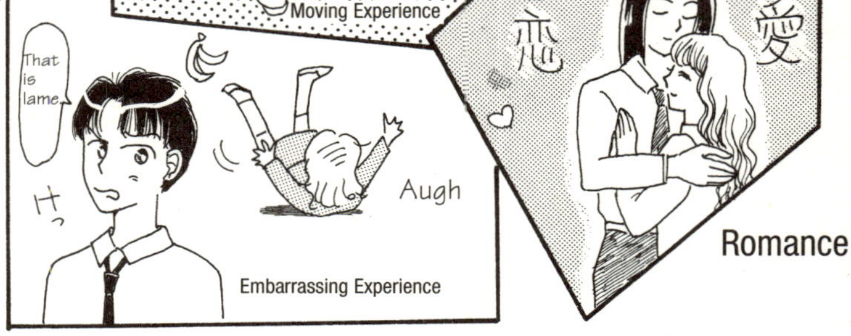

There are fun things and painful things. Curiosity is important. You may be motivated or moved by the surrounding environment. Actively look for things that are interesting.

What are episodes?

Episodes are connected incidents or circumstances that move a story along. The main episode of a story is always supported by other incidents. Episodes should be fresh.

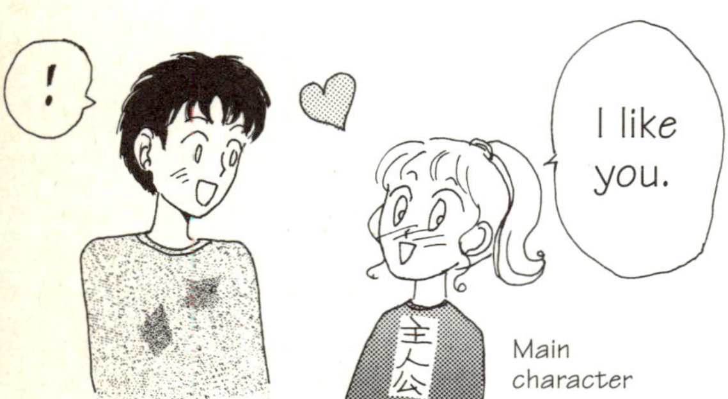

That could spark other events.

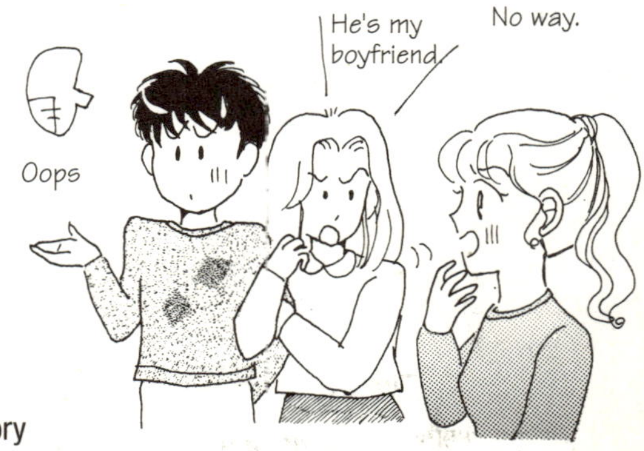

Episodes are connected incidents or circumstances that move a story along. The main episode of a story is always supported by other incidents. Episodes should be fresh.

How to Make the Story Development Interesting

It all boils down to ideas. This is the development part of the logical process of introduction, development, turn, and conclusion. Try using the five techniques below.

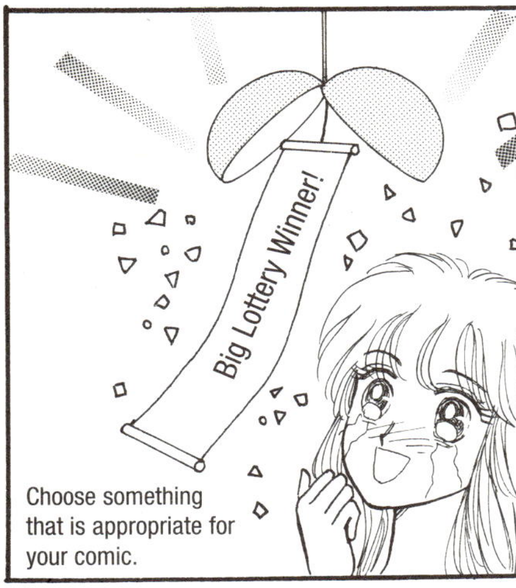

Choose something that is appropriate for your comic.

1 Incidents

This could be an accident, a sickness, a natural disaster, or suddenly receiving an award.

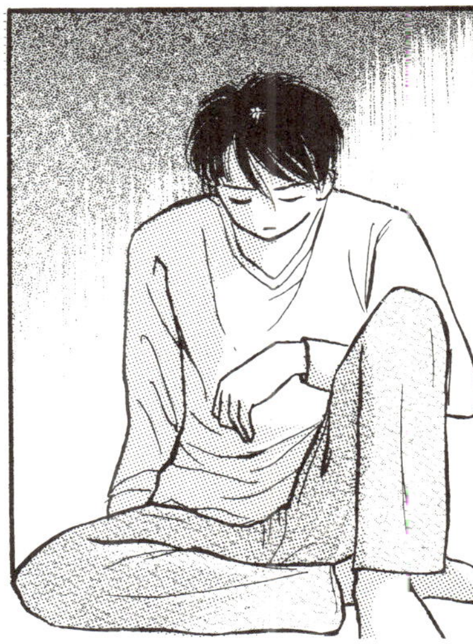

2 Circumstances

These are emotional circumstances such as family relations, human relations, a misunderstanding, or jealousy.

There are secrets that totally surprise people once told.

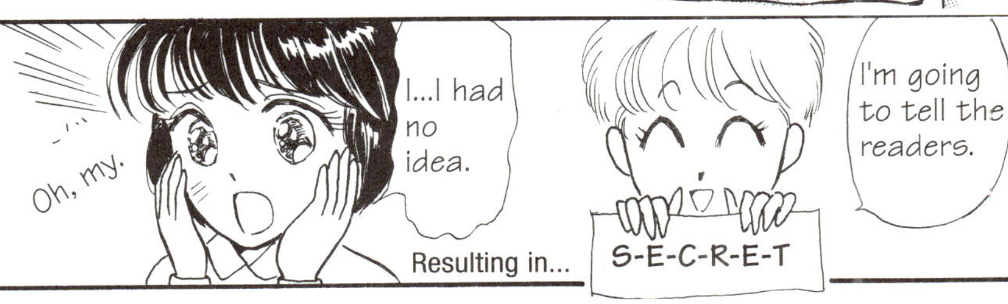

3 Secrecy

This could be something from your past that you want to keep quiet such as an extramarital affair.

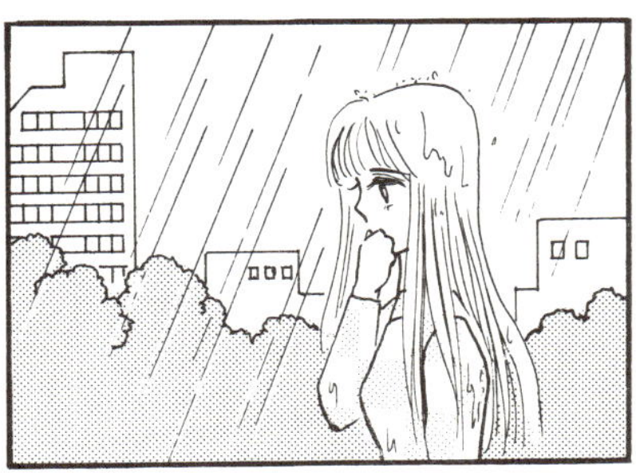

⬇

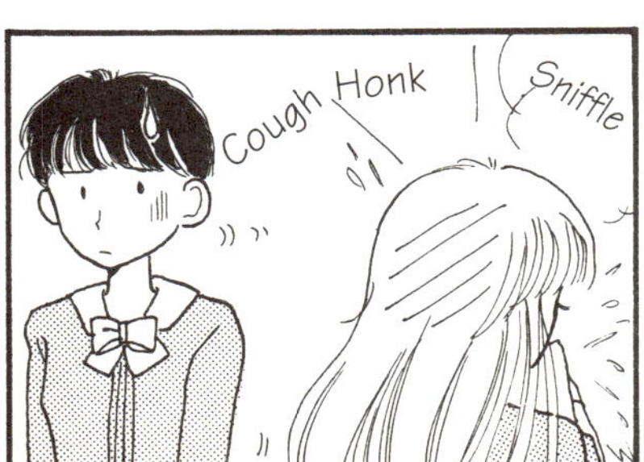

4 Foreshadowing

Drop advance hints without having too many coincidences or being too opportunistic.

The heroine should not catch a cold all of a sudden. You could add a scene where she is out in the rain all night for some reason before she catches a cold. This is foreshadowing.

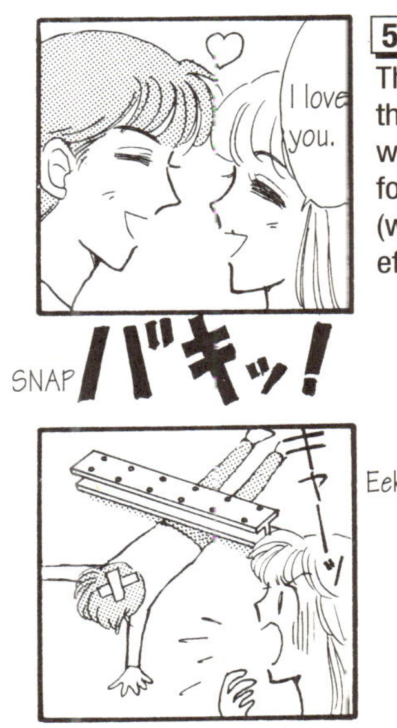

5 Foreshadowing

These are events that happen without any foreshadowing (which is more effective).

Element of Surprise (Attracting the Reader)

We talked earlier about the element of surprise and characters, but the element of surprise in the story is important too.

Here we have a nice, handsome mansion.

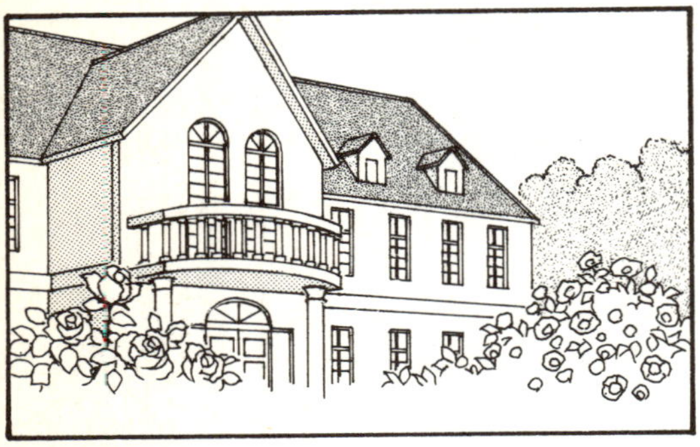

There are flowers everywhere and there is a pleasant aroma.
But, the truth is...

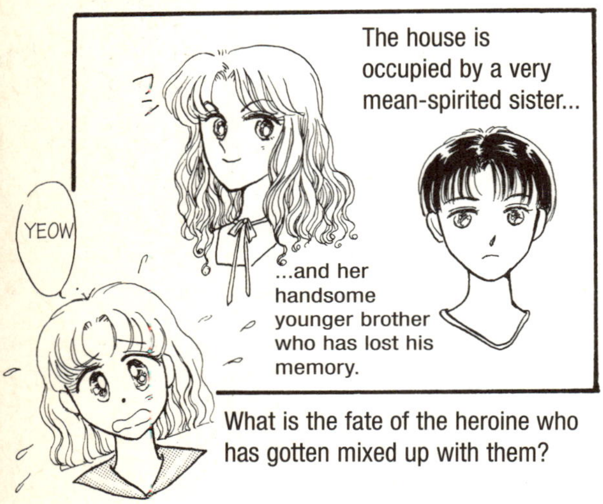

What is the fate of the heroine who has gotten mixed up with them?

Here we have an old house that looks like it is ready to collapse.

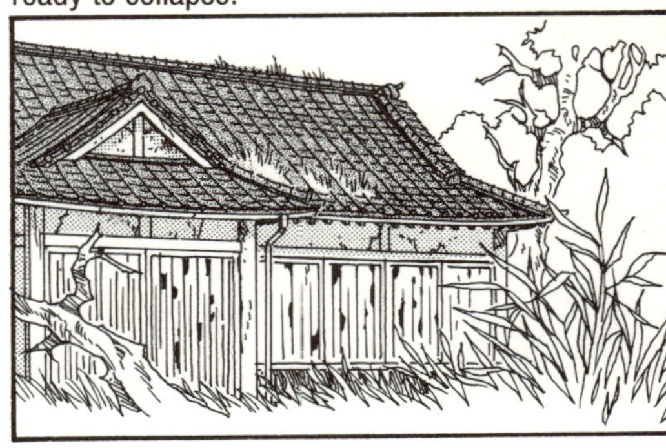

The trees are withered and forbidding.
But, the truth is...

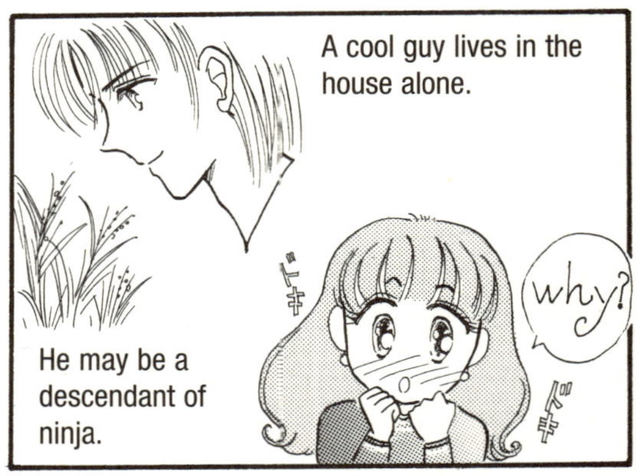

Dream Endings

The readers will feel betrayed if in the end you say the whole story was a dream. It is best if the story progresses in the present.

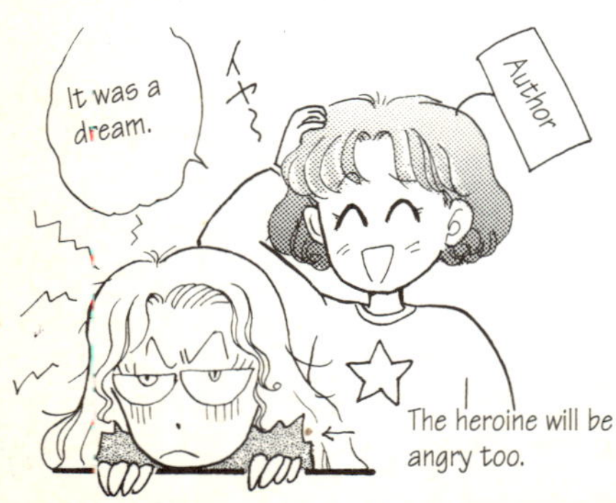

Significance of Episodes

For instance...

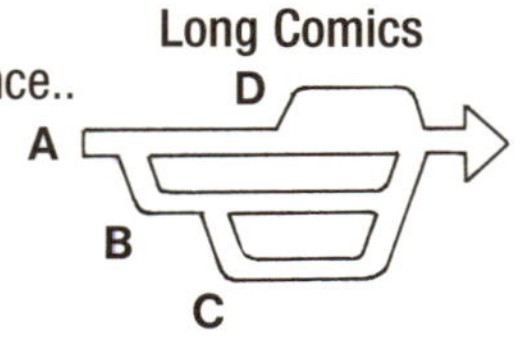

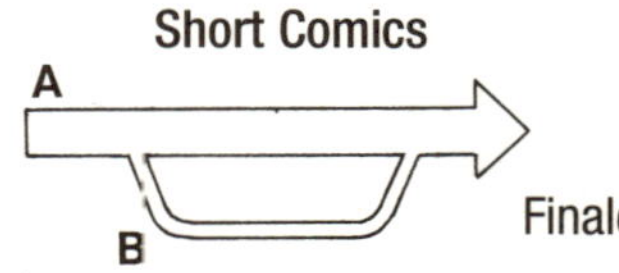

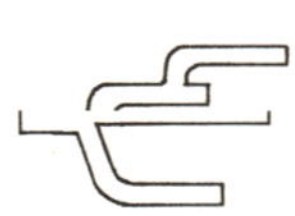

Poor Example

Make sure that the finale is not left unfinished.

As the main story (A) progresses, it branches out (B). In the end, A and B tie into each other, hopefully making the main story clearer.

Growth and Development of the Heroine

The heroine must grow emotionally and in terms of her skills (through effort) between the beginning and the end of the story. Find many chance events, which will be convincing to the readers, for the heroin to become stronger.

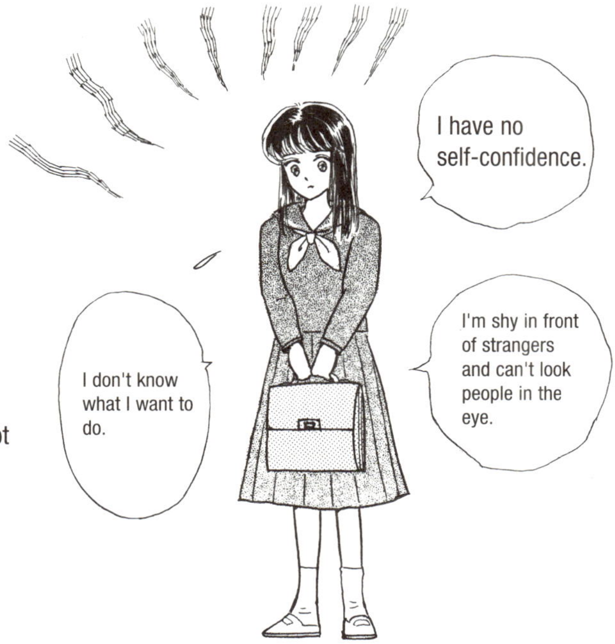

The heroine cannot have this personality from beginning to end.

Example: A somber heroine who is always looking down

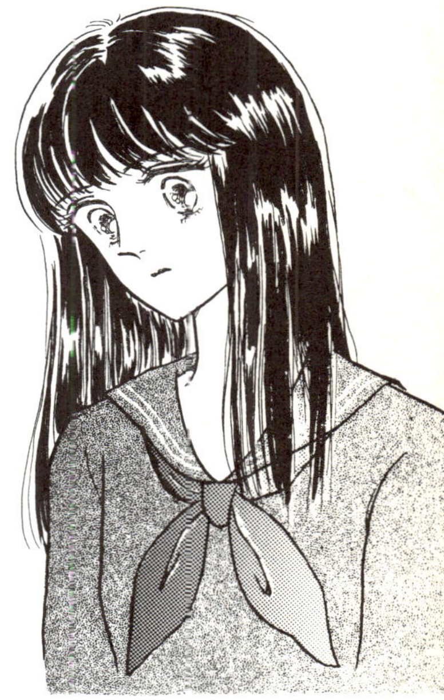

Part 1

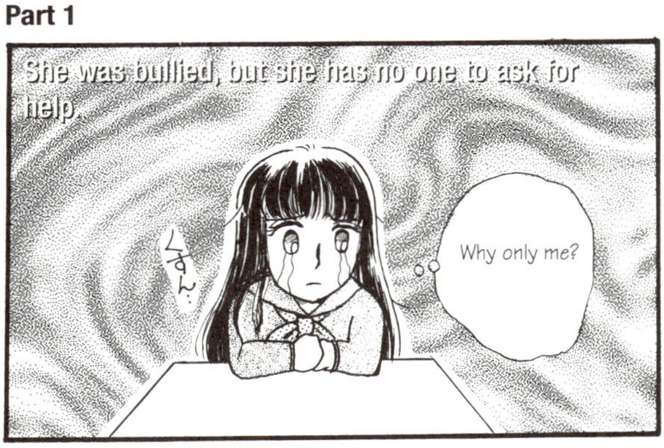

Part 2

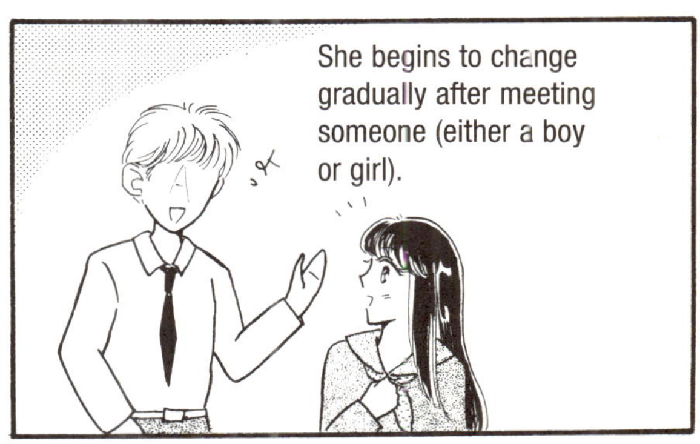

(Incident, hardship, love, etc.)

- A friend appears on the scene.
- (It will not be dramatic if the heroine accepts the situation and solves the problem all by herself.)
- She becomes able to clearly convey her opinions to others.
- The heroine becomes interested in pictures and makes the effort to begin drawing.
- Episode
- She discovers her true dream (she wins a prize for her drawing).

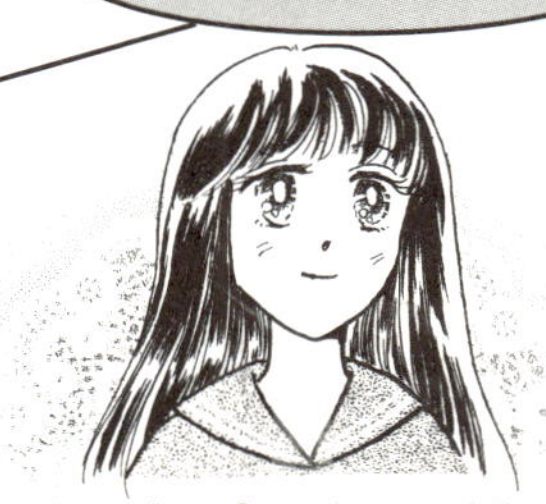

Heroine after Growing and Developing

Here the heroine is surrounded by good-looking boys.

If the heroine does not have a friend, a boyfriend, or other supporting character that can relate to her, adding another character such as a new friend will give more breadth to the story. Contingency is important including encounters and dialogue that do not appear to be self-serving.

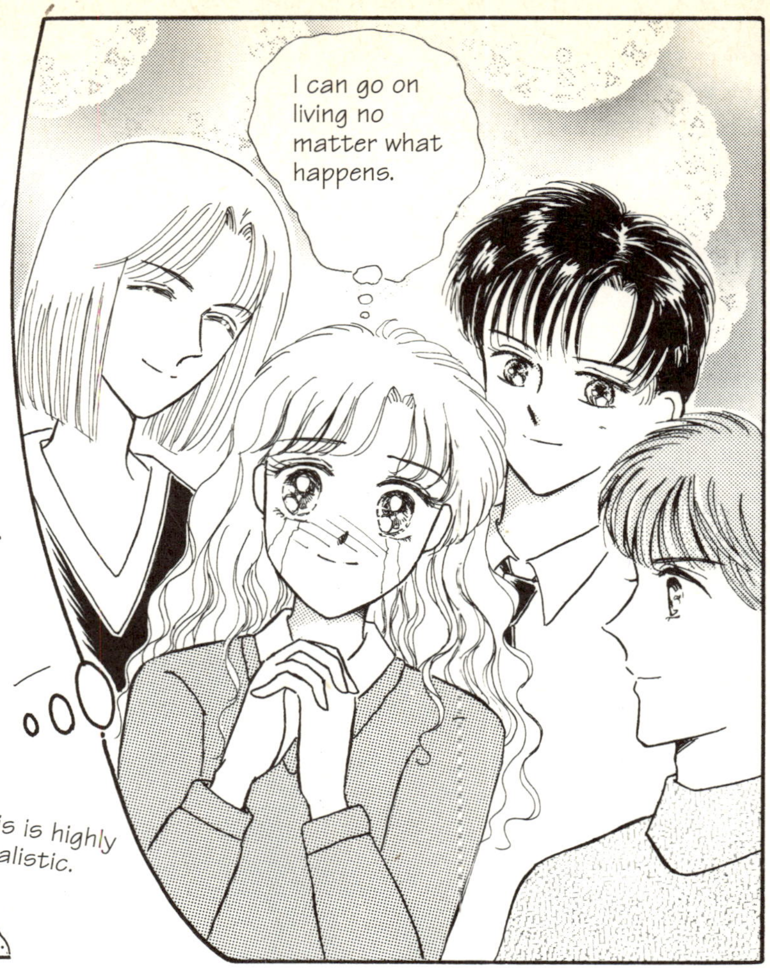

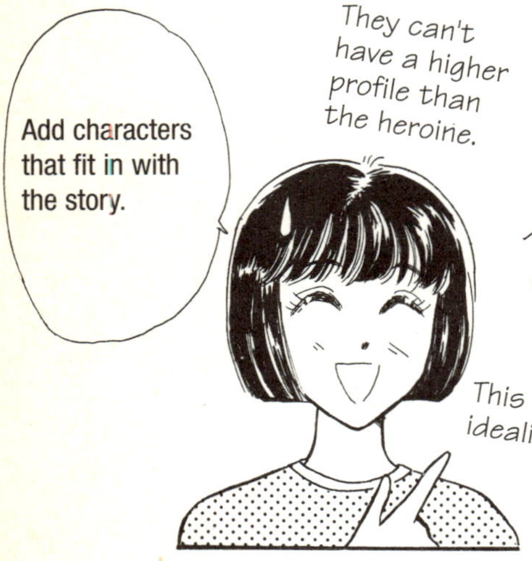

Notes on Giving Shape to the Story

Good Example

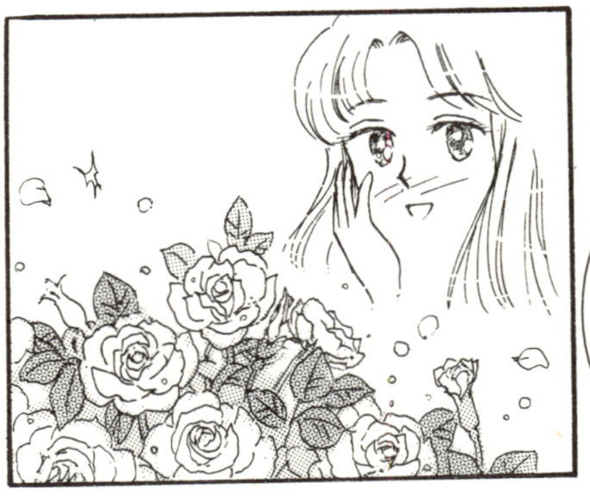

Poor Example

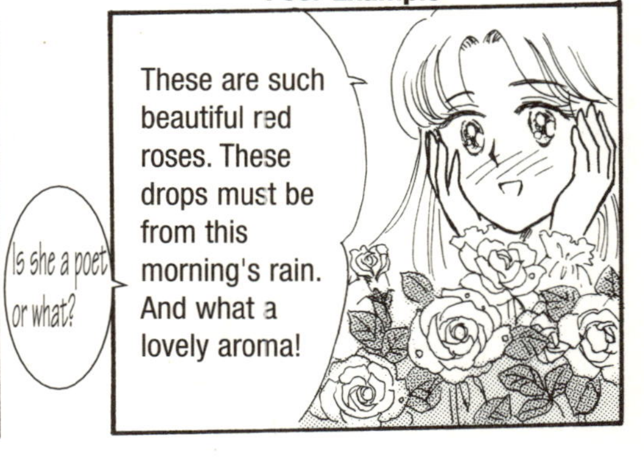

Convey the feelings of a character with a simple picture and not a lot of dialogue (must not be explanatory).
Omit superfluous characters and events to improve the tempo of the story.

Special Effects Used in Girls' Comics 3

There always seems to be someone crying at some point in every girls' comic. Whether it is a girl or a boy crying, tears have a very strong impact.

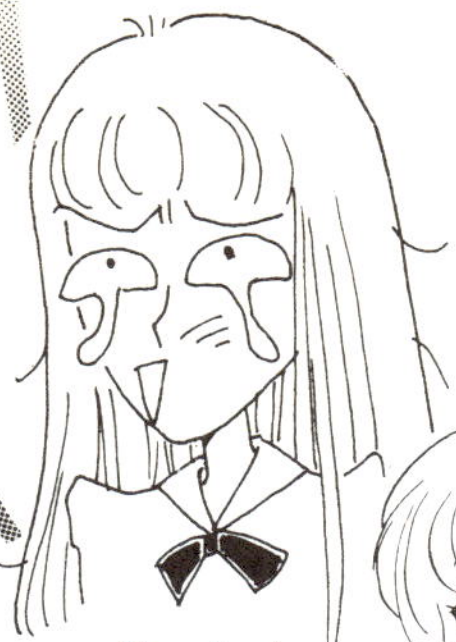

Comical

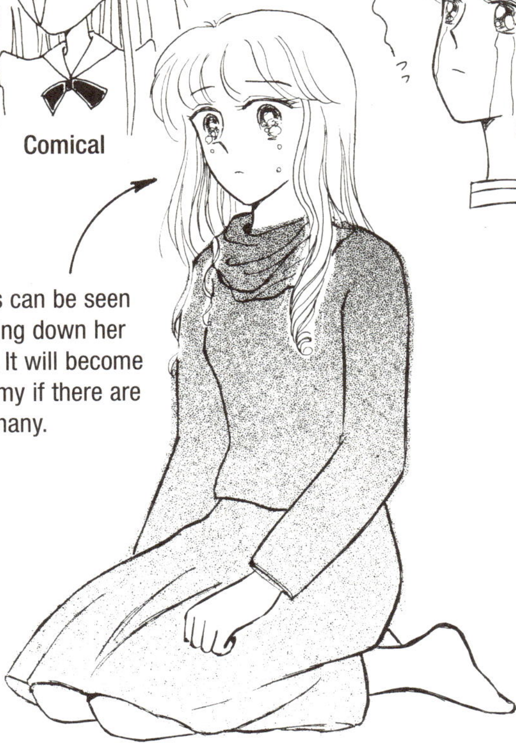

Tears can be seen running down her face. It will become rheumy if there are too many.

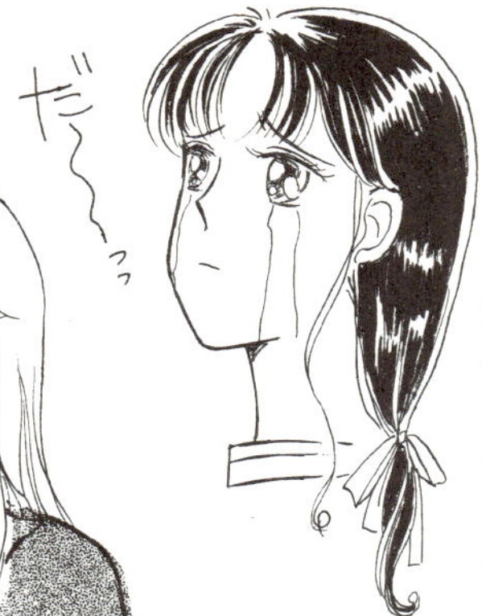

This is the type of person who is moved to tears and cannot be stopped by anyone.

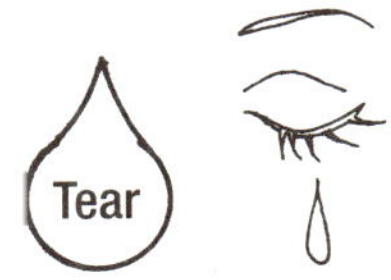

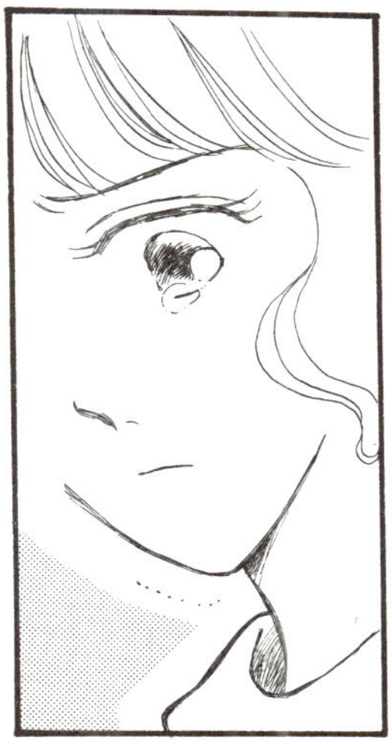

Single Tear Builds Up
Choking down tears.

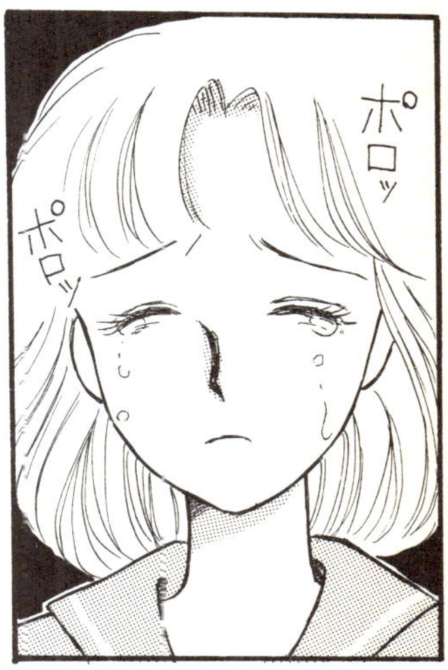

Streaming Tears
One tear after another spills out.

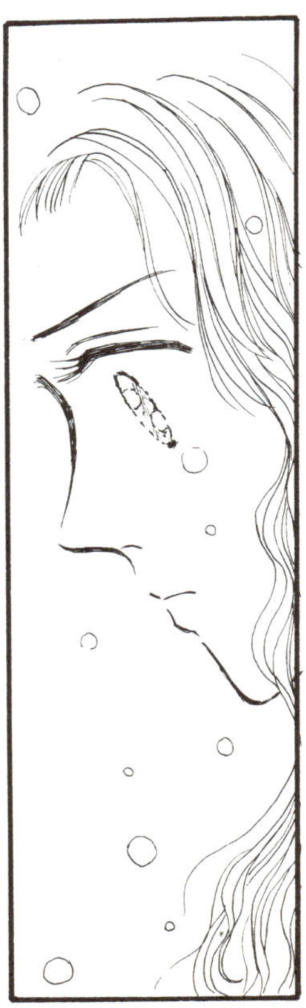

Here snow and tears were assimilated.

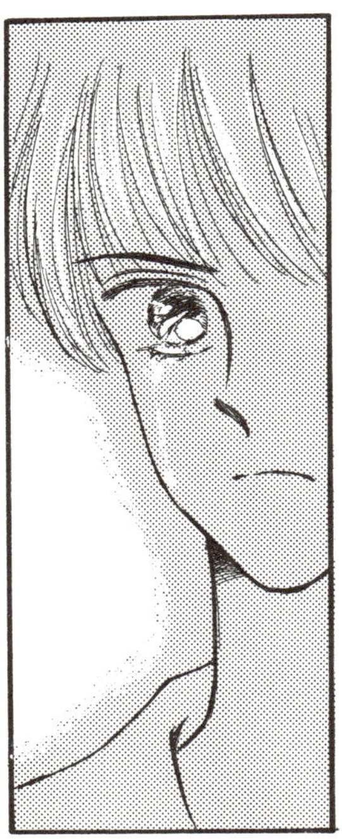

Tone was applied to the entire character and the tears were made by scraping with a cutter.

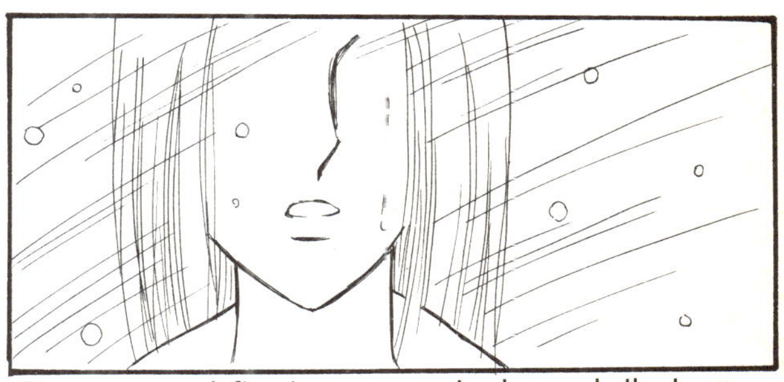

The eyes were left out on purpose to show only the tears.

There are many other situations where tears can be used for much greater effect by making an impact through the actions of characters and the plot.

4 Climax

This is where the story comes to a climax. It is where the characters' true feelings and actions are expressed. This is the high point of the comic, so use large frames and let the pictures do the talking.

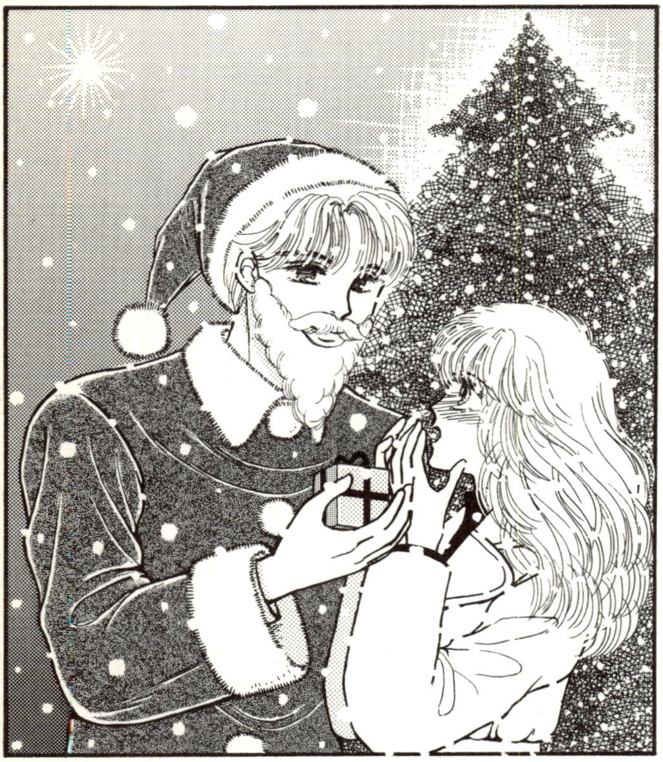

Example: Use Christmas to make the scene more romantic. Use the background effectively as well. Create a memorable scene!

Not good This is too mundane for a confession of love.

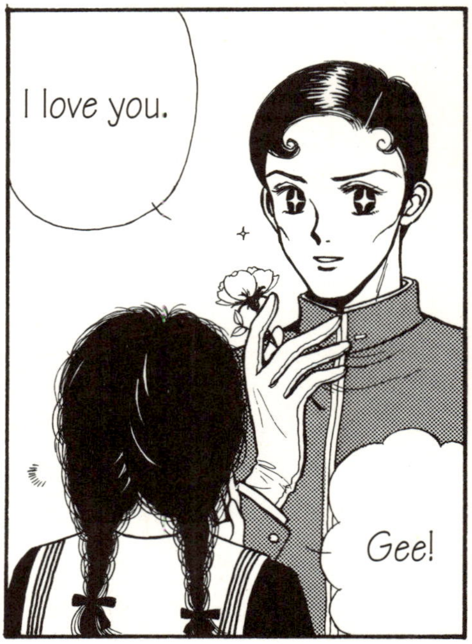

Example: A couple embracing in the rain.

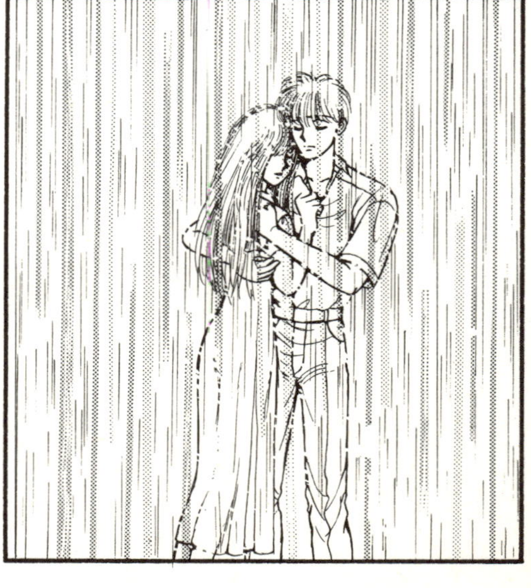

- When you want to convey a concept, try to show it to readers without use of lines and monologues.
- The climax is the place to demonstrate your concept. This is the place to express what you want to express.

5 Props

A prop is any object that can be picked up like a magazine or food. Use of props can eliminate the need for excess explanations and play a large hole in advancing the story.

Here are some examples:

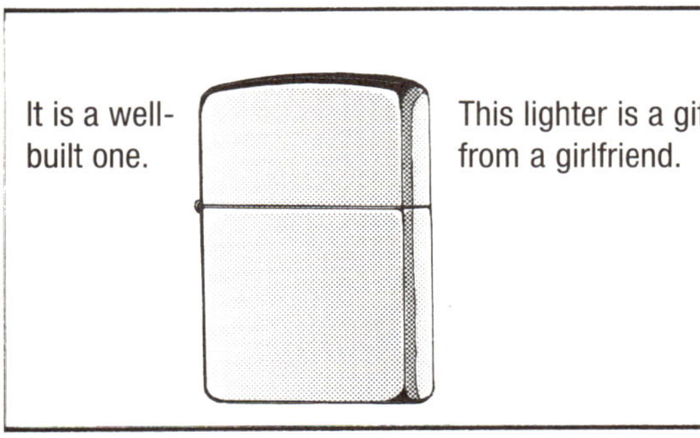

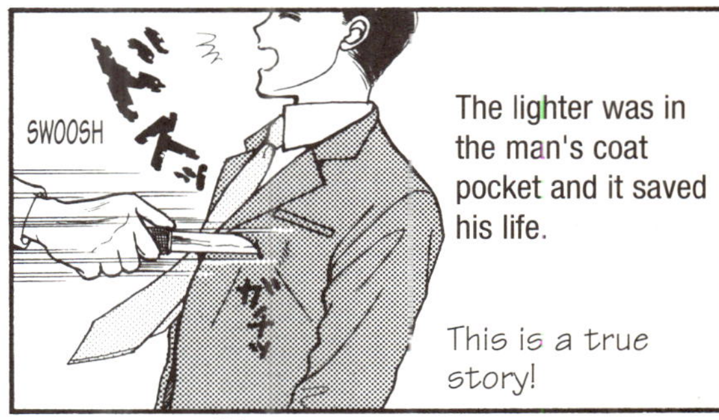

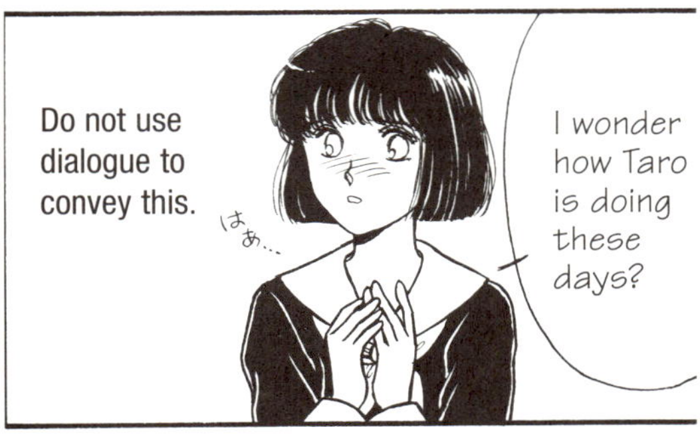

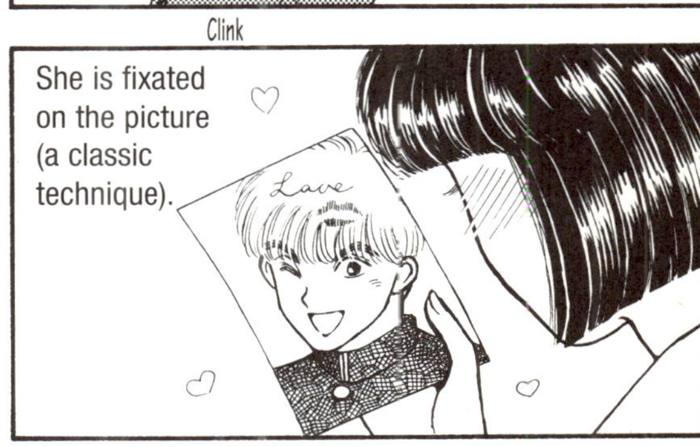

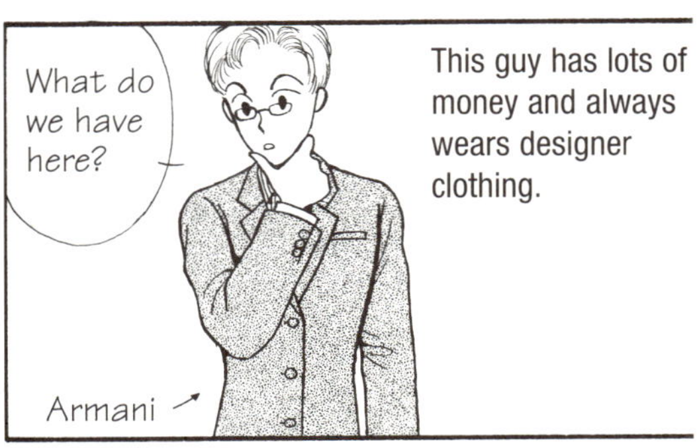

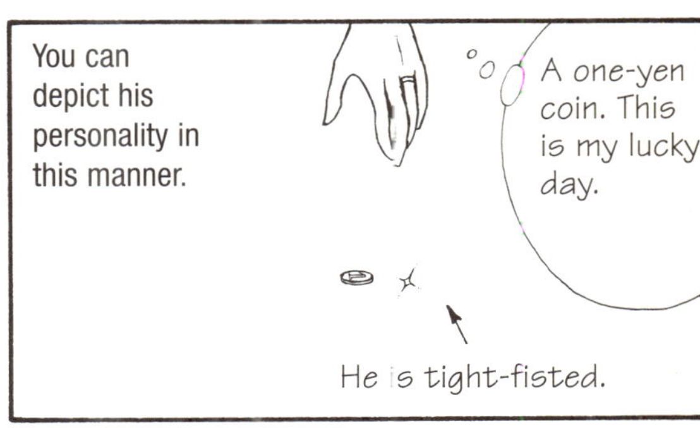

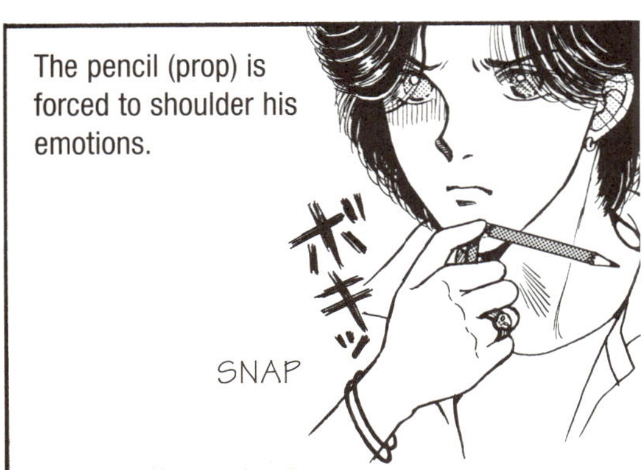

- Props can give you ideas for a story. You want to make good use of interesting ideas in your story.
- Collect information from a variety of sources to find hints for stories.

Chapter 4
How to Create Manga Manuscripts

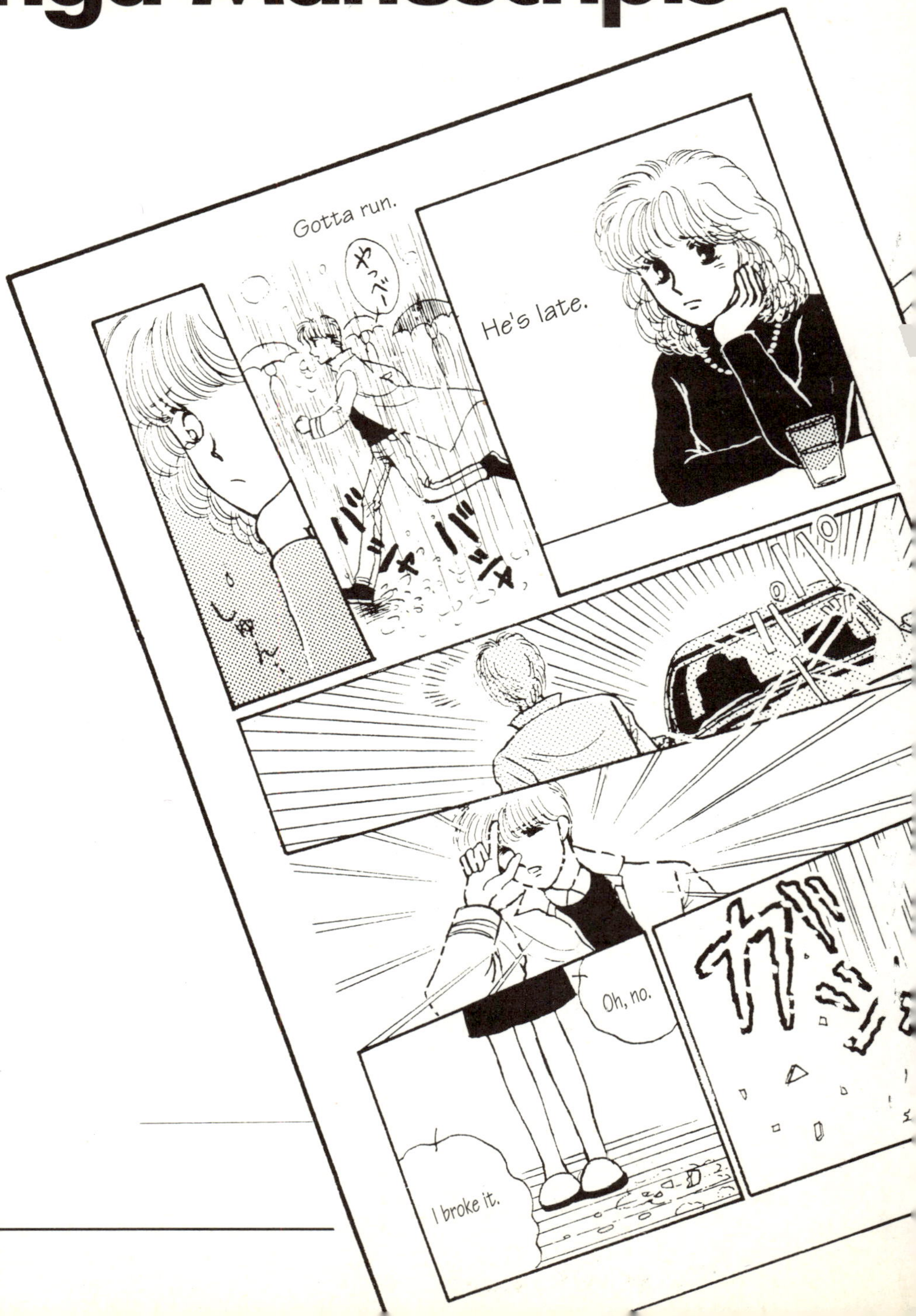

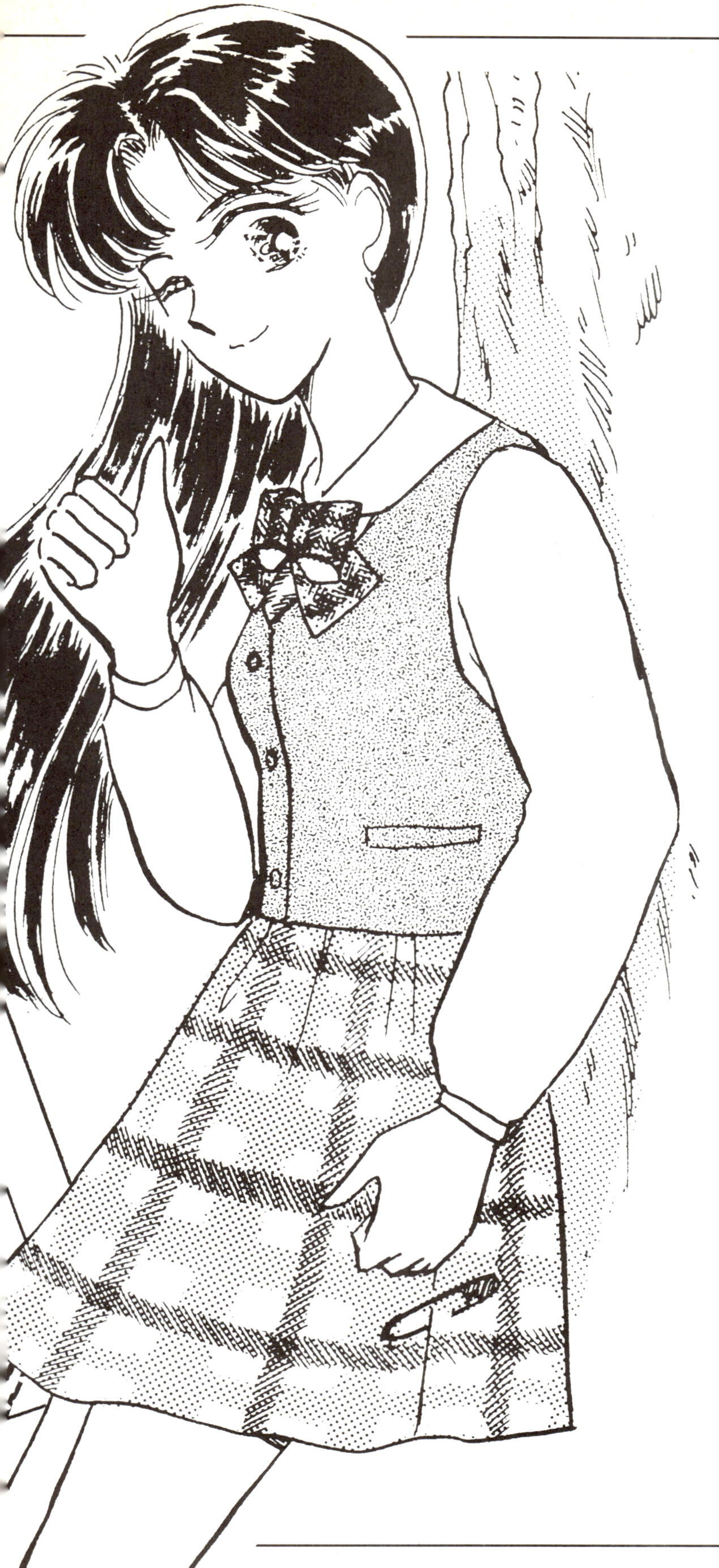

Writing a Plot

A plot is an outline of a story. For instance, the heroine and another character may fall in love. After deciding on the central part of the story, you flesh it out with an introduction, episodes, a main scene, and an ending scene.
Turn it into an enjoyable composition, paying attention to the following:

- Is the setting fully explained?
- Is the foreshadowing effective?
- Is the climax exiting?
- Is the story left unfinished?

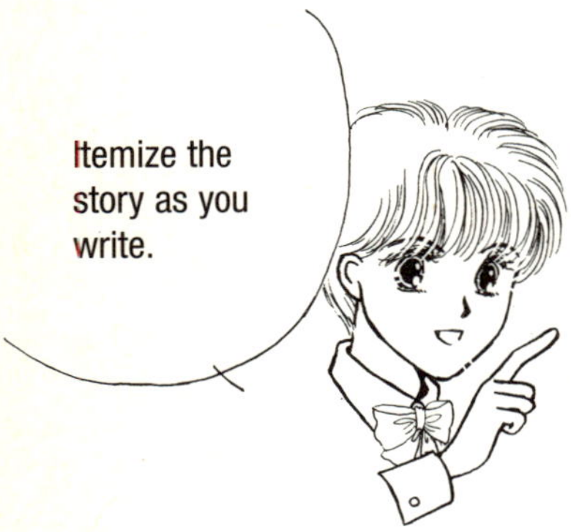

If you are going to draw a 16-page comic, write a plot that will fit within the 16 pages.

Example

Plot No.1

Page	
①	Title Page
② ③ (Two-Page Spread)	Picture of the heroine arriving at school in the morning. A boy runs up to her. He chides her on her new haircut.
④ ⑤	They are in the same class and sit next to each other. They have fights but are good friends. When the talk turns to what type of girl the boy likes, he indicates a type that is opposite that of the heroine.
⑥ ⑦	The next day, the boy runs into the hall and bumps into a girl in a neighboring class. He apologizes profusely. The heroine sees this and gets angry.

⑧ ⑨
⑩ ⑪
⑫ ⑬
⑭
⑮
⑯

END

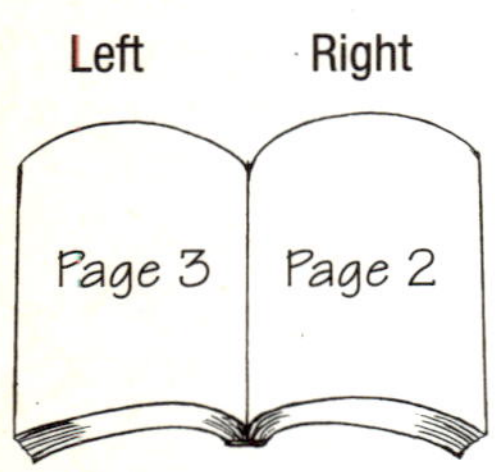

Even pages are on the right.
Odd pages are on the left.

Note: The pagination above is based on the Japanese right-side binding style. In the case of a left-side binding, the even pages should be on the left and odd pages should be on the right.

Storyboarding

Storyboarding is allocating frames based on the plot, drawing rough sketches, and adding dialogue in pencil on any old paper.
It is not always easy to fit the entire plot into the predetermined number of pages. Try narrowing down the story to the most important episodes. Discard any unnecessary episodes. Think about the composition in terms both left and right pages.
How you compose and present a work is important.

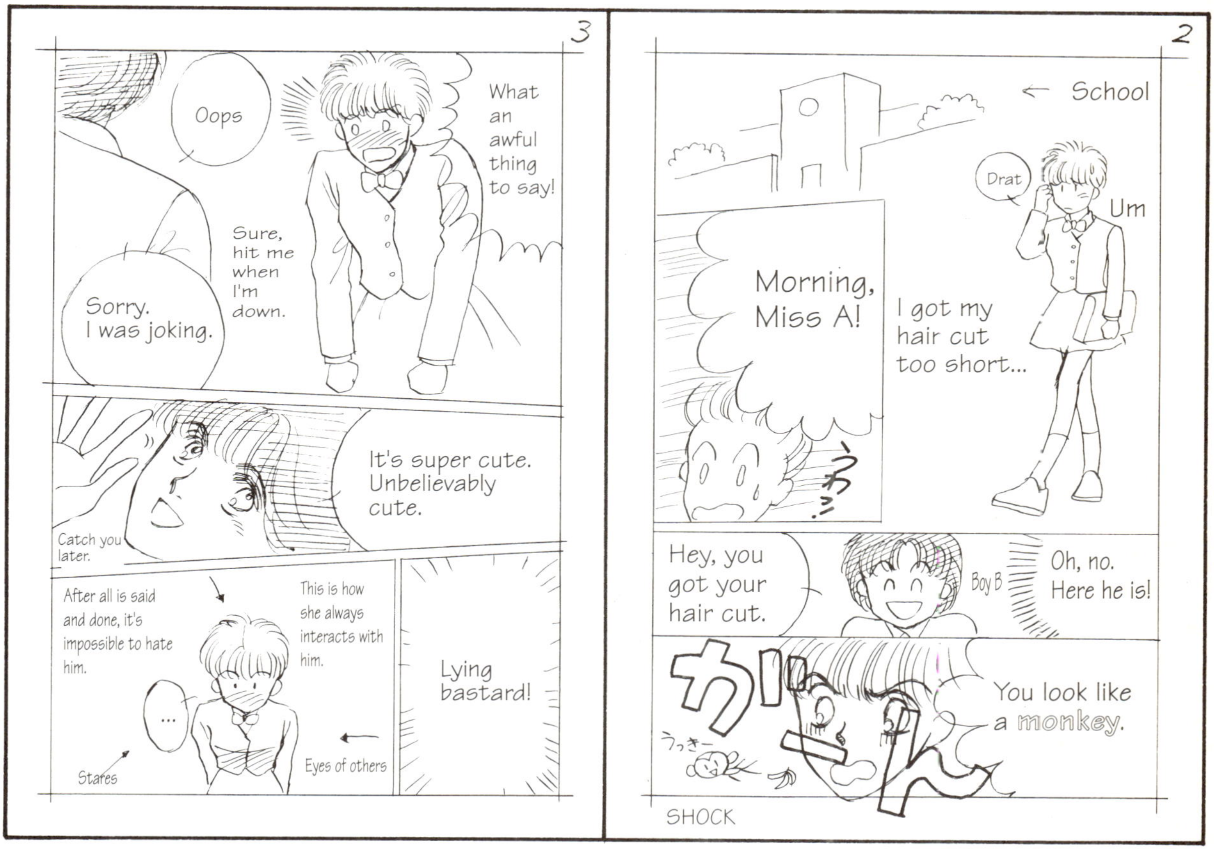

Left page　　　　Right Page

Note: The manga above is in their original layout. Please read from the right to the left.

Inner Margin and Bleeding

Bleeding is when elements of a page extend off any of the four sides. Bleeds are created by trimming the page after printing. Make sure that important drawings, dialogue, and drawn letters are always within the standard border line.

Magazine

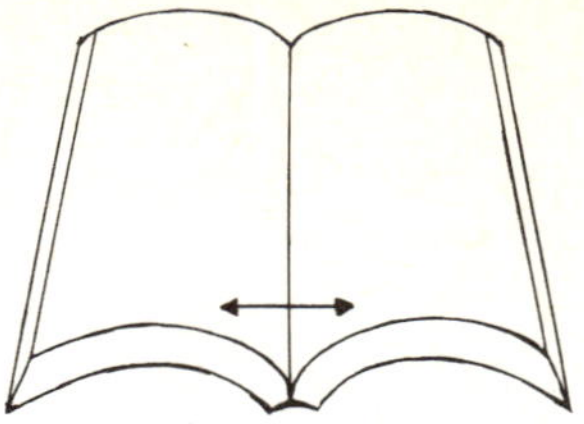

Inner margin

※The inner margin is hard to see, so do not put drawings and dialogue there.

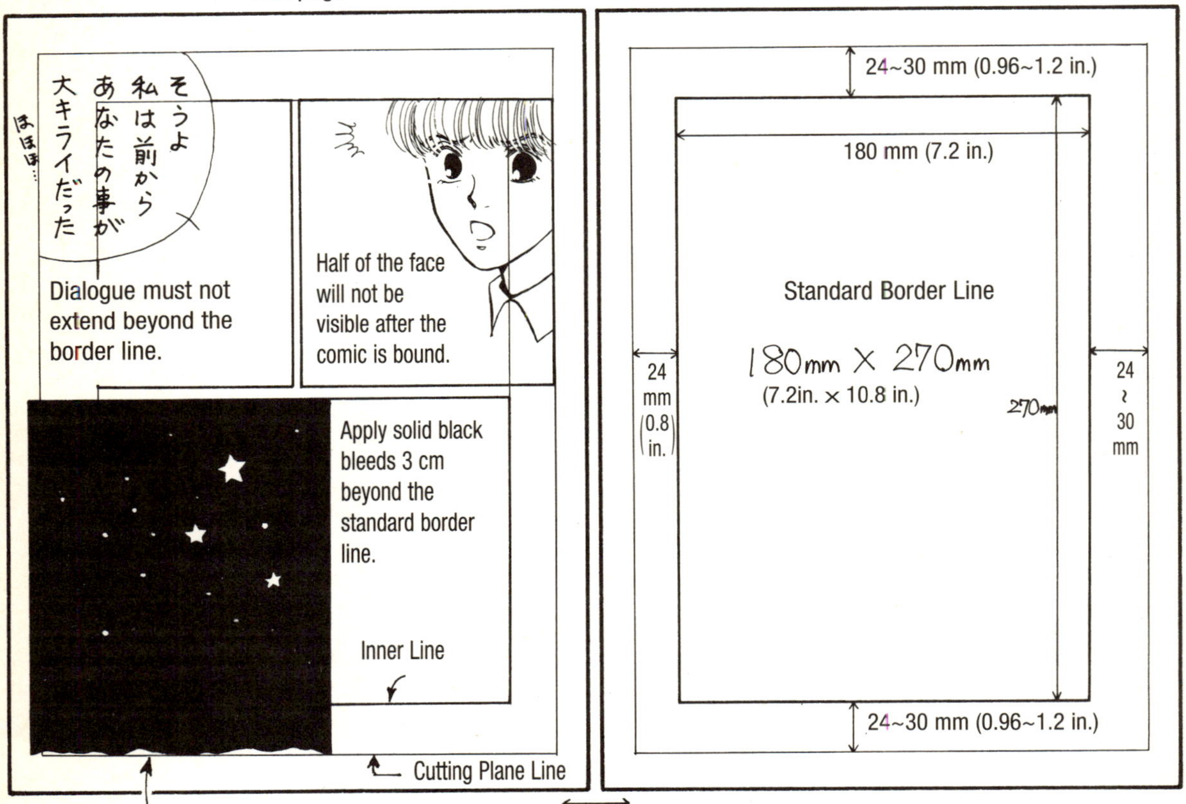

This will be printed as is. In this case it has not been painted properly.

Inner Margin

Bleeding Techniques

- Use bleeds when you want to emphasize the impact.
- Use bleeds to make a frame stand out from the rest.

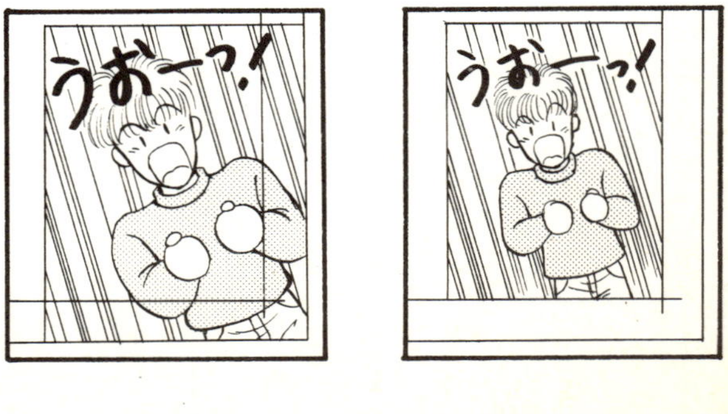

Overuse of runover will make the comic hard to read.

Speech Balloons and Letter Size

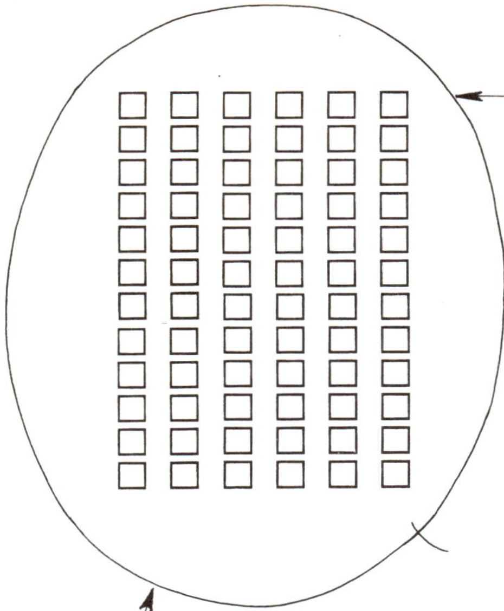

This border is called a speech balloon.

A single letter should be 4.5 mm (0.8 in.) square and the space between lines about 2.5 mm (0.1 in.).

Leave plenty of space between the words and the border of the speech balloon.

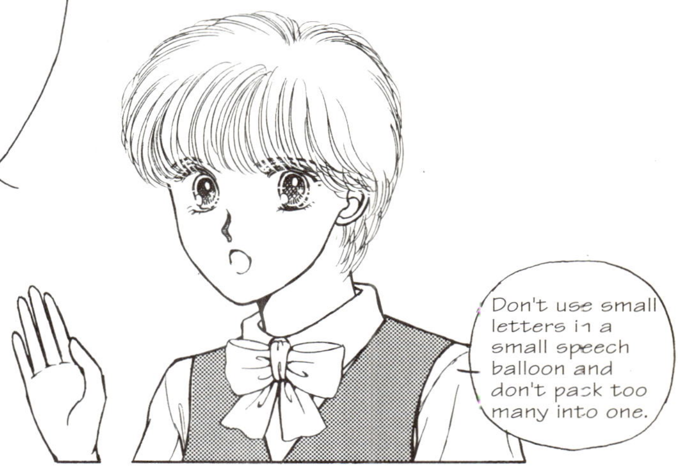

How to Draw a Two-Page Spread

You can draw on either two sheets of B4 paper or on one sheet of B3 paper. Two-page spreads are used for the high point of the comic and for the climax. Use this too much in short comics will often result in a simple story. It is suited more towards long comics.

Drawn on One Sheet of Paper (B3)

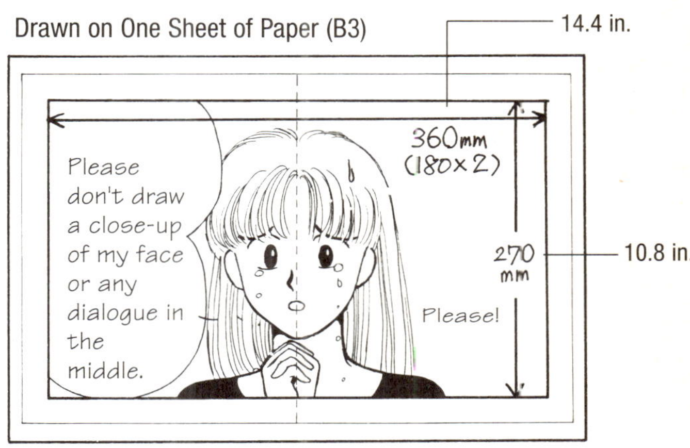

Drawn on Two Sheets of Paper

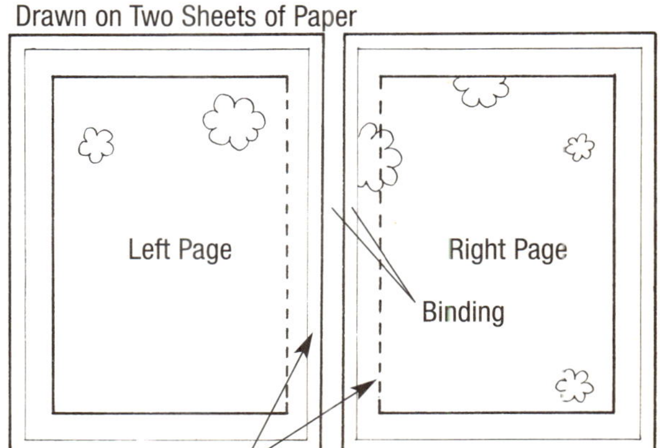

Do not draw this part of the border.

Borders, Speech Balloons, and Drawn Letters

Tools to Prepare

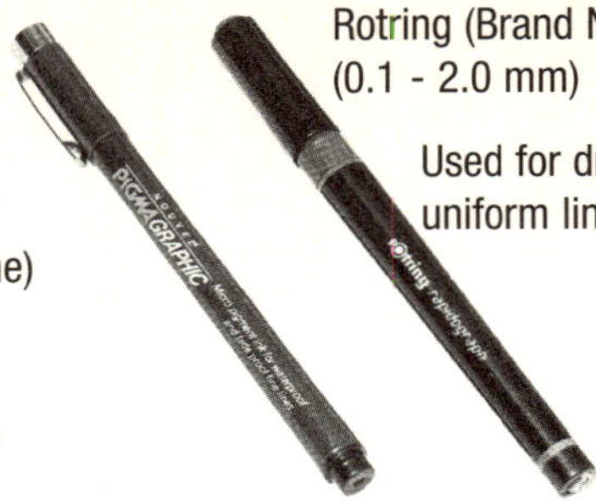

Rotring (Brand Name)
(0.1 - 2.0 mm)

Used for drawing uniform lines.

Pigma Graphic (Brand Name)
(0.05 - 3.0 mm)
Water-based pen
(water-resistant when dry).

Note: Lines will become lighter if an eraser is used on them later.

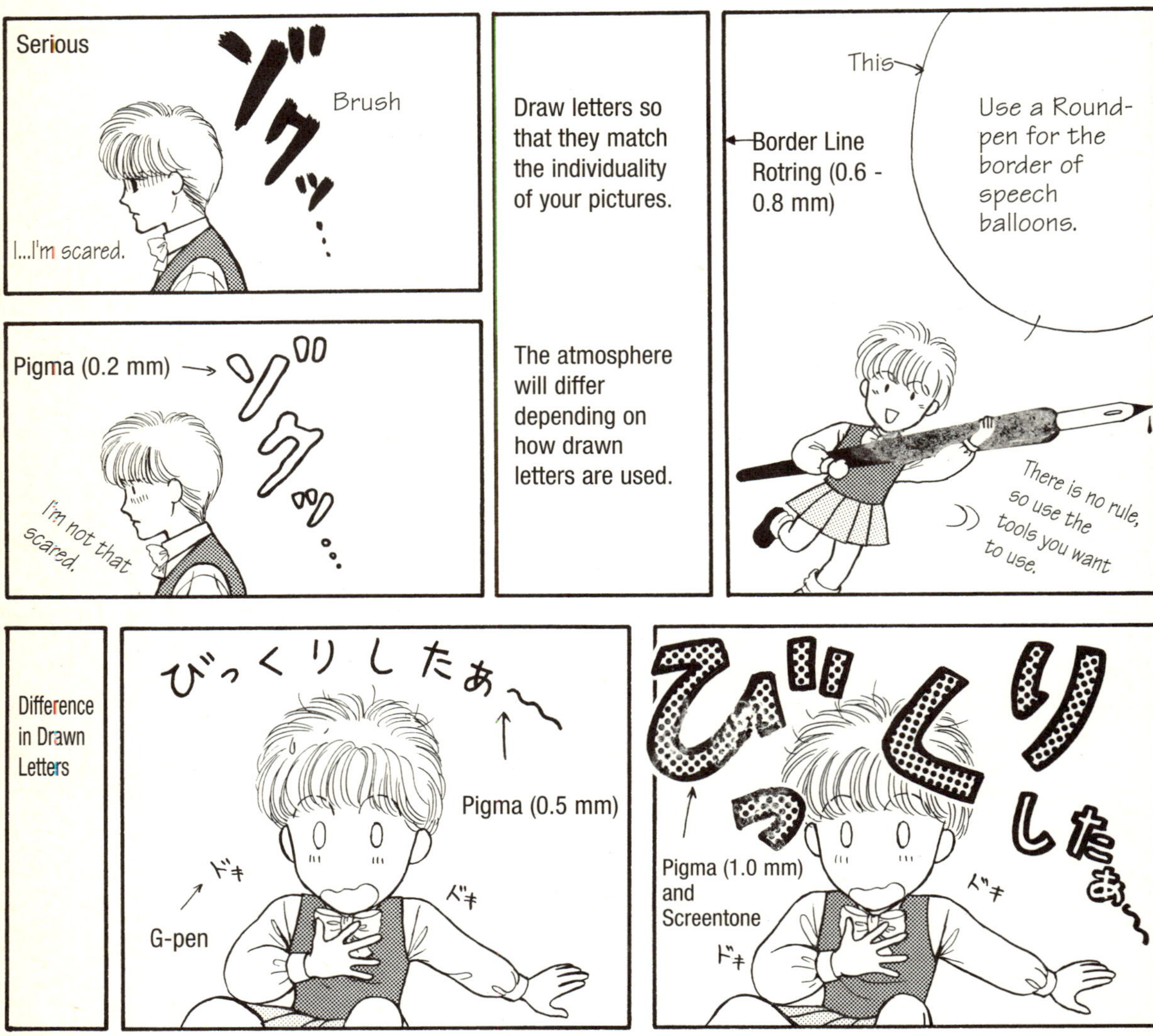

Attention

Using Water-Based Pens

☆They will smear and soil the paper if rubbed when not completely dry and the color will become lighter if an eraser is used on them (choose water-resistant ones since they are vulnerable to water).

Using Oil-Based Pens

☆They blur easily on paper.

Frame Allocation

Frame allocation is very important to the flow of the story. Think about the balance of the frames when looking at both left and right pages.

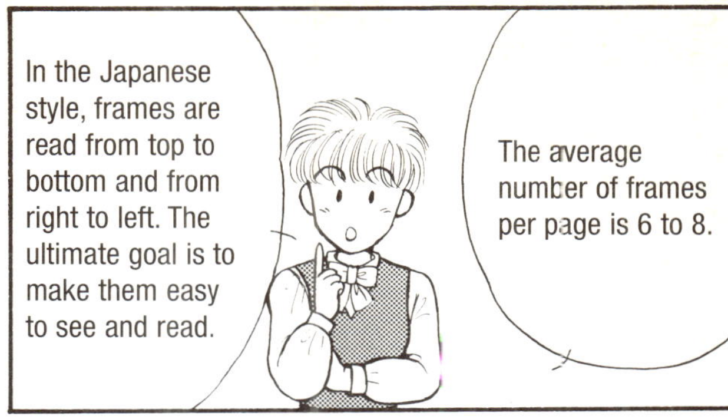

Correct Frame Allocation

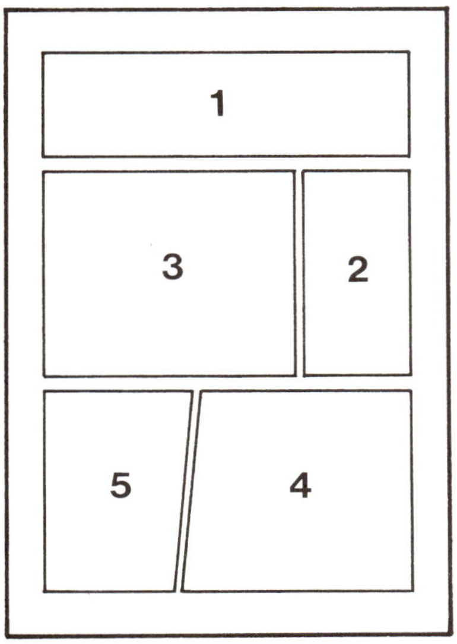

Order of Frames Indiscernible

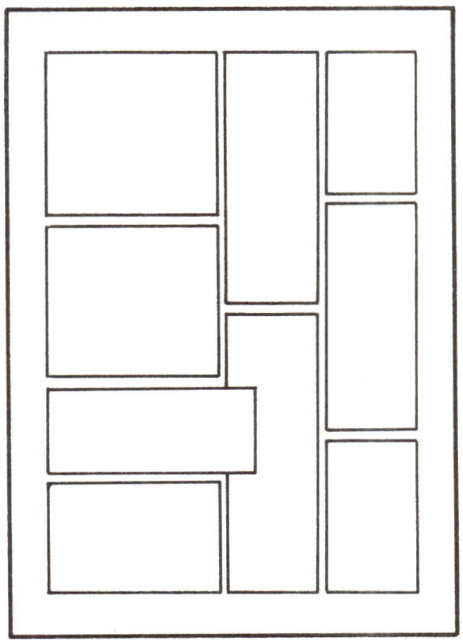

※Having too many frames makes it hard to read.

Too Simple

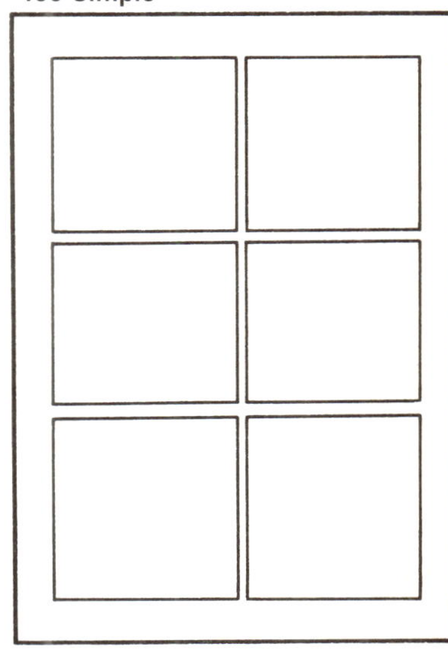

☆Do not allocate frames based on dialogue. Present the story using pictures, thinking about the high point of the page.

☆Large frames are effective when used for the climax.

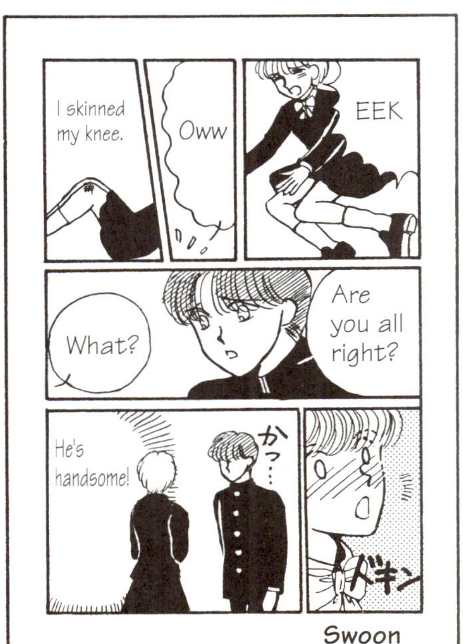

➡ Improvement

Present the knee injury using a picture.

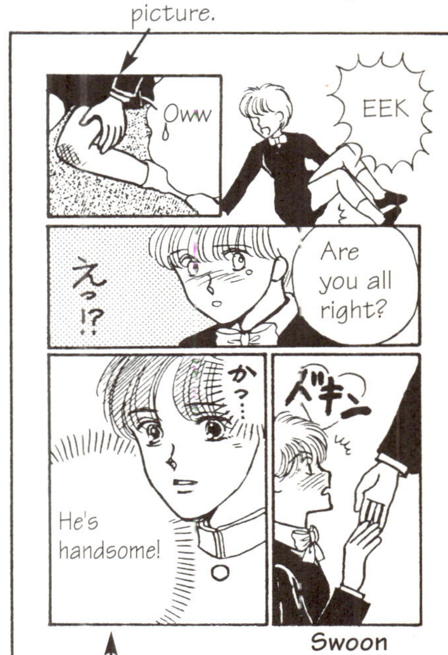

This frame is the high point.

Picture Composition

You can express the emotions of characters and add punch by rearranging the composition of pictures.

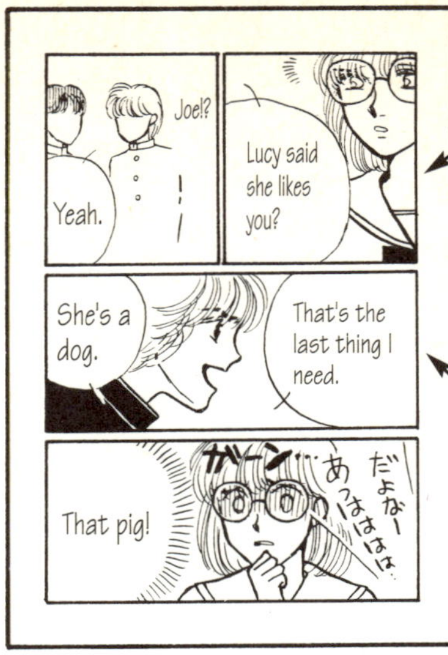

It is hard to discern where characters are and what they are doing if you always use close-ups and bust shots.

In this position, it is hard to tell whether it is Joe or his friend who is talking.

Poor Example

☆Make locations clear by adding a balanced amount of close-ups and wide-angle shots.

Good Example

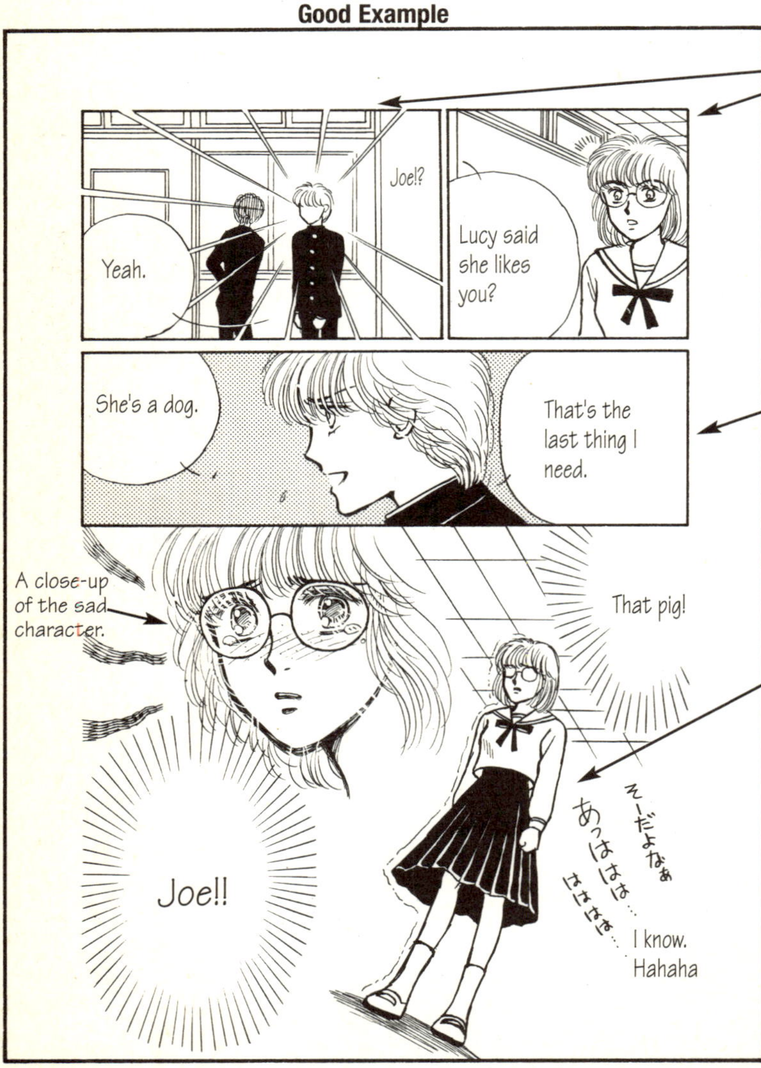

Adding a background will tell readers where the characters are.

The position of Joe was fixed.

The shock she feels is depicted using a low, wide-angle shot.

☆When you want to emphasize a part of the story or make a character stand out, think about effective frame allocation and picture composition.

☆A page will be appealing when there is a frame that catches the eye of the reader when a page is turned.

Shift of Scenery

This is one way to liven up story development. There is no need to go out of your way to shift the scenery, but when you need to do it for a change in location, passage of time, or a retrospective scene, for instance, then it is important to express it in an easy-to-understand manner. Make use of backgrounds and props that can express seasons and time.

Examples of Shifts in Place and Time

Add background such as a building.

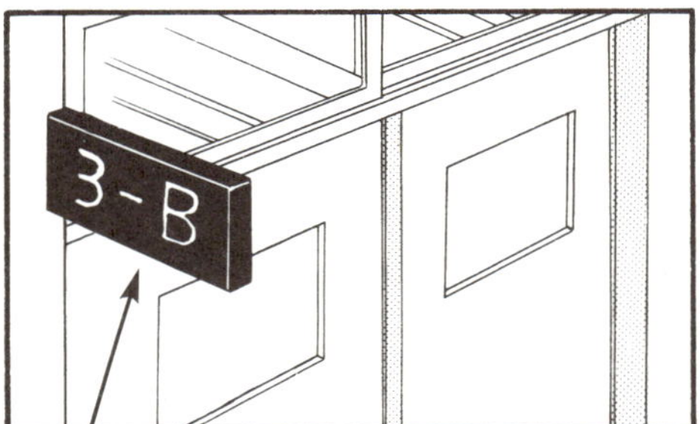

It is easier to understand with words included.

Explain using language.

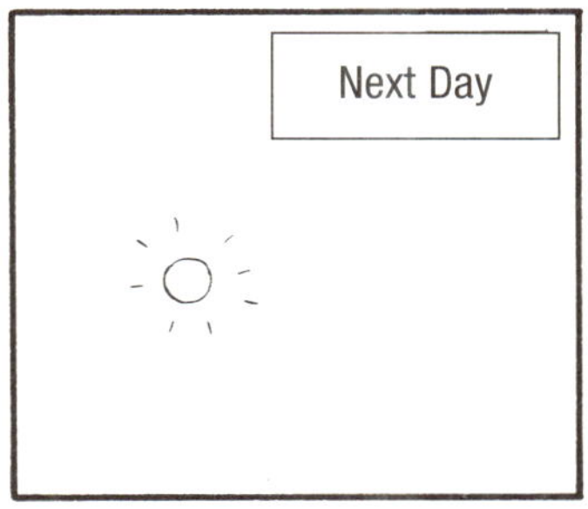

Night is falling.

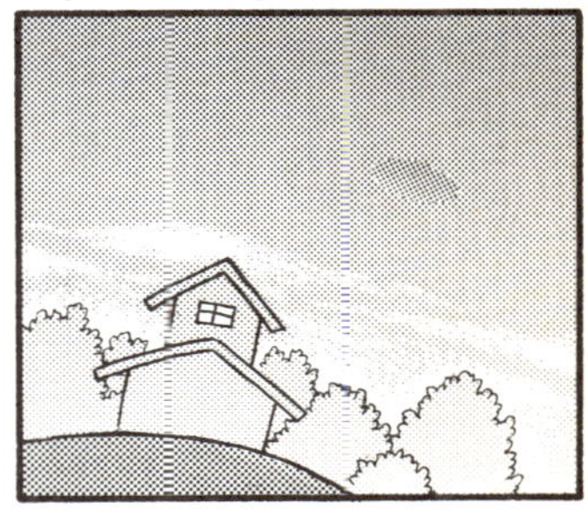

It is now night.

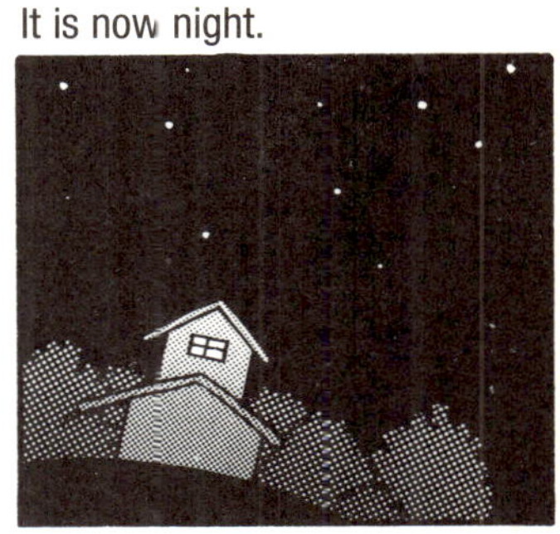

Add a wide-angle background.

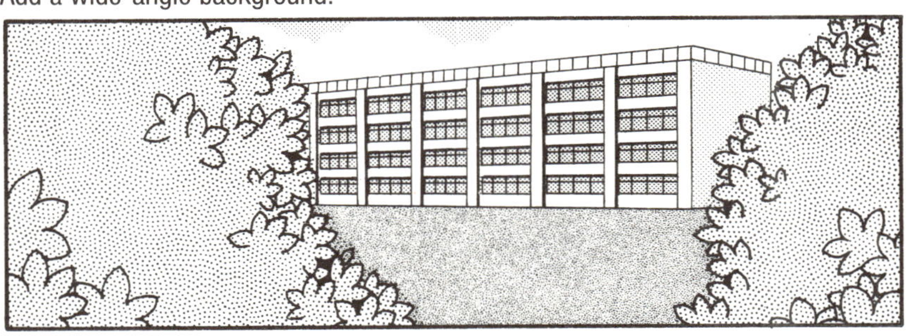

A frame was placed in between to show passage of time.

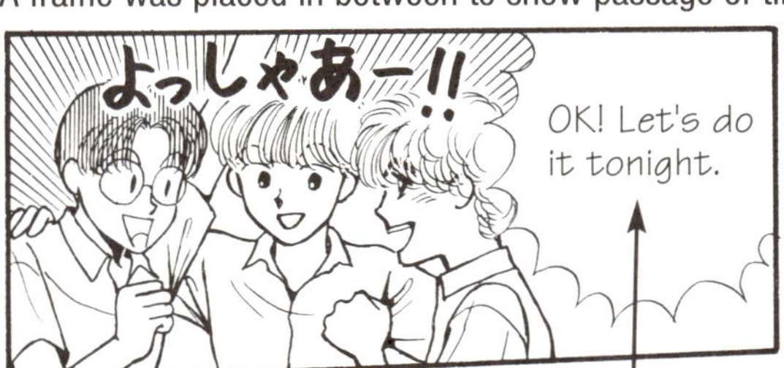

There is an explanation using dialogue as well.

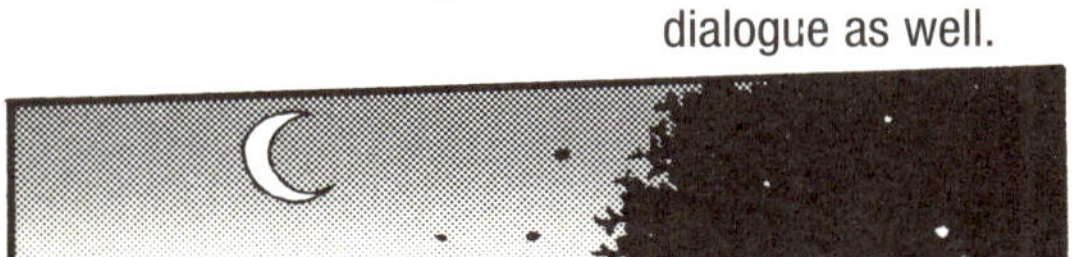

Retrospective Scene

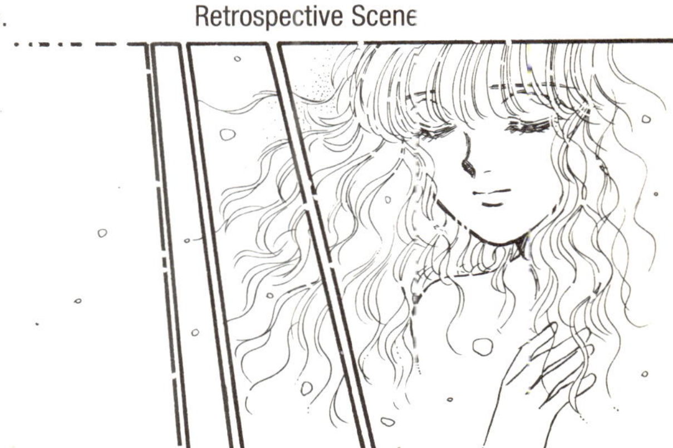

Consecutive frames are gradually made smaller.

Page Turning

Here are some ways to surprise readers when they turn a page. These can also be used to depict changes in scenery and passage of time.

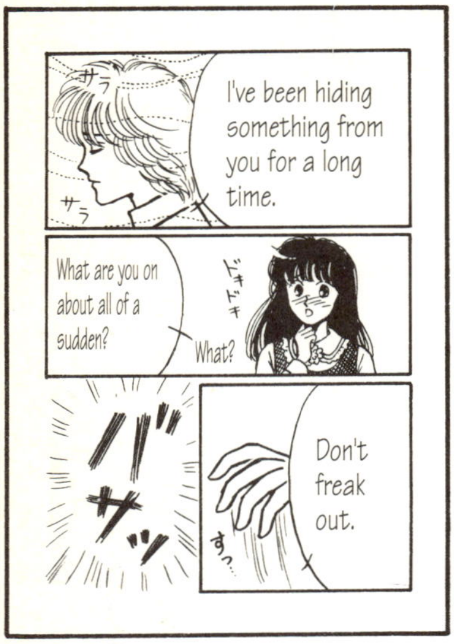

Turn the Page

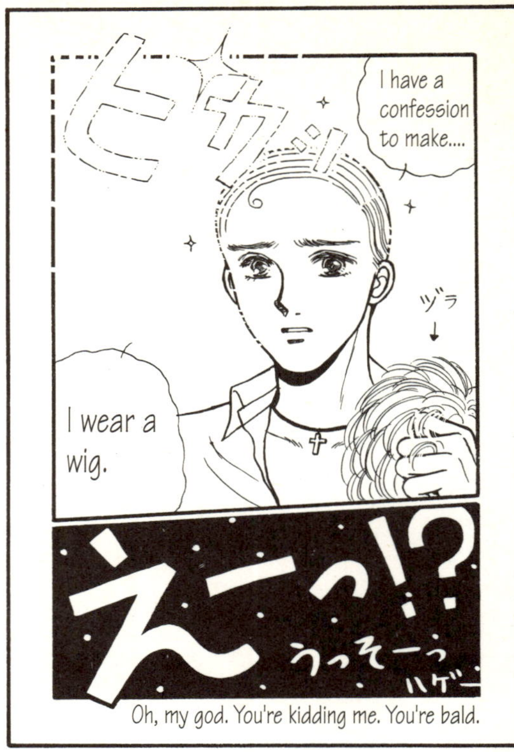

Use a large frame for the high point.

Surprise readers, make them laugh, or touch their hearts.

Shot Types

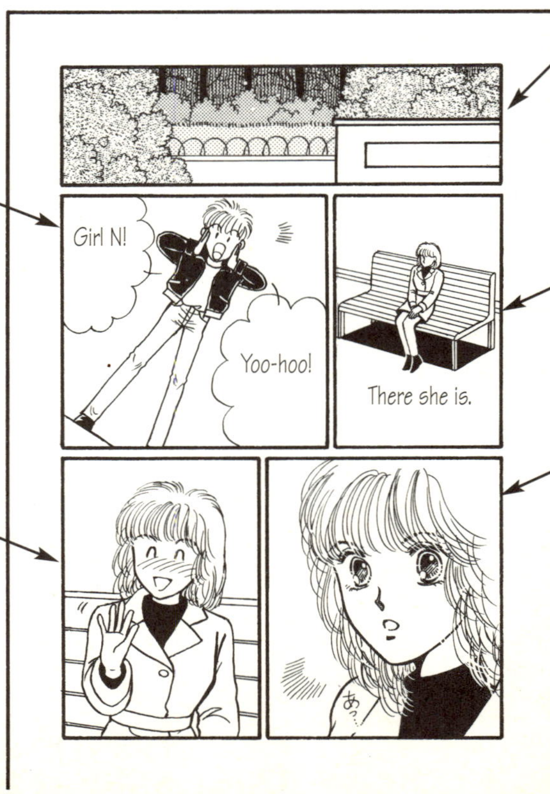

Wide-Angle Shots
- Used to depict places and

Full Shots
- This is a shot of the full length of a character. Can be used to depict personality and characteristics via body motions.

Middle Shots
- Convenient for explaining where characters are.

Bust Shots
- This is a shot of the upper body.

Close-Ups
- Used to depict facial expressions and emotions characters (make them attractive).

Vantage Point and Angles in Scenes with Characters

Do not allocate frames and compose pictures in a haphazard manner. Creative use of vantage point (position from which something is viewed) and angles will enrich the presentation.

As viewed from the camera.

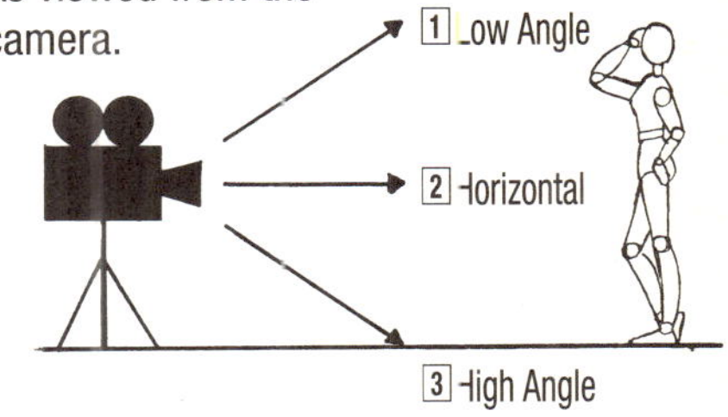

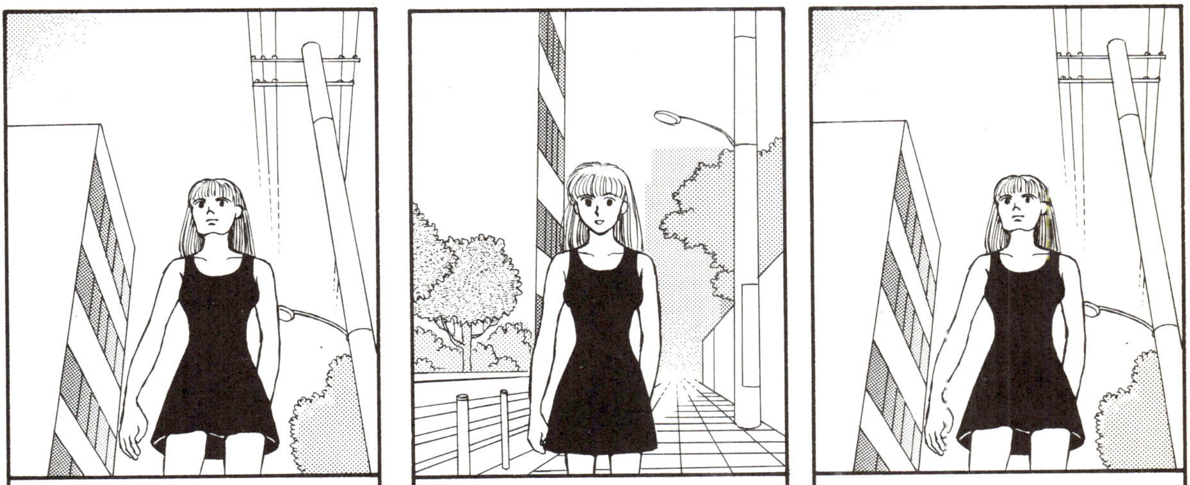

1 Low Angle

2 Horizontal

3 High Angle

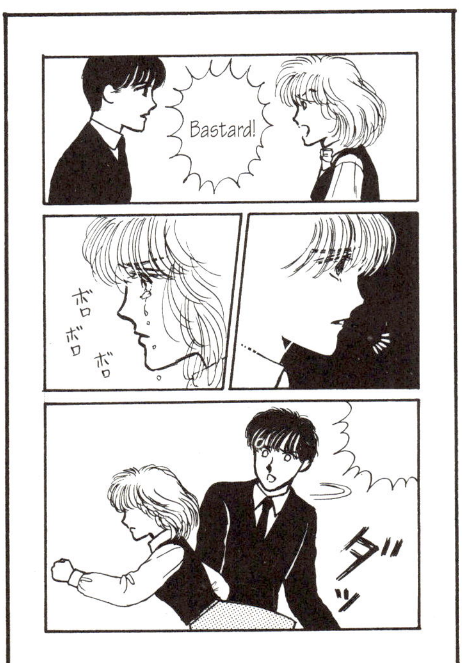

This is a normal angle. It has a quiet feel. This angle is used often.

The camera is fixed in a horizontal position.

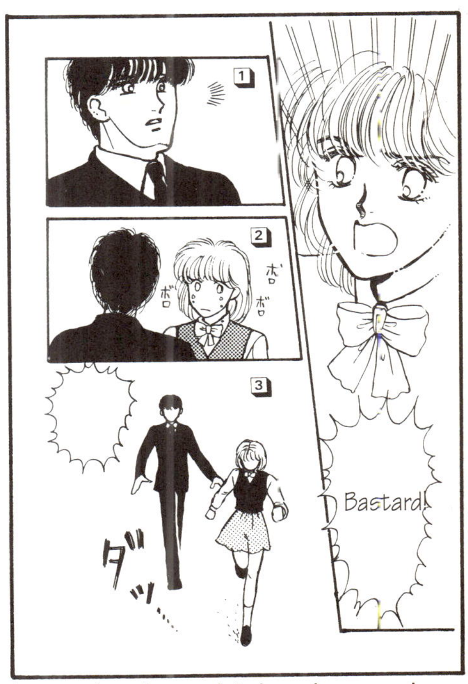

This is a slightly high angle view of a close-up.

A several vantage points have been used (perfect for powerful scenes, etc.).

Cut-Back

This is a method by which two or more different cuts are alternately inserted to build up tension or a sense of impending crisis.

Note: Do not use this technique excessively. It is effective when used before the climax.

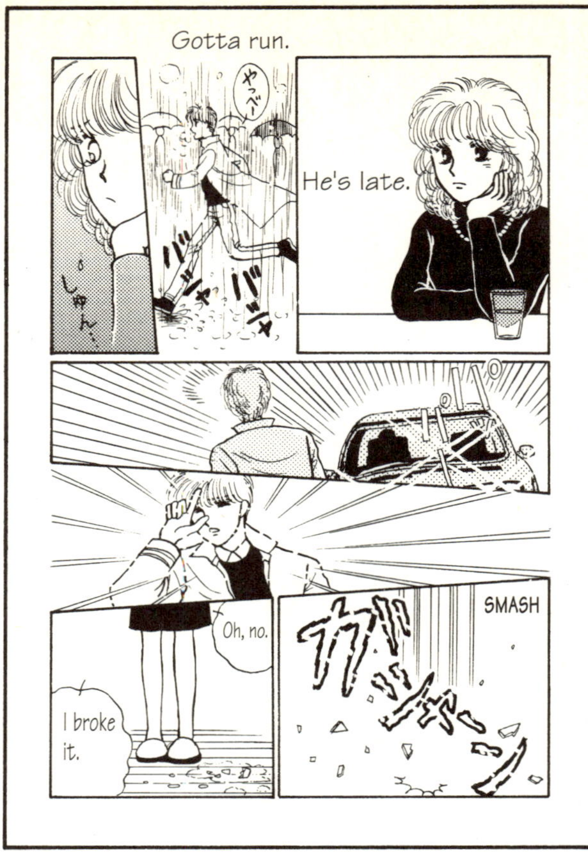

What is happening at the same time at two different places is depicted here.

How to Attach Tracing Paper

When there are going to be letters on solid black, a pattern, or tone, place tracing paper over the drawing paper, write the letters, and mark the position. This includes white letters printed on solid black and tone.

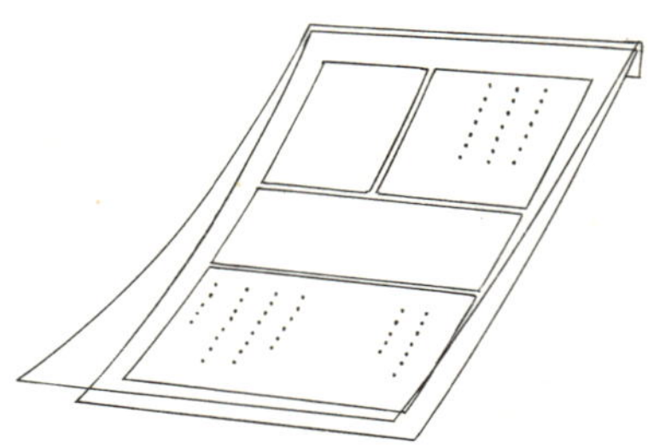

It is all right to cover the entire page with tracing paper.

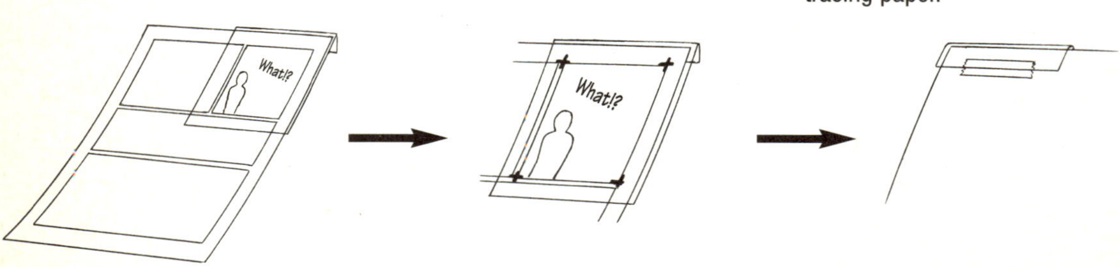

Here the tracing paper is placed on one portion of the page.

Write the letters on the tracing paper with a pencil and mark it (so you know the position).

Firmly attach the tracing paper to the back of the drawing paper with adhesive tape.

Title Page

This is the first page of a comic. It is important to compel readers to want to read the comic. Try to impress upon readers what you want to express most (the theme) in the comic.

Hints

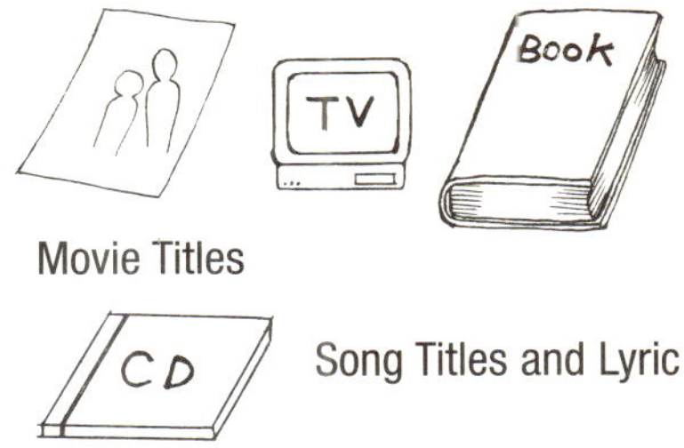

Movie Titles

Song Titles and Lyric Cards

You will find hints for titles hidden among these.

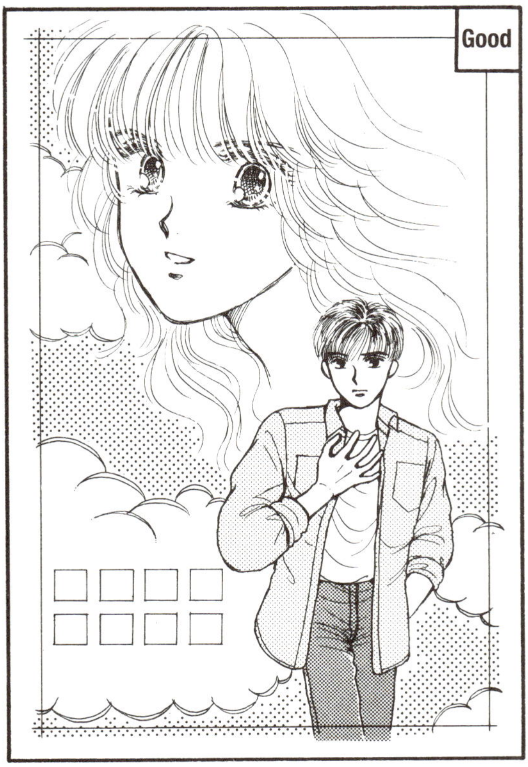

Leave space for the title. Keep the space for the title in mind when choosing the composition of the picture.

Write the title in a corner of the page in pencil.

Avoid titles that will give away the story. Titles should also not deviate too far from the story.
When you choose a foreign-language title that is not understandable, incorporate the meaning of the title in the story.

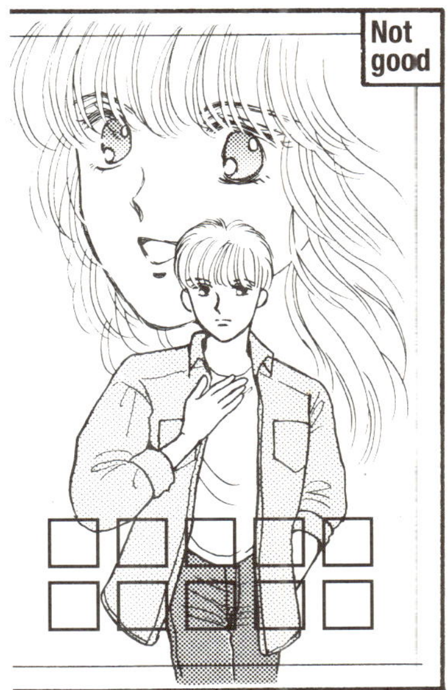

The title is on top of the character. The composition is no good either.

Uninspired Title Page

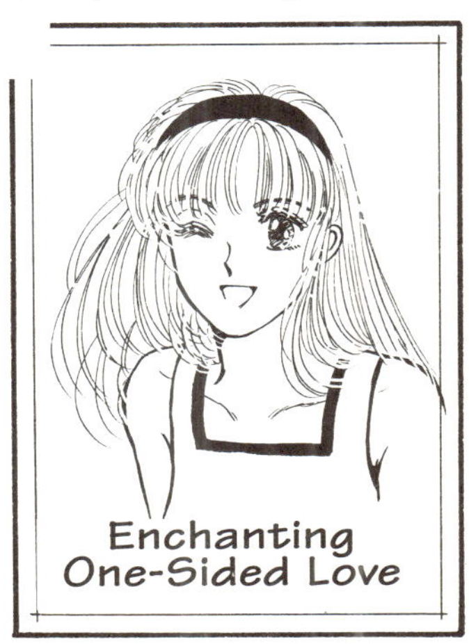

A close-up of the heroine in the middle of the page is mundane.

This garden-variety title should be redone.

Basic Tools

The ease of use of pens and brushes differs depending on the person. Try different types to find the right tools for you.

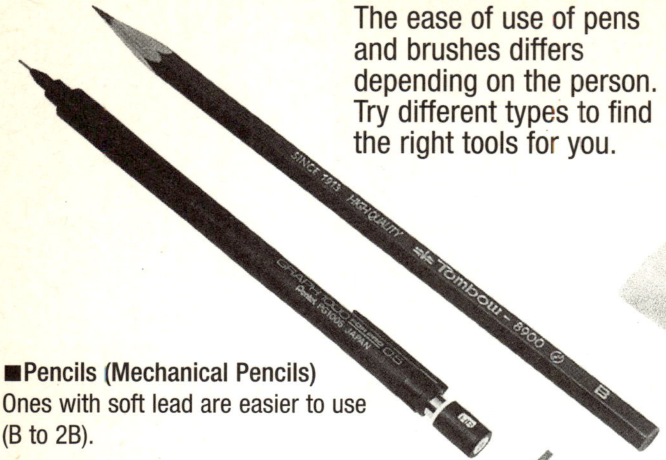

■**Pencils (Mechanical Pencils)**
Ones with soft lead are easier to use (B to 2B).

■**Erasers**
Ink eraser (Also used for erasing tone.)

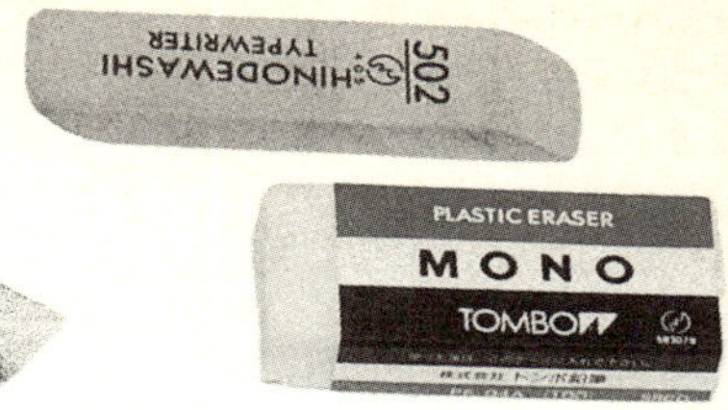

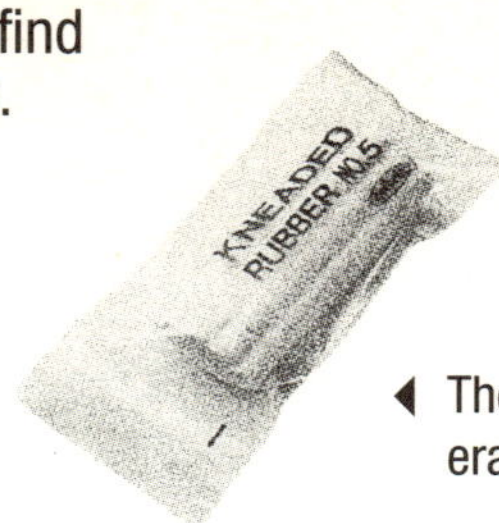

◀ There are also kneaded erasers for sketching.

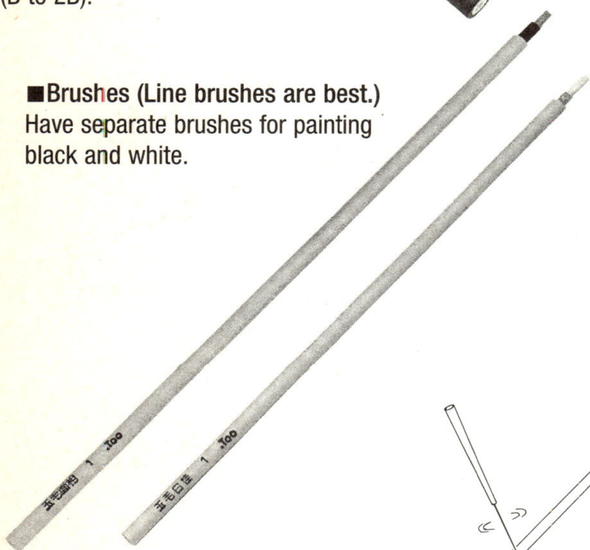

■**Brushes (Line brushes are best.)**
Have separate brushes for painting black and white.

■**Paper**
We recommend manga paper marketed by Too.

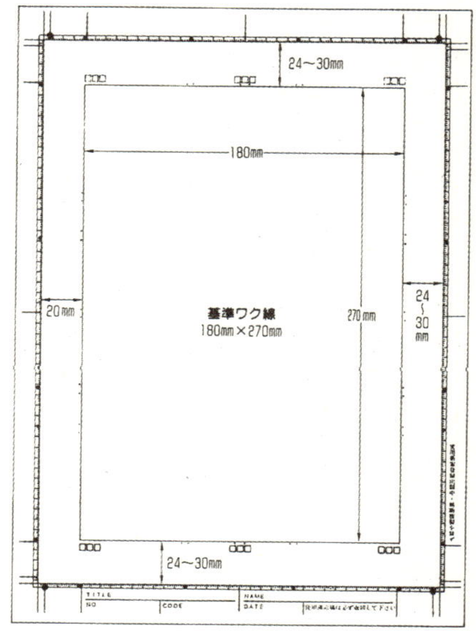

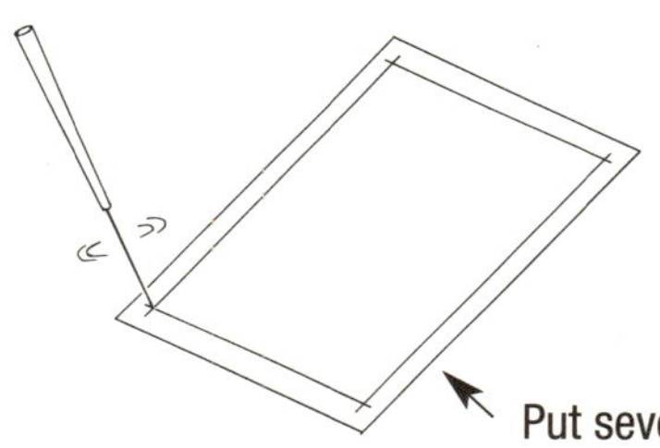

Put several layers on top of each other.

When drawing border lines yourself, you can measure the size of several sheets of paper at once by making holes in the four corners with an eyeleteer.

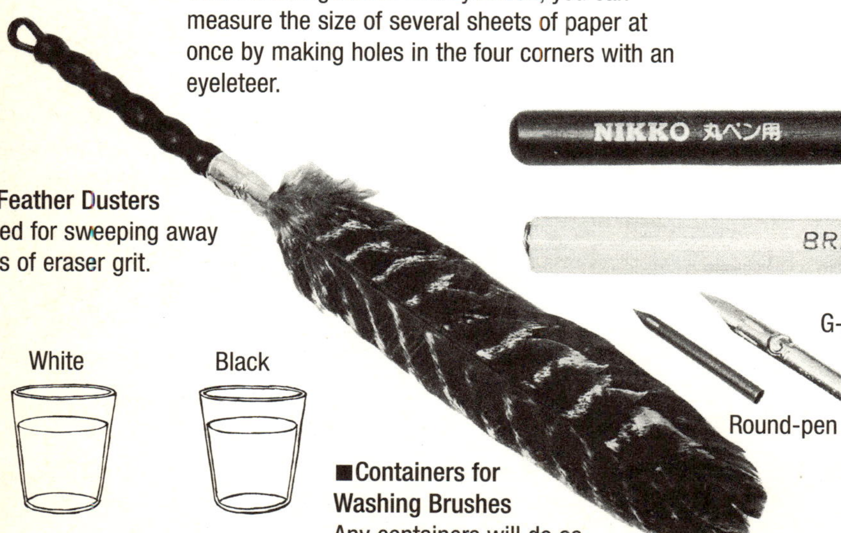

■**Feather Dusters**
Used for sweeping away bits of eraser grit.

■**Pen Nibs and Holders**

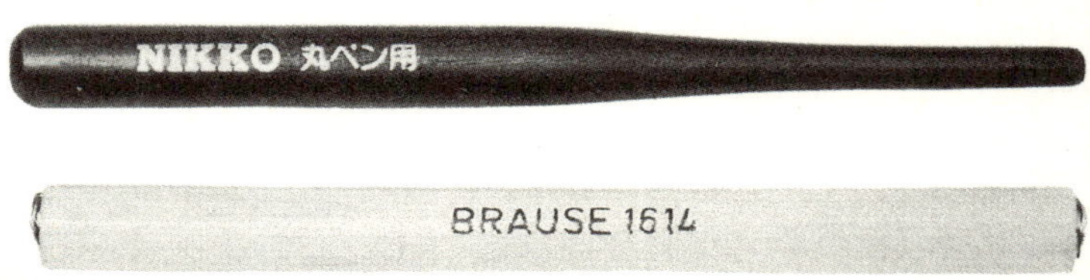

G-pen

Round-pen

White

Black

■**Containers for Washing Brushes**
Any containers will do as long as you have separate ones for black and white.

Here

Insert the nib here.

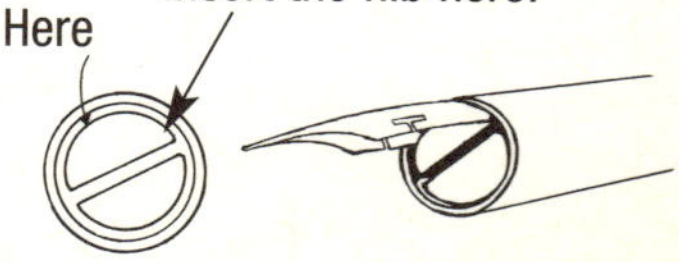

Overhead View of Pen Holder

Rulers with an edge are perfect for drawing India ink lines and drawing pen lines.

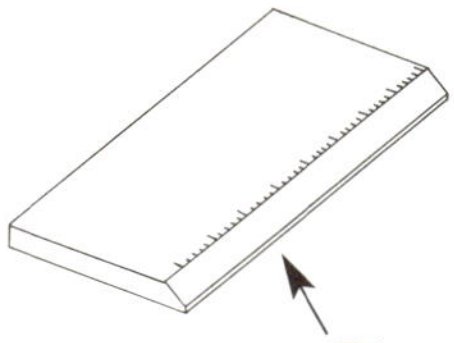

Edge

■**Rulers**

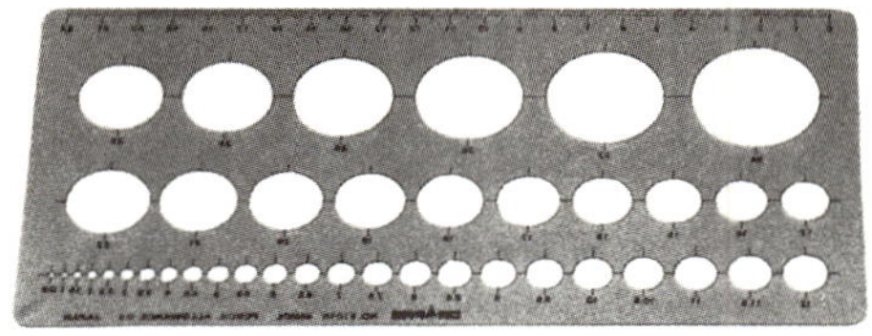

■**Templates**
Convenient for circles and ovals..

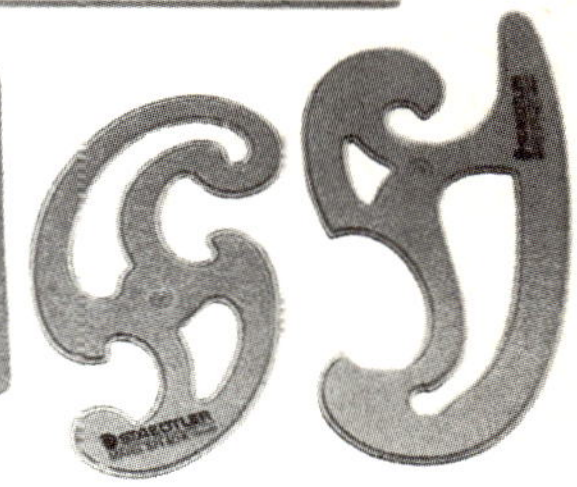

Curved Rule

■**Tone**
Letraset, Screen-Tone, and IC Screen tones are of high quality and are easy to use.

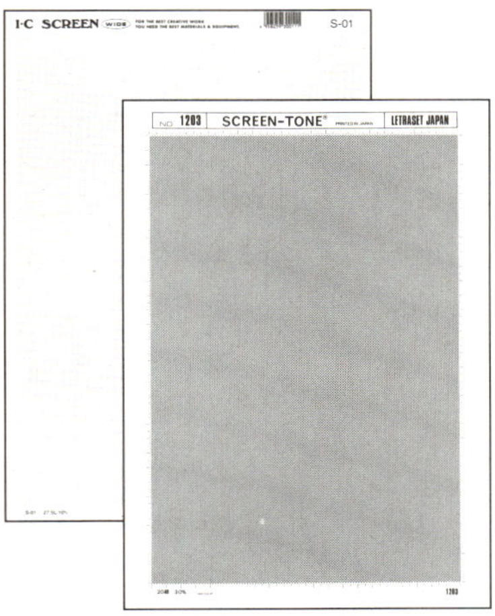

■**Tone Scrapers**
IC tone scrapers are easy to use.

■**Cutters**

■**Design Knife**

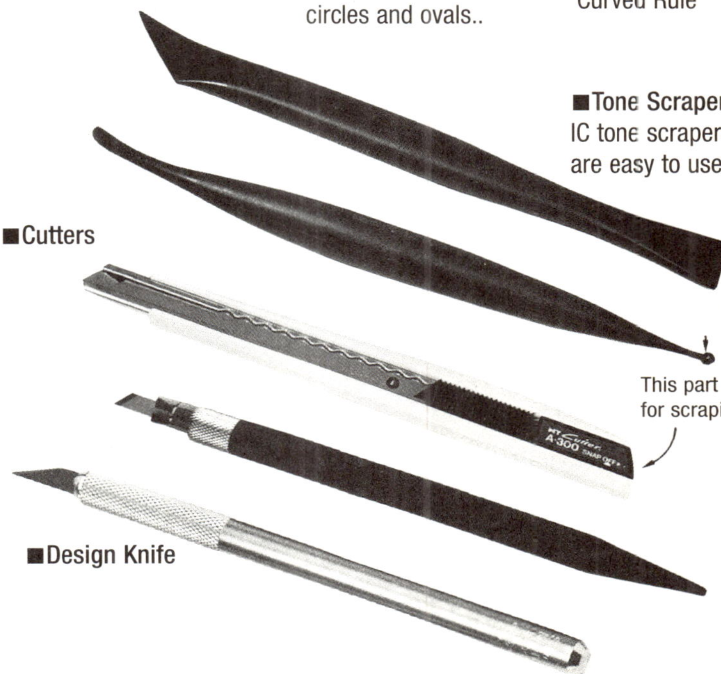

Convenient for minutiae.

This part can be used for scraping tone.

■**Ink/India Ink**

Lettering Sol (Dries Quickly)

Drawing Ink

Brush Pen (Both India ink and ink.)

Kaimei India Ink

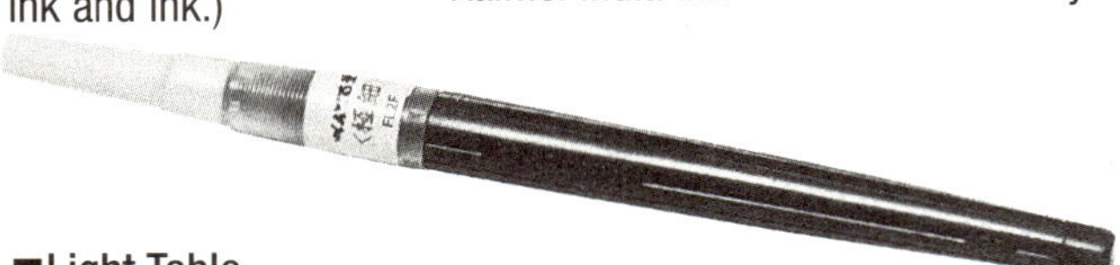

■**Items Used for Whitening**
Correction ink for comics and illustrations (The Correction Ink manufactured by Art Color dries quickly, is water-resistant, and is easy to paint over.)

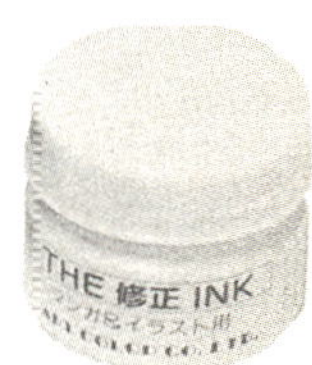

Misnon (Not suited to minutiae.)

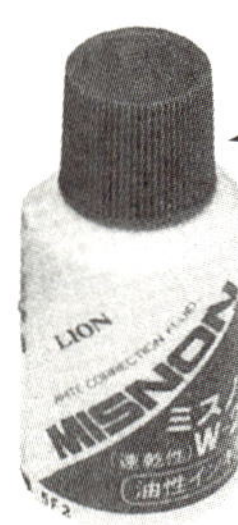

Correction Eraser Pens
Designed for both water-based and oil-based pens.

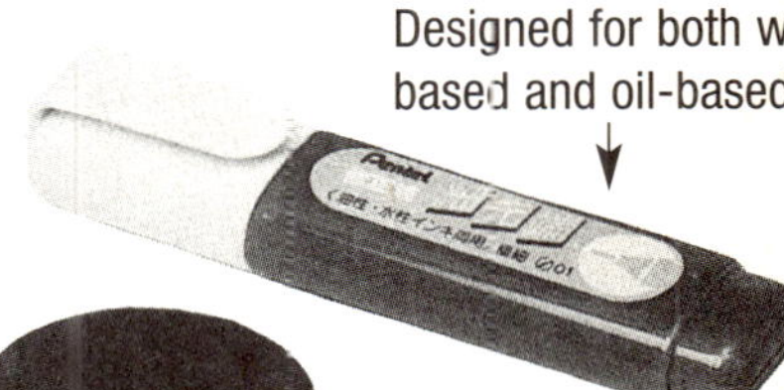

■**Light Table**
Convenient for tracing pictures, cutting tone, and finding deviations in drawings.

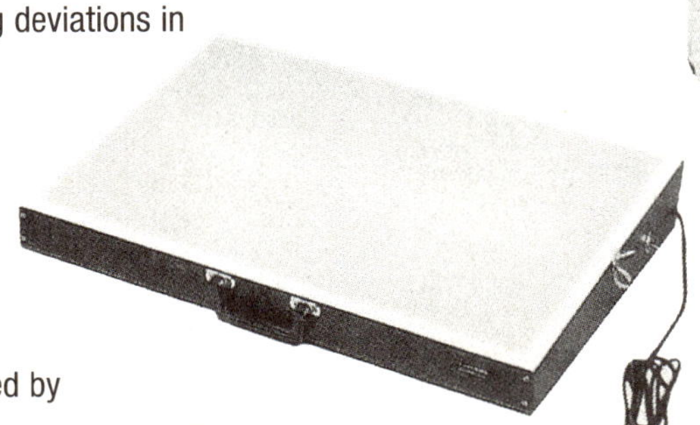

Light emanates from below.

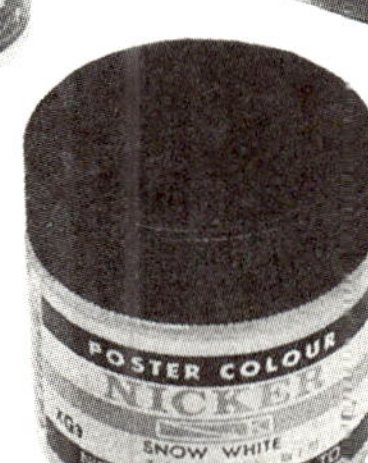

Poster Colors

Supplies provided by Sekaido Inc.

Types of Pen Nibs

Spoon-pen	Round-pen	G-pen
Delustered Type 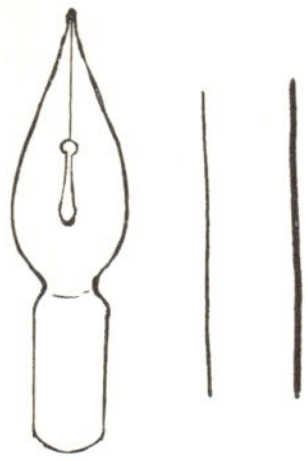	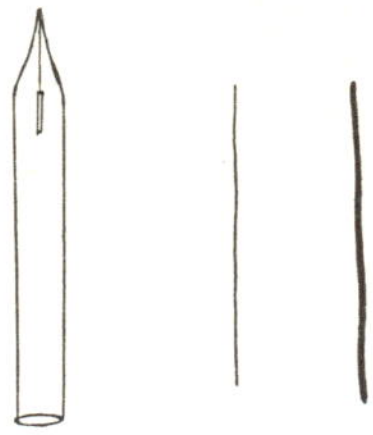	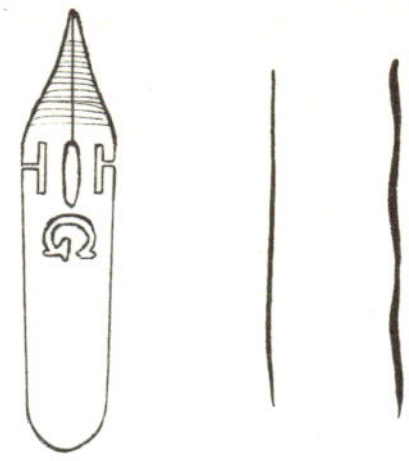
This pen cannot create the dynamics of the G-pen, but it can be used to draw thin lines. Though the shape is similar, the lustered type can be used to draw thick lines.	Convenient for drawing thin lines such as background lines and effect lines (a dedicated pen holder is required). This can also be used to draw dynamic lines.	Can be used to draw dynamic lines and thick lines depending on how much force is used.

❋There are other types of pens as well, like the school-pen (thin lines).

Example of Pen Work

At first, pen nibs repel oil, so wipe the tip before using it!

Replace pens when it becomes difficult to draw with them.

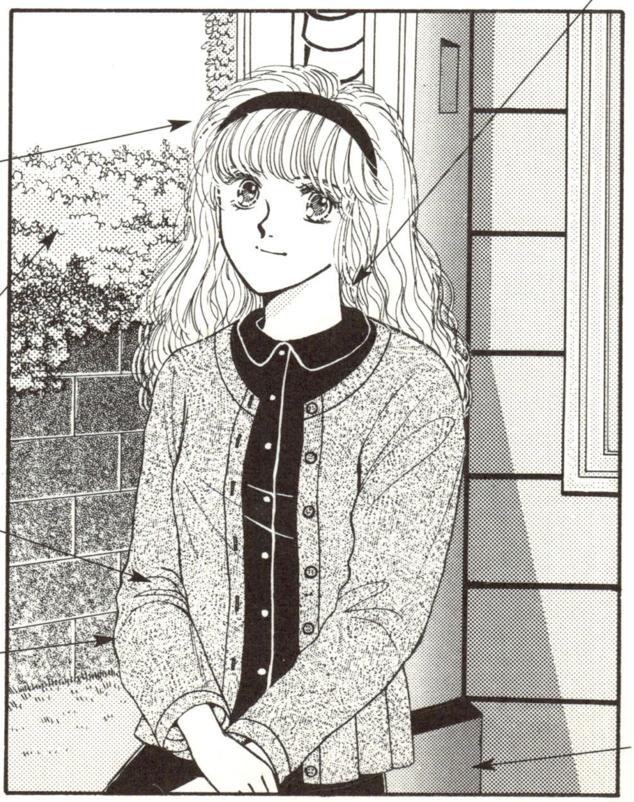

Main lines of character (G-pen)

Eyes, nose, mouth, eyebrows, and hair (Round-pen)

Plants (Round-pen)

Wrinkles in clothing (Round-pen)

Outer lines of clothing (G-pen)

Background lines (Spoon-pen)

Process from Beginning to Completion of Manuscript

1 Storyboard

2 Rough Sketch

3 Pen Work

4 Finishing Touches (Completion)

We will look at production in this order.

On pages 129 to 131, an original artwork is used to present the steps needed to complete a comic. See pages 114 and 115 of this book to learn about the story of this comic.

1 Storyboard

Create a rough storyboard on a separate sheet of paper.

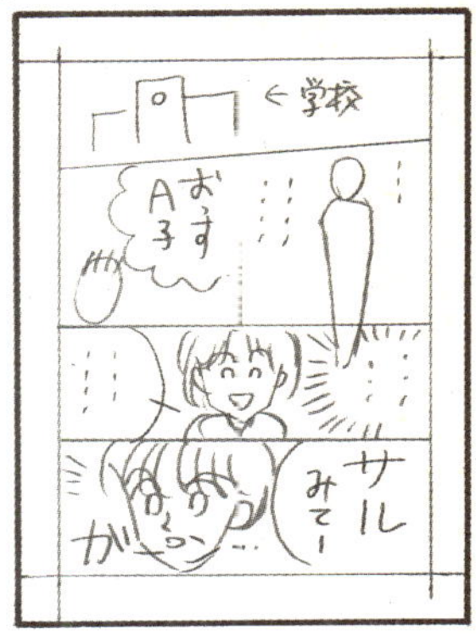

2 Rough Sketch

Transfer the storyboard to drawing paper. There is no need to copy the storyboard faithfully. Slight alterations are common (page changes are not allowed).

Note that a mark will be left after erasing if you draw with too much force.

☆Only leave necessary rough sketch lines so as not to become confused during pen work.

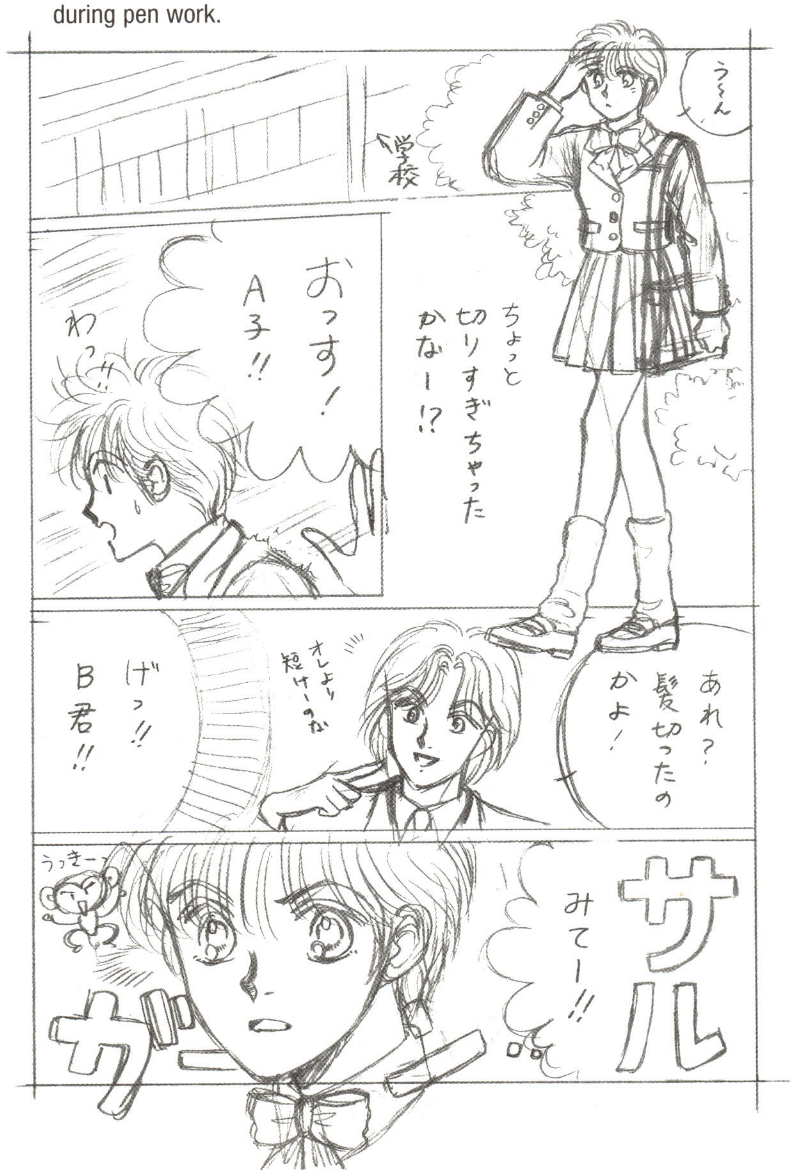

☆You may draw border lines and speech bubbles in ink at the rough sketch stage.

3 Pen Work

The building was drawn from a rough sketch after the character was penned in. For parts that are difficult to draw without being corrected at this stage, use correction fluid. Parts that will be solid black are sometimes marked with an X to act as a flag during the finishing touch stage.

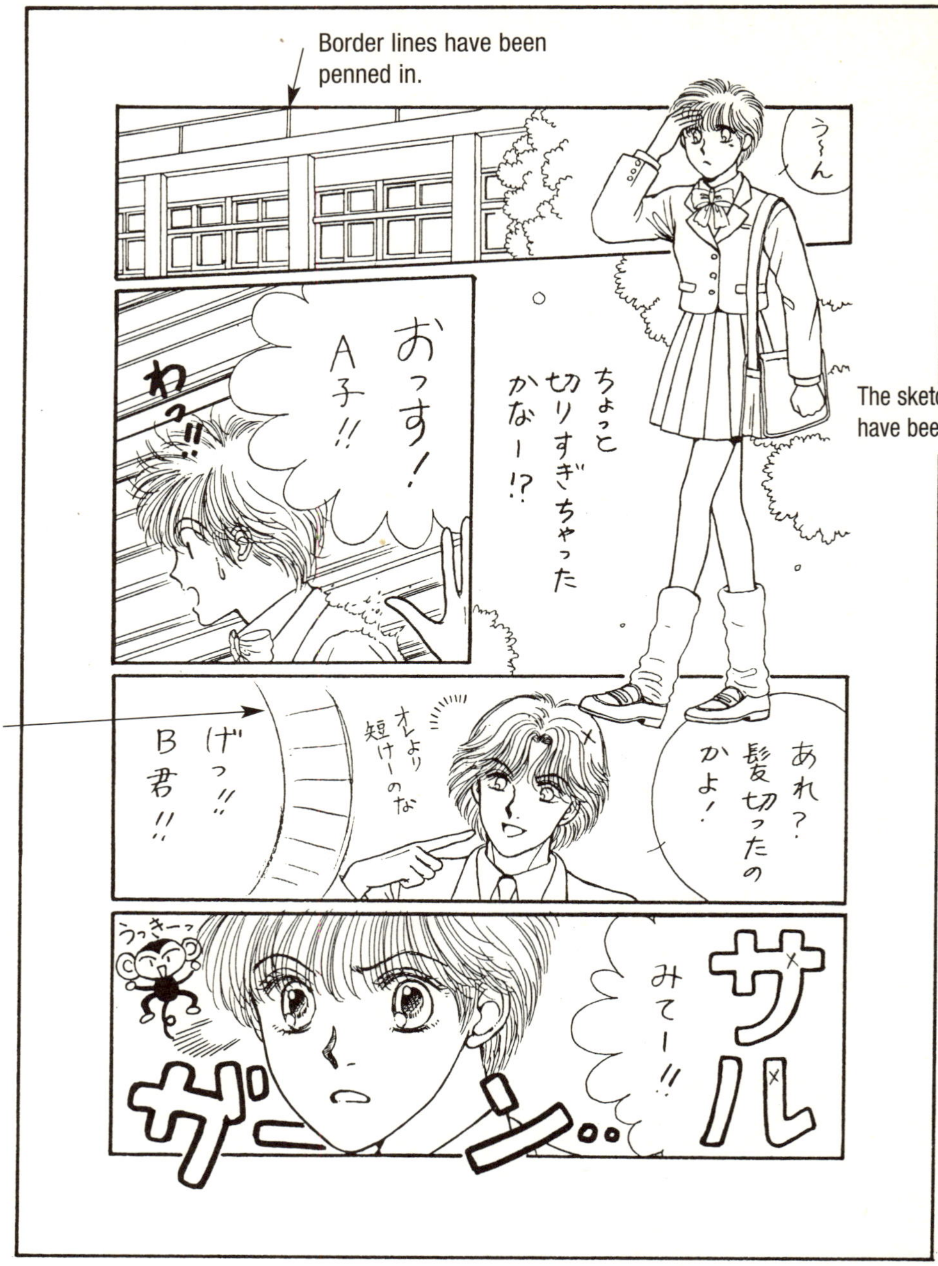

The sketch lines have been erased.

Tone will be used later for effect lines.

Supplement

- ■Start by penning in the characters. Some people start with the main lines (contour lines) while some people begin with the thin lines (eyes and hair).
- ■Pen work should be done from left to right (in the case of a right-handed person), so as not to rub ink lines that have not dried yet with your hand.
- ■Use the different types of pens in a suitable manner, and carefully draw the accents and minutiae.
- ■Draw the main pictures more clearly than backgrounds and effect lines. If the lines are all the same thickness, it will look flat.

4 Finishing Touches (Completion)

After erasing, check for lines you may have forgotten to draw and for lines not drawn correctly.

Dialogue may be left in pencil. The publisher will do the typesetting.

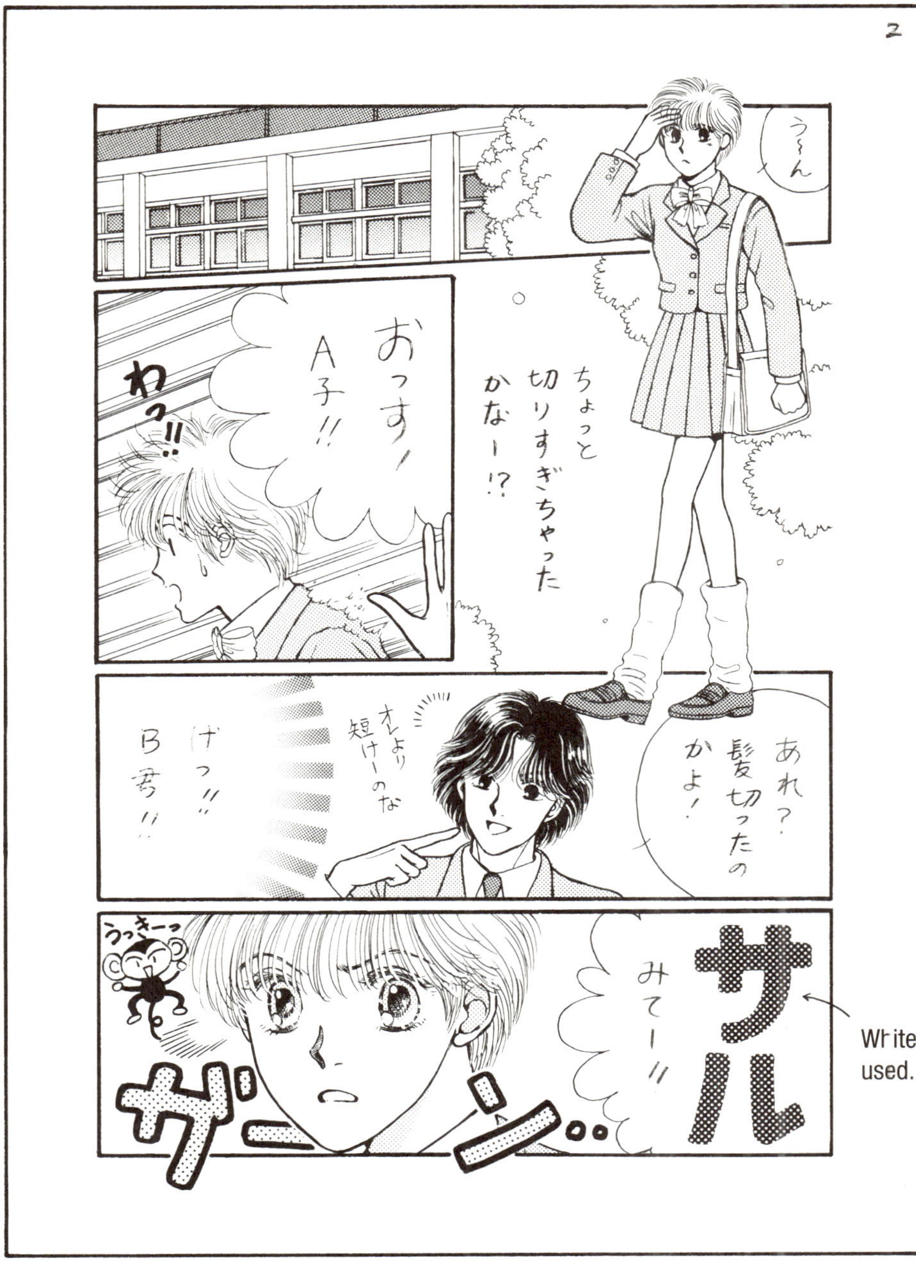

Add page number in pencil (above cutting plane line).

White tone was used.

Supplement

- ■After cleanly erasing the pencil lines that have been penned in, pen in converging lines and other effect lines.
- ■Next, paint the solid black parts. After they have dried, use correction fluid on any runover, smudges, and mistakes.
- ■Lastly, apply and scrape tone.
- ■Rewrite the dialogue where it has disappeared and check for errors and omissions. When there are letters on top of tone and solid black, attach tracing paper and write letters on it.
- ■Check to make sure the pages are numbered and you are done.

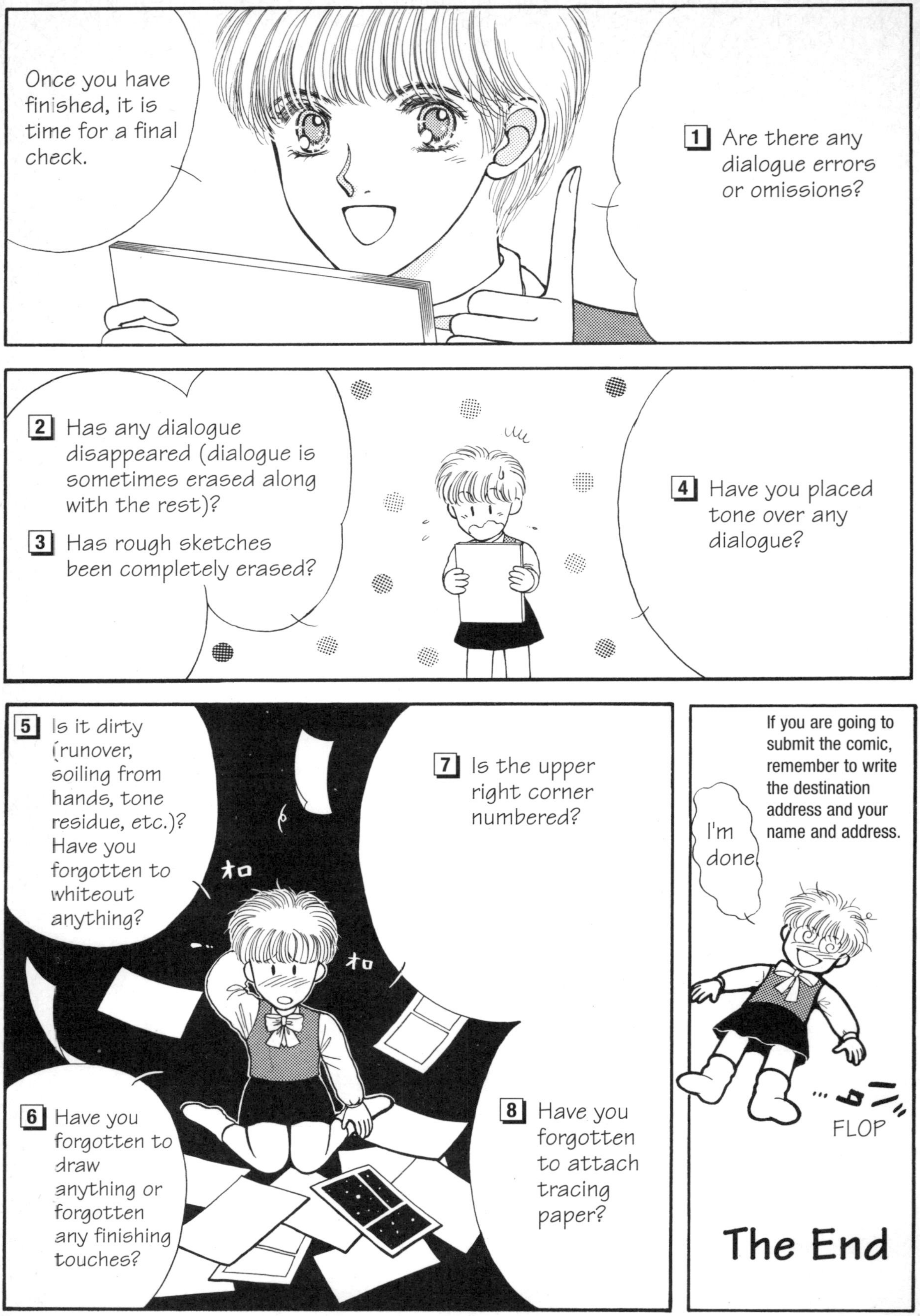
Once you have finished, it is time for a final check.
1 Are there any dialogue errors or omissions?
2 Has any dialogue disappeared (dialogue is sometimes erased along with the rest)?
3 Has rough sketches been completely erased?
4 Have you placed tone over any dialogue?
5 Is it dirty (runover, soiling from hands, tone residue, etc.)? Have you forgotten to whiteout anything?
オロ
オロ
7 Is the upper right corner numbered?
6 Have you forgotten to draw anything or forgotten any finishing touches?
8 Have you forgotten to attach tracing paper?
If you are going to submit the comic, remember to write the destination address and your name and address.
I'm done
FLOP
The End